Saving the Earth

Saving the Earth

The History of a Middle-Class Millenarian Movement

Steven M. Gelber

and

Martin L. Cook

UNIVERSITY OF CALIFORNIA PRESS

Berkeley / Los Angeles / Oxford

University of California Press
Berkeley and Los Angeles, California

University of California Press
Oxford, England

Library of Congress Cataloging-in-Publication Data

Gelber, Steven M.
   Saving the earth: the history of a middle-class millenarian
movement / Steven M. Gelber and Martin L. Cook.
      p. cm
   Includes bibliographical references.
   ISBN 0-520-06762-2 (alk. paper)
   1. Creative Initiative Foundation.   2. Cook, Martin L., 1951–
II. Title.
BP605.C74G45   1990   89-39606
299'.93—dc20   CIP

Printed in the United States of America
1   2   3   4   5   6   7   8   9

Contents

Preface

We were able to write this extensive and intimate history of the Creative Initiative movement only because several of the most senior leaders of the group gave us unrestricted access to their personal papers and many more agreed to long hours of oral history interviews. They were both candid and generous in their cooperation, and the result, we hope, gives the reader an unprecedented inside view of the intellectual, institutional, and spiritual evolution of a new religious movement. It was their hope, and ours, that we would chronicle the more than fifty years of experimentation and change that finally led this local group to blossom into a truly national movement.

A small group of Creative Initiative veterans reviewed the manuscript and gave us numerous suggestions concerning both fact and interpretation. Although we incorporated many of their points into the text, the final product reflects our scholarly interpretation, which, in significant ways, is at odds with their view of themselves. From their perspective, one of the major faults in the book is our failure to explore what could be called the "religious poetry" of the movement. They quite correctly believe that we have not explored the spiritual meaning of the new religion for the individual, or felt and appreciated the inner peace and sense of purpose it brought to so many of its adherents. Perhaps because we did not experience the personal transformations that they experienced, perhaps because we viewed this enterprise from the perspective of social scientists and, perhaps, in the final analysis, because we were skeptical outsiders and not spiritually driven insiders, the final product pleases us more than it does them. They also disagree with our emphasis on growth as a major focus of the group, feeling that such concerns have always been secondary to their primary goal of education. Finally, our friends in Creative Initiative are not entirely happy with our evaluation of their candor in presenting their religious position to the public.

We would therefore like to take this opportunity to apologize to any past or present members of the movement who may be offended by anything we say or fail to say. We have tried to be as complete and honest as possible, but a book like this involves a great deal of interpretation. As Creative Initiative itself taught in many of its courses, the way we see the world is a function of our personal "frame of reference," and we make no claims that what we have written here is anything but our own interpretation.

We have brought two complementary perspectives to this study. Steven Gelber is a social historian with a special interest in nineteenth- and twentieth-century America. Martin Cook, a professor of religious studies, specializes in philosophical theology and American Protestantism. Steven Gelber is responsible for all the historical research for this book, including the papers of Henry B. Sharman and those of Creative Initiative. The authors conducted most of the interviews jointly, although each of us did some alone. Gelber wrote the Introduction and all subsequent chapters, except chapter 3, of which Cook was the primary author. Each of the authors is responsible for the interpretations in the sections he wrote, but both of us have reviewed the entire manuscript.

We will not thank individually all the people who allowed us to interview them; they are listed in the notes. Our lack of individual thanks, however, in no way diminishes our deep appreciation for their time and honesty in exposing the most personal aspects of their lives. Special mention should be made, however, of some people connected with Creative Initiative who went beyond allowing themselves to be interviewed and gave unsparingly of their time and their ideas. Emilia and the late Harry Rathbun, whose papers provided us with the wealth of material we used, not only opened their long and fascinating lives to us through these papers and personal interviews but were also instrumental in encouraging others to do likewise. Jim and Wileta Burch also shared many of their Creative Initiative materials with us and, with their colleague Yale Jones, spent hours reviewing the manuscript. Creative Initiative librarian, Jackie Mathes, and their internal historian, Beverly

Sorensen, were invaluable guides through various aspects of Creative Initiative history.

Del Carlson, who was a mainstay of Sequoia Seminar prior to 1962, not only spoke candidly to us about his experiences there but also shared his personal journals and tapes from the 1940s and 1950s. Don Dodson, assistant academic vice-president at Santa Clara University, was always supportive and instrumental in helping us obtain internal grants to cover research costs. Donald Kirkey generously shared his unpublished work on Henry B. Sharman and the Student Christian Movement of Canada and allowed us to use invaluable material he had collected relating to the dispute at the last meeting at Camp Minnesing. We also wish to thank Melinda Bihn who assisted us with our four hundred questionnaires by entering the statistical data into the computer and helping us sort out the thousands of pages of narrative responses. Kang Hoang was our able transcriber of many hours of interview tapes. Finally, we owe a special debt of gratitude to our colleague Catherine Bell who read and commented in detail on the entire manuscript—and some sections more than once. Her thoughtful suggestions added substantially to whatever strengths this study has.

Introduction

Research into the phenomenon of "new religious movements" has become a major focus of attention for social scientists over the last twenty years. Sociologists in particular, but also historians and anthropologists, have been attracted to the unique quality of these groups—that of being both inside and outside the dominant culture.[1] Although, on the one hand, new religions are an expression of social trends and therefore a barometer of cultural values, on the other, by rejecting the established churches they place themselves beyond borders of mainstream society and its values. The emergence of new religions challenges traditional religions and thereby provides scholars with a special opportunity to examine the dynamics of religious belief and practice. So many new movements have emerged that scholarship about them has resulted in a body of work daunting in size and scope.[2]

Since new religious groups generally either do not keep archives or have been unwilling to make the papers they do have available to scholars, virtually all students of contemporary religious movements have been forced to obtain their data from interviews and/or participant-observation. These studies are, therefore, necessarily limited in their longitudinal analysis both of the leaders' lives and of the history of the movements. Confined to a several-year period at most, they tend to ignore change over time in favor of a detailed synchronic analysis of the groups as they exist during the period of field investigation.[3] As a result, the new religions are frequently perceived as static entities whose various qualities allow them to be fit into specific categories such as church or sect, charismatic or democratic, eastern or western, and so forth. As useful as such ahistorical categorization may be, it obscures the fact that religions are dynamic institutions that evolve over time in response to changes both in their external environment and in their internal relations. Due to our access to an unprecedented amount of historical documentation, this study can attempt to break through this fixed view of religious movements. We will specifically show how the complex mix of personalities, institutional needs, and social conditions interacted across time to move a religious group through several standard categories.

The grand tradition of pigeonholing religions into ideal types began, of course, with Max Weber, who first spoke of a church–sect dichotomy in *The Protestant Ethic and the Spirit of Capitalism*. His ideas were developed by his student, Ernst Troeltsch, according to whom sects were smaller groups that stood apart from society at large in their radical attempts to live the pure Christian message. Churches, in contrast, were integrated into society, took a much more conservative, that is, tolerant, view of living and implementing the Christian message, and, unlike the sects, were allied with the upper classes.[4] The Weber–Troeltsch model suffers from two major weaknesses. First, it is static, making no allowance for change; second, it is very difficult to apply beyond the European society from which the model was generated.

The problem of stasis was addressed by H. Richard Niebuhr, who suggested that sects almost always evolved into more churchlike denominations as the children of the founders softened the radical ideas of their parents.[5] In addition to adding a dynamic component to the description of religions, Niebuhr's approach was also more clearly compatible with a religiously heterogeneous society like that found in the United States. Yet that very heterogeneity seemed to beg for a set of new definitions that would enable scholars to categorize the wider variety of vendors in the American religious marketplace. Unfortunately, the number of suggested categories has grown to be almost as varied as the number of religions they have attempted to define.[6]

Although most of the more recent typologies acknowledge the possibility—even likelihood—of change, they still posit distinct categories into or out of which groups could move if and when they changed. This rather punctuated approach was effectively challenged in 1963 by sociologist Benton Johnson, who suggested that there is a continuum from church to sect in which churches are those religious groups that accept the status quo and sects are those that reject it.[7] The most obvious difficulty in the Johnson scheme is that of measuring just how much a religious group is rejecting or is being rejected by the dominant society.

That issue has recently been addressed in two closely related ways. First, in their book *The Future of Religion,* Rodney Stark and William S. Bainbridge have suggested that a group's location on the church–sect continuum can be determined by measuring the amount of "tension" that members feel vis-à-vis the broadly accepted secular values of society.[8] At one end of the spectrum are members of sects who experience high tension because they believe and behave in ways that are at odds with mainstream society, thus setting up a system of mutual rejection. Church members, by comparison, hold essentially the same values as the majority and suffer little if any tension. By asking group members specific questions about their attitudes toward society at-large, Stark and Bainbridge locate groups along a church–sect continuum.[9]

Stark and Bainbridge call one section of their book "The Religious Economy," and the image is an excellent one, even though they themselves do not use an economic model to describe the relationship of religion and society. A second work by economist Laurence Iannaccone, however, does. Avoiding discrete Procrustean categories and stressing the fluidity of a church–sect continuum, Iannaccone suggests that a group's position on the continuum can best be established by measuring an individual's "cost" of membership. Following Gary S. Becker's approach to analyzing nonmarket behavior, Iannaccone sees the individual's decision for or against membership in a religious group as an "economic" choice. In this sense "economic" does not simply refer to monetary exchange, but is used in a broader sense to refer to all limited resources that could include, in addition to time and money, psychic and physical effort, social reputation, and the like. He assumes that the individual will spend these resources in a way that will bring the greatest personal satisfaction. Because mainline churches have values and behavior expectations compatible with society at large, there is relatively little personal cost in being a member. Sects, however, depart dramatically from general social values; therefore joining a sect can be very "expensive."[10]

Obviously Stark and Bainbridge's "tension" and Iannaccone's "cost" are two ways of saying (and measuring) the same thing. They both assume, as have almost all scholars from the time of Weber, that churches are of society and sects are outside it. The major difference between the two is that Stark and Bainbridge limit their measurements of tension to what might roughly be called "psychic" items whereas Iannaccone's model includes all costs. Thus, the more the adherence to a religious group's values produces tension, the higher the cost of membership and the farther toward the sect end of the continuum a group would lie.

Since membership in a sect has very high costs in terms of secular rewards, sects must provide many of the benefits that their members would normally get from nonreligious sources. Although religious rewards might be the motivating factor attracting a person to a sect, people still need food, clothing, housing, companionship, and other forms of support. If membership in a religious sect makes it difficult to obtain these necessities from normal sources, then sect members must seek them from the group itself. It is, of course, in the sect's best interest to provide as much of this support as possible both to prevent defection and to build a feeling of thankfulness, if not actual dependency, on the part of members. Iannaccone points out that there is a corollary to this proposition: to provide the necessary support the sect must place high demands on its members, and thus high levels of active participation are characteristic of sects.[11]

The great strength of the economic model is that it can be used both synchronically to define the religion–society relationship in a particular moment and diachronically to track and explain variations over time. By examining changes in services provided to members or the demands made on them, students of a movement can make sense of the historical evolution of a group without discarding the still useful categories of church and sect. Thus history makes it possible to have a truly dynamic sociology, freed from the false confines of the synchronic moment as well as from the artificial walls of pure typologies. By actually watching a group operate over time in the religious marketplace we can see how it must provide more rewards as it demands higher costs and thus becomes more separate and sectlike, or, conversely, how it can drop support functions as it moves toward the social mainstream by becoming more churchlike. The economic model does not predict the direction of movement, but it does set up a correlation between supply and demand within the group. The more the group demands, the more it must supply, and the less the group supplies the less it can demand.

As noted above, most studies of new religious movements have been circumscribed not only by synchronic models but, more fundamentally, by a lack of historic materials. We have been able to undertake a unique longitudinal study of a new religion, the Creative Initiative movement, because its leaders allowed us access to approximately a hundred thousand pages of material spanning eighty years. These included the personal papers of the founders and their mentor and most of the records of the organization itself. This mass of material in conjunction with hundreds of questionnaires and dozens of interviews have enabled us to go beyond field study to reconstruct from the inside more than a half century of the history of Creative Initiative using its followers own words, both private and public. In doing so, we can explore the life-cycle of a new religion from its earliest beginnings as a Bible study group through its gradual development into a new religious sect and, finally, to its unexpected demise in favor of a totally secularized peace movement.

Members of Creative Initiative called themselves the "New Religion" (we follow their capitalization) and never used any other label such as denomination, sect, or cult. We refer to them as a *proto-sect* or *sect* depending upon where they seem to fall along the church–sect contin-uum at any particular point in their history. Students of religion some-times distinguish between cults and sects and, depending on which definition one follows, Creative Initiative might or might not be catego-rized as a cult.[12] Because of its pejorative connotations we have chosen to avoid using the term *cult* except in its commonly understood negative sense. As a new religion in California, Creative Initiative was under-standably sensitive about being labeled a cult. Because members did not slavishly follow a prophetic leader, did not engage in socially deviant practices, did not surrender their critical faculties or their wealth to the group, or engage in other extreme behaviors associated in the popular mind with cults, we have avoided that term, even when we might have applied it in a narrow technical sense, out of respect for their feelings.

Much of this book is the story of the group's husband and wife leaders, especially the wife, Emilia Rathbun, who had all the qualities of a charismatic leader, yet refused to become a guru or prophet. At the same time, this book is also the study of a group of people who dramati-cally belie the facile assumption that new religious groups appeal to marginal people suffering from some sort of relative deprivation. Mem-bers of Creative Initiative were the epitome of successful mainstream Americans. Ethnically, financially, educationally, and socially, they would seem to have been the least likely of people to deviate from the religious norm, and in some very profound ways they did not. Although on the surface Creative Initiative appears to have been a major departure from mainline religion, in fact it was in some ways also a continuation and even a rejuvenation of traditional American religious values.

The story begins in nineteenth-century rural Ontario and ends in 1982 in the suburban California headquarters of the antiwar group called

Beyond War. Beyond War's home office is in Palo Alto, California, but it has active groups in sixty-six cities in twenty-five states outside California and in more than four hundred cities and towns inside the state.[13] Although there is no formal membership, eighteen thousand people subscribe to its newsletter, and scores of full-time volunteers work both at its headquarters and in the field where they recruit new members and set up new local units. The movement sponsors an annual Beyond War Award for organizations or individuals who have been instrumental in furthering the cause of peace, and three times it has created televised intercontinental "space bridges" to carry the awards ceremony live to the Soviet Union and to several Latin American nations.

Yet unlike many other antiwar movements, Beyond War does not have a political agenda. It deliberately eschews institutional political action, believing that peace can best be achieved by teaching individuals how to adopt "a new way of thinking" in which they "pose no enemies" and renounce violence as a method of resolving conflict. Their focus on achieving peace in the world through individual transformation of attitudes would appear to place Beyond War in the company of numerous "New Age" groups that also make personal change a prerequisite for change in the world. Yet Beyond War is unique in a number of ways. First, the movement is not a product of the 1960s or 1970s but has roots that go back to the World War I era. Second, although it is a purely secular movement today, its immediate antecedents were decidedly religious. Finally, Beyond War grew out of a tradition that rejected the self-centered individualism of so many New Age movements and stressed the importance of community.

The process that eventually culminated in Beyond War began before the turn of the century with a Canadian scholar named Henry B. Sharman who, in the tradition of the "higher criticism," led Bible study seminars that emphasized Jesus as a model for life. After Sharman's semiretirement to California in 1933, Stanford University law professor Harry Rathbun and his wife Emilia joined the large body of university faculty who regularly studied with him. The Rathbuns took over leadership of the movement after Sharman's total retirement in 1946, and under their direction an organization called Sequoia Seminar continued to run programs that examined the teachings of Jesus.

For sixteen years Sequoia Seminar maintained the Sharman tradition. Then, in 1962, Emilia had a religious experience that she interpreted as a call to "practice the personal religion of Jesus" in a new context. Beginning with a few close women friends and spreading slowly, what had previously been a study group with some sectlike qualities became a distinct religious sect.

At first, the new sect was strictly private and had no name. It was simply referred to as "the work." As it sought additional members and became increasingly public the women adopted the name "New Sphere" in 1965. Two years later they changed their name to "Woman to Woman Building the Earth for the Children's Sake," which was eventually shortened to "Build the Earth." In 1968, as part of a project to promote voluntary national service, the group adopted the umbrella designation, "National Initiative Foundation," which in turn was changed to the "Creative Initiative Foundation" in 1972. In 1982, Creative Initiative began the Beyond War project, and in 1983 all the activities of Creative Initiative and Sequoia Seminar were suspended in order to concentrate exclusively on the new Beyond War movement.

The history of the Creative Initiative movement is a history of institutional evolution. During the fifteen years after they founded Sequoia Seminar in 1946, the Rathbuns and their circle slowly transformed the organization from a Bible study group working with and through the mainline churches into a quasi-sect. As it became more sectlike, demanding greater loyalty, developing a unique ideology, and increasing the "cost" of membership, participants found it increasingly difficult to be dedicated to the movement and at the same time to remain active in their churches. That tension between church and emerging sect was resolved after 1962 when Emilia's religious vision freed the movement to become an independent religious sect. The movement spent the next twenty years developing a full spectrum of sectarian activities that ranged from specialized ceremonies to social action.

Their unorthodox religious beliefs and their insistence on total commitment to work through the group limited the movement's growth, especially since they sought highly educated, financially successful and politically moderate members. Thus, so long as the movement remained a religious sect, it appeared that it would not have the worldwide effect its members envisioned. The emergence of Beyond War in 1982 marked the latest of the group's evolutionary transformations. By secularizing, it divested itself of those elements that could put off potential members and laid the groundwork for the growth necessary to achieve the goal of universal peace.

There were two characteristic themes of thought and action that wove through the history of Creative Initiative. The first, evolution, gave them a vision of hope for the future. The second, paradox, enabled them to integrate a number of apparently contradictory beliefs. Creative Initiative believed that individual transformation was the key mechanism in the ongoing evolution of the human species. Their use of the evolutionary model was both metaphorical and literal. Members saw themselves as a "peduncle," or link, between the old human race characterized by greed, competition, and conflict, and a new human race defined by generosity, cooperation, and peaceful resolution of conflict. Virtually all their philosophy flowed from that belief. The movement thought this final stage of evolution could be brought about through an act of will. This was an idea that appealed to the scientific and professional people who made up the overwhelming majority of Creative Initiative members. They were the kind of people who were accustomed to having control over their lives. They were rationalists who rejected fatalism and sought to mold their environments. Thus, they could act with the assurance that *they,* not some distant savior or political leader, could save the earth.

Whereas the idea of continuing evolution served to locate their philosophy in a scientific matrix, the second theme of paradox functioned to free them from the exclusively rational and create room for the spiritual. One of the most commonly referred to biblical texts in the movement's long history was Jesus' admonition in Luke 17:33 that "whoever seeks to gain his life will lose it, but whoever loses his life will preserve it." This was the "great paradox of Jesus" and was used both implicitly and explicitly to introduce the concept of paradox into Creative Initiative thought. Because in one sense a paradox is an extrarational statement, the truth or falsity of which cannot be proven logically, the incorporation of various paradoxical beliefs into their philosophy enabled them to move seamlessly from science to faith.

The most profoundly paradoxical aspects of Creative Initiative's ideology centered around the perennially difficult relationship between the individual and the community. In this area there were, in fact, two closely related paradoxes. The first involved the correct method to be used to bring about the changes in society they believed were needed. They rejected any political activity that sought change through coercive legislation and instead favored individual transformation. Somehow the group had to reconcile its theoretical emphasis on individual transformation with its working, and sometimes living, as an organized community. Because members believed that the smaller religious community was a model for the larger outside population, people who were active in the group were expected to live their lives in conformity with the group's values. Whereas the group rejected legal coercion as a valid method of changing society, it accepted a form of coercive personal confrontation as a method of maintaining proper community behavior.

The second paradox involved a conflict between the group's monistic and dualistic beliefs. Their belief that God and natural law were one led to a world-view that integrated all creation. Not only were all people members of the same human family, but humans were a vital part of the earth's biosystem. Further, the earth itself was part of, and ultimately at one with, the rest of the universe. Their belief in the unity and commonality of all people, however, might seem to have worked against the establishment of a distinct community of believers. Axiomatically, any self-defined organization exists only because it contains some elements that set it apart from the population at large. Indeed, the most important feature characteristic of a sect is the sharp distinction it sets up between those who are "in" and those who are "out." In other words, their very structure creates a dualism that conflicts with a monistic world-view. These paradoxes were never resolved in Creative Initiative—indeed they were hardly even acknowledged. Nevertheless, the conflicts they engendered were subconsciously but consistently coped with by recognizing that the religious life involved paradoxes that defied logical resolution and demanded leaps of faith.

Their belief in rationality on the one hand and their tolerance of paradox on the other raises the most intriguing and most difficult question to answer about Creative Initiative, What kind of people would be attracted to such a movement? Although outsiders would often look askance at the movement and sometimes accuse it of being a "cult," taken as a whole, the Creative Initiative ideology was consonant with traditional American values. Indeed, we would argue that Creative Initiative was successful in appealing to upper-middle-class people in part because it contained three important elements of the evangelical tradition. First, as an advocate of rigorism in the personal and family sphere, Creative Initiative was a refuge of probity in a society preoccupied with sex and drugs. Second, like so many nineteenth-century evangelicals, Creative Initiative advocated a life balanced between personal responsibility on one side and community welfare on the other. And finally, like traditional Protestants, Creative Initiative worried that material possessions could be a temptation and an end in themselves, and so it called upon its members to live lives of material moderation.

Members saw a teleological unfolding of history in which their community was to be a vital force in saving humankind from destruction by its own hand. They clearly thought of themselves as a "city upon a hill" that would be both a leader and model for bringing about the Kingdom of God on earth. Thus, despite the superficially strange elements of their religious beliefs, they actually tapped deeply into the core of American values. Those people who were willing to bear the costs of joining this unique sect found confirmation of their traditional middle-class values and a special sense that they were the vanguard of a new historical and religious epoch that would stop the destruction of the earth and initiate an age of peace and cooperation.

1

Genesis

Although Henry Burton Sharman is little more than a name for most current members of the movement, his influence is ubiquitous. Almost all members who joined prior to 1982 have studied the gospels using material written by Sharman. Newer members who have come into the movement since the transition to Beyond War, when they know the name at all, identify him as the legendary teacher of Harry and Emilia Rathbun. Old or new, most members of the movement know him mostly through anecdote and legend, and there is an overwhelming sense that his scholarly credentials legitimate the genesis of Creative Initiative.[1] Sharman, who died in 1953, is the founding father, a larger-than-life figure lost in the mists of time and the Canadian lake country, slowly fading from collective memory while his ideas live on, transformed but still recognizable. But Sharman was much more than the Rathbuns' mentor. He was a man who developed a system of religious thought that influenced several generations of Canadian students and, through them, prewar politics and education in Canada. He was an active participant in the scholarly debate about the nature of Jesus in the era before World War I, and many of the issues he raised in his writings and seminars sixty years ago continued to be discussed and debated in Creative Initiative until it launched the Beyond War movement in 1982.

The cardinal tenet in both Sharman's work and in Creative Initiative was that the individual had to align or "surrender" his or her personal will to the will of God. Much attention was focused on the process by which one shifted from the self to God, and then on how one in fact lived a life dedicated to God's will. Sharman's teachings created a tension between the private act of transformation of the will and the public acts that resulted from that transformation. Within his own work, Sharman never resolved that tension. He believed that the right path could be found through studying the teachings of Jesus, and such study was the core of his method.

His followers, however, differed on the implications of Jesus' teachings, and their differences tore the movement apart when Sharman retired in 1945. The basic dispute between the factions was simple, but its implications were immense. The Rathbuns believed that society could be altered for the better by changing the spiritual focus of individuals. The rival faction believed that people who had undergone the transformation had an obligation to act in the political arena to create a more just world. We call these two modes of thought "homocentric" (for those who wished to concentrate on the individual) and "sociocentric" (for those who centered their attention on society). Just how and where to draw the line between focus on the individual and the final goal of social transformation was a recurrent theme in the history of Creative Initiative.

Sharman and the "Records"

In 1884, when he was a nineteen-year-old agricultural student, Henry B. Sharman attended a religious revival with the express intention of challenging the Methodist evangelist H. T. Crossley. Sharman had grown skeptical about his faith when he had been unable to reconcile it with the scientific values taught at the Ontario Agricultural College, where he had studied for two years. But it was the evangelist who challenged Sharman when he told his audience that "every statement of Jesus could be proved as surely as the experiments the students were carrying on in their laboratories."[2] According to his friends, Sharman left the meeting profoundly moved, and before the night was over had dedicated his life to the will of God.[3]

Born in 1865, Sharman was the oldest child of a prominent pioneer family in Stratford, Ontario. The family owned a firm that manufactured agricultural machinery and was also involved in raising Hereford cattle. Sharman had attended the local public schools before entering college to study animal husbandry.[4] After a brief interruption during which he ran a family farm in Manitoba, Sharman graduated from college and accepted an appointment there as an instructor in chemistry.[5]

His interest in reconciling science and religion was further piqued when he read Henry Drummond's *Natural Law in the Spiritual World,* but he recoiled at Drummond's suggestion that Christ was the way to find God and the laws of the universe. "I could not see how or why it was necessary for Christ to come into the picture of God and the running of His universe," Sharman said.[6] Nevertheless, he did become increasingly interested in the person of Jesus, and in his own way would make the historical figure of Jesus much the same kind of path to God that Christ the savior was for Drummond.

After several years, Sharman, who had become very active in the Young Men's Christian Association (YMCA), realized that studying the Bible was more important to him than teaching science, and in 1893 he accepted the invitation of the renowned evangelist John R. Mott to become corresponding secretary of the Student Volunteer Movement of North America (SVM). SVM had been founded in 1886 by evangelist Dwight L. Moody and had as its goal "the evangelization of the world in this generation."[7] Concurrently Sharman held the unpaid position of Bible study secretary of the Student Department of the YMCA. He directed the Bible study programs of the SVM and the YMCA for seven years, during which time he began to develop his special interest in the synoptic gospels. The YMCA published a list of study questions he wrote, *Studies in the Life of Christ,* to facilitate discussion in his classes.[8]

Sharman's youthful rebellion against religion had been ended by the promise that the words of Jesus could be proven scientifically, and Sharman never wavered from the resulting commitment to the teachings of Jesus. As the analytic approach of "higher criticism" began making inroads among religious thinkers, Sharman was increasingly attracted to the new objective methodology and alienated from the leadership of the SVM and the YMCA.[9] Impressed by the success of his first set of questions on the gospels, the YMCA asked Sharman to prepare a similar series of study questions on "The Truth of the Apostolic Gospel." Sharman responded by saying that "the truth of the Apostolic gospel was confused, vague, and possibly in many respects quite outside of the mind of Christ." He suggested substituting a course on Paul—and Mott suggested that he might be happier in some other line of work. Sharman agreed, and in 1900 he resigned his position with the two groups and entered the University of Chicago to pursue a doctorate in New Testament studies.[10] Accompanying him was his wife,

Abbie Lyon Sharman, whom he had married in 1896, and who herself earned a Ph.D. in literature during their time in Chicago.[11]

Even before he received his degree, Sharman was offered a position at the Congregational Theological Seminary but turned it down to teach nondivinity students at the University of Chicago. When the department at Chicago told him it could not afford another position, he was confident enough of his own popularity to suggest a "docent" appointment that paid him a percentage of his students' tuition.[12] He received his doctorate in 1906 and his thesis, *The Teaching of Jesus about the Future,* was published in 1909.[13] That same year Chicago offered him a regular faculty appointment in the Department of Theology. Sharman turned it down.

Once more the problem raised by studying the gospels objectively was interfering with his career. Sharman was identified with a faction whose approach to biblical criticism alienated a lot of people. One of his students at the time remembered that some faculty in the theological school had developed a liberal reputation for advocating "higher criticism," and that many students were offended by "turning upon the Bible the same critical analysis taken for granted in the study of other literature, history or science." When a rumor circulated that Sharman was to be dismissed as a "radical," the same student organized a dinner for three deans at which Sharman's students testified to the importance of his work. Despite the strong student support, Sharman was unwilling to be caught in the cross fire between the warring factions. He declined the appointment and struck out on his own.[14]

Before Sharman could embark on what would be his lifetime vocation of leading independent Bible study groups, the forty-four-year-old scholar first had to add one more square to his already checkered career. If he were going to operate outside of the established support institutions like the SVM and the university, he would have to become financially independent. In 1908, Sharman returned to Canada to establish the Ontario Metal Culvert Company and then spent the following six years developing the firm into a highly successful business. Although he remained a director until 1931, Sharman was able to leave the day-to-day operation of the company in 1915 and return to Chicago to begin his true calling.[15]

From 1915 to 1945 Henry Burton Sharman spent almost all his time directing independent Bible study classes. The basis for these classes was *Records of the Life of Jesus,* his own arrangement of the synoptic gospels. Published in 1917 by the YMCA's Association Press, and later by

Harper, the book printed the gospels of Matthew, Mark, and Luke in parallel columns by topic in chronological order.[16] According to Harry Rathbun, Sharman believed that *Records of the Life of Jesus* provided the student with "a neutral display of the evidence" that made it possible to examine the gospels objectively. Rathbun further claimed that Sharman actually tried to suppress his earlier *Studies in the Life of Christ* since it was based on the assumption that the gospels could be "harmonized," a position he no longer adhered to.[17] One year after *Records of the Life of Jesus,* he published *Jesus in the Records,* a collection of questions to be used when studying "the Records," as the gospels were always called in Sharman's work.[18] Sharman had been influential in the formation of the Student Christian Movement of Canada (SCM) in 1921, and he worked in close conjunction with it when setting up the studies, conferences, and summer seminars that constituted his work in the thirty years after 1915.[19] With the exception of three years that he spent as an honorary lecturer in the Department of History at Yenching University in Beijing, China (returning each year to Canada to lead his summer seminars), and three years on the faculty of the Quaker study program at Pendle Hill, Pennsylvania, Sharman remained unaffiliated, working with college students and faculty and refining the method that would so influence the Rathbuns and the Creative Initiative movement.

Science and the Religion of Jesus

Although Sharman titled his first book *Studies in the Life of Christ,* all his subsequent work referred to "Jesus." The distinction was certainly intentional. Sharman was moving from the Christ of faith, perceived as God and eternal savior, to the Jesus of history, who was human and a model for this life. Although the YMCA labeled one of the early seminars he led while a graduate student, "The Life of Chirst," Sharman's own description of the course emphasized Jesus the man rather than Christ the savior. He told prospective students that he intended them to gain a "complete and accurate knowledge of the Life of Jesus, as that life was lived by Him," and went on to emphasize "the aim of the course is primarily and constantly *historical,* in seeking to know all that may be known of the course of events."[20] Sharman was quite convinced that if there were to be any future for religion, any basis for authority, it would be found "in one place and in one place only, namely, back where the religion of the modern world had its beginning—in Jesus."[21]

The historical Jesus was in the gospels but could be found only if he could be separated "from the mass of tradition which has grown up about him."[22] The idea was to examine the gospels with no presuppositions: Shaman and his students said that they did not assume Jesus was "Christ," they did not assume "that Jesus was related in some special way to God," they did not even assume a theistic position. "Jesus is not my authority," Sharman told his students, "The only reason that Jesus is of use to me is that he says so much that commands itself to me."[23] "Our approach," said Sharman, "is to be fresh, open, free from the limitations imposed by theories, doctrines and dogmas."[24] True to his skeptical beginnings and the liberal "higher criticism" of his graduate study, Sharman always insisted that his study technique was "scientific." He told his students, "THE METHOD OF STUDY we shall use in this work together is that generally known as the SCIENTIFIC METHOD." It was the method that had led to advances in the physical and biological sciences and was "the only known method which leads unfailingly to the discovery of truth," which was why they were going to use it in their "quest for the truth about Jesus."[25] Students were subjected to a very strict Socratic pedagogy. Sharman never lectured or instructed. His job was to ask questions and make sure that the responses were clear. As he explained, "if the leader makes no comment about your answer, it does not mean he does not like it—he may be quite excited about it. All his silence means is that your answer is intelligible and relevant." The leader's job in this Socratic dialogue was not to lead the students to the right conclusion but to get them to see all the evidence. Sharman admitted that he had his own opinions and convictions but did his utmost not to foist them on the study groups.[26]

According to all reports, Sharman was an imposing and somewhat intimidating presence. His students, even those who were highly placed academics, always referred to him as *Doctor* Sharman—only his immediate family called him Harry. He invariably wore tweed suits, high stiff white collars, and high lace-up shoes, even in the midsummer in the heart of the Canadian wilderness. He would sit for hours in a rocking chair but never move an inch, speaking only when necessary to clarify a point in his ponderous, measured tones. Sharman's aloof exterior was apparently matched by an equally cool interior. His relationship with close friends, and even with his wife, was quite formal. Emilia Rathbun always felt somewhat distant from him because he did not, in her words, "know the devil." By this she meant that Sharman had distanced himself from the weaknesses and foibles of human life and could deal only with the intellectual side of human existence.[27] Another of his students came to a similar conclusion when she charged that Sharman's most serious deficiency was his "almost total absence of consideration of the emotional life."[28] Ultimately the Rathbuns came to the same conclusion and included psychology as part of their search for a more fully developed philosophy of life.

Sharman's determination to keep his own conclusions to himself and allow seminar participants to reach their own understandings of the Records, plus his self-conscious emphasis on the scientific method, left most observers with the impression that the Sharman process was value-neutral and that Sharman either had no personal philosophy or that any personal philosophy he had was irrelevant to the Records seminars. Mary McDermott Shideler, who attended two Records seminars in the summers of 1937 and 1938, reported that "Dr. Sharman has made no attempt to present his own, personal philosophy of religion. He has been concerned, not with what we should learn from *him*, but with what we learned from Jesus."[29] Despite his best efforts to veil his own ideas, however, Sharman's personal philosophy inevitably colored his work and influenced his students. From Shideler's report and from other sources, a consistent pattern emerges that gives us a good picture of the structure of Sharman's thought and through it an understanding of those ideas that were germinal to Harry and Emilia Rathbun and the Creative Initiative movement.

Despite disclaimers based on the principle of scientific objectivity, it is clear that Sharman and most of his students did share a basic belief in the existence of God and furthermore believed that God could and would somehow save individual human beings. Sharman said that the key question he put to any theological position was, "what must I do to find the Kingdom of God, to inherit eternal life."[30] In his own mind, the answer was clear. The road to salvation was "really *knowing* the way of life after the manner of Jesus, not some blind alley that does not lead to that which is desired."[31] There is little question that Sharman's singular focus on studying the Records was predicated on the assumption that such study would lead the student to accepting the ideas of Jesus (although exactly what ideas, Sharman never specified). The ideas of the historical Jesus would in turn lead the students to dedicate their lives to God, which in Sharman's eyes was the essence of being religious. Sharman's Jesus was historical, but what was Sharman's God? Sharman's

God, like Sharman's theology, was a mixture of the evangelism of his youth and the scientific rationalism of his graduate student years. Sharman believed that there was a God and that God in some sense saved individuals. And yet his God was not the orthodox personal God of the evangelists who had first converted and then employed him. Sharman's God was "Direction, Purpose or Will." Sharman's God was a norm toward which people strived. Sharman's God was that to which religious people dedicated their lives, not knowing what such dedication would mean. They then studied the teachings of Jesus to find out.

Just what such dedication meant is nicely illustrated in a letter that Abbie Sharman sent to her sister, Sophia Fahs, in 1942. Attempting to patch up a dispute between her husband and her sister over situational ethics, Abbie explained that occasionally a seminar member would say, "a choice of the whole good and a commitment to choosing the good in future situations is psychologically impossible. The choice can only be made in concrete situations, and only when the time comes in which the situation arises."[32] In other words, the seminarian asserted that ethical choices were relative and had to be judged circumstantially. Such a position, wrote Abbie, "undercuts the central understanding of the teaching of Jesus and declares the 'religious' person impossible."[33] The Sharmans agreed that the religious person had to make a moral commitment to the concept of good (a commitment that Sharman hoped to bring about through the Records seminars) and stick to it no matter what the external circumstances. To charges that such a commitment was made *in vacuo*, Mrs. Sharman responded, "of course it's commitment *in vacuo* . . . it is the essence of the unified personality that it does not wait for concrete situations to arise in order to have a will to choose the good."[34] The merely ethical person was a creature of circumstance, but the religiously moral person had a code of values based on eternal truth.

Sharman confronted his students with the most difficult dilemma. On the one hand he encouraged them to choose the good, but on the other he told them that they would have to determine for themselves just what that good was. The key to being religious was recognizing that one had to draw a line between right and wrong. Although Sharman would not tell his students where to draw that line, he had no doubts that such a line existed and that it was ordained by the very structure of being. Sharman believed that there was a "moral order of the universe" that existed outside of human beings and that people ignored it at their peril because it was "ruthless, utterly ruthless in its destructiveness when crossed."

There was no room for relativism in Sharman's world. Sharman believed, and the Rathbuns accepted his view, that religion was not merely *like* science, it *was* science, and people disobeyed its laws at their own peril.[35] Sharman did not tell other people how to lead their lives. Jesus the man, stripped of myth and magic, might be a model, but a model that each person had to perceive, if not actually build, for him or herself.

Commitment and the World

Behind Sharman's concept of morality, behind all Sharman's ideas, lay his belief in the necessity of total commitment to God's will. This was the core of Sharman's belief and, as we shall see, continued to be the central idea and driving force in the work of Harry and Emilia Rathbun. To commit themselves to God's will, individuals had to first abdicate their own will "not in favor of another person, but to some force worthy of taking command."[36] The commitment, when it was made, was to be total, without reservation. The person making the decision had to pledge "that from this particular, concrete instant, until death or the voluntary revocation of the decision, I will do what I believe to be the will of God, regardless of the cost."[37]

Sharman justified his call for the destruction of the individual will and the dedication to God's will with the text of Luke 17:33: "He that seeketh to gain his life shall lose it, and he that loseth his life shall find it." Sharman interpreted the idea of "loss of life" as meaning "loss of will." The consequences of surrendering to the will of God were considerable and worth quoting at length:

Absence of conflict; ease, freedom, spontaneity; richness and variety of outlook; confidence, fearlessness; sense of unafraidness of challenge; disregard of anything the universe can do to me, knowing that neither people nor the universe can really touch me; quickening of ethical sensitivity, but without morbidity; absence of self-scrutiny and self-examination, because one has gotten away from an evaluation of specific acts and is moving in an area of peace; passage from intellectual obscurity and mistiness into clarity, luminosity; a hold upon an Ariadne's thread that leads you thru all the mazes; possession of outlook or viewpoint that lights every area, economic, philosophical or sociological; where one can see the wanderings of others and why they have gotten off the track; observations of intellectual disciplines; change of a sense of values which makes other things look stupid; hard tasks become easy; death of battle within, elimination of conflicts of drives, impulses, elemental human things.

Sharman concluded this catalog of treasures by assuring his audience, "I would not overdraw this picture for anything; it would be blasphemy."[38] Sharman did not claim that the committed person would exhibit perfect conduct—such perfection was unattainable. He did, however, believe that although perfect behavior was impossible, perfect attitude was not, and the religious person could do no less.

Sharman sometimes used the word *transformation* to describe the process of commitment. In doing so he came very close to describing what would usually be called a conversion experience, although he and his followers carefully avoided that term. Referring to the process as "purgation" in a statement that probably dates from the mid-1940s, Sharman said that the term did "not necessarily refer to religious conversion" (although that possibility apparently remained open). It was, he said, "merely the effect of opening the windows of one's moral life and allowing the freshening breezes of an exacting morality to sweep away the cobwebs."[39] Just how the act of commitment differed from conversion remained somewhat obscure in Sharman's writings, but he passed on to the Rathbuns the understanding that a specific decision had to be made before a person could be truly religious. People who made the kind of decision Sharman advocated would be willing to undergo not only discomfort but even torture and death before they would ever again put their will ahead of God's. Sharman told his students that one must be willing to "face the worst possible thing that one can conceive and then ask: would I go thru that for the right? If there is no hesitation, then one is ready to make the commitment." The committed person would face crucifixion just as Jesus did. The committed person would place God's will ahead of the marriage vow, ahead of the family, and ahead of material wealth.[40] This uncompromising expectation that truly religious people would totally subjugate themselves to the will of God, even at some great personal sacrifice, would continue as one of the core values in the movement as it evolved in the Rathbun era.

When it came to applying the idea of commitment to the outside world, Sharman was even less forthcoming than his usually reticent norm. He appears to have avoided most political and social issues on the grounds that transformation of the individual was a necessary precondition to social change. Despite his business background, Sharman seems to have been sympathetic to social reform (certainly many, if not most of his students were). One of his students quotes him as saying, "A Christian has got to be a social radical," and although he warned his students not to confuse society with the Kingdom of God, a social-gospel position was evident when he said, "religion has been the genetic force in the most significant social progress."[41]

The only systematic exposition of Sharman's views on the relationship between religion and politics appeared in a brief memo he wrote in November 1936. The circumstances that prompted this position paper are obscure, but it is clear that Sharman did not want his ideas on the subject disseminated. The memo was marked "*STRICTLY PRIVATE—* Neither to be printed nor any copy made."[42] In the paper Sharman sought to define the appropriate role of the "Christian Left," among whom he obviously counted himself.

According to Sharman, the first function of the Christian left was to "rediscover and recreate Christianity as a determining force in the contemporary world." Then, switching from the third to the first person, he said, "we have to work at a level that is above the political and social through inclusion of it." Sharman explicitly rejected the idea that his work was political in any way: "If we identify our task with the political one . . . then we should cut religion out entirely, and join in the most direct political effort in an effective political fashion."[43]

Having divorced religion from politics, Sharman said that his own and his followers' task was "the religious criticism of religion," that could "only be done through our own religious experience." This meant they had to fight against "nearly all modern religion," because it was based on the belief in "another world and immortality," and therefore had its central reference point "outside this world of contemporary existence." It also meant, however, they had to fight against the denial of all religion. Sharman distinguished between "European religions" and true Christianity. The latter presumably was the religion that grew out of the scientific study of the Records, whereas the former was an accumulation of historical accretions having little to do with Jesus. Thus Sharman was attempting to extricate himself from what he perceived to be the Marxist error of throwing out the baby of true Christianity with the bathwater of "European religion." He admitted that the Marxists were right in rejecting religion based on "another world and immortality." If that were all religion involved, then he believed that he and his group would have no reason for existing and that they might as well "accept atheism and join the communist party." But of course, he believed that the Marxist criticism was not fully correct, and that his role in the Christian left was to tease out true Christianity from the obscuring myths that had grown up around it—"To rediscover Christ and the revelation of truth in him in our own contemporary communal experience."[44]

It seems clear that Sharman was not insensitive to the social implications of his work. He simply did not perceive his role as furthering the efforts of political reform, although he presumably had no objection to others doing so. Whatever objections he may have had to Marxism were apparently based less on its political goals than on its opposition to all religion, and he found the "left wing" label congenial enough to apply it to himself, even if only in the religious sphere. Emilia Rathbun remembers that her exposure to Sharman caused her to begin thinking about political issues and spurred her, at least briefly, to think of herself as a socialist. Although her flirtation with the political left was fleeting, she said she never understood how anyone could go through a Sharman seminar and remain a Republican.[45] Although Sharman never defined the relationship between personal transformation and social action, many of his students took it upon themselves to apply their new values in the social sphere. Sharman, however, never encouraged such action and always believed that personal transformation was the first priority. Although they were a bit more willing than Sharman to address social problems directly, the Rathbuns shared his reluctance to become politically involved.

Inheriting the Sharman Tradition

In 1933 Sharman left his position at Pendle Hill and "retired" to Carmel, California. He nevertheless continued to lead Records seminars for another ten years. The center for much of his work in this last period of his active career was Camp Minnesing. Sharman first leased this rural retreat in Ontario's Algonquin Provincial Park from the Canadian National Railroad in 1925 after spending two summers at nearby Bon Echo. He later purchased it and held seminars there every summer until 1945.[46] Lack of paved roads in the park meant that seminar participants had to come by railroad and a ten-mile canoe trip before they reached the seven cedar-log lodges and seven cabins that made up the compound.[47] It was a place, explained Sharman, where nothing was "seen or heard of railways, automobiles, telephones or radios for the period of the Seminar."[48] Afternoons in this rustic setting were set aside for unstructured recreation, but mornings were devoted to the intensive study of the Records. It was there that he conducted his six-week "Jesus as Teacher" summer seminars, and it was there that the plans were laid—or perhaps waylaid—to continue Sharman's work when he finally gave up his active participation.

Over the years Sharman had retained his close ties to the Student Christian Movement of Canada, and the SCM sponsored the summer seminars until 1933. For both the summer seminars at Minnesing and winter meetings at various college locations, Sharman did most of the organizing, picked up most of the expenses, and led the Records study groups by himself. On several occasions he thought about formalizing his efforts and in 1923 actually drew up a plan for a Records study fraternity to be called Theta Pi Theta.[49] Although the fraternity never materialized, Sharman did adopt the Greek letter designation Alpha Psi Zeta to refer to the faculty members in Canada and the United States who worked with him in conducting Records seminars. Planned in 1923 and incorporated in 1928, Alpha Psi Zeta was not a fraternity. Sharman called it a "foundation," but it wasn't that either, at least when he first began using the term in the 1920s. Besides not being a foundation, Alpha Psi Zeta was "not an organization, not a society open or secret, not a movement, not a fellowship, not a body of people with a set of beliefs." It was, said Sharman, "a group of college and university faculty members who are interested in the unfettered and thorough study, the adequate understanding, and the sound evaluation of Jesus of Nazareth within the academic community."[50] Continuing his penchant for Greek, and confusing nomenclature even more, Sharman used the first and last letters of Jesus' Greek name, Iota Sigma, to refer to the seminars themselves.

Despite all the appearances of organization, Sharman shied away from establishing any formal structure that would further his work. He clearly felt great ambivalence toward the issue of organization. He once told Harry Rathbun, "All you need to do to kill anything is organize it. Then it will roll on long after it is dead."[51] Nevertheless, there were several isolated instances of organized efforts to spread the Sharman method. Seminar participants were always encouraged to organize their own Records study groups at their home institutions, and for three years, from 1931 to 1933, the Alpha Psi Zeta Foundation did encourage two women to start new groups at colleges in the San Francisco Bay Area. These two women, Elizabeth Boyden and Frances Warneke, were the people who introduced Emilia Rathbun to the Sharman method.[52] Other Sharman disciples maintained an informal network, but with the exception of a brief unsuccessful experiment at the very end of his career, Sharman never tried to extend his mission beyond his own efforts.[53]

Although Sharman never formalized his activity, his students were eager to preserve the tradition, so in the summer of 1944 a group of veteran "Minnesingers" drew up tentative plans to create a permanent organization that would carry on Sharman's work. They concluded that although it was sympathetic to their purpose, the SCM was not going to sponsor Records seminars and that if they wanted to further the cause they would have to do so with their own local units.[54] They adopted the name Alpha Psi Zeta Foundation that Sharman had been using since the 1920s and appointed a "Central Group" to continue developing plans through the winter.[55] As was his wont, Sharman remained aloof from the organizational discussions, in his own words, contributing "not even the extreme minimum of nothing." Nevertheless he was plainly pleased at the direction the group took, saying to them, "you have not only my approval but my commendation in the strongest possible terms."[56]

Despite adoption of a name and the creation of an administrative body, the group was still caught in the same bind that had trapped Sharman a decade before: they wanted to have the benefits of organization without actually becoming an organization. One member of the Central Group, Glenn Olds, articulated this ambivalence when he wrote that the foundation was not an institution. If it were, he said, he would be against it, presumably because he, like most of the others, did not want to set up a group that would appear to compete with the YMCA, the Student Christian Movement, or any other preexisting Christian organization, or that might even become a sect that would compete with mainline churches. He nevertheless described what, by almost any standard, was in fact a formal organizational structure involving material, method, leadership, participation, and membership.[57] Although it would be an open, nonexclusive kind of group whose only purpose would be to conduct seminars in the Sharman tradition, it would necessarily be a structured association with all of the bureaucracy attendant on such a venture.[58]

Most of Alpha Psi Zeta Foundation's Central Group met during the 1944 Christmas holiday and composed a draft letter describing the new direction and calling on seminar alumni to join the newly constituted foundation. The announcement was written by Sharman disciple Earl Willmott who had agreed to be in charge of the central office. In the draft, Willmott delightedly explained that Sharman had done nothing to promote the group, patiently trusting "the living vitality of the Word to work in us and others until a demand was felt."[59] Yet when the group presented its idea to Sharman he was so pleased that he gave them Camp Minnesing, saying "If you will use it for this one purpose; the study of the memorabilia about Jesus, the Camp is yours."[60] Although it appeared that the work of Henry B. Sharman had finally found an institutionalized means to perpetuate itself, it was never to be.

Four days after he mailed the draft to the others in the Central Group, Willmott received a telegram from Harry Rathbun informing the Central Group that Sharman would neither lead the 1945 summer seminar nor give the group his mailing list. Instead, according to Rathbun, Sharman was giving his "wholehearted cooperation" to a "more courageous and revolutionary program . . . based upon and requiring the total commitment central in the religion of Jesus." Rathbun asked the Central Group to give him and Emilia authorization to continue planning with Sharman for a "program of acting large and imaginative enough to meet the demands of the crisis of our time."[61]

The reaction of the Central Group was one of consternation and confusion. Willmott feared that Sharman was planning to make commitment a precondition for membership to the foundation and that, worried Willmott, would make it a sect. Others were concerned that Sharman had reached a dramatic conclusion on his own, ignoring the group process that had been so fruitful in the past. Finally, it was pointed out that the language of the telegram implied that the foundation could change the world. One critic commented that he had been working on what he could do for himself and he did not consider himself a great evangelist with a vision of transforming the world. "I don't see myself a John R. Mott, and I don't think the rest of us are John R. Motts either," he said.[62]

But the formidable model of evangelist John R. Mott did not scare the Rathbuns or their supporters. One of them conceded, "I realize none of us are John R. Motts," but, he continued, "neither was the John R. Mott we know until he launched forth to *do* the *impossible*."[63] They too were ready to do the impossible and become John R. Motts in the process. In a letter to Willmott, Harry reported Emilia's reaction to the draft letter plans for the new foundation: "That won't do! It won't work. There's nothing in that program to build a fire under people. If we think we've got the answer to the absolutely critical need of these times, we've got to get out and sell it to people in such a way as to set them on fire."[64]

The project the Rathbuns had in mind was ambitious beyond anything previously envisioned by Sharman or his followers, presaging both the style and content of the Creative Initiative movement. First, Willmott was correct in his assumption that commitment was to be a precondition of membership. Harry and Emilia suggested that the group "invite promising people to come to Minnesing the coming summer on the basis of their unqualified adoption of the way of life taught by Jesus."[65] Second, the Rathbuns were not interested in merely helping individuals achieve personal understanding. They also believed that they had an opportunity for a "large-scale program of 'selling' to the world the religion which can save it."[66] Here then, for the first time, is a clear expression of the sectarian messianic impulse in the Rathbuns' work. They perceived the world in crisis and they believed that they knew what needed to be done to save it.

To the charge that a precondition of commitment would be exclusionary, Ralph Odom, one of the Rathbun allies, countered that "this is not to 'exclude' anyone—it is to invite all to meet the conditions of mature religion." As though to concede the solipsistic nature of his own argument, however, he then went on to wonder "if perhaps we ought not be less fearful of being termed 'a sect.'" Like Emilia and Harry, Odom was unembarrassed by the profound religious implications of his position. He believed they had "a truth too significant to place in the old wine skins of customary organizational technique and procedure." Indeed, he believed that the times were ripe for a "new denomination, *a new religion* (1900 years old) with *real vitality* in a pagan world in which most of organised religion is *dead.*"[67] Although it would be thirty years before the Rathbuns would proclaim themselves members of a new religion, the seeds were already germinating in 1945.

In language that would become typical of the Rathbuns' uncompromising demand for complete dedication to the cause, Harry wrote, "Perhaps such a renewed and revitalized commitment to the will of God may mean for most of us who are members of the Central Group the giving up of our present jobs for a year—maybe permanently—and making *this* our sole job—for the year and perhaps the rest of our lives." Harry said that he was willing to ask for a leave of absence for the following year and he challenged the rest of the group to do likewise. "Are we serious about it?" he asked. "Are we really willing to sell all? Do we truly believe we have the answer to a desperately sick world's troubles?" The questions were obviously rhetorical. The answer was, "If we do, must we not face these implications and lay plans on a vastly greater scale than those we were thinking of as our first steps?"[68]

Dryden Phelps, another member of the Central Group, came to

California on personal business in early 1945 and had a chance to talk directly with the Rathbuns and Sharman. His report to the group makes it clear that Harry and Emilia, not Sharman, were the originators of the new plan. Emilia foresaw a community "on a communistic basis of religiously wholly committed people who have literally 'sold all' " and moved to a place where they could live and train others who in turn would go out into the world to spread the Sharman message and technique. She even suggested that this new community might be located near Trabuco in Southern California where Gerald Heard, a religious philosopher with whom both Rathbuns had studied in the mid-1930s and early 1940s, had his center.[69] Trabuco College, where followers of Heard lived and learned to practice his religious ideas, became something of a model for the Rathbuns, and they would refer to it constantly in their planning discussions.

Citing that bible of the social gospel movement, Walter Rauschenbusch's *Christianity and the Social Crisis,* Phelps attacked the basic premise of the Rathbuns' plan. He recalled that for two thousand years the finest minds of Christianity had withdrawn from the world to form elite communities, thus removing themselves from the very environment where they were most needed. Rather than try to provide a "solution by example," Phelps advocated bringing "the impact of Jesus to others through the seminar method, AND CONCURRENTLY to cooperate with men and women of good will and intelligence the world over to discover the generic causes of world chaos, and cooperate with them to eliminate those causes by the creation of a cooperative, non-competitive society."[70] Phelps's references to a "cooperative, non-competitive society" reflected his distinctly left-wing social gospel perspective. It was his belief that the reconstruction of society could not wait until large numbers of people had become committed to the religion of Jesus. Rather those with religious motivation had to cooperate with others motivated by economics and politics to work for a better world. Only in a new and decent society, he wrote, was it possible that "the Kingdom of God will have some chance of growth and survival."[71]

At a philosophical level, therefore, the group was split by the classic division between those who were homocentric, believing social reality derived from the ideas of individuals, and those who were sociocentric, believing that socioeconomic reality gave rise to individual beliefs. People with a homocentric outlook focus on the individual. For some, the homocentric focus is so narrow that it excludes the world beyond the single person. For others such an individualized focus is a way of influencing the collective whole. Sociocentrics approach the issue from the other end. They see the individual as more of a product than a component. For them it is not the collective sum of individuals who make up the social whole, but rather it is the ecology of the socioeconomic culture that molds the individual.

Within the context of religion, the homocentric–sociocentric split produces two very different sets of attitudes and activities. Religious homocentrics tend to be exclusive, believing that God's will can only be affected by those who have a special understanding, knowledge, or insight. At its purest, religious homocentrism holds individual salvation as the sole purpose of belief and regards the social implications of personal belief as irrelevant. Slightly less extreme are those religious homocentrics who do want to change society and believe the way to do so is by converting individuals to a new set of beliefs that lead to a new way of life. For them social change is the cumulative result of a large number of individual changes. They do not seek to force people to alter their behavior through the coercion of legal force, but rather to convert the individual to right thought and belief with the confidence that a good society will inevitably follow.

Sociocentric religious reformers, by contrast, see their role as getting out among and cooperating with others who share their goals, if not necessarily their values. They tend to place much greater stress on political action and advocate political solutions to social problems. Sociocentric reformers with a strong religious motivation adhere to what in America has come to be called the social gospel. Moving out into the world beyond the church, social gospelers seek to bring about change (reform or revolutionary) that will implement their idea of a just society. Individual conversion is still seen as a desirable goal, but not as a necessary precondition for genuine change. Indeed, a change in social conditions is frequently viewed as an important prerequisite for any change in the individual. Liberated from the oppression, corruption, and exploitation of the preexisting society, individual human beings would be free to realize their creative and spiritual potential.

The concept of religious community had a strong influence on the Rathbuns' position in the homocentric–sociocentric dichotomy. They always perceived themselves as part of a community of believers distinct from the rest of society, and they frequently talked of a physically discrete community as well. Homocentrics are much more likely than sociocentrics to separate themselves into a community of believers. Because their core value does not emphasize changing the world at large, they sacrifice little by withdrawing from it.

Homocentrics who divorce themselves more or less completely from the outside world when they move into communities, like the Shakers or the Amish, create an isolated society where they can live in an environment of mutual support with little regard for what might be going on in the rest of the world. Other communal homocentrics, like the Mormons and many political communitarians, use their community either as a base for missionary activity or as an example that they hope others will follow.

The Rathbuns fell into this last category. They hoped to establish a base in which believers could "live the life" nurtured by others who share their values. But it would not be a cloistered existence. The Rathbuns' projected community would be a school where people could learn about their beliefs and the techniques to be used to spread the word to others. It would be a place where believers could find practical as well as spiritual support, and from which they could venture into the outside world to spread the message. Unlike "pure" homocentrics who wish only to be left alone to lead a religious life, the Rathbuns always felt a compelling obligation to get as many people as possible to see the future of humankind as they saw it. Their homocentric approach was based on the ideal of saving the earth by awakening people to the dangers that faced them and getting them to change their religious values.

There were actually three factions in the Central Group. The most conservative were the pure homocentrics who had close ties to the mainline churches and felt that Sharman's work should be aimed solely at the individual, taking no position at all on broader social issues. The other two factions both believed they should work to create the Kingdom of God on earth. The sociocentrics, led by Willmott and Phelps, thought the good society could be created through political action with the help of converted people. The Rathbuns also wanted to create the good society, but their method was a synthesis of the first two positions. Like the pure homocentrics they wanted to concentrate their effort on converting individuals, but, like the sociocentrics, they hoped their actions would lead to major changes in society.

Thus the stage was set for a confrontation at Camp Minnesing in the summer of 1945 when, as it turned out, the debate was greatly complicated by the issue of communism. For Minnesingers, communism was inevitably linked with China because many of them had close personal ties with that country. Emilia's sister Elena had married Felix Greene, the sympathetic chronicler of the Chinese Communist revolution.[72] Sharman's wife, Abbie, had been born in Hangchow where her parents were missionaries. The Sharmans visited China in 1922 as the Canadian delegates of the SCM to the World Student Christian Federation Meeting in Beijing, and there the president of Yenching University, an old SVM colleague, invited Sharman to join the faculty. Sharman was a visiting professor of history in the Department of Religion from 1926 to 1929.[73] Finally, both Earl Willmott and Dryden Phelps had been missionaries in China before the war and would return at the war's end.

Their personal experience in China, and their objection to Marxist atheism, made both Sharmans unsympathetic to the Chinese Communist revolution, but the same was not true for Willmott and Phelps. The two younger men had taught together at West China University, an interdenominational school in Chengdu where Willmott had introduced Phelps to the Sharman approach. The two of them subsequently held Records seminars using Sharman's books, which they had translated into Chinese. Harry described Phelps as "an attractive, dynamic, powerful man" whom Sharman saw as his "St. Paul" and as the son he never had.[74] Perhaps because he himself was so assiduously nonpolitical, or perhaps because he did not want to see that the man to whom he was closest was a political radical, Sharman does not appear to have realized that his two disciples were sympathetic to the Communist revolution in China until the issue was brought to a head by others. [75]

The Confrontation at "Minnesing '45"

Rather than launching a new organization to promote Records seminars as originally planned, "Minnesing '45" turned into a confrontation between two groups with very different visions of the future of Sharman's work. Although they are brief, the minutes of these meetings vividly depict the clash between the Rathbuns' goal of a community of believers with selective entry and the Phelps–Willmott group's desire for a more open and decentralized structure.

At the very first meeting of the summer, the Rathbuns suggested that they expand beyond the academy to target people through churches and youth groups. Harry and Emilia had begun to doubt the receptiveness of students, whom they viewed as being even more conservative than their parents and infested "with the same germ of intellectual smugness which is deadly with the faculty."[76] Furthermore, students and faculty would be less likely to move into the separate community that they envisioned. Once more those worried about the Rathbun approach raised the caution that the group not become a cult. They did not want an organization that one had to become a member of. They believed that the group's only purpose was to promote the study of Jesus. The issue was joined again on the second day when "long, and at points heated" discussions took place on the question of who should be allowed into the foundation. The Phelps–Willmott faction, on the one hand, argued that the group "should be open to all who affirmed their intention to participate in the work of the F[oundation] for its specific purpose." The Rathbuns and their allies, on the other hand, "felt there should be definite restriction—preferably to those who affirmed their commitment to God."[77]

By the second week of argument tempers were frayed, goodwill had evaporated, and Camp Minnesing was a hotbed of rumors. Much of the actual debate focused on the peripheral issue of whether or not to have a full-time paid secretary. Earl Willmott was the existing secretary, so arguing over the position allowed the factions to use it as a symbolic way to address the deeper issues of inclusive versus exclusive membership and communism. Unable to reach any agreement, the feuding factions finally called a conference between Sharman and a select group of senior people. There, the pseudo-issue of organization was put aside and the real issue of communism finally broke into the open. Willmott accused the Rathbuns and their supporters of spreading a story that quoted Phelps as saying, "Earl and I lead Records groups to open students minds so that they will be ready for communism."[78] Phelps denied ever having used these words. Sharman, however, rejected the demurer saying that, whatever his exact words, Phelps had given a lot of people the impression that he agreed with the gist of the statement. Sharman said that he had received "floods of letters" from Canada's Maritime Provinces after a trip there by Willmott asking if the foundation "was interested in Jesus or in communism."[79]

Willmott and Phelps responded with a defense of their belief that religion could not be isolated from the social situation. They then counterattacked by charging that Emilia had said she would "wreck the foundation" if she did not get her way. Emilia, who had been the major source of the accusations against Willmott and Phelps, did not deny their charge, but explained that she had meant to act only if Phelps tried to use the group to spread communism.[80] Unpleasantness reigned and "for some time aspersions and recriminations were flying back and forth. There were many slurs and slams about fallible memories." Attempts to steer the course of discussion back to the administrative issue again foundered on the Communist issue. Harry Rathbun finally admitted that he was as much opposed to Earl Willmott as he was to the idea of a central secretary, and Willmott admitted that he had "spoken of the Chinese Communists with approbation" but still denied he had ever advocated communism.[81]

Finally, after six weeks of bickering, Sharman stepped in to put an end to the debate. He called off the Records seminar that he had been leading during the hours when people were not engaged in the political battle and roundly chastised everybody for the unseemly display of wrangling. The angry and dispirited leader was so appalled at "the willingness to impugn, to charge, to repeat, to go to others and report suspicions, sheer suspicions, of plots, maneuvering, politics," that he declared himself sapped of the will to carry on. Instead of holding additional Records meetings Sharman ordered the members of the group to go off by themselves and think about how they had contributed to the rancorous confrontation.[82]

Because the group was unable, or unwilling, to resolve the underlying conflict between the homocentric, community-oriented position of the Rathbuns, and the sociocentric, Communist-tainted position of Phelps and Willmott, the confrontation finally played itself out on the incidental question of organization. Although he appears to have had the support of a majority of the younger people, opposition from the Rathbuns and other senior people forced Willmott to tender his resignation both as secretary and as a member of the Central Group. The secretary job then went to Harry Rathbun. With Sharman already living in Carmel, close to the Rathbuns' Palo Alto home, Harry's new prominence in the group assured that the line of succession would pass to him (and Emilia) and not to the social activists.[83]

As secretary, Harry Rathbun did not assume the kind of aggressive role that either Phelps or Willmott would have. They were, after all, trained and experienced missionaries who had both the drive and the ability to organize. Indeed, despite their unhappy experience at Minnesing, Phelps and Willmott continued to be active in promoting Records study, even meeting with others (not including the Rathbuns) to put together a "Leaders' Handbook."[84] But, because they returned to

China, Sharman's work remained only loosely organized and, although Sharman himself was increasingly pleased by the Records study that Harry was leading in Palo Alto, no serious attempts were made to maintain any regular contact among the many Records study groups in the United States and Canada.[85] Without centralized leadership and with no institutional structure, whatever coherence there had been to Sharman's work evaporated.

The work in China effectively ended a few years after the Communist victory in 1949. Dryden Phelps remained in the People's Republic of China until 1952 when he was recalled by the American Baptist Foreign Missions Board for writing a public letter that called the Chinese Communist revolution "the most profoundly religious Christian experience I have ever been through."[86] Like Phelps, Willmott was one of a group of missionaries (all influenced by the Sharman method) who were invited to stay on in China by the Communist government.[87] When Willmott finally left with the last of the western missionaries in 1952, he crossed the border wearing a blue cotton peasant suit and had his picture taken giving the clenched-fist Communist salute.[88]

Records study groups in at least eight other nations besides the United States and Canada continued for some time after World War II. Sharman protégés were active in a number of Canadian colleges through the 1960s, and in the United States there were centers of Records study in the east associated with the Quaker facility at Pendle Hill.[89] In California, Elizabeth B. Howes, one of the women who originally introduced the Rathbuns to Sharman, continued to run Records seminars through her Guild for Psychological Studies.[90] But it was Harry and Emilia Rathbun's work that was destined to grow into an entirely new nationwide movement.

Harry and Emilia

Over a period of sixteen years, from 1946 to 1962, the Rathbuns slowly changed their movement from a Bible study group in the Sharman tradition to a de facto religious sect. The transition took place because Harry and Emilia Rathbun wished to create a permanent organization for which Sharman's work was a poor model. Assiduously nonsectarian, Sharman had rejected any kind of institutionalization for his movement. The Rathbuns, however, had a different vision. Rather than a stage through which people passed, they saw their movement as a permanent affiliation. In order to keep people in the organization they had to find a new source of members other than students, all of whom moved on after they graduated. Adults, by contrast, had roots in the community and could be counted on for more than a few years, but only if they could be kept involved. New courses were developed to provide members with a continuing variety of experiences, and new support systems emerged to give the participants the psychological and practical assistance necessary for continued participation.

Partially by design and partially by force of circumstances, the Rathbuns developed a structured social environment for group members. Their approach, like Sharman's, was still basically homocentric, but a permanent religious community emerged to support the individual transformations. The Rathbun group began to develop its own ideology that varied significantly from mainstream social and religious thought. It sought the primary loyalty of its members, weakening their ties to the churches; it developed its own organizational structure with a leadership of people who were perceived as spiritually advanced; and, most important, it began to provide participants with programs that compensated for the social and psychological cost incurred when they joined a group that held nontraditional beliefs.

Despite some significant differences in their leadership styles, there were a number of remarkable parallels in the lives of Harry Rathbun and Henry B. Sharman. Both were trained in the sciences. Both had brief careers in business and labor arbitration, and both ultimately saw themselves as teachers whose calling it was to spread the understanding of Jesus in the academy. Both also had very strong and independent wives who gave them a great deal of support in their missions. Emilia Rathbun, however, was much more an active partner to Harry than Abbie Lyon Sharman had been to Henry Sharman. And in the long run Emilia's role proved to be even more decisive than Harry's, for it was she who gave Sequoia Seminar the spiritual leadership that changed it from a group study of religion into a self-proclaimed new religion.

Harry Rathbun's ancestors had settled in Rhode Island in the colonial period and over the course of the next five generations moved steadily westward to Ohio, Iowa, South Dakota (where Harry was born), and California (where his children Juana Beth and Richard were born). At the time of his birth Harry's parents lived in Mitchell in the Dakota Territory, where his father owned a grocery.[91] He had identical twin brothers nine years older than he and a sister four years younger.

Harry remembers being a timid child, somewhat intimidated by his older brothers who were both rather troublesome, a fact that Harry believes accounts for the nine-year gap between their birth and his. Indeed, his shyness was acute. He would never recite his elocution pieces for family guests and, when a Sunday school teacher assigned him a part in the Christmas play, he refused to go back for six months. Despite the Christmas play trauma, Sunday school proved to be of great importance to Harry's spiritual development. Although neither of his parents was a regular churchgoer, they sent him to Methodist Sunday school and reared him with what Harry called "a strict Protestant ethic." Harry never questioned the basic validity of the values taught by the Methodist church—continuing to adhere, for example, to the non-drinking pledge he had signed as a youth even after he left the church.[92]

When he was thirteen, a favorite Sunday school teacher invited a group of young men to join the church formally. Although he would have been too shy to make a public profession of faith on his own, in the security of the group he joined the church at the Easter service. The collective nature of the act did not diminish its importance to Harry. He understood his action as a public commitment to the idea that he would do his best to do what was right. He feared, however, that this might oblige him to be a minister or a missionary, and he was not at all sure how, given his shyness, he could be either. But he reasoned that God would not ask him to be anything that God had not equipped him to do.[93]

Harry understood his new religious commitment to mean that he had to take his school work more seriously, which he did. But this too raised a serious problem. In his small-town high school the bright and hard-working young man quickly moved to the head of his class, and as early as his freshman year he realized that if he continued to do well he would graduate as the class valedictorian. For four years he lived in constant dread of the day when he would have to get up before the commencement audience and speak, all alone, in public.[94]

The feared day finally arrived, and Harry had carefully prepared an address inspired by the antiwar ideas of Stanford University president David Starr Jordan. The young scholar was somewhat nonplussed when the principal speaker, who preceded him, also chose peace as his topic. Nevertheless, he forged ahead with his memorized speech explaining that war was the result of selfishness and suggesting that international disputes be settled through arbitration enforced by a body of international police. It was an unduly optimistic talk, coming just three years before the outbreak of the First World War, but the ideas of peace, rational settlement of disputes, and the necessity of worldwide cooperation were already present in the mind of the seventeen-year-old youth.[95]

After Harry's graduation his father decided to retire and move to Los Angeles, where the family lived for several months. Following the footsteps of an older brother who had gone to MIT, Harry wanted to become an engineer. He had seen the introduction of the first telephone and the first electric light into his hometown and reasoned that engineers would be in high demand as this new technology continued to grow. His father had to return to South Dakota to finish up some business, and Harry persuaded him to move the family to San Jose so that he could attend Stanford University and live at home with his mother and sister while his father was gone. Stanford was only twenty years old and still tuition-free when Harry presented himself to the director of admissions one morning in September of 1912. On the strength of his high school record and a flowery letter of recommendation from his principal, he was admitted to the class of 1916 that same afternoon.[96]

He received his degree in mechanical engineering (electrical engineering was not yet a separate discipline) and spent the war years working for the Federal Telegraph Company designing high-power transmitters for the navy. Because the firm designated him as "essential" he was exempt from the draft—and subject to a certain amount of social opprobrium as a "slacker." Despite the antiwar sentiments of his valedictory he supported the conflict and was proud of his civilian role in the war effort. Even though the movement he founded eventually became Beyond War, an organization opposing all violent conflict, Harry was never a pacifist. He supported both World Wars, although there is some indication that he was influenced by Emilia's antiwar sentiments just before America's entry into World War II.[97]

Although he went back to Stanford after the war to get his engineer's degree (a postgraduate degree), he had serious doubts about his abilities in this field. He was not very good with his hands and always did poorly in machine shop and in other direct applications of theoretical knowledge. He was spared the need to test his skills in the field when he was offered an administrative position with the Colin B. Kennedy Company, a new San Francisco firm that was manufacturing radio receivers. He stayed with the Kennedy Company until it folded in 1926, moving with it to St. Louis and working variously as treasurer, general manager, and vice-president. When the owners liquidated the firm in the face of the new RCA patent pool, Harry decided to pursue his interest in the interaction of business and the law and, putting aside his engineering skills, he took his profits from the sale of the firm and returned to Stanford to enter law school.[98]

By the time he graduated from law school in 1929, Harry Rathbun was thirty-three years old and ready to start an entirely new life. But before he could launch his legal career he was offered a position on the Stanford faculty. A popular business law professor had quit to go into private practice, and the dean asked Harry if he would take over the position for a year while they conducted a full search. He did, and on the strength of his business experience was appointed to the position full time in 1930. Although he passed the California Bar, Harry never practiced law and spent his entire professional career until his retirement in 1959 on the faculty of the Stanford Law School.[99]

The courses that Harry taught were all intended for undergraduates and graduate business students. He never taught a regular course to law students except during summer school and during the World War II teacher shortage. He called his courses, "an approach to law for the layman."[100] Harry's scholarly accomplishments were modest. He had one contract to do a textbook on business law but abandoned that project when he and the publisher could not agree on the content. Then as now, being a good teacher was only part of what was expected from university professors. Harry was denied raises for focusing on Jesus when the university thought he should have been doing scholarly research. One year, when both of his deans (law and business) asked the acting president to give him a long-delayed raise, the president responded, "No, not while Rathbun is wasting so much time on religion."[101] His lack of scholarly activity meant that he was constantly passed over for merit pay increases, and he eventually resigned himself to the fact that he would never make as much as his more widely published colleagues. Like many other popular but low-paid faculty members he periodically fed his resentment by figuring out how much more the university was making from the tuition in his large classes than it was paying him.[102]

Yet what Harry lacked in scholarly accomplishments, he more than made up for in teaching success. By all reports he was a gifted and widely loved teacher both in the classroom and in his religious work. He had a deep and genuine commitment to the well-being of his students. He and Emilia constantly had students to their home for coffee and dinner, and even after Harry's retirement the Rathbuns were

among the first faculty couples to occupy faculty quarters in the Stanford fraternity clusters in 1962.[103] Their children, who both attended
Stanford, commented later how surprised they were to have never once
been invited to a faculty home during their undergraduate years,
wrongly assuming that all professors were as generous with their hospi-
tality as their parents had been.[104]

Reading the *Stanford Daily* one day toward the end of the spring
term in 1937, Harry came across a column in which the student author
complained, "We who are about to graduate are not individuals living
our lives as we should have taught ourselves to live. We are stereotyped
forms cast in the shape of that outworn likeness of a sacrosanct individual called the American college student." Harry was struck by the de-
spair of the column, by the hopelessness of a student who after four
years of a Stanford education could write, "I'm not looking forward to
June. Personally I'm scared to death."[105] Mulling over the implications
of the column, Harry decided not to give his planned final lecture in
Business Law that day, but instead to address himself to the column. It
was, he admitted, a sermon in which he told the class that the meaning
of life was up to them. Just as nobody else could eat their breakfasts for
them, nobody else could save their souls for them. He told them they
had to find the meaning of life for themselves, and that by finding their
destinies they would be saving their souls. The class gave him a standing
ovation that continued for the whole time it took him to walk out of the
classroom, across the inner quad, and to his office in the law school.
That began a tradition that lasted for twenty-five years during which
Harry ended every course with the same talk. The lecture was so popular that students brought their friends and it had to be moved from the
regular classroom to a large auditorium.[106]

In 1950, at the invitation of *Life* magazine, the student government
named Harry one of two "great teachers" on the Stanford campus. In
his final year of teaching in 1959, the administration moved his class to
the seventeen-hundred-seat Memorial Auditorium, and when he retired
they retired his business law course along with him.[107]

Harry's inspirational teaching was not limited to the academic classroom. Alumni of his Jesus as Teacher seminars are virtually unanimous in
remembering him as an outstanding teacher and group leader. Unlike the
stiff and forbidding Henry B. Sharman, Harry Rathbun was much more
approachable and inspired love as well as respect. Writing to Sharman, a
1946 seminar participant called Harry "one of the finest teachers that is
or has ever been our privilege to study under."[108]

Harry's religious journey had begun with his Methodist Sunday school experience. Although he adhered to his childhood precepts of morality thoughout his life, he had increasing problems with creedal theology. The first seeds of doubt had been sown in high school when he studied comparative religion and realized that other people believed as fervently as he that their religions were as true as his, and he wondered how one could know who was right. As an undergraduate at Stanford he attended the San Jose Methodist church but found that he was caught in a trap of his own honesty. At age thirteen, upon joining the church, he had pledged to be truthful. Yet each church service started out with a recitation of the Apostle's Creed, certain parts of which he did not believe. Thus by attending church and reciting the creed he was lying. Although it was not the proximate cause of his leaving the church, Harry remembers going to a lecture by Abdul Baha, the leader of the Bahai faith. This man's honesty impressed him and made him think that he, himself, was not being honest in his own religion. Eventually he left the church, not to repudiate his religious beliefs but to live up to them.[109]

Between the time that he left the church as an undergraduate and the time he met Emilia, Harry was not active in any social or religious activities. His energies were completely devoted to his business career, his study of law, and finally to preparing and teaching classes. But all of that would change when he met Emilia Lindeman. Emilia would become the major influence in Harry's life. It was she who encouraged Harry to become involved in religion again, and there, as in his classroom teaching, he found success and satisfaction. Near the end of his life, Harry wrote, "Thank God for Emilia who has been my teacher, but whom I have resisted, who has taken the brunt of my hostility, but has persisted in the job of helping me save my soul!"[110]

Emilia Lindeman was born in the Mexican city of Colima in 1906. Her father had been born and raised in North Carolina and had gone to Mexico as a young civil engineer to work on the construction of Mexican ports and railroads. Emilia's maternal grandfather was a low-level German diplomat whose family connections had enabled him to go to Mexico rather than to prison when he refused to join the army. He married a Mexican woman of mixed Indian and Spanish background, purchased large tracts of land, and ran a series of haciendas where he raised cattle, sugar cane, and coffee.[111]

Emilia and her three younger sisters grew up bilingual and somewhat bicultural, although Emilia thinks of her early years as being primarily upper-class Mexican. The family had no single home but moved from hacienda to hacienda as her grandfather supervised his holdings and her father traveled to the location of his latest engineering project. She remembers her grandfather as lord of the manor, a benevolent despot who provided his Indian workers with schools, medical care, and periodic fiestas where she was exposed to the colorful folk culture that expressed itself in her dress and surroundings for the rest of her life. Her experience as the pampered granddaughter of a grandee left her with a strong sense of noblesse oblige.[112] On the one hand, Emilia was always very sure of her own high social status. Her powerful self-confidence and finely developed social skills made her extremely popular and socially successful throughout her life. On the other hand, she was imbued with a sense of concern and sympathy for those less fortunate and, because she was so sure of her own place in life, she had no reservations about reaching out and helping others of lower status.

Neither her grandfather, who had converted to Catholicism in order to marry her grandmother, nor her parents were religious. Although they supported churches and priests for the workers and attended services on holidays, the family viewed the Catholic church of Mexico as practically pagan and inappropriate for people of high rank. Emilia does remember being fascinated by the mysterious ritual and ceremony of the mass, as well as the powerful religious symbols of the crucified Christ that were so prevalent in Mexican churches. Although they may not have had any immediate religious significance for her, these church rituals would later express themselves as she (and her daughter, Juana) worked out the details of her own religious vision.[113]

Until the time she was sixteen, Emilia was educated by American tutors who stressed the traditional women's accomplishments of art and music. These skills, and a love of literature that she inherited from her father, were her major intellectual accomplishments. Neither background nor education disposed her toward systematic, analytic thinking. She thought of herself as an intuitively creative person who worked better with people than with ideas.[114]

Several times during her childhood Emilia had fled to Los Angeles with her mother and sisters to escape political unrest in the aftermath of the 1910 revolution. In 1922, when she was sixteen years old, her father decided that she was being "raised like a savage" and had to be sent to the United States to get an American high school education. She spent two years attending San Jose High School while living with relatives of her father. Then in 1924 her mother moved to San Jose and she transferred to the Convent of the Sacred Heart High School, but even there she managed to avoid taking any courses in religion. After graduation Emilia enrolled at San Jose State College with the intention of becoming a teacher.[115]

In the meantime, her family's circumstances had taken a definite turn for the worse. After her grandparents' deaths, her parents relinquished all claims of the family estate rather than risk confrontation with and alienation from other relatives. Her father joined her mother in San Jose, but with the onset of the Depression, he could not find employment as an engineer and eventually had to go to work on the WPA. After her father died, Emilia herself dropped out of school for a year to help earn money to support her mother and sisters.[116]

When she entered college, Emilia was even less involved in organized religious activities than Harry had been. She was very active socially, however, joining the YWCA at San Jose State, an important center of women's activities. Emilia remembers the "Y" of the late 1920s as being concerned less with religion than with social justice. Their great interest in the plight of the poor, especially blacks and migrant workers, was especially congenial to Emilia, with her family tradition of concern for the poor. Equally attractive was the Y's interest in campus social activity. Situated in the center of rural Santa Clara County, San Jose State attracted large numbers of women from the fruit farms that were the area's major industry. The more sophisticated Y girls took on the obligation of introducing their country cousins to the ways of the city, instructing them in proper dress, etiquette, and other social graces.[117] Emilia's college experiences teaching other women how to look and act set a pattern that would continue through her work in Creative Initiative.

The YWCA was so removed from the ordinary religious concerns of Christian life that when the group's leader, Dorothy Phillips, came back from a Sharman seminar and began talking about Jesus, the other women were mildly shocked. But Emilia was intrigued. She had become good friends with Phillips and made it her business to meet Sharman at the annual YMCA–YWCA conferences that were held each year at the Asilomar conference center in Pacific Grove, near Sharman's retirement home in Carmel. Emilia admits that while she was impressed with Sharman as an individual, his rigorous intellectual approach to the gospels did not excite her. Nevertheless, she was increasingly attracted to a more serious study of religion, which blossomed into a full commitment when she finally attended her first Jesus as Teacher summer seminar in 1934.[118]

By that time, Emilia was married to Harry and had had her first child. Emilia had met Harry at a Stanford faculty party where she had been invited to entertain. Her work in the YWCA had introduced her to a number of Stanford faculty wives who would invite her and her sisters to perform at their parties. In fact, the Lindeman sisters had organized a semiprofessional group, "Las Tapatias," that performed Mexican folk songs around the Bay Area in the early 1930s.[119] At one particular party in 1931, she spotted Harry leaning against the mantle and said to herself, "that is the man I am going to marry." Discovering that he was a law professor who had a background in engineering, she invited him home to meet her father, who quickly realized that he was not the true object of the visit and left. Harry admits to having been a bit overwhelmed by this "aggressive female," who was not at all awed either by his professional position or by the fact that he was twelve years her senior. They met in February, were engaged in April, and married in August.[120]

By 1934, although happily married and the proud mother of an eighteen-month-old daughter, Emilia felt dissatisfied. She had given up any thought of teaching when she married (in 1934, wives of employed men did not work) and found the prospect of a life of endless faculty wives' teas a dreary one. She had previously thought about going to Minnesing, but six weeks and a six-thousand-mile roundtrip made that impossible for a young wife and mother. Then, two women who had been active disciples of Sharman started their own summer seminar in California, and the full experience of the Sharman technique became available to Emilia.[121]

Becoming Sharman Disciples

The two women responsible for starting the Sharman seminar in California, Frances Warnecke and Elizabeth Boyden, had met while both were undergraduates at the University of California, Berkeley. Warnecke had been introduced to Sharman at a YWCA Asilomar conference in 1929 and had attended a seminar at Minnesing the same year. She introduced Boyden to the Sharman method and the two of them spent several years promoting Records study in the Bay Area with money that Boyden had inherited after the death of her parents in a car accident. Much of their work was focused on Stanford, and there they inevitably met Emilia Rathbun who had also moved into the Sharman orbit.[122]

Warnecke, Boyden, and the Rathbuns were soon working together on the Stanford campus recruiting students and faculty for the summer seminars at Minnesing, even though neither of the Rathbuns had ever attended one. Thus, when Emilia attended the Warnecke–Boyden seminar in the summer of 1934, she had already been active in Records work for a number of years. By her own admission, however, she had never really understood the points they were trying to make, and her involvement lacked genuine commitment.[123]

Perhaps because she had achieved the goals of her early adult life, a husband, a child, and social position, and found that she needed something more, the Records seminar proved to be a major turning point in her religious life. Sharman had always insisted that all people had to discover the truth for themselves, and that is what Emilia did that summer in the California redwoods. The seminar's focus on the first great commandment of Jesus, "You shall love the Lord your God with all your heart and with all your soul, and with all you mind," and its demand for complete obedience to God, provided Emilia with the purpose that was missing in her life. She felt that up to that moment she had always gotten her own way. She had been able to manipulate her parents, her teachers, and her friends to get what she wanted. Now she realized that God wanted her to stop working for herself and to start working for him. She believed that he was a God "who demanded all or nothing" and "a God that would demand everything, was the right God" for her.[124]

She took the great Christian paradox, "Whoever seeks to gain his life will lose it, but whoever loses his life will preserve it," to mean that she must give up her social activities and devote her life one hundred percent to God. Upon returning home she resigned from the various clubs in which she was active, went down to the local Baptist church, and asked the pastor if he would let her lead a gospel study group among the church women. He agreed, and Emilia launched a career of work among the churches that would last for more than a quarter of a century. Lacking the academic credentials of Sharman and Harry, Emilia saw other wives and mothers as her natural constituency, and she appears to have been the first Sharman disciple to move beyond the academy in her work. Emilia worked at a series of churches in the Palo Alto area, frequently asking the pastors for the names of women who sent their children to Sunday school but did not themselves attend church. She would take these "dumpers" (because they dumped their kids on Sunday) into a study group and, according to Emilia, turned many of them into the most active people in their churches.[125]

While working in the churches beginning in the late 1930s, Emilia first encountered the situation in which her instinctively powerful style ("charismatic" would not be too strong a word) intruded on what she perceived to be the appropriate role of the religious leader. Unlike Sharman, Emilia did not have a naturally reticent personality. She was a performer who enjoyed the limelight and had spent most of her life successfully seeking to become the center of attention. She discovered in the church groups that many of the women were attributing their spiritual growth not to the study of the gospels but to the leadership of Emilia Rathbun.[126] She did not want her study groups to become personality cults centered around her, and she arranged to share the limelight by having certain women help her in the study sessions and then calling in ill to force them to take over the whole burden of leading a meeting.[127] Emilia's conviction that when she surrendered herself to the will of God she also surrendered the right to be the center of attention may not have led to a life of self-conscious effacement, but her belief in submission and the model of Sharman did restrain what might otherwise have been an overwhelming temptation to become the charismatic prophet of a personality-centered cult.

While Emilia was spreading the method-according-to-Sharman to women through the churches, Harry was also becoming increasingly involved in Sharman's work. Harry had been attracted to Sharman's method because it made sense to him "as a lawyer and as a scientist." The press of university business prevented him, however, from attending any of the longer seminars, including the one that Emilia went to in the summer of 1934. He could only take time to drive her up to the site and stay for the first day. Warnecke and Boyden were so pleased to have a member of the Stanford faculty there that they violated one of the basic rules of the seminar and told him he could return any time. The initial session was an eye-opener for Harry. For the first time since he had left the Methodist church as an undergraduate, he perceived the possibility of reconciling his beliefs with the teachings of Jesus. He was able to return for the last nine days of the four-week seminar and found the experience as important to him as it was to Emilia. Unlike his wife, Harry did not feel compelled to change his life style, but he did discover that the supernatural aspects of religious faith that had made him uncomfortable were subject to rational explanation, and that Jesus regarded as a teacher could point the way to finding God.[128]

As a result of his experience at the California summer seminar, Harry felt moved to begin leading Records study groups through the Stanford Methodist student organization. In the following year, 1935, he and Emilia attended their first summer seminar with Sharman at Camp Minnesing. For approximately the next ten years the Rathbuns actively engaged in a religious life that centered on teaching Records study in the Palo Alto area, recruiting participants for the summer seminars in Canada, and helping in the work of the California seminar that continued to be run by Elizabeth Boyden after she and Frances Warnecke parted company. In the immediate postwar period Harry was particularly successful with students, many of whom were ex-GI's looking for answers to questions raised by their war experience.[129] During the 1950s however, the Rathbuns' attention turned increasingly away from students and toward adults in the community at large.

The Rathbuns' assumption of leadership positions within the Sharman movement occurred rather quickly after their initial exposure to Records study. The year after attending their first Records seminar run by Elizabeth Boyden they were listed as contact people for the 1935 California seminar and by 1936, immediately after their first seminar with Sharman, Harry's Stanford office had become the mailing address for the Minnesing seminars as well.[130] Then in 1941 Harry got his first opportunity to lead a seminar on his own. Fred Howes, a Sharman disciple from Canada who had been leading a summer seminar in New Mexico was unable to leave the country because of the war. Harry was recruited to substitute for Howes and repeated his role the next year.[131]

Sequoia Seminar: The Rathbuns on their own

When, for personal reasons that will be discussed in chapter 3, Elizabeth Boyden was read out of the Sharman movement and went on to found her own Records study group, California was left without an "authorized" summer seminar. The highly motivated could still go to Canada to study with Sharman, but when the Minnesing seminars ended in the acrimony of 1945, the Rathbuns moved to fill the seminar vacuum by establishing their own summer program. Dubbed "Sequoia Seminar," the new summer Records program did not really replace Minnesing as a fountainhead of Sharman-style Records study but did become the largest and most active of the twenty-five or so Records study groups that existed after the 1945 breakup.[132]

The first Sequoia Seminar was held in July of 1946 in a rented fishing lodge on the Klamath River on the northern California coast. This isolated site proved inconvenient, and for the next four years the summer seminar moved to the conference center at Asilomar in Pacific Grove, closer to the Bay Area and to Henry Sharman, who occasionally attended sessions.[133] The Rathbuns' dream, however, was to have a place of their own, their own West Coast Camp Minnesing.

In October of 1945, just after the Minnesing breakup, Harry and Emilia met with a group of men in their Palo Alto home and outlined a plan to establish a permanent center for Sharman's work. Harry's notes for the meeting make it clear that he envisioned a hybrid of Sharman's Camp Minnesing and a teaching–living religious center like Gerald Heard's Trabuco College. Unlike the restricted academic focus that Sharman preferred, Harry wanted to recruit widely among other professionals, such as doctors, psychiatrists, clergy, teachers, and managers. Somewhat incongruously, he also hoped to recruit members from Alcoholics Anonymous. A fellow Methodist Sunday school teacher and member of his Records study group was an AA member and had attended the first Sequoia Seminar. This man had persuaded Harry to speak to AA meetings about the religious meaning of the Alcoholics Anonymous message. Since Alcoholics Anonymous had its origins in the religious fellowship of the Oxford Group (in which Emilia was active for several years before the war), it was easy enough for Harry to speak to the significant parallels between their work and the ideas of AA.[134]

The purpose of Harry's proposed center would be to teach "the way" to financially and educationally privileged people. Since the teaching process would involve meetings, conferences, and summer seminars, Harry wanted a center situated on a large secluded site with good views and basic improvements. Thus far he was merely envisioning a Minnesing-like retreat. But he went on to speculate that the center might grow into a partially self-supporting community growing its own food and running its own handicraft shops. Workers could go out from this center to serve and teach in the world, and return to it for support and rejuvenation.[135] It was in fact the same plan that had caused so much confusion among Sharman's followers the previous year. The Rathbuns were serious enough about this idea to approach philanthropists for donations to get the project started.[136]

Funds were not forthcoming, however, and after a few years the Rathbuns had given up their dream of a permanent home for the Sequoia Seminar. Writing to Sharman in 1948, Emilia told him, "We are through with the experiment of buying property. God doesn't want it as all attempts have failed. I see now that it would greatly handicap our freedom in teaching the *pure* truth because we might fall into all sorts of errors stemming from the need for finances to keep property up." In an afterthought Emilia expressed her wonder at the way God worked. "In time," she said, "He shows us the error of our ways if we are sensitive to read his signs and not too proud to admit our mistakes."[137] The comment was ironic because in the same letter she reported the death of Irving Hellman, one of the most active students in the Records study. Although Emilia did not know it at the time, Hellman had made Sequoia Seminar the beneficiary of his ten thousand dollar GI life insurance policy. Emilia subsequently interpreted the windfall of the Hellman inheritance as divine beneficence, signaling that land should be acquired, even though at the time she was writing to Sharman she also confidently stated that God wanted exactly the opposite.[138]

When the Rathbuns, who had always been close to the Quakers, heard that the American Friends Service Committee had been given 50 acres of land in Ben Lomond in the Santa Cruz Mountains, Harry proposed that Sequoia Seminar develop the land jointly with the Friends. In exchange for the money from the Hellman legacy, the Friends gave Sequoia Seminar the right to use certain portions of the Ben Lomond land. The funds were used to buy materials for three buildings that were erected with volunteer labor. The Quakers used the kitchen for their interracial boys' camp, and Sequoia Seminar used it for their meetings. Each group provided its own sleeping and meeting facilities.[139] Through the purchase of adjoining property and the construction of additional meeting lodges and sleeping cabins over the next twenty years, the Ben Lomond camp grew to 233 acres with several meeting lodges and numerous sleeping cabins, a large central kitchen, and a caretaker's cottage, but it never did become a permanent residence and refuge for followers of the Sharman method. In this sense, Ben Lomond was always more a Camp Minnesing than a Trabuco College.

The Rathbuns' vision of an actual camp for their community of believers was not completely fulfilled by a duplicate of Camp Minnesing, because their sense of mission differed considerably from that of Henry B. Sharman. Yet it would take the Rathbuns sixteen years before they reached the logical conclusion of their religious philosophy.

During this time they experimented with both the form and content of their group, emerging finally as a distinct sect whose members were willing, at least among themselves, to speak of their own "New Religion." The process of transformation from lay Bible study group to religious sect was both the cause and effect of tension with the established churches through whom they worked.

Functioning as a Proto-Sect

Sharman's Records study groups had been distinct from, but completely consonant with, the churches, and so there was very little cost to the people who participated in them. When Harry and Emilia picked up the program in 1946 they initially continued the original pattern. Over the next fifteen years, however, Sequoia Seminar underwent a series of changes that made it demand greater and greater commitment from its members, and so in turn it had to provide them with increased measures of support. By the end of the decade the group had moved so far from its original social context (the mainline churches) that it had become a competitor with them for the limited social, economic, and psychological resources of participants. It had become what could be called a proto-sect.

The story of the first fifteen years of Sequoia Seminar is the story of the drift away from the norms of the churches and even further away from the norms of secular society. Accompanying this movement were the changes that the economic model would predict. First, as Sequoia Seminar became more highly structured, both organizationally and ideologically, it became increasingly intolerant of those who were less than fully committed. Second, unlike churches, whose beliefs are relatively flexible in response to changing social values, the philosophical foundations established by the Rathbuns in the late 1930s remained essentially intact and became even more fixed, increasing the tension between members and society. Third, Sequoia Seminar provided increasing services for its members to compensate them for the growing costs of belonging and, at the same time, made increasing demands on the members to give to the group. Finally, the group's initial appeal was to women, a marginal social category that had fewer opportunities in society at large and therefore experienced less cost in joining the movement.

Following the tradition established by Henry B. Sharman, the

Rathbuns preferred not to think of Sequoia Seminar as an organization during its formative years. They sought to work with the churches and were careful to assure potential participants that they posed no threat to established religious groups. The very first announcement for the Sequoia Seminar in 1946 stated, "Those who are sponsoring this seminar are not connected with any institution or organization in common."[140] As late as 1959 and 1960 the group's annual report was still insisting that Sequoia Seminar was making "a conscious effort to avoid institutionalization and development of a systematic ideology." The very fact that Sequoia Seminar was issuing an annual report belied the claim that it was not an organization, a paradox admitted by the report itself when it pointed out that they owned property, held meetings, conducted seminars, and, they might have added, had a budget of almost twenty thousand dollars a year. Nevertheless, the report noted that the group had "no officers, no elections, no voting on decisions; we, as a group, have no denominational preference; we advocate no creeds or dogmas, nor do we purport to have 'the' answer to man's religious problems."[141]

Despite continued protestations of noncompetition through the 1950s, Sequoia Seminar people became increasingly concerned with the growth of their own movement and wanted to be sure that they could carve a role for themselves within the churches with which they were affiliated. They ruled out "authoritarian" churches, churches whose doctrines and creeds were incompatible with their beliefs (although they still claimed to have no established dogma of their own) and churches that already had a heavy schedule of study groups and prayer meetings (although they did not want to identify themselves with stagnating churches either).[142]

Sequoia Seminar simultaneously wanted to work within the churches and transcend them. It wanted to be a distinct entity with its own membership while not competing with the traditional churches. There were models for such a group. Sharman had done it, so had the Y's and laymen's movements like Frank Buchman's Oxford Group. The great potential for conflict between the churches and Sequoia Seminar grew, nevertheless, as the latter organization slowly evolved a bureaucratic structure. To the extent that potential members had a finite amount of time and money that they were willing to invest in their religious life, what they gave to one group they would have to take from the other. As long as Sequoia Seminar was running its study groups within the churches, and as long as its own operating budget remained modest, the conflict was minimal. Between 1946, when it held its first summer seminar, and around 1955, Sequoia Seminar and the churches appear to have had the kind of symbiotic relationship envisioned by Sharman.

After 1955, however, Sequoia Seminar entered a phase of organizational development that led to it becoming a proto-sect. Members were expressing more individual identification with the organization, while the religious life of the group was becoming more highly structured through the creation of a nascent bureaucracy. Increasingly the study groups and courses demanded more time and effort from participants, and Sequoia Seminar had to grapple with the issues of recruiting participants and new leaders. There appear to be a number of reasons for the change. First, Sharman had died in 1953 at the age of eighty-eight, removing his restraining influence. Second, Harry was nearing the end of his career at Stanford and probably envisioned being able to spend more time on the group. Finally, and most important, Sequoia Seminar had completed the first buildings on the Ben Lomond property giving it the sense of permanence and institutional identity that it had previously lacked. The organization had put down roots in its own real estate and was looking for a direction in which to grow.

Some of these new themes were expressed at a conference of leaders in 1955. They rejected Sharman's willingness to leave the leadership of study groups in the hands of relatively untrained people and concluded that "the leader must be 'on the spot' and actually lead." Even more significantly, the leadership seminar took the unprecedented step of actually downgrading the scholarly approach advocated by Sharman. "Sharman's approach was somewhat intellectual and aloof," they noted. Then they went on to stress the strong collective orientation that so clearly differentiated Sequoia Seminar from Camp Minnesing: "We feel it is necessary to live the life in the group—to practice love in the group situation."[143] This stress on community indicates how far the group had drifted from the principles that had motivated Sharman. Although Sharman's books and the Jesus as Teacher seminars would remain the intellectual heart and soul of the movement, the group was now self-consciously aware that it had evolved to a new stage of development in which it had to forge an identity of its own. In conformity to the Rathbuns' interest in group solidarity, this new identity would be much more communal in nature than anything that had taken place during the Sharman era. The lure of collective commitment was very strong, and although the movement never withdrew into itself to the point of becoming what is commonly called a "cult," Harry felt comfortable telling movement members that "the age of the rugged individualist is past. Some societies are given over to collectives. We prefer to stress community. Each of us considers himself expendable for others."[144]

Organization and Membership of Sequoia Seminar

On the day before Christmas, 1955, Sequoia Seminar published a formal statement of its new organization and operating principles. This was part of a general restructuring of the way the group was administered that had been going on for several years and included the formation of a new legal entity, the Sequoia Seminar Foundation.[145] The new formal organization consisted of a planning commmittee and four operating committees. Those whose lack of commitment did not yet qualify them for the planning committee (which chose its own members) could serve on one of the four operating committees: administration, public relations, property, and personnel.[146] Ever cautious of the possibility of conflict between themselves and the churches with whom they worked, the planning committee members carefully warned that work on the operating committees should not divert people who were "already productively engaged in creative activities such as church work." For those, however, who were not so engaged, the committee meetings themselves were supposed to be one of the ways in which people "would live the life in the group." Indeed, "live the life," a phrase of Emilia's that became standard Creative Initiative terminology, meant to behave in a way dedicated to the will of God and the principles of Jesus as interpreted by the group.[147]

The organizational plan of 1955 continued to serve Sequoia Seminar through the transition period that culminated in 1962. This seven-year period was one in which the leadership of the movement gained experience in running a large organization with the many complications that came from trying to coordinate the efforts of volunteer group leaders, study group participants, and the development of permanent facilities at Ben Lomond. By 1956, when the group initiated a newsletter, there were hundreds of Sequoia Seminar alumni, mostly in the Bay Area, in addition to the participants in local study groups run by graduates of leadership training programs offered at Ben Lomond.[148] The new organizational structure was far from perfect and not without its critics.

Perhaps in response to a new member who charged the leadership with being an oligarchy and called for more democratic participation, there was a move toward decentralization in 1959.[149]

It became increasingly clear through this period that the original Sharman vision of work within the academic community was too constraining for a group that wished to grow but could attract people only from a geographically limited area. Although Harry continued to recruit actively on the Stanford campus, the specific reference to students was dropped from Sequoia Seminar announcements. Roll books indicate that during the first few years of Sequoia Seminar more than half and as many as three-quarters of those attending were active students; most of the others were recent graduates. By 1955, the year of the structural reorganization, less than one-tenth of those attending the summer seminar were students.[150]

Harry and Emilia did not have Sharman's broad international base from which to draw participants. Their source of students was Stanford University, and Stanford did not have a large enough student population to provide the numbers needed to make Ben Lomond practical. By actively recruiting participants from the larger community, the Rathbuns were able to attract sufficient numbers of people to run the kind of weekend and summer seminars for which they had bought Ben Lomond. As long as the university had been the major source of participants, however, the Rathbuns did not have to worry about the "quality" of those they attracted—the university admissions office and faculty selection committees did that for them. But as they increasingly looked beyond the academy for members, they had to make a more conscious effort to maintain the highly educated, upper-middle-class image that marked the group since the Sharman era. Internal recruiting documents emphasized that they were looking for "people with mature minds—leaders, thinkers, doers," and that recruiters should "concentrate on professional people."[151]

This switch from students to the general population was to have an unforeseen effect; the proportion of men to women fell dramatically. During the first three years of Sequoia Seminar the numbers of men and women attending were roughly equal, with a slight preponderance of men. After 1953 the ratio was almost always 60 percent or more women. The actual proportion of women in discussion groups held during the year was probably even higher since there was a tendency for couples to attend the two-week summer seminars together.[152] On at least one occasion in 1957, Harry held a special dinner for the "husbands and friends" of the women discussion group participants with an eye to setting up all-male groups if there were sufficient interest. There is no indication that there was.[153] Concomitantly, as larger numbers of more mature women attended meetings, the need for child care became acute. In 1951 one of the summer seminars made special arrangements for child care so both husbands and wives could attend sessions and, throughout the 1950s, many couples participated in ad hoc exchanges of children. The child care program eventually grew into a summer camp run for the first time in 1961.[154] Unlike college students whose personal needs were met by their schools, married people needed specific support like child care if they were to participate, and by providing that support Sequoia Seminar took further steps toward establishing a sectlike institutionalized support system.

Financially, Sequoia Seminar was always a rather modest operation. Some of the disaffected members of the old Camp Minnesing Central Group have hinted darkly that the Rathbuns' inherited a substantial amount from the Sharman estate. Money was in fact left to the Alpha Psi Zeta Foundation of which Harry was secretary and one of the trustees. He was also the executor of the Sharman estate, which may account for the implication of ill-gotten gains.[155] But Sharman's will specifically prohibited the money from being spent on the acquisition of property, limited its use to promoting gospel study among university people, and required that it be spent within fifteen years of his death. Thus, there was very little Harry could have done to use it to develop the Sequoia Seminar.[156] By the time of Abbie Lyon Sharman's death in 1955, no more than $25,000 remained in the estate, and most of it seems to have been spent in support of the several Jesus as Teacher study groups still functioning in the United States and Canada at that time.[157]

Like much else connected with the seminar before 1955, accounting procedures were rather casual. There are no account books among the Rathbun papers, and only simplified financial statements were issued. Scattered references to money indicate that the thirty-five dollar fee for the seminars just about covered all expenses. Since there were no employees, and the Rathbuns never took a penny for their time and services, overall costs were minimal. The expense of constructing additional buildings at Ben Lomond with volunteer labor was met through contributions from members and an occasional bank loan.[158] The first complete balance sheet, put out in 1955, indicates that the group actually lost a bit more than five hundred dollars on their seminars. Their general operating costs were a modest seven hundred dollars and, with an income of about ten thousand dollars made up mostly of contributions, they were actually able to save money against future expenses. Hence by no stretch of the imagination was Sequoia Seminar a big budget operation. In 1955 the group's net worth, including the property and buildings at Ben Lomond, was $43,450.[159] This pattern remained relatively stable for the period up through 1962. Seminars paid for themselves, total contributions ranged from seven to eleven thousand dollars a year, and expenses—principally continued expansion of the Ben Lomond camp—kept the cash on hand quite low.[160]

Although donations and expenses remained stable throughout the 1950s, participation grew appreciably during most of the decade. No records are available for 1946, the year of the first seminar, but 59 people attended the two held in 1947. In 1953, after the move to Ben Lomond, Sequoia Seminar offered five seminars and the number of participants jumped to 86. Those figures steadily grew until 1959 when 217 people attended seminars at Ben Lomond, but after that the numbers dropped by more than a quarter to around 160.[161]

The membership problem caught the group in a dilemma. They wanted to expand, yet at the same time they wanted to admit only those people who were serious in their desire to explore the gospels and open themselves to the possibility of living a new life.[162] Seminar leaders also needed to tread cautiously in asking for funds from new members since they were still working within the churches and money that went to Sequoia Seminar might well be money taken from the churches. If local ministers believed they were losing money to Sequoia Seminar, they could have easily cut the group off from its major source of participants. Besides having to worry about the sincerity of members and possible conflict with the churches, Sequoia Seminar was not prepared to move beyond a very narrow geographic focus. The Palo Alto organization gave encouragement to Records study groups in other areas, including Boise, Los Angeles, and Chicago, but expected that they would "become completely independent and self-sufficient, including providing their own leadership."[163] During the peak year of this period, 1959, about five hundred people in the Bay Area were actively involved in local study groups and/or in the summer seminars.[164]

By the end of the decade the strain of ambivalence was showing more clearly. Special meetings were held about ways to attract new people, while at the same time the annual report admitted that "numerical growth does not necessarily indicate that anything of real significance is taking place."[165] Much of the growth, moreover, had taken place in so-called continuation seminars designed for people who had already attended the basic Jesus as Teacher seminar. Whereas only 20 more people attended basic seminars in 1959 than in 1955, attendance in continuation seminars had almost quadrupled from 33 to 121.[166] This was one more sign that Sequoia Seminar was becoming more sectlike in both its form and function. It was evolving into a place of continuing spiritual fellowship where people could find a coherent religious philosophy and support for transforming their lives.

2

Philosophy and Action in a Proto-Sect

Despite their deep attachment and respect for Henry B. Sharman, Emilia and Harry Rathbun did not freeze the movement as Sharman had left it at the end of his active career in 1945. Intellectually as well as organizationally, Sequoia Seminar became a much more complex undertaking than anything Sharman had ever attempted. Sharman's techniques for studying the teachings of Jesus remained the backbone of the Rathbuns' work, but just as they moved toward a more institutional structure for carrying out their mission, they also developed a more systematic ideology. By the end of the 1950s the combination of a more formalized organization supporting a more formalized religious philosophy began to define the group as a new religious sect.

The Rathbuns made almost weekly trips to Carmel to visit Sharman and keep him abreast of their progress and to ask his advice for the work that they always saw as building on his. Emilia told Sharman that she and Harry had "a tremendous sense of the destiny we must play in the next step toward the fulfillment of your dream." "Give us fifteen, twenty years more," she wrote, "and we will have been to you what Paul was for Jesus." Noting that he was in his eighties and ill, she asked him if he would write "a farewell prayer and discourse something like Jesus did in his life for his disciples."[1] He seems to have resisted the temptation. Although he may have been a reluctant prophet, Sharman was not unappreciative of the work that the Rathbuns were doing, indicating in 1948 that he believed that the Stanford activity was the most productive any-where.[2] Harry Rathbun, for his part, never pretended to be Henry B. Sharman. He was his own man with his own religious agenda. Unlike Sharman, who had always worked from the gospels themselves, Harry used Sharman's book, *Jesus as Teacher,* as the basis of his teaching.[3] As time went on, Harry deviated even further from the style and content of the Minnesing model. After Sharman's death in 1953, Harry, and espe-cially Emilia, accelerated the rate of change until they had moved their work well beyond the narrow academic boundaries in which Sharman had operated.

Many of the early changes introduced by Harry involved such techni-calities as the exact order in which issues from the Records would be raised. There were also important differences in style, however. Harry enjoyed participating more actively in the discussions than Sharman had; he also made some structural changes in how the seminars were run.[4] The thirty to forty students that usually comprised a Minnesing seminar were eventually reduced to as few as a dozen. The original six-week seminar period that was so convenient to college students on summer vacation was reduced first to four and then to two weeks, which was more realistic for working adults. Although there continued to be references to the "vacation" aspects of attending a seminar, in fact, Sequoia Seminar placed much more stress on study and less on leisure than Camp Minnesing.[5] Harry evoked deep respect for his personal warmth and teaching excellence. Younger participants in particular, who called him "prof" in the early days, valued their contact with him. "The most impressive single aspect for me," reported one Berkeley graduate student in economics, "was the outstanding example of intel-lectual and emotional maturity set by 'the prof.' "[6]

The raison d'être of Sequoia Seminar was the study of the Records. But exploring the life and teachings of Jesus was not an end in itself. Understanding Jesus was a way to understand God. Understanding God meant living new lives doing the will of God. Whereas Sharman had been content to help students discover the religious life, the Rathbuns had a grander vision. Right from the beginning at "Minnesing '45" when they proposed establishing a religious community, they had wanted to create a collective situation in which members could help one another "live the life." Within two years of the demise of Minnesing, and before the found-ing of Ben Lomond, they launched the first experiment to put their ideas into practice.

Students Concerned: Practicing their Beliefs

Fired by the vision of total commitment and the possibilities presented by the unsettled postwar conditions, Emilia and a group of students who had attended the 1947 seminar at Asilomar began to draw up plans for a permanent organization that would turn commitment into action. With her complete support, and possibly at her instigation, the students decided to take a term off from school to engage in a period of intensive study and planning.[7] As she later admitted, Emilia was oblivious to the implications of a large number of students leaving school for the tutelage of a professor's wife; she saw simply an opportunity to stop talking and start doing. Despite widespread opposition from parents, other faculty, and some members of the Stanford administration, the students launched a new group called Students Concerned.[8] Ten of the forty students who had attended the 1947 summer seminar formed the core of the new group. They, in turn, recruited additional students from thirteen colleges throughout the country. Thus, when the ten-week special study session opened on April 1, there were twenty-five men and twelve women in residence.[9]

Many of the students were veterans of World War II. Trying to make sense of the horrors they had seen and afraid of a third world war, they had been motivated by Sequoia Seminar and now sought some specific way to work for international peace in those first years of the atomic age and the cold war.

Students Concerned had a dual purpose. The first was to achieve complete commitment to the will of God, and the second was to put that commitment into practice in order to forestall the end of the world. The students testified that their study of the life of Jesus enabled them to perceive what had "prevented his return to the carpenter shop." "We see the action he initiated as the only adequate action today," they concluded.[10] They were "Committed to unlimited responsibility for making real One World," and, having "understood the import of his message for our day," had "no alternative but to accept the full responsibility as demonstrators." They declared that joining Students Concerned was their surrender to God's will and required them "to leave school, our hopes of professions, and our personal lives, in order to devote ourselves entirely to this one purpose."[11]

They had to act because the very fate of the earth was at stake. As one of their position papers warned: "Any thinking person recognizes that war is out—the term itself is simply obsolete. It should rather be called: extinction."[12] The philosophical core of the new movement was summed up in a statement that could have been lifted word for word from Beyond War literature of the 1980s: "The creative resolution of any dispute, difference, or disagreement depends upon the adoption of the attitude which can break through the impasse of closed minds." "Peace among men," it continued, "is possible if each man will foresake his blindness and adopt the attitude of discovery." Students Concerned explained that they had been led to their position through "the study of Jesus," and members were "assuming personal and group responsibility for conveying this attitude to many minds over the nation and the world."[13] Even though almost forty years separate Students Concerned from Beyond War, the fundamental message is identical: the way to end war is through the transformation of the individual.

Originally the group intended to achieve this purpose through a three-step process. First, the 1948 spring quarter was spent studying the gospels and the works of St. Paul.[14] This was done primarily under Emilia's leadership, although on weekends Harry went to the camp they had rented. Second, having obtained "a solid foundation in constant principles," the students hoped to go to Europe for ten weeks so that they could "serve where the needs are greatest."[15] Finally, upon their return from Europe, they intended to disperse to other campuses in order to "arouse student concern by indicating the seriousness of the world situation and suggesting that the positive answer lies in a fundamental change in men themselves."[16]

In fact, Students Concerned effectively disbanded after June 10, 1948, when the ten-week seminar ended. As one participant remembered, "At the end of the training program the 29 of us had 29 different ideas about the greatest significance of Jesus and about the most effective plans and action."[17] An illustrated journal kept by Del Carlson, a marine veteran and aspiring artist with an accrbic sense of humor, reflected some of the problems that arose. Along with several mocking cartoons of Emilia being worshipped by the participants, Carlson drew a group of smug, self-satisfied students topped with halos, delivering food to starving people eating worms. Closer to home, one cartoon indicated that ambivalence toward the mainline churches was present almost from the beginning, when it showed members of the group emulating Jesus by "overthrowing the tables at the Wed. night BINGO game at the Redwood City Methodist Church." Perhaps most telling was the wry description of a group discussion. Carlson depicted members of the group presenting their positions with effusive apologies: "Now, correct me if I am wrong," and "Please feel free to straighten me out if my thinking has been bad," and so forth. Then, Carlson noted, when the others did criticize them, "they smother their negative reactions under a smile tinted with a subjective–objective tone, and bow backwards with: 'Oh, thank you, you're so right,' " only to return with another proposal and begin the process anew.[18]

In addition to illustrating the conflicts within Students Concerned, the Carlson cartoons also highlight the homocentric–sociocentric tension that plagued the group and, indeed, marked all the Rathbuns' work. Carlson showed the students delivering food to the hungry and scattering bingo cards in the church hall. He showed them, in other words, taking concrete social action to further their vision of a just society. Social action was seen as the inevitable consequence of surrendering to the will of God. In fact, however, the group was much less clear on exactly what, if anything, they could do to eliminate suffering. The only specific suggestion made was to encourage others to think the way Students Concerned did, to see the light as they themselves had seen it. Everyone in Students Concerned appeared to have agreed that the objective study of the gospels would lead to the surrendering of the individual will to the will of God. The sociocentrics wanted to go further and apply their beliefs through specific social action. But, as it almost always would in the Rathbuns' work, the homocentric view carried the day, and the group finally sought only to convert others to their philosophical position.

Students Concerned was the high point of the Rathbuns' early work among students. It was also the low point. The naive enthusiasm of the young people struck even Emilia as unrealistic. She remembers going through boxes of clothing they had collected to give to the poor to rescue the students' hand-knit sweaters and expensive jackets, which, she said, in the sober light of day they were happy to get back.[19] The lack of any permanent accomplishments coupled with the opposition from parents and colleagues helped convince the Rathbuns that the future of the movement lay outside the university. They did not abandon Sharman's constituency—Harry continued to lead study groups on campus—but after 1948 the focus permanently switched from students to adults.

Individual Conversion and Social Action: Resolving the Tension

During the late 1940s and early 1950s, when Sequoia Seminar was limiting itself to fairly straightforward Records study, participants who were inclined toward social action found outlets for their activism in other groups. Many Records-study alumni worked in social service divisions of churches, and a significant number went into the ministries of liberal Protestant denominations. At least one Jewish participant entered the rabbinate. A large number were attracted to The Church for the Fellowship of All Peoples, a nondenominational, interracial Protestant church in San Francisco under the pastorate of a black minister, Howard Thurman. The issue of racial justice was of great concern to group members, including Emilia who was actively involved in the Palo Alto celebration of National Negro History Week during this period. Others worked through the Quakers, especially with the European relief activities of the American Friends Service Committee. Informal alumni newsletters of the early 1950s indicate Sequoia Seminar encouraged many of its graduates to participate actively in teaching Sunday school and pursue careers in the helping professions.[20]

Because transformation of the person was primary and social action only consequential, the Rathbuns at first focused on the individual conversion and ignored the resulting community activity. Such a position, however, was potentially self-destructive for Sequoia Seminar. Since the group itself did not sponsor any social action, persons whose transformation induced them to work directly in the community had to look outside of Sequoia Seminar for opportunities and could no longer devote their complete energies to the movement. A permanent organization that depended on continuing membership to survive could not afford to infuse its members with the desire to go beyond it. Thus, as the movement evolved into a sect, it became increasingly unambiguous in its purely homocentric focus.

Occasionaly at first, and more often toward the end of the 1950s, the Rathbuns began to claim that personal transformation was the sole function of the movement. The appropriate social action was to remain within the group and help it spread the word because in a homocentric world view spreading the word *was* the way to change the world. Their homocentric position was an ideological compromise between those who worried most about the next life and tended to ignore this one, and the social gospel adherents whose concern for this life led them to support collective acts of social, political, and economic reform. The Rathbuns sought to bring about the Kingdom of God in this life through mass transformation of individuals. "Economic and social change is a waste of time, as is fighting through law courts to change the social structure," wrote a seminar student in 1952. She believed such victories were transitory and that "the fruit of this activity fades away in time."[21] What was permanent was the transformation of the individual. "Ours is not the responsibility of reforming the world," wrote a participant in a 1953 seminar, "for through individual enlightenment, and *only* through individual enlightenment, shall the world be reformed."[22]

As the homocentric philosophy became increasingly explicit, there was mounting criticism of those who took the sociocentric position. The idea that the world's problems could be solved by politics was labeled "political messianism." They contrasted political messianism with their own position, which they characterized as "realism": "realism stresses that the only way I can do something about you is to get myself straightened out. My problem is not my mother, my conditioning, my values, etc., but *myself*."[23] Thus, the responsibility of Sequoia Seminar, wrote Emilia, was "to present an opportunity for persons to progressively put themselves at the disposal of a creative power greater than themselves that will result in a fulfilled life for the individual and effect a transformation in the life of the community in ever widening circles of inclusiveness, ultimately to encompass all mankind."[24]

A New Constituency

The Rathbuns countered the tendency of people to leave for social action by emphasizing the social implications of individual transformation. But they still had to keep people involved beyond the first round of Records study. The Records study approach was inherently self-limiting. Although some particularly dedicated individuals would come back year after year to plow the same ground, most people were satisfied with one or, at the most, two seminars and then moved on to apply what they had learned in their lives. Although some did start their own Records study groups, there was no central direction or control from Palo Alto, and most other groups appear to have been short-lived. The high turnover had been no problem for Sharman or for the Rathbuns at first, because they saw students as their primary constituency, and every year brought a new crop of potential recruits. Records study seminars no more needed to change than did Harry's final lecture. It might be the same sermon year after year, but there was always a new congregation to hear it. However, after the collapse of Students Concerned, when the Rathbuns increasingly turned their attention to Bay Area adults, they discovered that if they wanted to keep people involved they would have to introduce not only new techniques, such as shorter summer seminars, but some entirely new course work as well.

By beginning to develop new material that went beyond the scope of Sharman's approach, the Rathbuns were taking yet another step toward the development of an independent sect. This growing proto-sect status derived in part from the philosophical content of the new courses that encouraged the development of a distinct religious ideology, and probably in part from the economic realities of the new camp at Ben Lomond. To keep Ben Lomond full, to justify its existence, to pay its bills, to develop it into the kind of facility that the Rathbuns long envisioned, it was necessary to have a lot of people making use of the facilities. One way to get more people was to develop a greater number and variety of seminars.

New advanced or "continuation" seminars were created to meet the demand for continuing study from people who were becoming permanent members of the movement. From 1951 through 1955 one continuation seminar was held each summer and, according to one participant, "the discussions ranged over Eastern religions, modern psychology with particular reference to the problems of the individuals present, and prayer and meditation."[25] In 1953 for the first time the group held a special leadership seminar to train people who had taken the basic course and now wanted to lead study groups on their own.

With these newly trained leaders the summer seminar schedule fairly exploded in the mid-1950s. Gerald Heard, whose ideas were so influential with the Rathbuns, gave guest lectures and led seminars at Ben Lomond in 1954 and 1955, and during the summer of 1956 there were eight seminars, including two continuation groups and a leadership seminar. There were fifteen in the summer of 1958 and seventeen the next year. Six of the seminars were the basic Jesus as Teacher groups, but not one of them was led by Harry or Emilia. They had moved up to the continuation seminars that dealt with such issues as "methods and procedures for implementing the way of life implicit in the teachings of Jesus," "knowing the self," and "Prayer and Meditation." Yet, the Rathbuns did not carry the full load of the continuation seminars alone. An inner circle of leaders was beginning to emerge, some of whom would remain into the Beyond War era of the 1980s.[26]

Of particular interest was the special seminar that Emilia led in 1956 at the request of group leaders who felt the need "for renewal of fellowship and inspiration."[27] The fact that some members of the group went to Emilia to ask her to lead this seminar indicates that, for them, Sequoia Seminar and not their churches had become their social and spiritual touchstone. They saw nothing inappropriate in requesting additional institutional support from the group. The movement was not unaware that its structure was becoming more sectlike, and they took pains to disavow any such purpose. In that same year, 1956, the Sequoia Seminar newsletter assured its readers, "we are keenly aware that it is not our chosen mission to become a new sect nor promulgate any dogma or creed."[28]

Unlike the Jesus as Teacher groups that had their framework established by Sharman, the continuation and postseminar meetings were in a state of constant flux seeking some kind of coherent theme and methodology. The 1960 annual report acknowledged that the groups varied "considerably in content and approach." It admitted that they sometimes wished, "rather wistfully," that they could develop a uniform structure similar to the Jesus as Teacher groups, but it concluded, "to date we have not found one and we are not sure there is one."[29] Although it would take ten years to develop a coherent pattern of additional courses, many of the ideas eventually used by Creative Initiative were first tried out in the continuation courses of the 1950s. In particular, they began the process of what would later be called "deconditioning," that is having people examine their lives to see what forces had shaped them, and then freeing themselves of those chains to the past so that they could move forward in their commitment to God.[30]

The shift from students to more mature members and the introduction of the continuation seminars were organizational changes that significantly altered the nature of the movement. The postseminar groups both provided more activity for existing participants and more opportunity to expand the membership base. Toward the end of the Sequoia Seminar era, in 1957, both Harry and Emilia began giving public lecture series outside the churches in an attempt to attract more people into the work. The Rathbuns shifted Sharman's clientele and, while they did not change his message, they augmented it. From being the end, Jesus as Teacher became the beginning. Where Sharman had left it to the individual to determine how to implement the teachings of Jesus, the Sequoia Seminar movement sought to become a vehicle not only through which individuals could change their lives but through which they could live them as well.

Philosophical Sources: Jung, Buchman, and Heard

The changes in style and content took place incrementally through the 1940s and 1950s so that the transformed seminars as they finally emerged in the beginning of the 1960s were an amalgam of the ideas of Henry B. Sharman and of several other people whose philosophies were synthesized by the Rathbuns into a total world view. Indeed, the philosophical and spiritual foundations of Creative Initiative were firmly established in the 1950s. The three most important influences other than Sharman were C. G. Jung, as received through Elizabeth Boyden and her mentor, the German psychologist Fritz Kunkel; the Oxford Group Movement (Moral Re-Armament) of Frank Buchman; and the English popular philosopher Gerald Heard.

Elizabeth Boyden had been introduced to the Sharman method by Frances Warnecke in 1929 and had attended four summer seminars at Camp Minnesing.[31] She went to Europe several times before the war to study psychology with Fritz Kunkel and returned with him to this country where they worked together between 1942 and 1948.[32] Kunkel's work closely paralleled that of C. G. Jung. Both Kunkel and Jung stressed the importance of religion in the process that Jung called "individuation," by which a person comes to integrate all aspects of the personality into the subconscious. By coupling the Sharman study method with the techniques of psychotherapy, Boyden was supplying one of the components that many of his disciples felt was missing from Sharman's work. Since psychology was perceived as a science, and Records study had always been seen as a scientific process, it was easy enough to include the search for psychological as well as religious truth in the seminar process. When Kunkel came to this country for the first time in 1936, the Rathbuns and Henry Sharman traveled to Los Angeles to attend seminars he was leading at Holmby College.[33]

Elizabeth Boyden eventually founded her own center, the Guild for Psychological Studies, which combined Jungian psychology with Sharman's Records study. Other Sharman students followed similar paths. The Rathbuns, however, never fully committed themselves to a particular school of psychotherapy. Kunkel and Jung would provide themes for much of their work over the years, as would other psychologists such as Carl Rogers and Erich Fromm. Psychological issues were never far below the surface of the Creative Initiative movement, and at some points threatened to take over. But Harry, with his single-minded loyalty to Records study, and Emilia, who was always more attracted to the intuitive than to the rational, ultimately followed a different road to personal fulfillment.

The Oxford Group was the second major outside influence on the Rathbuns in this early period. Founded by Frank N. Buchman in 1921, the Oxford Group was a somewhat amorphous religious movement that stressed individual conversion, confession of sins, adherence to a strict code of morality, and listening to God for guidance in daily life. In 1938 Buchman rechristened his movement "Moral Re-Armament" and took a stand opposing America's involvement in the growing conflicts of Asia and Europe. He advocated the idea that Americans remain neutral and live a philosophy of love and cooperation in their families, workplaces, and government.[34]

As a toiler in the vineyards of religion, Sharman was well aware of the Oxford Group and had himself attended one of their huge "house party" conventions in Briarcliff Manor, New York, in 1932.[35] Although he did not join the followers of Buchman, Sharman did consider them to be "the most vital religious movement of the time" and urged any of his followers who were interested to examine the group for themselves. Harry never had much use for the movement's minimizing intellectual understanding and emphasizing a purely emotional surrender to the will of God. Emilia, however, found the Buchmanite approach more to her liking.[36]

When Emilia attended an Oxford Group house party in Stockbridge, Massachusetts, around 1935, it was even more important to her than her first Sharman seminar because, unlike the seminar, the Oxford Group addressed her feelings. At the seminar she had made the decision to dedicate her life to the will of God, but at the house party she was forced to confront her own human weakness. She was shocked by being placed in a group of the "unchanged" (that is, unconverted), where she was constantly urged to confess her sins so that she could open herself to the voice of God. Having led a rather traditional and somewhat cloistered life, the only sins Emilia could think of were having taken a book from the YWCA lost-and-found and having been rude to her mother. She traveled to Los Angeles to return the book in person, as required by the Buchmanite theory of restitution, and then waited for a "leading" from God. What she felt frightened her enormously. She had the strong sense that God wanted her to put on a black velvet dress and visit William Randolph Hearst to urge him to use his fortune to end all wars. She feared that such behavior would be not merely eccentric but a sign of serious mental illness. After discussing the matter with Harry, she decided not to follow the leading.[37]

Although worried that she might be "cracking up," Emilia remained active within the Oxford Group in California. For several years after 1935 she dropped all work on the Sharman Records study and devoted her time to the Buchmanites. Harry continued to lead study groups, while Emilia did individual counseling that included the hearing of confessions of sin. This was an eye-opening experience for her. Although her worst conscious sin might have been filching a book from the Y lost-and-found, others had indulged more fully in life's forbidden behavior, and their recounting of it to Emilia served as her education in the broad range of human weakness.[38]

In the years before the outbreak of the war, Buchman and some members of his inner circle were clearly sympathetic to Hitler and at least marginally anti-Semitic. Although the quasi-fascist elements of the movement were not publicly stressed by the Oxford Group leadership, they were pointed out by the group's critics.[39] Harry and Emilia appear to have been unaware of the unsavory aspects of the Oxford Group's politics, although they went along with Moral Re-Armament's strong isolationist position. Several months after Buchman launched his Moral Re-Armament campaign to keep the United States out of the European and Asian conflicts, Emilia and a small group of others sponsored an advertisement in the *Palo Alto Times* calling for continued American neutrality.[40] And as late as October 1941, just two months before the Japanese attack on Pearl Harbor, Harry and twelve others who took the "peace position" signed an appeal for funds to help defray the expenses of conscientious objectors.[41] There is no indication that the Rathbuns were either pro-German or anti-Semitic, so their opposition to American involvement in the war probably stemmed as much from the antiwar position that Harry had taken since his high school years and from their sympathy with the Quakers as it did from the influence of the Oxford Group.

Emilia has said that she eventually drifted away from the Oxford Group because she felt that it lacked substance. She came to agree with Harry that the Oxford Group depended too much on emotionalism, wishful thinking, and intuition. She also objected to its aggressive proselytizing—an ironic position given the later evangelical zeal of both Creative Initiative and Beyond War. Although she returned to the Sharman model of Records study, Emilia brought with her a permanent legacy from her Oxford Group involvement. Her experience hearing confessions left her with "an education in how the devil worked in life" and prepared her for the role of confidante and counselor that she would play in the future. Although she rejected as inappropriate the message she received when she prayed for God's guidance, the idea that God could communicate directly with people—which had no role at all in Sharman's academic approach—was immensely appealing to Emilia. Subsequent leadings and revelations would have a major influence in directing the course of her life. Finally, Emilia accepted the Buchmanite demand that all followers adhere to the four absolutes: absolute purity, absolute honesty, absolute unselfishness, and absolute love.[42] Observing these absolutes meant surrendering to the will of God, a concept that dovetailed neatly with the ideas of Sharman, so the four absolutes would become an integral part of the teachings of the Creative Initiative movement.[43]

In addition to the psychology of Kunkel and Jung and the religious beliefs of the Buchmanites, the Rathbuns were influenced in the Sequoia Seminar period by the philosophy of Gerald Heard. Gerald Heard was one of those hard-to-define intellectuals who combined science, philosophy, and mysticism in a life lived in the murky penumbra between academics and journalism. Reared in England, he studied philosophy and philosophy of religion at Cambridge University. He was a friend of H. G. Wells, Julian and Aldous Huxley, and others of that left-wing humanist circle in the 1930s and 1940s. He spent his early career writing, teaching extension courses, and commenting on current events and science on the BBC. In 1937 he was offered a position at Duke University but, after a brief stay in North Carolina, decided instead to move to California where he eventually opened his own school in Trabuco Canyon near Los Angeles.[44]

Although it was called Trabuco College, Heard's school was really more an ashram. Trabuco was not merely a place to teach the religious life; it was a place to live it. Students were expected to do the work necessary to keep the school running, and monastic rules governed much of their behavior. "All the amusements and distractions of secular living," including smoking, were prohibited. Silence was to be maintained from supper until breakfast, and all food was simple and vegetarian. Students meditated for an hour three times a day in pursuit of the school's purpose, the "attainment of a quality of consciousness above the ego." But such enlightenment was not an end in itself. Like Sharman and the Rathbuns, Heard believed that religious ideas could change the world, and his theory of social change was solidly homocentric. He thought that, although enlightenment was not an end in itself, it was sufficient in itself to bring on the necessary change. Once enlightenment was obtained, Heard claimed, "our individual, our group, our international issues are solved."[45]

The Rathbuns had read some of Heard's work and attended a lecture in San Francisco where they met him in 1937, the first year he was in this country. Then, in 1942, Emilia, who was ending her affiliation with the Buchmanites, enrolled in a seminar on mysticism at Trabuco. Because her mother was ill, she was forced to miss the first week of the three-week course, but undaunted she went down late to Los Angeles where she received a very chilly reception. After hitching a ride from the mailman into the canyon, hiking up a long dusty road carrying her suitcase, and being forced to wait outside the gates "like a peon," she was told to go home because she was late. Emilia had gone down to Trabuco to study and she was not about to be turned away. She simply refused to leave. Rather than make a fuss, Heard allowed her to stay and work in the kitchen, but she was otherwise virtually ignored.[46]

Emilia found the time she spent at Trabuco extremely important. The silence, the three hours a day of meditation, and the time to explore books on prayer in the college library all contributed to a new attitude. Harry said that she came back "a new woman . . . at a higher level of being."[47] The Rathbuns were so impressed with Heard and Trabuco that they hoped to hold one of their seminars there in 1946.[48] Although those plans fell through, Heard journeyed north on several occasions in 1954 and 1955 to give public lectures and private seminars to the Sequoia Seminar. It would appear that Heard provided the necessary bridge between the scientific analysis of Sharman and Emilia's strong intuitive bent. Just as the work of Kunkel and Jung reconciled the science of psychology with religion, the work of Heard reconciled science with mysticism. Heard's philosophy made it possible to accept science and still engage in the apparently extrarational behavior of eastern mysticism.

Since many of Heard's ideas were transferred wholecloth into the philosophy of Creative Initiative, they are worth a closer look if we are to understand the intellectual grounding of the Rathbuns' movement. Gerald Heard saw religion and science as complementary. Science was the process of finding facts. Religion was the process of finding meaning. At the very heart of Heard's philosophy, and subsequently at the very heart of the ideology of Creative Initiative, lay the idea of the evolution of human consciousness. According to Heard, pre-Paleolithic people lived in a state of economic, social, and psychological integration. As humans began to develop tools they experienced a breakdown of this integration and started down the road of objective reason, a road that eventually led them to reject intuition in favor of science. Heard believed modern people had to transcend the dualism of objective and rational science on the one hand and psychology and religion on the other by developing techniques that would allow them to generate the same kinds of insight in the intuitive areas as they had in the scientific.[49]

Heard argued that reintegration was possible because in the evolutionary process human beings had not become overspecialized and had retained the power to decide among options. Human consciousness and the human psyche were not results of evolution, but its cause. In a neo-Lamarckian inversion of standard Darwinian principles, Heard made humankind the master rather than the servant of its biology. He was unabashed in his teleology. There was an explicit right direction in evolution and human beings were heading toward a specific and final stage of existence. Heard contended that once they had reached the end of their physical evolution, human beings had then entered a stage of technical evolution during which an emphasis on the rational had led to the systematic suppression of extrasensory abilities. He placed great stress on extrasensory perception and other aspects of parapsychology, frequently citing parapsychological studies as evidence for his belief that consciousness, or the mind, had a reality of its own outside the body. It was Heard's contention that human beings were on the threshold of a new age, the "Tertiary Age" that would replace the "Age of Technique." In the new age, the mind or consciousness would grow as much as the body had in the first and the mechanical world had in the second. Humankind would come to recognize how each individual was an integral part of the comprehensive consciousness that was nature.[50]

Heard found evidence that people had the potential to evolve into this third age by the way they responded to pain and sex. He argued that both pain and sexual desire were the result of redirected psychic energy and claimed that when people focused on developing their consciousness, as in the mystic traditions of both east and west, both sensitivity to pain and sexual desire were considerably diminished.[51]

Since Heard believed that people were still evolving, that the next stage of evolution lay in the development of human consciousness, that achieving the new state of consciousness was the same thing as understanding the will of God, and that this next step up the evolutionary ladder was within the conscious control of individuals, clearly there had to be some method to achieve this end. That method was prayer: "Prayer is the only way in which our evolution may be continued and there is no other way."[52] Heard discussed prayer at some length and concluded that meditative and contemplative prayer, or what he called "high prayer," was the way to achieve a unity not only of mind and body but also of human and God.[53]

Gerald Heard published no fewer than eighteen books between 1931 and 1959, and all of them were variations on the theme just described. The Rathbuns appear to have been particularly influenced by *Pain, Sex and Time,* published in 1939, and *A Preface to Prayer,* published in 1944. The ideas in these two books, plus what they learned during several meetings and seminars with Heard, infused their personal beliefs and established the philosophical framework for the Creative Initiative movement.[54]

The ideas of Kunkel, Buchman, and Heard found their way into the Rathbuns' thinking within two years of their first exposure to Records study in 1934. Thus, although the concepts gleaned from these three men were alien to the long tradition of Sharman's study groups, they were all part and parcel of the Rathbuns' religious philosophy from its inception. Sequoia Seminar may have been the institutional successor to Camp Minnesing, but it grew out of a more complex ideological tradition than Sharman's Records study alone. By itself, the Records study movement was able to survive only as long as it had the personality of Henry B. Sharman at its head. Once he was gone, all Records study groups gradually faded away except the two in California, Elizabeth Boyden's Guild for Psychologial Studies and Harry and Emilia Rathbuns' Creative Initiative Foundation, both of which had enriched the core of gospel study with additional ideas.

In Search of an Ideology

From its beginning as an independent entity in 1946, therefore, Sequoia Seminar adopted a different tone than that which had characterized earlier Records study groups. The first announcement of the Rathbuns' Sequoia Seminar owed as much to Gerald Heard as it did to Henry B. Sharman. It proclaimed that the world was in danger and that people had to act immediately if the earth were to be saved. Pointing to the recent advent of the atomic age, it warned, "the very existence of our species is seriously threatened." The announcement went on to say that people had the choice to use this power dangerously and, if that were to be avoided, human nature had to be changed: "The *ultimate* and basic need has to do with the nature, the character, the spirit of man himself; it is the need to achieve so radical a change in human nature that man no longer will be his own worst enemy."[55]

It is clear from the language here and in similar statements contained in the 1947 announcement that the Rathbuns did not perceive of their seminar merely as an opportunity to explore the teachings of Jesus in order to gain personal insight. Rather, it was a place to learn the solution to the problem that might end civilization. The method was still the critical study of the Records of the life of Jesus, but now its purpose was to "discover the thought behind his teaching and action, and thereby the psychological secret of his insight, his maturity and his vitality." The method was the study of the gospels, but the purpose was to change the person. This was not change in Sharman's somewhat limited sense of commitment to the will of God. This was change in the sense of Gerald Heard's theory of human evolution. As the announcement put it:

It must be obvious to all thinking persons that our problem is man himself. His psychological development has failed to keep pace with his matchless technological advances. The need is for a body of mature men and women, ready to pay whatever personal price is necessary to preserve and enhance the actual and potential values which are inherent in humanity. A small band of such mature people committed to objective and persistent effort to discover the demands of the situation and to such fearless action as the discovery may entail, can alter the course of history, can prevent the disaster which imminently threatens, and can direct man's feet again into the path of his evolutionary ascent.[56]

These early statements of purpose are important because in the first flush of enthusiasm at having their own group and an opportunity to do something about the new danger of the atomic age, the Rathbuns did very little to soften the public appearance of their movement. Their apocalyptic language, their frank avowal of a cosmic framework for future human evolution, and the centrality of individual psychological change were presented in bald, uncompromising language. Forty years later these same ideas would form the ideological heart of the Beyond War movement, but they would be presented in a way less at odds with popular values. Indeed, popular ideas about nuclear war had changed by the 1980s, but the movement also learned that religious true believers could not attract a large following among educated, professional, middle-class Americans and that the message and the medium had to be secularized if the movement were to have broad appeal.

By the mid-1950s even, the apocalyptic tone of the first announcement had been toned down considerably. The emphasis had shifted from changing people to save the world to helping individuals find greater fulfillment and meaning in life. Ever sensitive to the shifting whims of popular culture, Sequoia Seminar, like the rest of the country, moved from the high anxiety of the early cold war to the introspective psychology of the 1950s. In 1956 Sequoia Seminar published a little booklet that sought to describe the purpose of the group. Under the subheading "The Need of Our Time," the booklet referred to an age of uncertainty in which old values had broken down but no new ones had taken their place. "We don't know what we want or feel," it said, "we don't know ourselves." Echoing the era's concern with the mindlessness of the "organization man," the booklet warned that "conformity with the crowd has taken on higher value than the development of one's individuality." Without ever quite saying so, it strongly implied that the seminar would provide individuals with what was missing in their lives by helping them find a new and more mature understanding of religion.[57]

When the Rathbuns used the term "religion" they did not mean Christianity. They felt that too often Christianity had become the belief that "being polite to God will bring powers which insure prosperity and success," "an anaesthetic that brings peace of mind and obliviousness to the unpleasant realities about us," in other words, a socially acceptable neurosis that allowed one to avoid facing up to the real world, or "a lot of false ideas and superstitions stemming from wishful thinking."[58] What they sought was a mature religion that they believed could be found through studying the teachings of Jesus not as the words of God (both Rathbuns doubted that Jesus was divine) but as the reflections of "one who thought deeply about human life and what it could be."[59]

Studying Jesus brought one to God. For Sharman, God was the "ceaseless dispenser of that which makes for man's evolution, growth, creative motivation," and humans were the vessels that had to open themselves to what God was willing to dispense.[60] Harry too, emphasized the absolute centrality of God to the work. There was no point, Harry argued, in asking whether God was or why God was: "The basic assumption at this point is that one is no longer fighting God, but taking God on the faith in a Being that is." Like Sharman's God, Harry's God was the power that allowed "the self and all else . . . to function growingly." Harry's "minimal definition of God" was truth, goodness, and beauty: "Goodness is that which I must do. Truth is to be used in terms of goodness. Beauty is to be appreciated and enjoyed."[61]

Both Sharman's and Harry's definitions of God deemphasized any personal aspect of God's nature, but Emilia was less comfortable with a depersonalized God. At the same seminar in which Harry gave the definition of God just quoted, Emilia told the participants, "God is personal." She was concerned that people understand that prayer was efficacious. Yet, when she defined "personal," it becomes clear that she was no more talking about an anthropomorphic God than were Sharman or Harry. By personal she said she meant "the capacity to project unrealized meanings into the future." God was then defined as "unrealized Purpose, the unrealized meaning who can, through prayer, be translated into concrete being."[62] Murky as this definition was, it nevertheless captured the essence of Sequoia Seminar's message—humans have the potential for evolution which could be achieved by following the will of God, a process facilitated through prayer.

A Codification of Ideas

In 1959, as the result of two years of experimenting with postseminar groups, the leadership of the movement prepared a "leadership handbook" to provide some common approaches and methods for the work being carried on in a wide variety of postseminar meetings. This handbook was the most comprehensive attempt during the 1950s to codify the philosophical structure of Sequoia Seminar and represented a major step toward the establishment of a distinct religious sect.

Of course, nothing even remotely comparable had been produced by Sharman, who only issued an occasional manifesto about the importance of studying the teachings of Jesus. Even though the group continued to insist that it had no interest in establishing its own creed, the leadership handbook had all the appearance of a compendium of dogma. Its importance lies not in the originality of its contents, since almost everything in the book was the result of years of discussion and development, but in the fact that the group felt the need to commit its beliefs to writing and thereby begin an independent tradition of passing on its ideals through the printed word.

The first few pages of the handbook placed great stress on the concept of community, and this time there were no cautions about conflict with peoples' church activities. It reminded the leaders that "the God-centered life is the shared life" and urged them to make it clear that one of the purposes of the group was to build a spirit of community. Participants were to be told that they would all "be expected to do some work, to take some responsibility, to be willing to give something in return for what they are receiving."[63] Community meant commitment, and participants frequently found it very difficult to distinguish in their own minds where commitment to God's will ended and loyalty to the Sequoia Seminar community began.[64] Intentionally or not, the demand for sacrifice from the members functioned as a device that built loyalty to the group. The more people could be persuaded to invest in terms of time, effort, and money, the greater stake they would have psychologically in justifying their participation and confirming the truth of the group's values to themselves.

Sequoia Seminar was not yet ready to announce that it had fathomed the will of God and was going to teach it to participants in the seminars. It was willing however, to go beyond anything done by Sharman to instruct followers about the meaning of Jesus' teachings as they applied to life. The leaders' handbook laid out a way of thinking and a way of living that it deemed appropriate for people who had dedicated their lives to the will of God. These intellectual, emotional, and behavioral prescriptions (and proscriptions) amounted to a blueprint for a specific life style lived within the Sequoia Seminar religious community that would be different from a life led within one of the mainline churches. It followed, then, that "living the life" within the community was an indication of obeying the will of God—although not the only way, because neither Sequoia Seminar nor Creative Initiative ever claimed exclusive knowledge of the will of God.

One of the first changes that Harry had made when he began to lead his own Jesus as Teacher seminars was to start the study with the two great commandments of Jesus, "Thou shalt love the Lord thy God with all thy heart, and with all thy soul, and with all thy mind and with all thy strength," and "Thou shalt love thy neighbor as thyself." These became the central teaching for Sequoia Seminar participants, requiring people to love God, love themselves, and love other people. As part of the emerging ideology of the proto-sect, Sequoia Seminar developed its own nomenclature to refer to these three requirements. Love of God was called authority, love of self was called integrity, and love of others was called responsibility.

Love of God was called authority because love meant surrendering to the authority of God. When discussing this concept the leadership handbook used terminology that minimized the significance of the human individual and stressed that people could choose neither the ends nor the means of their lives. God had determined what was to be done and how it was to be done, and "our function is simply one of opening ourselves so as to be able to discover what is required of us and of responding to what we discover as required." "Do you really see that you have no choice, and that you never will?" asked one of the clarifying questions suggested for discussion.[65]

The issue of authority led directly to the discussion of the problem of evil. The handbook explained that "followers of Jesus *see no external evil:* the 'evil,' the duality is within." The group believed that to call something or someone evil was to assume a prerogative open only to God—judgment. Instead of looking outside for something to blame, instead of passing judgment on others, participants were told "any 'evil' effect is traceable to a root cause of ignorance—usually the ignorance of thinking that you can be the first cause, the authority."[66] As a consequence members took the position that evil should not be resisted and that they should make no enemies. Much seminar time was devoted to discussions of what this meant in practical terms. How did one respond to crooked politicians, road hogs, people who threw garbage out of their cars, and the like?[67] Even if one did not act judgmentally and vindictively, what did you do to cope with the anger? There were no simple answers to these specific questions, but there was an obvious personal style that emerged as a result of this philosophical orientation. Sequoia Seminar people had a gentle and benign attitude toward the world and its occupants. Individually and collectively, when they were wronged they did not strike back but sought a "creative" solution to the conflict.

It followed naturally that if individuals could have no enemies, neither could groups of people, and thus war, which assumed collective enemies, was not a way to solve problems.

Their refusal to resist evil was integral to the homocentric orientation of the movement. If there were no external enemies, then neither could ultimate solutions be external, that is, political. Politics was a method of passing on the responsibility for things that individuals needed to do for themselves. Political leaders were neither the cause of nor the solution to the world's problems. The movement also held that the source of evil did not lie in the "old order" and therefore would not be solved by the coming of a savior. As an extension of the logic that rejected political action and as a consequence of their rejection of Jesus as the messiah, this idea made perfect sense. Yet, when one remembers that they also believed that people were capable of evolving into a third stage, the idea that the "old order" was not the cause of the world's problems becomes less clear.

The handbook then dealt with a series of other problems related to the issue of authority. It explained that since the function of the individual was "simply to be aware, to be," people should not seek identity through traditional customs and institutions. They should not think of themselves simply as members of churches, or nationalities, or ethinic groups, or professions, or any other category that divided people from one another. Categories tend to separate people, and the entire Sequoia Seminar philosophy was based on the unity of human beings and the world: "We were created to be part of the whole. Atonement (at-one-ment) is the exhortation to drop our separation."[68]

Just as the philosophy of the group promoted the unity of people with one another, it also stressed the necessity of individuals to integrate themselves. The integration of the self was "integrity," the second major theme derived from the commandments. Integrity meant coming to grips with personal hopes and fears, and being honest with one's self. The handbook urged leaders to challenge all participants to see if they had been open with themselves and with others, using Jesus as the appropriate model for achieving personal integration. The purpose of this self-exploration was not to solve personal problems, not to make individuals happy, and not to let people live lives successfully on their own terms. Nor was it merely psychotherapy. Although a happier and more satisfying life in which doubts and fears had been overcome was seen as a beneficial side effect, integrity was primarily "a means toward the goal of full acceptance of authority."[69]

The third form of love that members of the group were urged to develop was responsibility, or love of others. As interpreted by the handbook, love for others was more than another way of saying "make no enemies." Being responsible meant accepting a special obligation toward the others in the group. "Responsibility leads us to community—the brotherhood of those who are serving God," stated the handbook. It distinguished clearly between a community, which was a group working to carry out God's will, and a collective, which was working for immediate human goals and thus was not expressive of authority. Participation in the community meant that individuals were expected to join others in working at carrying out the will of God, and that meant teaching others the ideas they were learning in the seminar.[70]

It is in the discussion of this third area that the movement came closest to declaring itself a sect. A series of questions were laid out in the handbook that leaders might use to clarify the issue of responsibility. These questions were obviously not meant to open a Socratic dialogue. Each of them was designed to elicit a specific response, and those responses constituted a virtual definition of a sect. The very first one asked, "Does it seem that in order to work most effectively toward helping people to meet their real needs you must join yourself with others who are working together for the same cause?" This was more than a simple invitation to join a community of believers, it was a demand for the surrender of self to the group: "This means the surrender of your illusory freedom so as to multiply your effectiveness by joining together with others who are working for God." The handbook conceded that this question might well "initiate a rather intensive discussion of community."[71]

As stated in the handbook, the way people could demonstrate their acceptance of authority, that is, commitment to God's will, was by joining a group dedicated to that end. Here at last was a clear demand for specific behavior that was a test of authenticity. Sharman had never posited any test of commitment, but the Rathbuns were doing exactly that. Commitment to God now meant commitment to the group to the point of surrendering individual freedom for the community good. There was an implication that those who refusd to sacrifice their individual freedom for the effort of the group lacked genuine commitment to the will of God and were therefore not among those who would be the harbingers of the third age. But the addition of a final qualifier kept open the possibility that people could do the will of God outside the movement and prevented the handbook from being an open declaration of independence from the established churches and a public admission that they were indeed a sect. "We need people to join with us in the work we are doing," the handbook declared, but it went on to provide people with an escape clause: "If this doesn't seem to be the place for you to function, then quit wasting time and go out and find the place where you can serve God most effectively."[72] Aware of the dangers of absolutism, the leadership refrained from declaring themselves either the only or best medium for carrying out the will of God.

Harry Rathbun Interprets the Philosophy

As the intellectual spokesman for the movement, Harry developed a speech, given repeatedly, that summed up the Sequoia Seminar philosophy. The philosophical consistency of Harry's speech over many years demonstrates a sectarian reluctance to change even in the face of shifting social values. The form changed, the institutional support structure changed, but the core truths that the Rathbuns had perceived in the late 1930s were immutable. The first version of the speech was delivered to two different conventions of educators in 1942. More than forty years later, the authors heard Harry give basically the same talk to a meeting of Beyond War leaders. In fact, it seems to have been the only speech that Harry gave through most of his life. Notes to some of the last of the "final lectures" that he delivered to his Stanford classes indicate they too covered the same ground and used most of the same illustrative material. Mixing the order in which he presented his points from speech to speech, Harry invariably mentioned science, evolution, psychological maturity, individual obligation to the group, and Jesus as a model for thought and action. He liked to set up the speech, when possible, with a dramatic statement about the danger the world was in. This was easy enough during World War II, and later he usually managed to mention the possibility of the end of civilization from nuclear war somewhere in the talk. Soon after the war, in 1947, he used for the first time a quote from Albert Einstein that would later become the virtual motto of Beyond War: "The unleashed power of the atom has changed everything save our modes of thinking, and we thus drift toward unparalleled catastrophe."[73]

Having established the danger, Harry proceeded to imply a solution by describing Heard's theory of human evolution.[74] In a 1959 version of the speech that was reprinted and apparently widely distributed, he argued that there was a direction in the evolutionary process toward greater complexity, greater specialization, and greater understanding. He then likened each of these ideas to one of Heard's stages of human development: "The first, the biological or organic state, was that in which we developed the characteristics that made us men. . . . The second stage has been called the technic stage, and we are in the middle of that now. . . . The third is the psychic stage in which we learn how to use this equipment above our ears more effectively."[75]

The speech then usually moved into a section dealing with the importance of psychologically mature individuals, "men and women adequate to the situations in which they will find themselves."[76] And always, in every speech, he illustrated what he meant by reciting that paean to bourgeois self-sufficiency, Rudyard Kipling's poem, "If." The selection of Kipling's poem was understandable on most counts since it defined maturity—"you'll be a Man, my son!"—in terms of sobriety, hard work, and emotional control. But it also stressed the importance of personal independence from others, an idea that ran directly counter to the great emphasis within Sequoia Seminar on interdependence. Harry was apparently untroubled by the fact that the poem could be considered inconsistent with the goal of community because it described a person of great inner strength derived from solid middle-class values.[77] Finally, Harry came to the logical conclusion of his talk: the way to achieve the next step in evolution, the way to attain psychological maturity, the way to insure human cooperation and the survival of civilization—religion. He always insisted that religion was universal. "I contend that everyone has a religion whether he knows it or not," Harry told an audience in 1960. "I say that," he continued, "because it seems to me that historically it is true that what we encompass by the word religion is a person's views of the universe in which he lives, his relationship to that universe, the way things are, the things that are valuable and so on."[78] His definition of religion might not have passed muster in an academic setting, but it had another purpose. Since everybody had a religion, then it was "extraordinarily important for a person to have a realistic religion instead of one based upon illusion; . . . a mature rather than a childish one."[79] He defined mature religion in Sequoia Seminar terms as total loyalty to the highest good, that is, the surrender of the individual's will to the will of God, and pointed out that Jesus was one of the finest exemplars of that mature religious approach to life. The purpose of accepting a mature religion, as he defined it, remained constant through Harry's speeches, but the wording was softened somewhat in the later years. The first full-blown example of the standard speech, delivered in 1942, pulled no punches. Man, he explained, had to "cast off the shell of separateness in which he is imprisoned and emerge . . . into the next stage of human evolution which is not organic evolution but that of his psyche, his spirit, his essential nature." Using an explicitly biological term, he stated that this "*mutation* is attained by giving one's complete and total loyalty to the underlying spirit of ultimate and total good, call it by whatever name you like. Such is the essence of the teaching of Jesus of Nazareth." Harry had no doubt that what he was saying was scientifically true and would someday be proven through psychology, but, he declared, "we can't wait for that. We must save civilization now so the psychologist will have an opportunity to make that discovery."[80]

Psychology in Sequoia Seminar

Psychology was the most poorly defined of all the elements that made up Sequoia Seminar's philosophy, yet it was one of the most important and, even more than the ideas of Buchman or Heard, it set Sequoia Seminar apart from the tradition of Henry B. Sharman. Since Harry always argued that psychology would eventually prove what religion already knew, why bother with psychology at all? Because, among the three appropriate objects of love—God, self, and other—love of self or integrity required that people come to understand their subconscious needs and fears so that they could be free to carry out the will of God. The movement believed psychology could help people toward religion, and religion could help them psychologically. A physician participating in a 1953 seminar wrote that he had learned that psychiatry taught, "To be happy you must be properly oriented to your environment and totally integrated, so that every action is a productive one leading to full potentiality." The seminar taught him that Jesus had said the same thing two thousand years ago and, he concluded, "a well-adjusted person is, by definition, religious."[81]

Psychology was, nevertheless, also perceived as potentially dangerous; when wrongly used it could either undermine the religious message or become the primary purpose of the group, relegating the teachings of Jesus to a secondary role. Freudian psychology, which defined religious belief as neurotic, was an example of the first danger. Harry believed that "Freudian psychology leads to a mechanistic view of the universe and to a philosophy of meaninglessness."[82] There is some indication that the Rathbuns felt, not without reason, that Boyden and her followers fell into the second danger when they split off from the main Sharman group in 1941 and began their own work.[83] The Rathbuns referred to them as "the psychologizers."

The exact role that psychology played in Sequoia Seminar meetings prior to 1955 is not clear, although its flavor is suggested by a list of recommended readings from 1950 that included works by Rollo May and Erich Fromm in addition to books by Kunkel, Jung, and Heard.[84] Much of the psychological activity that did occur took place under the direction of Emilia with the assistance of Betty Eisner. Eisner had been a student of Harry's in the business law course. She had attended a Records study group at the Rathbuns' home in 1936 and was at the first Sequoia Seminar in 1946. She had gone on to earn a Ph.D. in clinical psychology and came up from her home in southern California to help lead some special seminars in the mid-1950s.[85]

A set of very complete notes from a 1952 continuation seminar gives some insight into the kind of psychological activity that took place in the sessions. A parenthetical comment near the beginning of the notes indicate that there were "several sessions during which Seminar participants verbalized their 'seventh veil' matter, their inmost blocks to further growth and progress on the Way."[86] These group confessions may have owed something to Emilia's years of experience hearing confessions in her Oxford Group work. When she told the participants, "nothing that has been said is a surprise, at least to me," she was repeating language she had used to describe her Buchmanite experience. Emilia assured the group that they became more lovable when they opened up and admitted their "inmost natures and problems," and explained that it was all part of the process of discovering what they could be so that they could see where they were and how they could move toward what God intended them to be.[87]

As the decade progressed the role of psychology in the group's activities increased. In 1956 Emilia and Betty Eisner were coleaders of a group that wrote spontaneously on themes suggested by Emilia, "trying to express their own feelings rather than intellectual concepts."[88] In addition to spontaneous writing, they also did Jungian dream interpretation in groups and used art to express their feelings.[89] The 1958 annual report explained, "painting and other art work is becoming an increasingly important part of our program, particularly at the Continuation seminars. We are learning how such activities can contribute to the process of individual change with which we are concerned."[90] So pervasive was the psychological approach by 1958 and 1959 that almost all of the continuation seminars given in those summers were psychologically focused and many included art. The most explicit was a seminar entitled "Group Therapy" led by Betty Eisner. It was described as "an intensive group therapy situation and will be conducted on a very personal level aimed at removing barriers within the individual which obstruct his growth in creative living. . . . The use of art materials will play an important role."[91]

Two comments made in 1959 indicate that the heavy emphasis on psychology may have gotten out of hand. The announcement letter for the 1959 seminar season cautioned potential participants that the leaders were "neither qualified nor intended to perform the function of psychotherapy," and they would not accept anybody who seemed more interested in that than in pursuing a religious life. About the same time, a handwritten memo from Emilia asked if people should not be "well grounded in the teachings of Jesus and have made the decision to follow the 'way' before they are enrolled in any group which has as its objective the process of introspection (therapy)." And, conversely, she asked if people who started work in psychotherapy should be "told that the process in the seminar structure leads to a choice of 'the way' of life commended by Jesus (commitment)?"[92]

Emilia's fear that the psychotherapeutic aspects of the work might have begun to take precedence over the religious purpose seems particularly apt in retrospect. Although nobody knew it at the time, Sequoia Seminar was one of a stream of sources for what would become the "human potential" movement of the 1960s. Their stress of religious values kept them from total involvement, but for several years in the late 1950s they were the place where some of the California activists in the human potential movement got their start. One was Del Carlson. Carlson was a Marine Corps veteran who had been attracted to a Records study group at San Jose State College in 1947 and who had participated actively in Students Concerned. He stayed with the movement after the demise of Students Concerned and was, for a dozen years, one of the mainstays of the group. A high school art teacher, he had his summers free and devoted them to Sequoia Seminar. He was the group's registrar, business manager, and leader of art therapy sessions until 1962.[93]

Carlson was also a friend of Michael Murphy, the man who founded Esalen. In fact, Carlson was a coleader of the first formal seminar ever held at Esalen in 1962, when it was still called Slate's Hot Springs.[94]

Even more important, both to Sequoia Seminar and the human potential movement, was Willis Harman. An engineering professor at Stanford, Harman had attended a study group led by Harry and then had gone to a Sequoia Seminar in 1954. He had not expected the heavy emphasis on meditation, introspection, and self-exposure, but he found that his engineer's rational world view was "permanently destroyed" as a result of his experience there. He embarked on an extended period of self-education in mysticism and psychic phenomena and moved into the inner circle of Sequoia Seminar.[95]

Harman had been very impressed by Gerald Heard's lectures on his experience with mescaline; he also made contact with Myron Stolaroff, one of the original American experimenters with LSD, who was also briefly involved with Sequoia Seminar. On November 16, 1956, eight of the Sequoia Seminar leadership group accompanied Harman to the home of a physician member of the movement, where Harman took LSD for the first time. In subsequent years almost every member of the Sequoia Seminar inner leadership group experimented with LSD on a number of occasions. Many of the drug sessions were led by Betty Eisner who was very interested in the psychotherapeutic possibilities of low doses of the then legal hallucinogen. She and Harman disagreed strongly, however, on how the drug should be used since he preferred larger doses that would provide the user with mystical experiences, rather than the milder effects that Eisner sought.[96]

Even though LSD was still a noncontrolled substance and, therefore, legal to use, Sequoia Seminar employed it very cautiously. It was never distributed to anyone other than group leaders, and their sessions were carefully planned and supervised, usually with the presence of one of the planning group members who was a medical doctor. There appear to have been few if any "bad trips," and the drug-induced mystical experiences and psychotherapeutic sessions are usually remembered positively by those who partook of them. Experimentation with LSD stopped after 1959 because most of those involved felt there was nothing more to be gained from continued use and perhaps also because of a difficult confrontation between Emilia and Betty Eisner that may have involved the use of the drug. Those, like Harman, who wished to pursue further interests in the drug left Sequoia Seminar and became active in other groups such as Esalen and the International Foundation for Internal Freedom.[97]

Just how far the Rathbuns had moved from the tradition of Henry B. Sharman by the end of the decade is illustrated by the controversy that surrounded the last meeting of the trustees of the Sharman will in 1959. Harry was not only one of the trustees of the self-liquidating foundation set up by the will; he was also its executor. In 1958 plans were made to dispose of the last twenty-five thousand dollars of the funds from Sharman's estate, and Harry apparently hoped that the bulk of the money could go to Sequoia Seminar. To convince the others that his group met the intention of the will, Harry invited them out to California for a seminar.[98] Opposition from the other trustees to the kind of program that the Rathbuns were running killed both the visit and any hope Harry had of getting Sharman funds, although Harry did lead a seminar for the trustees the next year at Springfield College in Massachusetts.

Word of the psychological emphasis had spread, and those who toed the orthodox Sharman line were not pleased with what they had heard. One trustee reported that a number of students of his had gone to Stanford and had reported back unfavorably on the Rathbuns' work. Another summed up his objections by telling Harry that he believed Sequoia Seminar was "quite different from those led by Dr. Sharman. Very little serious study of the Records themselves seems to be attempted and much time is devoted to the personal problems of the individual members. Training and skill in psychology and psychiatry seem to be very important."[99] And finally, a third pointed out that Sharman had wanted efforts directed at students and faculty, but Harry and Emilia were working mainly with nonacademic adults.[100]

The alienation of the trustees and the experimentation with LSD were both aspects of the way psychology had come to dominate the work of the group. This domination could have made the group an ongoing force within the new human potential movement in California. That course was not followed, however, because in the period between 1959 and 1962 Emilia underwent a number of severe personal strains that eventually climaxed in a religious revelation. This revelation was the basis for a reclarification of the whole meaning and purpose of the movement. The psychologizing that Emilia had first questioned back in the early 1940s when it was led by Elizabeth Boyden had slowly worked its way into her own group, and by the end of the decade it threatened to eclipse the religious work completely. The philosophy that had evolved was based in part on the validity of psychology as a means for personal insight, but it also used the evolutionary and mystical theories of Gerald Heard, and always the objective study of the life of Jesus in the Sharman tradition. Emilia's personal crisis of the period after 1959 would have the effect of redressing the balance and putting psychology back into a secondary role. Psychology would be exchanged for a new interpretation of the religious message that would finally move Sequoia Seminar from proto-sect to a fully self-conscious religious movement.

The increasing stress on psychology toward the end of the 1950s, and the growing formalization of ideology, were both indications that the group was moving away from the churches (both literally and theoretically) and toward the sect end of the church–sect continuum. The codification of the movement's ideology decreased the likelihood that they would change to go along with trends in the larger society. The focus on psychology was perceived by members as a "service," exactly the kind of service predicted by the economic model as compensation for the increased cost of sect membership. The transition was not yet complete. The most obvious component of a sect is its divergence from standard church values. It is that divergence that makes membership so costly. At the end of the 1950s, Sequoia Seminar was still primarily a gospel study group that could operate from within the churches. There were signs of uniqueness beginning to appear, but they would not be fully embraced until after Emilia had her vision of a New Religion for the Third Age.

3

The New Religion of the Third Age

The most decisive transition of the many that Creative Initiative went through in its history occurred in 1962. In that year, Emilia had a religious revelation that resolved a series of personal and collective crises and radically changed the organization and style of the group. Yet, as with all their changes, no matter how radical in appearance, a backbone of core beliefs remained immutable. On the one hand, the group abandoned all pretense of working through the churches and realized its long-standing dream of building a community of believers by supplementing the academic study of the teachings of Jesus with a self-conscious new religion complete with its own rituals. On the other hand, these new religious forms were colorful trappings for an ideology that remained in most respects unchanged.

A Time of Crisis

Betwen 1959 and 1962 Emilia underwent her trial in the wilderness. Although Harry had always been her partner in their religious endeavors, and, indeed, Harry had done most of the actual teaching of the Sharman method, it was Emilia who suffered the crises and it was Emilia who led the group in its new direction. Events in three distinct areas began to come to a head in the mid- to late 1950s and produced in Emilia and in the group a profound sense of religious and psychological distress. First, she and other leaders became increasingly disillusioned with the mainline Protestant churches where they worked as Sunday school teachers and youth leaders. Second, there was a growing concern about sexual morality and other issues of "life style" (including the social use of alcohol). And finally, Emilia had to confront a series of problems related to Harry's retirement, her employment, and her health. These culminated in an experience that she believed was a call by a divine source to alter the direction of the movement. This experience resolved the crises and, at the age of fifty-six, Emilia emerged as the charismatic leader of a new sect—indeed, a new religion—which saw itself both as the fulfillment of the Jewish and Christian traditions and as their successor.

The relationship between Sequoia Seminar and the mainline Christian churches in which Emilia and other members of the group had been working was greatly strained by the end of the 1950s. These tensions appear to have arisen as a consequence of the increasingly sectlike role that Sequoia Seminar was playing in the lives of its participants. As the demands of Sequoia Seminar increased, both pastors and congregations came to view the movement less as a supplement to their own programs and more as an organization in direct competition with them.[1] Emilia, however, did not see the strain arising from an unavoidable conflict growing out of the changing structure of Sequoia Seminar. She believed the split occurred because the church leadership resisted the movement's ideas regarding Jesus and because movement people objected to sexual immorality on the part of many clergy.[2]

Emilia's conflicts with the churches played themselves out in several events of the late 1950s. First, she had some sharp differences with the ministerial leaders of a Methodist women's conference at which she taught about the historical Jesus in a way that they felt conflicted with church doctrine. She claimed the clergymen were upset particularly because her lectures drew huge audiences even though they had been deliberately scheduled at inconvenient hours. A second conflict occurred closer to home. Emilia had been appointed superintendent of the local Methodist Sunday school but was forced to resign after some of the congregation complained that her style was too "Catholic." It appears that she decorated her Sunday School room with an altar and introduced some distinctly un-Protestant rituals and ceremonies into school activities.[3]

Aside from specific incidents such as these, there was the more general problem of Sequoia Seminar competing for the time and effort of church members. Pastors were becoming suspicious that Emilia was taking advantage of her role within the churches to find participants for Sequoia Seminar, and other members of Sequoia Seminar's core working in other churches found that their enthusiasm and commitment threatened clergy and fellow church members.[4] John Levy, a prominent member of the group during this period, recalled that Emilia was indeed "anti-church," and that she worked in the churches "in a kind of subversive way to try to lure the poor people who weren't getting the message from the church over to us."[5] Although not denying that Sequoia Seminar recruited from the churches, Emilia always argued that she targeted only those women who were marginal participants in church activity and that their involvement in Sequoia Seminar actually strengthened their commitment to the churches. It seems clear, however, that the Protestant clergy had their doubts about her and other group members.[6]

In their work with the women church members Emilia and others increasingly heard stories of sexual impropriety among the clergy.[7] The thought that religious leaders, who should have been setting an example, would fail in this area was particularly intolerable to Emilia, who claimed that she had "met only one minister that was not into predicaments of his own."[8] The concern of Emilia and the group with "living the life" often found its clearest focus in the areas of sexual purity and the sanctity of marriage. Failures by the clergy in these areas therefore seemed to invalidate their religious leadership and to reinforce Emilia's conviction that "literally, the Christian era [was] over."

The group's tendency to focus on the personal behavior of the clergy rather than on institutional competition as a source of tension between the churches and Sequoia Seminar has two apparent sources. First, seminar activists had always had a very strong sense of right and wrong, and thus they concentrated on those issues about which there was no moral ambiguity. It was much easier to condemn immoral ministers than to acknowledge that Sequoia Seminar as an organization was in competition with the churches for the time, money, and religious energy of their members. Second, there was a long tradition, dating back to Sharman, of resisting the formation of a separate group in favor of working through the churches and para-church agencies such as the YMCA. For that reason, prior to 1962 Emilia felt they were obliged to cooperate with the churches. Nothing in her history or that of the group would have given them a philosophical justification for divorcing Sequoia Seminar from the churches. But that did not stop them from condemning the churches because of the behavior of their ministerial representatives and thus finding a legitimate reason for the increasing tension and the impending split.

It is not surprising that Emilia concentrated on the issue of sexual morality in her growing disillusionment with the churches. Insistence on marital fidelity was part of the tradition inherited from Sharman and was reinforced by Harry and Emilia's personal experiences and attitudes. Emilia's early upbringing in Mexico was quite traditional, and Harry was as unworldly as she in sexual matters.[9] Harry rejected a double standard in the area of sex and believed that men should enter marriage as pure as their wives.[10] Emilia has said that it was not until her work with the Oxford Group in the late 1930s that she came into direct contact with people who behaved in less than exemplary ways regarding sex. Even there, however, her experience (like Harry's with Alcoholics Anonymous) was with people who were repenting their previous personal behavior and turning to God and conventional values as a means to finding absolution and peace.

Sharman's views on sex and marriage had become clear in an event that took place toward the close of the 1930s, at about the same time that Emilia became involved with the Oxford Group. Elizabeth Boyden and Frances Warnecke, who both worked together at a number of Bay Area colleges and who had first introduced Emilia to the Sharman method, fell in love with the same man: Fred Howes, a Sharman disciple and an engineering professor at McGill University. Frances Warnecke was expecting to marry him when he told her that he realized he loved Elizabeth instead. Frances was devastated and severed her relationship with Elizabeth, who went on to marry Howes.[11]

The marriage was not a happy one, and within a short time Elizabeth had become involved with another man. After four years of negotiations and accusations, they were finally divorced in 1941.[12] Sharman became involved in the Howes' domestic drama because both parties were very close to him, and both clearly wanted his support for their positions. Sharman did not so much support Fred as he opposed Elizabeth. When, in 1939, she suggested that she stop by to visit and talk with him about the situation, Sharman responded with a letter that essentially "excommunicated" her.[13] He called the issue between them "profoundly cleaving" and warned her "*not* to come to see us." The final paragraph of his letter left no doubt that his alienation from her stemmed from the sexual and marital situation:

Your letter lacks completely any evidence of the one essential for your recovery, namely, deep loathing because of your relations with Don, overwhelming disgust that you should have prostituted yourself for the satisfaction of mutual lust—in a word the only way to your salvation, which is REPENTANCE.[14]

In her response to his rejection, Elizabeth was not repentant in the slightest. She defended her conduct and feelings and told Sharman that they were not communicating because he lived by a code rather than by individual insight. She accused him of never letting the word "love" enter his religious thinking and explained that she based her religious ideals on it. She wrote that she was willing to be the scapegoat for all those at Minnesing who had extramarital relations, but she was amazed that Sharman would take upon himself the right to sit in judgment of others.[15] She was subsequently dropped from the list of those who could lead sanctioned seminars and thereafter struck out on her own. Boyden Howes founded the Guild for Psychological Studies, a group that offers seminars that use the Sharman study technique in conjunction with Jungian psychology, and, since 1982, the only organized group that continues the Sharman tradition.[16]

The Rathbuns were not directly involved in the split between Sharman and Elizabeth Boyden Howes, although Sharman kept them apprised of his role in the situation and their loyalty remained with him. The legacy of this controversy stayed with the Rathbuns in the form of a willingness to expect and to enforce very traditional codes of personal sexual conduct and a commitment to the indissolubility of marriage under almost any circumstances.

Emilia's attitudes and moral expectations were put to a personal test in the late 1940s—roughly at the time of Students Concerned—when she became emotionally entangled with a married neighbor who was also very active in Sequoia Seminar. Their mutual attraction was common knowledge among many of the people in the movement at the time. Although the man claimed otherwise, Emilia told confidantes that, despite their strong feelings for one another, the relationship was never consummated.[17] Eventually the man asked her to leave Harry and said he would leave his family so that they could get married. She refused and rededicated herself to her marriage. The rumors and accusations of a possible affair eventually necessitated a meeting of the core leadership with Emilia and the man. At that meeting, she refused either to affirm or deny the charges, feeling that the others' knowledge of her and her character should speak for itself.[18]

Whatever the specific facts of this event, it is clear that it served to reinforce Emilia's commitment to the inviolability of the traditional marriage relationship. Either because of her successful resistance to the power of passion over commitment, or because of guilt and denial, Emilia became even more critical of other peoples' failings in such matters. By the 1950s her personal attitude toward sex had become one of grudging tolerance. In 1952 she claimed that the "animal drive" for sexual union with another person could never be successful because true union could come only through God. She then praised psychology as a useful tool for helping people free themselves from the "repression of basic, animal drives" and observed that "sex life, even in happily married people, will last for only a time anyway."[19]

This final comment seems to imply that Emilia had suppressed her own sexual feelings, an interpretation supported by a remark she made some years later while discussing the incident with a friend. She admitted that she had been strongly attracted to the man but said that she had refrained from acting on her feelings. She went on to say that a person either had to free herself from sexual feelings altogether or else repress them and live a lie, and that "God gave me the answer that there is freedom," which appeared to mean freedom from sexual desire itself.[20] She further said that she would have to "relinquish what it meant to be a woman" because "you can't be a woman and be an instrument of God both."[21] Being a woman meant being attracted to men, and being attracted to men meant "you have to look deep, deep down . . . and see whether you want to leave this completely and never have it anymore in order to be with God."[22]

There was still one other crisis involving sexual behavior that affected Emilia deeply, perhaps because it echoed the earlier confrontation between Sharman and Elizabeth Boyden Howes. In 1959, Emilia became aware that a woman whom she considered one of her protégés, Norma Rosenquist, was having marital difficulties. Possibly as a consequence of her work with the Oxford Group, possibly because of her experience in her own marriage, Emilia saw other people's marriage crises as personal challenges. For more than a year, she and a small group of the inner circle of Sequoia Seminar met weekly with Rosenquist and her husband to try to help them resolve their problems. Their help was to no avail, and the Rosenquists were eventually divorced.[23]

Discussions of the Rosenquist marriage were complicated by Emilia's suspicion, never voiced in the group, that Norma Rosenquist was having an affair with John Levy, a member of the planning group and the first full-time volunteer worker in the movement. Both Levy and Rosenquist have denied that there was an affair, although they admit to having been strongly attracted to each other. Indeed, Rosenquist observed that Emilia "taught her better than she knew," because she would not have dreamed of having a relationship with another man while she was married.[24]

Nevertheless, Emilia believed there was an affair and, when she realized that Norma and John were scheduled to lead a seminar together, she "went into a spasm." From her perspective, it was clear that someone even suspected of having an extramarital affair and clearly unable to preserve her own marriage could not lead a seminar. She therefore refused to allow either Rosenquist or Levy to direct the seminar. This situation brought to head problems that had been developing for some time. Seven members of the Sequoia Seminar leadership group, including Rosenquist and Levy, met for a week of intensive discussion and at the end decided that they needed to strike out on their own. They were extremely grateful for the Rathbuns' love, friendship, and instruction, but they also were beginning to feel confined by the two founders' strongly paternalistic approach and concluded that the time had come to break free of the Rathbuns' close rein. In addition to sexual values, there were differences in attitudes toward alcohol, prayer, and other religious practices.[25]

In addition to the conflict with the churches and the issue of sexual morality, Emilia experienced a third set of crises that involved a broad range of personal issues. The year 1959 was Harry's last as a member of the Stanford faculty, and retirement meant a considerable drop in his already relatively low income. Casting about for a way to supplement the family earnings, Emilia decided to return to college and get a credential that would allow her to teach in the public school system. She enrolled in her alma mater, San Jose State College, took the necessary courses, and got a job teaching in a predominantly Mexican American elementary school in San Jose. Although she thought she did well as a teacher (and got the principal involved in Sequoia Seminar), she kept the job for only three years. She seemed to feel that her changed circumstances involved a serious loss of status. In the first place she found it "humiliating and embarrassing" to have to work, since she did not believe that married women should be employed outside the home if their husbands could support them. This feeling was exacerbated by her assignment to a school that served predominantly lower-income families. Revealing the status-conscious attitudes that occasionally showed through the group's liberal position, she recalled, "I didn't want to work in that school. I wanted to work in a high class school that has good kids to work with, and these were all blacks and kind of deprived kids."[26]

Added to these changes in financial and career circumstances, there was growing unhappiness with the religious process in Sequoia Seminar. Emilia came to feel that "somehow Jesus wasn't working anymore, that people would write these great papers about their commitments and what they've got and somehow it wasn't working, it wasn't taking hold."[27] A close associate at the time recalled that she began to question the Sharman method's ability to bring about individual change and at the same time raised questions about Harry's ability to lead the group, complaining that he "didn't have it anymore."[28] Ever impatient to see dramatic change as a result of the seminar process and to see in tangible terms the formation of a community dedicated to common purpose, Emilia was rapidly losing faith in the efficacy of the Sharman method to bring about those ends. As Emilia herself recognized, she was seriously depressed and "in trouble."[29] She began to talk about the necessity of gathering a group of ten women who would fully and totally commit themselves to "live the life" and made fitful starts in this direction, but nothing organized emerged from those early efforts.[30]

Emilia's sense of personal crisis was further aggravated by problems she had with Betty Eisner, who had first joined the group while a student at Stanford. After she became a psychotherapist, Eisner led therapy sessions at Sequoia Seminar where she commonly used low doses of LSD to relax people. Her relationship to Emilia was characterized by tension and apparent competitiveness.[31] At one point in 1959, Eisner had conducted a meeting with the leadership at the Ben Lomond camp on the condition that Emilia not be present or even on the camp grounds. People who were there say she used the meeting to try to turn the group against Emilia.[32] Later, Emilia participated in a therapy session under Eisner's guidance in which Eisner urged Emilia to confess that there was violence in her, which Emilia refused to do.[33] Depending on the source of the story, Eisner either succumbed to her competitiveness with Emilia and took advantage of a situation in which Emilia was drugged and vulnerable, or merely used the therapy situation, without LSD, to get Emilia to confront deeply buried problems. In either case, it is agreed that this experience, coming on the heels of the adultery accusations and the departure of valued and long-time members of the group, was powerful enough that Emilia had to leave the religious work and take some months of rest and recovery.[34]

The cumulative problems placed Emilia in an untenable psychological position that demanded some kind of resolution. Given her personality and religious preoccupations, it was perhaps inevitable that the resolution would take a religious form. Emilia herself was well aware at the time that "something had to give." In a long handwritten memo from Emilia to the membership in 1960 she expressed the expectation that something had to change and that she would be the force behind a purification and revitalization of the movement.[35] Like much of Emilia's writing, the memo was vague. It appears, however, to have been a reaction against the heavy psychological emphasis of the late 1950s and a reassertion of the fundamental purpose of the work to act as "a dynamic intermediary between the individual and the living God."[36] Ostensibly this represented a return to the religious purity of the Sharman legacy. Yet, there was a simultaneous sense that Sharman had been only a beginning and now was the time to move in the direction of a new and unambiguous religious commitment. Although that direction had not yet emerged clearly, the organization was demanding unprecedented dedication from its members and was taking another step in the process of becoming a sect.

How was this fundamental clarity of purpose to be restored? Emilia began to see the movement as awaiting a true charismatic leader who, armed with an infusion of insight from God, would be able to marshal the forces of the group and lead it in a new direction. As her crisis deepened, Emilia increasingly speculated whether she might not be that leader, and whether the tensions and crises she felt might not be attributable to her failure to discern her mission. A participant from this period remembers that in one "revelation," she "went into one of her trances and she said she saw a movement coming where the men that were needed were the men that were there" in the group, and that she expected them to commit themselves to her and she would be their leader.[37] In an undated fragment from about this period Emilia wrote that God intended the work to go into a second phase in which Harry would play the role of "stabilizer & anchor," while she would be the visionary "with all the vicissitudes & characteristics that make the role precarious."[38]

As early as 1958 the various tensions and stresses bearing on Emilia began to manifest themselves in headaches and other ailments for which she sought professional help.[39] The turmoil of 1959 and 1960 that ended with the defection of much of the leadership group, Harry's retirement, Emilia's brief experiment with teaching, the confrontation with Betty Eisner, and the end of the connection with the churches, brought on additional illnesses that provided temporary escapes from the unsettled state of her life.

The Revelation of the Third Age

Leaving school one day, Emilia felt that "something happened" to her back. She remained bedridden, waiting for an appointment with an osteopath, who diagnosed her as having a very serious problem with cartilage in her spine. As quickly as it began, however, her pain disappeared, and Emilia concluded that "somebody had done something" to her and that she "was in the hands of something."[40]

This was followed by a second experience in which she felt very ill and told the principal that he had better get a substitute for her because she was not coming back. He commiserated, telling her that he understood that the work had gotten to her. She responded that it was not the work, that she felt happy and fulfilled in her teaching. She went home, nevertheless, and "slept for three days solid," eventually waking up and complaining to Harry that the doctor must have prescribed "some medication with dope."[41]

But it was not Emilia's style to retreat into invalidism or to allow the religious flame to be extinguished. She was to find a more creative solution.[42] As she lay in her depressed state she remembers that she woke up thinking, "I am emptied. I have no feeling for God, and Jesus somehow has removed himself, and I can't work."[43] Having reached her nadir, physically, psychologically, and religiously, Emilia recognized that her old resources and old patterns would not be adequate to extricate her from her problems. She had reached the end of a three-year process during which she had prayed to God asking him to find a leader, to raise up somebody "because I can't do it, I can't do the work anymore."[44]

The crisis was finally resolved in a dramatic religious experience that cut the Gordian knot of her conflicts:

In the middle of the night from a sound sleep I woke up . . . and I felt the presence of Christ in the room—not Jesus—Christ. . . . Always when you come to the end of the life of Jesus as we study him, he says, "I will not drink of the fruit of the vine until I drink it new in the kingdom of God." And every time I come to that passage I've wondered what that meant. Because I know Jesus didn't believe that he's coming back . . . and I knew he didn't believe he's going to go to heaven and sit up there drinking new with God in heaven. I didn't believe that and still don't, so then I would say what does it mean, this passage? What is God going to do with the Passover? That's one question that I've always asked. So when this presence of Christ came into the room, he said to me, "Lazara, arise! I'm going to have communion with you in the new covenant and drink it anew from the kingdom of God."[45]

Emilia concluded that the presence could be trusted because "it snapped me out of the condition I was in."[46] She believed that she had been "raised" by a higher power, for, as she explained, "I don't think it's possible to understand the depth of the thing I was into and how I was slipped out of it like that. I had to interpret it as something I hadn't done for myself—that had been done for me."[47]

Emilia explained the significance of the fact that it was Christ, not Jesus, who had appeared to her by saying the vision was "something more universally attainable by everybody, but not particularized in that one individual in history."[48] A merely historical figure like Jesus could not, of course, appear in contemporary religious visions, and a figure who could do so must surely transcend in some sense the limitations of history. Because this vision was a direct communication from "the other side" and a radical departure from the prior theology of the group, it had a dramatic effect on Emilia's views and, through her, on the shape and focus of the movement. Emilia now felt divinely authorized to move beyond the historical focus on Sharman's Jesus. No longer was she confined to deducing the meaning of the historical Jesus as constructed with the tools of biblical scholarship. The way was clear for her to pursue an explicitly mystical path of present communion with Christ. The rationalism and intellectualism of the Sharman tradition was now supplemented with a more explicitly religious spiritualism. Harry would continue to honor the academic approach by leading Records seminars, but Emilia could begin to move off in new and creative directions.

Although conscious of the danger that her own personal story might interfere with the "message," in fact Emilia's experience validated her role as the new prophet who could guide the movement through direct revelation. The new "condition for the movement succeeding was to surrender Jesus," she explained, but it was not her idea to do that: "Never in this world would I ever think that—come out of my head? surrender Jesus?"[49] If it were not her idea, then it must have come from a higher power and therefore be legitimate. Continuity with Sharman's interpretation of Jesus was preserved through the position that true religion consisted of absolute submission of the individual to a higher authority and that that understanding could be achieved through the study of the gospels. As the movement transmuted itself, however, into a sect in the months and years following the vision, the Sharman legacy was recast with a radically new context of mythology, rituals, and a vision of the group as a religion in its own right.

Unlike Sharman, who thought he could influence established groups by osmotically permeating them with individually transformed people, Emilia understood her vision as divine permission for the group to fully express the sectarian impulses that had been building for many years. Individual transformation now took place in a collectivity, and it was the group as much as the person that would bring about social change. Emilia wrote at the time that it was her

commitment to God to help Him . . . attain a head for the human body of a group of educated, intelligent persons willing to step out of the boundaries of organized religion. . . . A group of one mind so identified with the purpose of God in this age that they will work to gain the numbers to shift the balance of history by a great event.[50]

The implication of this change was clear: God was calling for a new convenant community, based on a new revelation that would be a "successor religion" to the earlier covenants of Judaism and Christianity. The movement would be an expression of the third age in which "people will resurrect that spirit that was once in Jesus and affirm the truth that he once spoke."[51] Although she was unwilling to make the claim in public, in private Emilia was willing to affirm that she was to the covenant of the third age what Jesus was to the second and Moses was to the first. The idea was not a passing one. As late as 1976 Emilia wrote a long meditation that expressed these same ideas. All religions, she wrote, had found their fulfillment in Creative Initiative, a fact that she illustrated by describing a meeting that included Zoroaster, Buddha, Abraham, Isaac, Jacob, Moses, Peter, Paul, and "someone in actual life now"—clearly herself.[52]

Emilia's special role in the new covenant was always problematic. On the one hand, she consciously resisted the temptation to allow a cult of personality to grow up about her. On the other hand, both she and many movement participants viewed her as a woman of special insight, if not special powers. She, for example, held a strong belief in reincarnation, as did many others in the group, and spoke of herself as drawing on the experience of "many lifetimes" to make herself "pliable to the law and will hidden in the stars and yet close, as close to me as soul."[53] Reincarnation never achieved official sanction as part of group philosophy, but the idea of an alternative plane of being did. As Emilia's sense of her mission developed, so did the concept of the "gnostic world," or "gnostic plane," from which instructions were delivered through a process of mystical insight into the earth plane of ordinary existence. In a private meditation that reflected the broader group belief in the powers of the gnostic plane, Emilia wrote, "There is a Gnostic plane of existence where a higher intelligence has planned how to lift us from lower to higher states of awareness."[54]

The belief that individuals could, in some special way, be chosen to receive wisdom from the gnostic plane generated a distinctive tension in the group. Emilia expressed this problem in her concern for "the intrusion of the self." Nevertheless she reasoned that "God must use human vehicles for expression." She tried to resolve the tension by consciously renouncing her ego. "My person is now named 'Sin nombre,' " she wrote, "which means without a name." There is a play on words here too because when spelled "sinombre" it means "without a man." Having taken on a symbolic cloak of anonymity, she then went on to pledge, "I, Sin nombre . . . set out with a banner—a steel bracelet, a burning world, a twelve-pointed star, twelve candles, twelve golden cloaks of light, one burning wooden cross, on God's mission. I will cry, 'Women of the World unite.' End the fight. Accept the light. Exert the might of the right."[55]

The Gathering of the Thousand

The call for a new covenant community was immediately followed by details for a ritual to initiate the third age, revealed to Emilia by means of automatic writing on the day after her vision of Christ.[56] She was told to gather a group of ten women to perform the rites that would bring the third age into being. In language that the group developed later, this ritual was supposed to "fix the third age into the time stream," or "bring it down from the gnostic plane to the earth plane." Emilia prepared the details of the ceremony in secret, telling the women who were to participate only when and where to gather. They were psychologically prepared for something like this event by the sense of crisis that had pervaded the group for the previous several years. Those years had been

an "environment of holding . . . a stillness, a biding of time" comple-
mented with a "tremendous faith" that "there would be a movement."[57]
These mystical experiences of Emilia's, although recognized by the other
women as especially valuable and meaningful for the whole group, were
more easily accepted because others had been equally conscious of the
need for a new breakthrough and were also having mystical experiences
and intensive prayer times of their own.[58]

The first "Dawn" ceremony, as it came to be called, was held on
February 2, 1962, at a lodge on the Ben Lomond property. Although
the date was chosen simply because it was convenient, the women were
delighted to discover that it was an astronomically auspicious time
because on that day seven planets aligned themselves behind the sun.
The fact that their random date turned out to be one on which people
all over the world expected great events was taken as one more sign that
their enterprise was blessed.[59] On the evening before the ceremony the
ten women and Emilia gathered at the lodge to help decorate it. The
next day at dawn they entered a room "aglow with hundreds of lighted
gold votives. The fragrance of fresh roses permeated the air." Ten chairs,
each draped with a gold robe, were arranged in a circle around a large
felt twelve-pointed star with a candle at each point. The women put on
the robes to symbolize their inclusion in the new age and subordination
of their personal identities into the uniform of the collaborative work.
As they lit the candles, each pledged to gather ten more women who in
turn would gather ten more and so on until a thousand women had
been brought into the movement. The pledge spoke of them passing
"the threshold into the secret fellowship of Hermanas en la Luz [sisters
in the light]" and taking on the new name of "Sin nombre [without a
name]."[60]

The use of a twelve-pointed star as the centerpiece for the ritual was
the first time that symbol had appeared in the work. In a modified form,
as a cross composed of six intersecting lines, it would survive for many
years as the central symbol of the movement, their equivalent of the cross
for Christians or the Star of David for the Jews. Designated the "cross of
fulfillment," it was embellished with a plethora of additional features.
Each point was marked with a word standing for a basic teaching of the
group, the first letters of which, when read in a clockwise direction,
formed a mantra used by the group for collective meditation.[61]

Having lit their candles and pledged to help build the movement, the
one black woman of the original ten placed a bracelet on each of the

other women to symbolize that she was becoming a "free slave of God." The women then drank a "communion of the new age." One woman drank for Judas the betrayer; one for Cain, the first homicide; and one for the "living presence" that was guiding the movement. The drink for the new communion was orange juice—the golden fruit—to symbolize the golden third age.[62]

Women were thought to have a decisive role to play in the new age. They were to reappropriate the direct connection to the divine that had been broken by Eve. The new woman would return to an age of communion with God armed with new power, both uniquely feminine and yet equal to that of men. Unlike the previous covenants in history that had been introduced by men, the new covenant was to be mediated by women. For the first time in history, Emilia told them, "we are promoted by God to be equal."[63] To achieve this new equality women had to make a conscious effort to change themselves. When they did so, they would benefit themselves, their husbands, and all humanity.[64] To affirm this new role of women in the Dawn ceremony, the participants lifted the crown of thorns from Jesus and replaced it with a crown of yellow roses to mark the fulfillment of Jesus' mission and the beginning of an era of direct connection between God and individual persons.

As the ceremony concluded and the women walked out of the lodge into the early mountain dawn, one participant remembers that they looked at the rising sun and all of them saw it take the form of the twelve-pointed star they had just used in the ceremony. Like the lining up of the seven planets, the astronomical event was taken as a sign that their efforts had been favorably received.[65]

There was a very real sense among the participants in the first Dawn ceremony that they were the nucleus of a movement that would expand to fill the world. Each of the original ten was charged with the responsibility of recruiting ten more women for a second round of initiations. Although the process would later become much more elaborate, the first initiates did their recruiting on a one-to-one basis, inviting friends to their homes to discuss the two core documents of the New Religion. The first document, "The Blue, Blue Lake," was a guided meditation that described "the predicament and solution." In it the participant imagined herself standing on the edge of a beautiful lake, witnessing a growing fire coming over a hill. Feeling a powerful urge to do something to contain the fire, she suddenly finds herself amid a host of women, marching and singing a dirge. Together, they "abandon all" and "claim lessons of the past and bring into reality . . . the New Jerusalem."[66] The second document, entitled "The First Paper," constituted a creed for the new movement:

We, the women of the world unite, under God, to change the course of history. As instruments of a higher cause, God, we conceive, nurture and give birth to the human race. We arise from our unconscious sleep and will act now, in this present world emergency, to will a great, powerful, absolute spiritual force to work through us.[67]

After the first two groups had been initiated, a "Ceremony of Twenty" was held to cement the unity of the women gathered thus far. Ceremonies continued apace and, on April 26, 1964, two years after the first Dawn ceremony, a "Ceremony of 100" commemorated their reaching that milestone in the drive for one thousand. It was not precisely specified what would happen when a thousand women were assembled, and speculation on the point was discouraged in favor of "just working for that thousand." Yet there seems to have been a millenarian hope that when the thousand were gathered God would at last have "a mighty instrument through which to work" and their task would then be made plain.[68]

While the process of gathering women into the movement progressed, the first men were introduced to the New Religion. More than in the earlier days of Sequoia Seminar, the group began to shift toward bringing couples into the group together in order not to cause marital dissension over the level of commitment required. Indeed, Emilia came to the conclusion that "it had to be a couple, and if a woman got too interested and the husband wasn't interested, we eased her out— suggested to her that she work someplace else."[69]

Initially, Emilia and the other women had hoped that the men would find their own independent role in the New Religion and that a ceremony would be "given" to one of the men just as the Dawn ceremony had been given to her. Harry, however, failed to share her enthusiasm for ritual, continuing to prefer the more academic Sharman Records study. "I never got excited about the ceremonies and that sort of thing," he admitted.[70] Still, Emilia insisted that the men had to "have a ceremony, but the Lord will have to instruct somebody or give somebody the instructions."[71] The decisive signal for change came during a July seminar for leaders. Twelve men and a few women were meeting together in the Casa de Luz lodge on the Ben Lomond property discussing the question of male participation in the New Religion. They had just agreed to begin such work when one of the men looked at the stone fireplace in the room and saw the "shadow of the Star of David which had been made by the lines from the wooden skylight frame overhead." Everyone present interpreted this as a divine sign, calculating that such an apparition "was an unusual occurrence which could only happen once each year at exactly twelve noon, when the sun was at its highest point in the heavens." Further reflection on the fact that there were twelve men in the gathering, that the time was twelve noon, and that the sun, which symbolized enlightenment, was at its highest point in the sky, reinforced the sense that the time was indeed right to begin.[72]

Predictably, it was Emilia who ultimately received instructions for the men's ceremony shortly after this event. This first "Able" (Abel) ceremony was enacted on November 3, 1963, and was far more complicated than the women's Dawn ceremony, graphically illustrating the elaboration of symbols and rituals already taking place. The men gathered before dawn, dressed simply in white cotton shirts and dark-colored slacks. The women of the group had prepared the altar and placed votive candles around the room. A special chair draped with a purple velvet cape, "to honor Jesus of Nazareth," was placed near the altar. On the altar itself were a large "God candle," the Bible, a statue of a lion, a statue of the Buddha, "Jewish symbols," a globe, and a dozen white stones.

The ceremony began with each man being called by name. As he entered the room, he crossed over a black and white yin/yang symbol on the floor which signified "his choosing to pass over from the darkness of ignorance into the light." In the center of the room on the floor was a large felt Star of David with a red rose at its center. Small gold swords with twelve-pointed crosses were placed at the points of the Star of David symbol and, beyond them, twelve chairs were arrayed in a circle. Each chair was draped with a long blue cape lined with gold satin cloth. The blue "symbolized the world of which each was a part," the gold, "the inner life, dedicated to attaining enlightenment." A four-sectioned gold satin cap rested at the foot of each chair. The four points of the cap represented the four corners of the earth and alluded to the prophecy of Jesus that all people would come from the east and the west into the Kingdom of God (Luke 13:29). The number twelve stood for "the masculine principle" in the group's numerology, and the fact that twelve men participated in the ceremony meant "the establishment of the correct masculine principle" through which men "would be motivated from a God-centered base and would work in the world to bring others into this same knowledge."

Each man took a red votive candle and extinguished it, symbolically eliminating "the red fire of hatred, selfishness, and the war within him." He then lit a white votive from the central God candle and placed it on the altar next to the globe "to symbolize his willingness to use the light of God in his life." All then received a white stone symbolic of the purified will that made each man Able (Abel). This "Able" stone referred with deliberate orthographic ambiguity both to the slain brother of Cain, renouncing of violence in the new age, and to the ability of each man to fulfill his vow. Taking red roses, traditionally given in love to women, the men offered them instead to God as an expression of their first loyalty and devotion to Him. A crown of red roses was put on the altar to replace the crown of thorns that Jesus had worn, and a "brotherhood with Jesus" was declared as each man committed himself to carry out the unfinished task of Jesus—to realize the Kingdom of God.

They put on the gold caps and the gold-lined robes signifying their willingness to take up the task and commitment. Finally, the participants raised the flaming swords of truth as they rose to affirm their willingness to battle for God and to work vigorously to spread His truth. The elaborate ceremony concluded with a male version of Emilia's "drinking together," as they drank grape juice from red goblets to represent living fellowship with Jesus, their brother in the light.[73]

At the end of the ceremony the men received gold rings embossed with the twelve-rayed cross of fulfillment. These rings were the men's sign of initiation, the equivalent of the women's bracelets, and many of the men inducted during this period have continued to wear their rings to the present day. Harry, however, dryly ascribed theological significance to the fact that, as the movement continued to evolve into Beyond War (and he lost weight), his "just dropped off."[74] Groups of twelve men at a time were initiated and, like the women, new members were expected to gather groups of their own.

Like the women, the men recited a pledge that was in fact a creed of the new sect. In it they declared themselves to be "the nucleus of the new collective, the new community, the new church, the new race, the new species, the new world."[75] They continued, "I affirm my faith that by the continued expansion of community through this process mankind can and will become united in a continuously growing organism wholly dedicated to fulfilling God's purpose for man on planet Earth."[76] The ostensible goal of the community gathered through these initiation rituals was, therefore, nothing short of messianic. It was the community itself, however, that was the means of redemption—not anything specific that they would do, but simply their existence as a collectivity dedicated to following the principles of Jesus. Thus, the proximate goal and practical focus of activity was spreading the educational message that would lead to the augmentation of the community itself. This created a particular tension that would plague the movement throughout its subsequent history: although the growth of the community was believed to be an end to a grander (indeed, cosmically important) goal, in practice the function of the movement was simply to enhance its own numerical growth. The link between the growth of the community and the rectification of all the social, political, and ecological evils that fueled the fervor of the recruiters was vague at best, and often wholly an affirmation of faith. Indeed, questioning the mechanism by which the numerical growth was supposed to bring about sweeping social change was dismissed as "cynical" and a distraction from the urgency of expanding the group itself.

The Dawn and Able ceremonies were the core rituals of the 1960s. Although they would be joined later by a wide variety of additional rites, all attention was focused on these two ceremonies during the first few years of the New Religion. These two original ceremonies addressed one of the major issues that made the new covenant new—the role of women. Although the movement's ideas on the place of women in the new religious age probably originated in Emilia's personal perspectives on sexuality and gender roles, the group's aversion to having a single individual as the sole source of insight led them to look elsewhere for confirmation. Much was borrowed from the ideas of C. G. Jung, especially his notions of the *animus* and *anima*.[77] But a most potent reinforcement came unexpectedly from a visiting professor.

In 1967, Robert G. Albertson, chairman of the humanities department at the University of Puget Sound, was invited by a Stanford fraternity to take part in their week-long scholar-in-residence program. At a lunch with several Creative Initiative members, including Harry and Emilia, Albertson became intrigued by the New Religion. He introduced the group to a number of sources that they felt gave their beliefs an "intellectual and concrete basis."[78] These included Jeremiah 31:31 that affirmed the message of the new age; Joseph Campbell's book *The Hero with a Thousand Faces,* which described the life-cycle of heroes and which the group then applied to their own lives; and finally the Gnostic Gospel of Thomas, which confirmed their own peculiar understanding of gender roles.[79]

Emilia recalled Albertson saying, "What you just said to me explains to me the ending of the book of Thomas."[80] Albertson was referring to the final passage of the Gospel of Thomas, one of the recently discovered Nag Hammadi gnostic Christian documents. In it, Simon Peter suggests to Jesus that Mary should leave the disciples, since "females are not worthy of life." Jesus replies cryptically, "See, I shall lead, so that I will make her male, that she too might become a living spirit resembling you males. For every woman who makes herself male will enter the Kingdom of Heaven."[81] Emilia understood this to be "an affirmation" of "exactly what [she] had been telling the women"—that they needed "to rise up out of the collective unconscious of femaleness" and "become like men—strong."[82]

Thus, the study of the Gospel of Thomas bolstered some gnosticlike tendencies already present in the group. These included the belief that the major human shortcoming was ignorance, that "salvation" was to be had by knowledge of a special truth initially available only to a leadership group, and the conviction that knowledge could be communicated by special mystical means to those gifted with the ability to receive it. The group was already accustomed to speaking of bringing insights and rituals down from the "gnostic plane" to the "earth plane." Ideas from the Gospel of Thomas helped to complete the transition from exclusive reliance on the relatively objective authority of the teachings of Jesus as learned through the Sharman method, to a state in which the unfettered authority of personal mystical experience, Emilia's in particular, could supplement the Records study.

The 1962 Transition: A Descriptive Model

This remarkable reshaping of the Sequoia Seminar, from quasi-academic study group, through proto-sect, into full-blown New Religion, was driven by the engine of Emilia's religious vision. She was a "religious virtuoso" whose private struggles played themselves out in the arena of public faith. Yet she did not travel on her religious journey alone, but in the company of others who were usually men and women of wealth, education, and social position ultimately willing to follow her as she deviated from the main road and sought to blaze a new trail to enlightenment. The history of Creative Initiative is much more than the story of one woman's religious life writ large. The response of the group to her charismatic leadership was an essential element in the dynamic process that institutionalized her insights and produced the New Religion of the Third Age.

One standard account of such events is Max Weber's now classic notion of the charismatic individual who brings forth new insights and perspectives and then has his or her work "routinized" by later followers.[83] Descriptively, however, this model has limited application to the Creative Initiative transition of 1962. In Weber's model the charismatic figure operates outside the framework of organization and, indeed, resists it. Emilia began her religious life inside the churches and functioned for all of her charismatic career within a highly organized group. Most importantly, however, Emilia's role differs from that of the Weberian model because both she and her followers struggled mightily to restrain her charismatic appeal and prevent her from becoming the single fountainhead of truth for the movement.

A useful descriptive model of the way a charismatic figure, even a reluctant one like Emilia, can affect the structure and values of a group is provided by the recently published work of Raymond Trevor Bradley.[84] As Bradley defines it, charisma involves two elements: the idea that an individual is endowed with extraordinary powers and abilities, and "the belief that there is a divine or supernatural basis to the exceptional powers."[85] On the basis of the presence or absence of such beliefs, Bradley divides communal groups into four categories. Those in which these beliefs are not present at all he labels "low charismatic potential" groups. The other three types share a belief in the existence of persons with such powers. In one type, which he calls "high charismatic potential" groups, despite the acceptance of such persons and powers *in principle,* the group does not believe that anyone within it possesses these powers *in fact.* Indeed, these groups are often conscious of waiting for such a leader to emerge to show them the direction in which they should go. The remaining two types believe that there are such powers at work within their group at the present and differ with respect to whether the powers reside in a given individual solely on the basis of his or her *individual* qualities (charismatic leadership type), or because he or she bears an *office* that is viewed as the routinized locus of such powers (charismatic authority type).[86]

Using Bradley's typology, Sequoia Seminar prior to 1962 can be described as a "high charismatic potential" group—one that accepted in principle the existence and communication of higher powers but was at least ambivalent about claims that any member actually possessed them. After 1962, however, the movement became a "resident charismatic leader" group. Although Emilia and others had explored the mystical aspects of religious experience prior to this transition, those explorations had remained subordinate to the rationalistic Sharman method. Like Bradley's high charismatic potential groups, Emilia was convinced that the movement was languishing, "not working anymore," and eagerly entreated God to help her "find you a leader, raise you up somebody." With the revelatory vision of Christ, the ceremonies that were "given" by automatic writing, the confirmations from astronomical signs, and the support from the Gospel of Thomas, the path was cleared for full-blown charismatic leadership to emerge.

Bradley analyzes the differences between these types of groups by studying two major dimensions of social organization. The first, which he calls "communion," is a measure of the "intense emotional bond that fuses the group into an undifferentiated whole."[87] The second, "power," is in dialectical tension with the first but is needed to maintain group stability and control over the emotional power released by communion. He argues that two relational patterns differentiate charismatic systems from noncharismatic forms of social organization. First, they have an interlocking pattern of highly charged bonds of fraternal love in which virtually every member is connected to everyone else, and, second, there is an interlocking, transitively ordered, power hierarchy, aligned under the charismatic leader or, if absent, the leader's lieutenant.[88] He further notes that these patterns vary and are more apparent in collectivities where the charismatic leader is resident than where the leader is absent.[89]

There was an intermittently strong sense of community in Sequoia Seminar prior to 1962, but, except for a relatively few top leaders, the sense of group tended to be episodic, largely limited to the summer seminar periods. For most participants in the seminars the exposure was intense but lacking in staying power. After 1962, however, an almost "communal" atmosphere developed as a result of the emotionally intense rituals and bonding experiences that followed from their new sense of themselves as a collective messiah. Such a profound communion could not take place unless there were a powerful sense of the unity among group members. Since intimate relationships between individuals, even married ones, could weaken that unity, the philosophy of the New Religion taught that the love of God took precedence over all other relationships, including spousal affection.[90] The movement as it emerged after 1962 deemphasized special love between particular members and emphasized instead the mutual ties of each person to every other—an approach reflected in its tendency to make all important decisions through long, loosely structured "group think" sessions rather than through a formal apparatus of committees and subgroups.

Bradley shows that groups with a charismatic resident leader have a unique structure of relations among their members. Three features distinguish such groups. First, the experience of communion generates a sense of "collective unity" and "oneness." With the appearance of a clear line of supernatural authority, the group no longer sees itself as a loose assembly of disparate individuals striving to find a common purpose, but rather as a whole that is more important than its parts. Second, such groups share a "strong feeling of optimism about the future" that "follows from the belief in the efficacy of charismatic leadership as the means to achieve the desired utopia."[91] They are confident that, having found the leadership they were awaiting, they are in fundamental harmony with the direction, will, and purpose of the deity or universe, and that their plans will inevitably succeed. Finally, they experience an exuberant bond of euphoria and excitement from the fact that they are privileged to be part of such a movement.[92] All of these features clearly characterize the movement in the aftermath of Emilia's revelations and the ceremonies the group enacted in the years after 1962.

Bradley has found that the love felt among members of charismatic groups is more "a universal bond embracing all members" and "not personalized or particularized" to properties unique to specific individuals.[93] Members tend to think of one another in familial terms (brother, sister, etc.) and seem to experience something of an incest taboo in interpersonal relations, thus strongly reducing intimacy within the group. Thus, Creative Initiative's deemphasis of sexuality in general, even in the context of marriage, can be seen as much more than the imposition of Emilia's and Harry's own attitudes on the movement. It was, according to Bradley, typical of groups with a charismatic leader, groups in which the participants expected to sacrifice their individuality to the collective—or, as Emilia put it, to be "sin nombre" (without a name).

Despite their sense of closeness, Bradley says that there is frequently little personal intimacy in such groups (for example, they might know very little about members' families outside the group). Although members of Creative Initiative always maintained very close personal relations with one another, there was a symbolic shift after 1962 as the new Dawn and Able ceremonies emphasized the overcoming of individuality and the donning of the "cloak of anonymity." Clearly, what was important in the new age was not assisting individuals with their perceived psychological problems but rather reorienting them to identify the goals and values of the group as their own. As Emilia said regarding the Christ who appeared in her vision, it was no longer Jesus as a historically particular individual but "the impersonal consciousness . . . that Jesus personalized in his lifetime. Something more universally attainable by everybody."[94] Hence, Creative Initiative followed the pattern of groups led by charismatic leaders, promoting the group itself as a whole rather than attempting to accommodate individuals and their differences.

Finally, Bradley's model provides insight into the survival and behavior of the group during this period. On the one hand, his model predicts a very high rate of instability and dissolution for resident charismatic movements during the first years of their lives—and as we saw, there were major defections during the transition period. On the other hand, many of the features that he predicts would tend to stabilize such movements quickly appeared in Creative Initiative. Most importantly, Bradley says that the channeling of the energy of communion into exclusive "dyads" (couples) while retaining a very strong sense of communal control over the dyads "would seem to reduce the destabilizing consequences of higher levels of communion."[95] Thus the pattern the group developed after 1962 with its strong emphasis on bonded pairs of married couples (and indeed, the virtual exclusion of "isolates"— unbonded individuals), while maintaining effective collective control over many aspects of the internal lives of those couples, served a valuable social purpose. It effectively stabilized the intensity of communion while not routinizing the charisma.

Ultimately Emilia emerged from the difficulties that culminated in 1962 with a recipe for a relatively stable religious group. It was a group that simultaneously provided each individual with a strong sense of his or her place in the secure relational system of the community while keeping open the possibility of new interventions from the charismatic leader that could reshape, rename, and redirect the energies of the collective. In many ways, indeed, it would appear that the Creative Initiative's frequent changes of direction into new all-consuming campaigns and activities served to recreate and regenerate the experience of communion that might have otherwise flagged under a visible and stable power structure.

Rituals for the Third Age

With the transition in 1962, Sequoia Seminar was decisively changed in ways that would endure for twenty years. When ceremonies given in Emilia's automatic writing were enacted by the group, the door was opened to further innovation both in rituals and in doctrines. Emilia's rich religious imagination was set free to shape a movement more to her temperament and style. Other members of the movement as well, now that communal acceptance of charismatic leadership was well established, were also free to seek direct religious experience and to look for guidance from the gnostic plane. No longer a simple ecumenical group organized for intensive Bible study but a de facto sect, the movement proceeded to develop additional ceremonies and symbols appropriate to its status as the New Religion of the Third Age.

New ceremonies emerged in different ways at different points in the development of the movement. In the earliest period rituals were "given" to Emilia through direct religious experience and automatic writing. Drawing on a mix of biblical myth, Jungian archetypes, and new myths spun from the insights that occurred in the context of religious meditation and prayer, the early ceremonies emerged directly from what must be described either as Emilia's unconscious but powerful mythogenic personality or from direct revelation to her. Emilia, however, was by no means the sole source of new religious practice. Over time, the group became extremely self-conscious of its need to develop a host of new ceremonies, and most of these were products of a group process. They eventually included a complete ritual calendar (a kind of new liturgical year), as well as rituals for some of the major life events of the members. In the earliest period of the New Religion phase of the group's history, rituals were wholly focused on conversion and commitment to the movement—what they called "identification." This focus was a consequence of the millennial expectation that preoccupied the group in this period: the urgency of attracting the mystical one thousand required before the next step would be revealed. All ceremonies in the first three years marked the progress of the group toward that goal. The first and most long-lived of the rituals developed in this period were the Dawn ceremony for women and the Able ceremony for men. This initial phase came to a close in 1965 when the group took on the name New Sphere. Although it had only about three hundred identified women, the group ritualized the *symbolic* achievement of its goal of one thousand members and began to diversify the style and purpose of its work. It was at this point that rituals devoted to other purposes and goals begin to appear and proliferate.

Because of the ages of the adults identified with the group, children created one obvious group for new ceremonies. As the children of the group matured, a need arose for their religious education and for ritualizing their coming of age. The first such ritual was a "Spring Maiden" ceremony, originally held in 1965, to symbolize the passage of girls from childhood to young womanhood. Preparation for the ritual involved learning traditional women's crafts (macrame, crocheting, flower arranging, etc.), as well as discussions of drugs and sex which inculcated the group's beliefs and values. The ceremony itself was artistically elaborate, as were almost all Creative Initiative activities. Butterflies were used for decoration as symbols of transformation. The central event of the ceremony occurred when the girls were brought from a room decorated in pink (symbolic of girlhood) into a room decorated with yellow roses (symbolic of maidenhood, as gold roses were of full womanhood). Each guest presented the maiden with a gift and gave her a blessing, lighting a candle at the same time. Eventually, as the ceremony evolved, girls were asked to give a short speech on the subject of their intended careers, and the adult women present discussed with them the nature of "the feminine" and motherhood.[96]

Not to be neglected, boys were given an equivalent to the Spring Maiden ceremony in the "Eagle" ceremony, which ritualized their coming into manhood. Preparation for this ceremony required a series of three annual "ordeals" chosen by the candidate and approved by his father. The boy also had to participate in an Outward Bound style trip, undertake a twenty-four hour solo hike, and hold a steady paying job. Boys were trained in speech and debate and taken on a variety of tours of courts, manufacturing plants, and academic institutions.[97] The ceremony itself took place in a room with an altar bearing twelve large white candles and the "God candle," and decorated with lions and eagles. The central event, as for the girls, was the lighting of candles and the giving of blessings to the initiate.[98]

In addition to the youth ceremonies, one might have expected the group to evolve a full set of "rites of passage" for marriage, death, and infancy. For these predictable stages of human growth and development, however, the movement was largely content to make do with ad hoc arrangements. Pixie Hammond, a woman minister ordained by the

Unity School of Religion and attached to Methodist churches before joining the Creative Initiative movement, was available to develop syncretistic rituals appropriate to the group. She conducted ceremonies of dedication for infants in which the parents and other adults present committed themselves to the religious and spiritual nurture of the child, and she also performed marriages and funerals. None of these rites, however, was codified into anything that could be called a Creative Initiative ritual. Despite the fact that they evolved a calendar for the full liturgical year, there was no equivalent of a *Book of Common Prayer* to provide rituals for predictable life transitions. The fear of excessive formalization seems to have prevented the group from stabilizing even those rituals that came to be repeated frequently. Although the Dawn and Able ceremonies did achieve a fairly standard form for a time, the Spring Maiden and Eagle ceremonies varied substantially in detail from year to year. Indeed, individuals were encouraged to develop their own ceremonies for any event of personal significance to themselves. Emilia described the groups attitudes toward the ceremonies by saying, "They have been part of the unfoldment of the movement and they have not stayed permanently."[99]

Another class of ceremonies involved what appeared on the surface to be public presentations, plays, or programs marking cultural holidays. Whereas outsiders may have perceived these as entertainments or holiday celebrations, to insiders they were profound and mystically efficacious ritual events—collective enactments of religious reality.

The first of these "public ceremonies" was the development in 1965 of a "Tree of Light" event to replace the traditional Christian Christmas. This was the time during which the community was working closely with several black Protestant churches in East Palo Alto. The new ceremony was presented jointly with one of those churches as a "Christmas show" even though the symbolism of the "Secret of Light" program (as it was called) actually presented the movement's theology of the new age. The replacement for the traditional Christmas "bathrobe pageant" was a symbolic children's story entitled "Hark the Harold," Harold being the angel–narrator in the account. Beneath the surface of a Christmas program accessible to all, and close enough in its symbolism to pass as vaguely Christian, the story presented the whole revelation of the New Age.[100] After two years of pageants in black churches, in 1967 the venue shifted to the Rathbuns' Stanford University home where it was ostensibly sponsored by four organizations, two of which were really different facets of the group itself. The tie to the black community was maintained, however, by including the Strivers (a group dedicated to raising scholarship money for the college education of blacks) and the Stanford Black Student Union among the sponsors. Called the "Christmas House," the home was decorated with seven beautiful life-sized angels representing the seven angels in the book of Revelation, elaborate symbolic banners representing the great world religions and religious leaders, and a prominently displayed Tree of Life crowned with the Cross of Fulfillment. Once again, whereas the casual observer may have experienced merely a festive Christmas display, the group had presented its solution to the world's problems through a synthesis of major religious teachings.[101]

These colorful public presentations, filled with symbolism at once obvious to the uninitiated yet profound for the insider, were the first of a long series of such events the movement would mount in the ensuing years.[102] Their function in the inner life of the group was complex. On the one hand, they served (with greater obscurity than the movement probably grasped) to communicate their ideas to the public. Equally important from an internal perspective, however, was the enactment of the ritual for its own sake. The members of the black churches who participated in these events, like many other outsiders who worked with the movement over the years, served in effect as unwitting "extras" in the enactment of a gnostic drama that was far more than symbolic. From the point of view of the group, these events, in the terminology of the movement, "brought down from the cosmic plane" new moral and religious realities, "fixing them in the time stream." More than morality plays, these activities served, in the view of the movement, to *literally* change the world, to bring about the reality of the third age, even though only the enlightened consciously recognized those realities. Such conscious recognition was desirable but secondary to the metaphysical reality of the ritual performance itself. Emilia called them "shadow plays [of] what will be reality someday."[103]

It was this belief in the efficacy of the ceremonial enactment of religious truth that motivated a plethora of dramatic presentations and multimedia events in the next few years. "The Universal Song" was a play on forgiveness given three times in 1966, as was a multimedia presentation entitled "People, War, and Destiny," followed in 1968 by "Building the Earth," which presented the idea of a national service corps. Such programs remained an abiding feature of the group even after it secularized. The current Beyond War award ceremonies and convocations are described by some Creative Initiative veterans as "ceremonies" to replace those that were dropped. In each case, although accessible as theater to outsiders, the core of the movement experienced them as powerfully effective events whose enactment contributed to world–historical transformation.[104]

A New Liturgical Calendar

Ultimately more important for the inner life of the movement than these large public events were the rituals with which the movement began to formalize its status as the New Religion. Starting in 1965, and reaching full development in 1977, Creative Initiative elaborated a series of ceremonies and symbols appropriate to the new age. A major impetus to the formalization of these rituals occurred during 1975, when Juana Mueller, Emilia's daughter, remained with the skeleton staff of Creative Initiative as most members temporarily focused their energy on an anti-nuclear-power ballot initiative. Sensing a need to "ground" those working "out in the world" in the deeper religious significance of that involvement, she became especially interested in maintaining the ceremonies.[105] Her concern led to the production of the first of a series of pictorial calendars that listed the dates for major ceremonies.

This trend toward explicit ritual formation increased sharply after the group underwent an episode of intensive introspection and recommitment in 1977. Families who elected to remain in the movement signed a "Book of Life," rededicating themselves to the moral and spiritual goals of the group. In the midst of this process of self-criticism and renewal, a major issue emerged concerning the discomfort of members from Jewish backgrounds with what they perceived to be the essentially Christian symbolism of the movement. To meet those concerns, and to ritualize the reconstitution of the group, an ad hoc ceremony was devised to distinguish those who had made that commitment, or "Passed Over," from the earlier phase in the life of the movement.[106] As the name indicated, this ceremony was based loosely on the traditional Jewish Passover. Beginning with the sounding of a *shofar,* the ritual culminated in a passing of the cup as the group affirmed its willingness to "accept the conditions of the new covenant."[107] Special prayers were included for the Jews indicating their willingness to surrender all separateness and for the Gentiles to confirm their "passing over from Christianity to Universality." It was at this point that Creative Initiative changed its central symbol from the twelve-rayed *"cross* of fulfillment" to the twelve-pointed *"star* of fulfillment." The star, actually two superimposed Stars of David, was intended to replace both the five-pointed Christian star and the six-pointed Jewish star with a new universal star.[108]

This ceremony was viewed as such a success by the group that, in the summer of 1978, Emilia assigned Juana to convene a "ceremony committee" charged with developing rituals for the movement. The result of the committee's efforts was the production for five years of a well-designed and printed liturgical calendar, called the "Blessman Calendar." These calendars listed major religious holidays for the New Religion, along with "preparation periods" during which prescribed meditations and self-examinations were expected.[109] The calendar began with New Year's Day, but the first uniquely Creative Initiative holiday was February 2, the anniversary of the original Dawn ceremony, when they performed the Dawn and Able initiations. On April 8 they marked the "Adam and Eve" ceremony that subsumed both the Jewish Passover and the Christian Holy Week in a spring celebration. "Mary Day," May 13, was a time to acknowledge the new status of women in the third age as they took on characteristics previously reserved for males. July 4 was Interdependence Day and September 21 and 22 were the Celebration of New Beginnings and the Day of At-One-Ment. These two autumnal equinox holidays took the place of the Jewish High Holy Days and stressed the movement's belief that major historical events took place at thousand-year intervals and that it was preparing for the next great transformation. In addition to these holidays, the calendar displayed the moon phases, solstices, and equinoxes, reflecting the vague but significant function of astronomical (or astrological) motifs in the group. These were described as "a reminder that all nature works in harmony and rhythm."[110]

Most important and in many ways typical of the regularized rituals during this period was a weekly home ceremony, roughly modeled on the Jewish sabbath eve service but moved from Friday to Sunday night. Instead of the two candles of the Jewish service, four candles were lit in the Creative Initiative version. The first was the large God candle prominent in numerous Creative Initiative rituals. From it, a second smaller candle was lit symbolizing the first age of the "Golden Thread" of divine revelation in the Bible. As it was lit, those gathered "affirmed the light." A third candle, lit from the second candle, symbolized Jesus as the fulfillment of the Old Testament tradition and elicited the response,

"We receive the light." The fourth candle, representing the third age, was lit from the third candle with the response, "We pass on the light." The ceremony concluded with the recitation of the "Shema of the New Age," which read, in part, "Hear, O Sons of Light, The Lord our God, the Lord is One; for He makes His sun to rise on the evil and the good, and makes His rain to fall on the just and the unjust."[111] Dinner followed, along with various activities intended to form a "family night." This ceremony, then, was the most significant way in which the ideas of the movement were communicated and reinforced on a regular and family-centered basis. It provided the mechanism by which each family could affirm its common bond, both as itself and as a family identified with Creative Initiative. Despite the official disbanding of Creative Initiative in 1982, the Sunday night ceremony continued to be a regular event in many older Creative Initiative homes.

The Dissolution of the Ceremonial Tradition

Although there was always a strong fascination with ceremony in the movement from Emilia's days in Methodist Sunday Schools through the establishment of the ceremonial calendars of the later 1970s and early 1980s, there was also always an undercurrent of ambivalence about them. Juana's ceremony committee had conducted its work under the assumption that its rituals would "fix in the time stream" and communicate to succeeding generations the full richness of Creative Initiative's ideas and experience. Yet, as will be discussed in chapter 8, within only a few years all official rituals were abandoned and the secular Beyond War movement initiated. The decision and method of bringing this ceremonial New Religion phase of the movement to an end is remarkable, both in its rationale and in its form.

The ambivalence toward ceremony arose from two conflicting ideas about ritual. On the one hand, there was a sense that rituals were an important way to transcend the flat-footedly rational when expressing ideas and thus served to evoke commitments beyond the ordinary. On the other hand, the group's strong bias against institutional religion led to a deep suspicion that ritual forms tended to become rigid and inflexible, losing their meaning over time. Hence, the quest was always for ways to find sufficient stability in ceremonial form to sustain the movement from year to year, while at the same time insuring that the ceremonies remained fresh and that participants would grasp the significance and purpose of the ritual. This tension was handled during their "liturgical calendar period" by means of highly didactic preparation for and explanation of each ritual. The symbols and ceremonies were explained, rationalized, and studied, thereby attempting to insure that they retained their significance and clarity of meaning for participants. Also, even though there was a period of relative stability in the *names* of the ceremonies used, there was an annual review and revision of the prescribed symbols and ritual actions.

As Beyond War began to recruit individuals into the movement who had no prior experience of these ceremonies, a new and more difficult issue arose. What relationship should new members of Beyond War have to the ceremonies, rituals, and initiation rites of Creative Initiative? As Juana deliberated about this problem, she said she was struck by the prophecy in Jeremiah 31:31–33, in which the Lord says He will write a new covenant on the hearts of the people. She understood this to mean that Creative Initiative too should "write its tradition on the hearts of the people," lest it be lost in the new and unfamiliar land in which they found themselves. In light of this insight and prophecy, the ceremony committee concluded that it was time to plan a ceremony to end all ceremonies, a ritual that would mark the end of common ritual performances for the group. Referring to the great paradox of Jesus, Juana explained they would "have to lose their lives to save them," giving up the last vestiges of Creative Initiative as an exclusive religious movement in order to become Beyond War wholly and without reservation.[112] There was an urgency to prepare and execute this termination of the old so that it would not hold up the Beyond War movement. They realized that February 2, which was coming in only a few weeks, would mark the twenty-first anniversary of the first Dawn ceremony. This anniversary struck them as a particularly appropriate one on which to have the ceremony, since the number twenty-one represents adulthood in our culture. That anniversary, therefore, could symbolically represent the "coming of age" of the New Religion. A ritual would be planned that would mark that anniversary and represent the "writing on the heart" of all that had been publicly and overtly ritualized in the past. This would transcend and eliminate the need for such public ritualization in the future.[113]

Small groups gathered on the evening of February 2, 1982, in various houses where they found the God candle, gold votives, and globe typical of so many Creative Initiative rituals. Between eleven o'clock and midnight the groups enacted a symbolic ritual by means of guided meditation rather than by literal performance. Different rituals were prescribed for men and women. The women in their ritual imaginatively reenacted the original Dawn ceremony, putting on gold capes of anonymity and bracelets. Then mentally each took a gold rose and placed it on the altar, blessing the world with the light and writing the ceremony on their hearts. Similarly, in guided meditation the men took red roses from the women and their Cross of Fulfillment rings and placed them on the altar, thereby surrendering all external trappings of Creative Initiative to God's will and purpose, which they now believed would be enacted through Beyond War.[114] Thus, with a single nonliteral ceremony, twenty years of New Religion ritual came to an end.

4

Surrendering: The Process of Personal Transformation

Emilia's religious experience of 1962 led her to formally transform the proto-sect of Sequoia Seminar into a self-defined new religion—"the New Religion of the Third Age." For Emilia and for the first ten women who joined her in the original Dawn initiation ceremony, the supranormal aspects of the vision and automatic-writing episodes that followed were instructions from the gnostic plane to move from a proto-sect within the Christian tradition to a sect meant to transcend Christianity and usher in the third dispensation.

For Creative Initiative, the process of sect formation was neither sudden nor dramatic. Emilia's revelation confirmed, rather than created, the New Religion. She was a compelling personality who attracted people, especially women, to the movement, but she did not claim that she was essential to its continuation. People certainly found her fascinating, but she was not the reason they were attracted to nor remained in the movement. Initially, most individuals appear to have been drawn by the sense that here was a group of people like themselves—white, educated, refined, and financially successful—who had gathered together to give one another support and friendship based on a sense of grand purpose. The full details of just how grand that purpose was were not revealed immediately but emerged slowly as the new members entered into a multiyear process that engaged them ever more deeply into a psychological and religious commitment to the movement. For new members what had been an attraction to a group eventually became a new life style.

Individual involvement was multifaceted. Psychologically, members substituted God and sometimes the group itself for previously held authority figures in their lives. People found new understandings of themselves and of their relationships with others that were continually reinforced by the intimate social interaction within the movement. The process that drew them into group commitment made it increasingly more difficult to leave, although they were always free to do so. They were willing to stay in the group because the psychological cost of leaving would have been higher than the social and economic costs of staying.

In addition to the psychological benefits of participation, members also found strong religious reasons for staying. They came to believe that they were playing a key part in God's plan for humankind and that by participating in the movement they were performing a messianic role that would save the earth. Although their messianic self-image, unique ceremonies, and unorthodox theology would seem to have placed the movement outside the mainstream of traditional American religious values, in fact, most of the beliefs were quite compatible with the American value system and, indeed, provided members with a way to synthesize and reconcile some of the inherent conflicts within the mainstream ethos. Superficially the sect appeared to be another New Age monistic movement that preached the oneness of humankind and the unity of humanity and nature. As a democratic and ecology-minded group it fit neatly into its liberal Palo Alto environment. But under the monistic exterior beat a dualistic heart. The movement's philosophy had as much in common with its Calvinist antecedents as it did with its transcendentalist ones. While espousing the humanistic liberalism that derived from their monistic beliefs, they also adhered to a strict code of conservative personal behavior and believed sincerely that there were absolutes of good and bad, right and wrong, God and "the Devil."

This group of solid citizens could remain solid citizens because, in their own view, they were not captives of a guru and were not sacrificing their values or basic life style to the group. They believed they were involved in a rational educational process whose objective approach should make sense to any educated person. For that reason, among others, the new religious sect that emerged after 1962 did *not* base its legitimacy on Emilia's revelation. Although it was the decisive confirmation of their belief system for the original initiates, the fact that the revelation happened at all was something very close to a secret that was shared by only a few of the oldest and closest allies of the Rathbuns.

Although the details of the way in which Emilia received her insight into the third age were never widely disseminated, the new theological justification for the movement that grew out of Emilia's experience became part of the group's most fundamental beliefs and was learned by all participants.

There were several reasons for keeping the revelatory experience quiet. First, mystical revelation had no place at all in the rational style of Henry B. Sharman, and very little, if any, in the teachings of Gerald Heard and C. G. Jung. The vision had served the purpose of resolving Emilia's psychological crisis and legitimizing the proto-sect as a sect, but it could not be presented to the membership at large because there was no intellectual tradition within the movement to legitimize it. Second, Emilia was intellectually committed to a nonhierarchical movement free of a charismatic leadership cult. Although her powerful personality and commanding style made her the de facto prophet of the movement, her unwillingness to have others see her as a supernaturally anointed savior led her to keep the vision private and not use it as a base for building the New Religion.

The philosophy that evolved in the wake of Emilia's vision consisted of an end and a means. The end was God's purpose for mankind. The means was the Creative Initiative method of education that would lead individuals to accept the will of God and transform themselves into new people who would be instruments of God's purpose. Over the years the movement developed a cycle of courses and seminars that took as long to complete as a college education and had as its purpose the breaking down of old psychic and intellectual structures and replacing them with new constructs that were appropriate to the new people of the third age. Unlike the common liberal ideal of a college education, the Creative Initiative process had no sympathy for relativism. On the contrary, it sought to erase relativism (although not tolerance) and build a new structure of dualism.

The Nature of God and the God of Nature

Creative Initiative was, at its very core, a theistic movement. Every article of belief and every individual and collective action was predicated on a belief in God and in God's plan for the human race. Most of the group's thinking and writing about the nature of God appears to have been done by Harry, who was the movement's acknowledged philosopher, although his ideas were augmented by Emilia, and the resulting views went virtually unchallenged by their followers. Creative Initiative's description of God began, but did not end, with God as first cause. Taking their clue from Genesis—"In the beginning God created the heavens and the earth"—the movement attributed the existence of the universe to the hand of God. If asked, then, "Who created God?" Harry responded, "Here we are indeed up against an aspect of Ultimate Mystery, the aspect of *First Cause*. . . . Why not admit that we cannot answer the mystery of First Cause, accept the fact of Ultimate Mystery and include that in our content for the word God?"[1] At this most basic level the philosophy of Creative Initiative retreated from the scientific formulations that marked most of their ideas and rested its case on faith and mystery. As a seminar outline from 1974 put it, "There is no way to prove God as Source, so you finally give up and either accept it or not."[2]

The standard problem with the God-as-first-cause argument is that it makes God remote and perhaps even irrelevant. Creative Initiative obtained a divine immediacy by equating God not only with the origins of the universe but with the universe itself. God was not only the creator, but also the created. God was understood to be present everywhere in the physical universe, and therefore everything in it was of God. In this definition of God, Creative Initiative was positing a monistic world view in which all and everything were part of a fully integrated whole.[3] Creative Initiative usually summed up this idea by saying that God was reality. It followed, then, that if God were reality and all reality were God, and if humans were part of reality, which they clearly were, then in some sense God and humans must be one. And, indeed, that is just what the movement believed. This idea was occasionally expressed in the startling formulation, "Men are walking Gods."[4] So central was the monistic world view to Creative Initiative's philosophy that the three-word article of faith, "We are one," became the movement's most visible public expression in the late 1970s, appearing on everything from Christmas cards to bumper stickers. A meditation prayer from 1973 started out with the the refrain, "We are 'ONE' before birth. . . . We are 'One' with origins. . . . We are 'ONE' with the earth," and ended, "Take the old divisions into the setting sun. March to the ancient drum made new. It has a single beat. Face together the rising sun. We Are One. We Are One. We Are One."[5]

Although making God imminent in all creation, including human beings, certainly solved the problem of a remote first cause, it still left the question of meaning. Creative Initiative answered that question by attributing teleology to the creation that was God. "We believe," wrote Emilia in an early statement of faith, "in the purpose of God, the guidance of God, and the power of God."[6] Harry explained that science could find the answers to "how" but was unable to help with the question "why?" But his response was hardly more enlightening. Once more he was forced back to an explanation based on faith: "The only answer that can be made at our present level of consciousness is, 'That's just the way it is!' Or if we don't object to the use of religious language, 'That's the way God decided to have it!' "[7] Creative Initiative believed that the way things are, "reality," had to be faced and accepted. But reality was neither static nor directionless. "God is Direction," proclaimed a 1979 "Meditation on God." "His plan is set before us. Within his plan, his will is the blueprint for life, and we can choose to follow it or not. When we decide to obey, we become co-creators with God."[8]

When Creative Initiative used the word "direction" in relationship to God's plan, its members really had two things in mind. First, they believed that there was a development direction for each individual that could take him or her from the basic survival needs of food and shelter up through steps of mental and aesthetic development to reach a final stage of "spiritual discernment" in which the person embodied knowledge, understanding, mercy, and love.[9] A second document put it more briefly, if ambiguously: "The plan is the movement to fuller and higher consciousness which both enables and requires us to co-operate and execute God's plan."[10] In other words, they believed that God had a plan for individuals that would enable them to carry out a second plan for human beings as a whole. This second plan was God's intention for the human race. It was God's will. "What is God's will or desire for mankind?" asked one of a series of handwritten questions in the Creative Initiative files. "Is God's will for mankind being done? What part do you personally play in God's plan for mankind? What is keeping you from doing God's will?" the writer ended.[11] Although sometimes couched in an interrogative form, there was no doubt what the answers were supposed to be. Queried one discussion-course question, "What would you say in response to the proposal that God seems to have an *intention* or *purpose* for 'his' Creation, and that it is beneficent?"[12] People who did not respond in the affirmative could hardly have remained active in Creative Initiative.

To do God's will, one had to know God's will, and one could know it by studying his plan, the direction that was God—the process of evolution. The Rathbuns were convinced by their studies with Gerald Heard in the 1940s, and by later reading Pierre Teilhard de Chardin, that humans had not finished evolving, but were capable of another step up the evolutionary ladder. They made this theory of evolution one of the core beliefs in their philosophy. Evolution was a major mechanism through which God worked, and because it was a theory confirmed by a hundred years of biology and paleontology, evolution was the nexus between faith and science. Like Sharman before them, the Rathbuns insisted not only that there was no conflict between science and religion but that despite their belief in mystic revelation and the gnostic plane their religious enterprise was conducted in a scientific manner. "The seven basic concepts of the Challenge to Change [introductory course] process are really the 'scientific method' restated in the context of every-day life," they told new members of the movement.[13]

Because Creative Initiative believed that God was the first cause and did not intercede miraculously in nature—indeed, God could not because nature *was* God—then it followed that the laws of nature were the laws of God. The essence of their scientific approach to the study of human beings and religion was "cause and effect." Just as God was the first cause and all creation was the effect, so all the relationships within that creation, "reality," could be understood through "natural law, or 'the laws of science,'—the *cause and effect* dependability built into the *structure* of Reality."[14] By getting neophytes to accept the validity of the premise that all creation was subject to natural law and that scientific knowledge consisted of understanding cause and effect, and then by couching all its philosophic and religious propositions in scientific language, Creative Initiative was able to draw large numbers of technically educated people into the movement, appealing directly to their predisposition to accept the legitimacy of ideas proven by objective scientific logic. For example, the "Leader's Manual" for one course listed a sample question for discussion, "When our goal is personal fulfillment, what do we need to know?" and then informed the leaders (in direct contradiction to the Socratic tradition of H. B. Sharman) that the discussion should "bring out answers such as . . . 'the cause-and-effect relationships which must be observed or obeyed in order to reach it.' "[15]

Members believed that God worked his will through science (natural law) and, therefore, by studying science they could come to know God's will. That was particularly true for evolution, because evolution, as understood by Creative Initiative, both explained the past and pointed to the future. So crucial was their interpretation of evolution that it formed the basis for one of the first and most frequently repeated courses in the

Creative Initiative curriculum, "The Challenge of Time." The Challenge of Time was a simplified synthesis and recasting of the works of Gerald Heard and Pierre Teilhard de Chardin. From Teilhard the Rathbuns borrowed the concept of "complexification" and much specific terminology.[16] From Heard they borrowed the idea that there were three distinct stages of human development. They agreed with both men that human beings were on the threshold of a new stage in evolutionary growth.

The idea that the human evolutionary journey was incomplete really constituted the essence of Creative Initiative's message. Their discussion of biological evolution was always a preface to the main text, and it served two purposes: it established their credentials as a group that took a scientific approach, and it grounded the course in a universally accepted theory that established the basis for the more problematic step of predicating direction in future evolution. By using Teilhard's and Heard's theories in the courses, people were led from scientifically and historically known facts to a speculative future. Teilhard's description of the biological evolution of Homo sapiens suggested that the process of "complexification" would bring a higher consciousness. Heard's three stages of human development began with biological evolution, passed through technic evolution, to predict a third stage in which "man hatches a soul."[17] Educating people so they could partake in this third, and least scientifically grounded, aspect of the human journey was the raison d'être for Creative Initiative.[18]

Unless individuals were willing to accept the evolutionary premise of Creative Initiative's system of beliefs, there was no reason for them to become active members of the group. Hence, the idea of evolution and a personal journey to the final stage was made the subject of the first intense weekend course that new members attended after they had completed the initial introductory courses.[19] They taught that each person's individual journey toward personal fulfillment went through four stages (an idea loosely based on the concept of the hero's journey as described by Joseph Campbell in his book *The Hero with a Thousand Faces*) and augmented with Erik Erikson's ideas of the stages of childhood.[20] The first three stages involved growing up and taking on traditional adult roles. Although such roles might be temporarily satisfying, eventually people experienced "a growing dissatisfaction with life and a vague yearning for something more. . . . Those goals which at one point were thought to bring happiness no longer satisfy." This dissatisfaction corresponded to Jung's belief that there was a natural crisis in midlife that could act as the stimulus to increased "individuation" and a more mature second half of life.[21] This Jungian theory was certainly compatible with the goals of Creative Initiative and also dovetailed neatly with Emilia's personal history. Thus, the Creative Initiative view of life reflected both the theoretical view of C. G. Jung and a projection and universalization of Emilia's own midlife crisis. The course listed a number of things people did when faced with a midlife crisis: "job changes, excess seeking of pleasure, changing houses, returning to school, divorce, affairs, depression, etc."[22] With the exception of divorce and excess seeking of pleasure, Emilia engaged in (or was as least tempted by) each of these deadend roads to finding meaning.

Although many, perhaps most, adults remained mired in the unsatisfying self-indulgences of their later years, Creative Initiative believed that some few would choose to enter the fourth stage where they could learn to experience a new unity with all life. As Harry explained, the individual's evolution into the fourth stage was "neither automatic nor a matter of chance" but rather a matter of the person's "conscious choice." One key was to find "a wise one, a teacher" who would awaken the individual's "inborn capacity to perceive and inspire him to undertake the journey to fulfillment, to maturity, to the wholeness which is his birthright!"[23] At the final stage of personal maturity, Creative Initiative believed that a person was at last able "to take his position as an active co-creator of an unfolding universe. He becomes a creative initiator at the frontier of time."[24]

The belief that human beings could, through their own volition, break through into a new dimension of life gave the ultimate sanction to the group's homocentric approach to reform. They were not merely trying to get individuals to adopt a more benign stance in the world. They were trying to transform the very essence of the race itself. "The dead end is to assume the internal environment to be fixed, and respond by seeking only to change the external world of objects and other beings," explained a document from the early 1970s.[25] The movement argued that such a sociocentric approach ignored the opportunity for personal growth and evolutionary change. Although they recognized that whatever change was supposed to take place would not be genetic, they nevertheless frequently used Darwinian language that carried all the implications of biological transformation.[26] A formal introduction to a course in 1979 declared that people had to accept the responsibility to do God's will, and when they did, "in large enough numbers, evolution continues, a *new mutation* occurs (a loving, responsive human being), and life is open-ended."[27] It would be easy to dismiss the reference to a "new mutation" as hyperbole except that it fits a language pattern that manifested itself throughout Creative Initiative's writings, not only on evolution, but generally. An early pledge signed by new men who joined the movement said, in part, "We declare ourselves to be the nucleus of the new collective, the new community, the new church, the *new race,* the *new species,* the new world."[28] The combined references to a mass movement and to a new race are the key to the final complication in the concept of continued evolutionary progress. The movement taught that the time was right for the next stage to be achieved through a three-step process. First the individual would change, then the changed individuals would gather in a community, and finally the whole world would undergo a transformation.[29]

Teilhard's ideas were the essential ingredient in allowing the movement to believe that it could change the entire earth even when it was obviously having trouble reaching more than a few thousand people in the San Francisco Bay Area. Teilhard had explained that each new phylum was begun by just a few radically different individuals. When such biological sports found an unexploited ecological niche their numbers exploded and the few actual pioneering individuals (the peduncle, or stem, he called them) would quickly be overwhelmed by their successful offspring and be lost to the fossil record.[30] Thus, even a very few individuals, or a "creative minority," could be the root stock of an entire new race so long as they appeared when the time was ripe for their growth.[31]

Creative Initiative people knew that there could be change and they knew how to bring that change about; they even knew what the changed people would be like; but what they did not know were the exact details. They admitted that the community could not "tell any of its members that he or she must evolve in a certain manner or at a certain rate of speed," and although they claimed to be "as gods" in the limited sense that their "imaginations, willpower and dedication [did] bring about change," they also admitted "exactly how and when and where the change occurs is not ours to determine—that is subject to a higher control of a more universal sweep than any one man's intelligence, or any group's foresight." But they did think that if they could gather one thousand "clear" persons (a term apparently borrowed from Scientology) in one place, "public opinion on the war–peace issue could never again return to its old level."[32]

The Supranatural

Because it had not yet occurred, and because it dealt with ideas that fell outside of the normal boundaries of the natural sciences, the exact nature of the next step of evolution remained somewhat vague in Creative Initiative writings. Even more vague were a number of other extrascientific issues that were frequently discussed under the same rubric. They included higher consciousness, spirituality, mysticism, the soul, and the gnostic plane.

"We are a community of men and women who are committed to discover and operate at a new higher level of consciousness. We seek to pioneer the next step in the evolutionary growth of man," said a statement of principle from the mid-1960s.[33] Although they talked at great length about the attitudes, values, and feelings of people who had obtained this higher consciousness, those human responses were thought to be reflections of a state in which the individual was in connection with some extramundane force. Borrowing heavily from Teilhard, particularly in their earlier period, they sometimes referred to this force as the "noosphere." Teilhard used the term to designate a presumed aura that surrounded the world as a result of the thought of human beings.[34] So influential was Teilhard's vision and terminology that two of the group's early names were borrowed directly from him. In 1965 they began calling themselves "New Sphere," an admitted play on the term "noosphere," and in 1968 the women's part of the movement adopted the name "Building the Earth," the title of a brief, nontechnical summary of Teilhard's ideas.

There was, however, much more to Creative Initiative's view of the supranatural than an invisible envelope of collective human thought. There was also the aspect of the human psyche that sought communion with God, an aspect that Creative Initiative variously called "spirit," "mysticism," and "soul." According to Creative Initiative beliefs, there were three levels of reality: the physical with its laws of biology, chemistry, and physics; the mental–emotional with its laws of psychology; and the world of the spirit, which was "more nebulous, less tangible than the physical and mental categories."[35] Harry defined the spiritual level of existence as the one in which the intuitive plays a central role. "It is in this, the field of direct perception of reality, that people have their communication with Ultimate Reality, with God," he wrote.[36]

What Harry referred to as the "Ultimate Reality," or God, was more frequently called the "gnostic plane." Like other terms that referred to the supranatural, *gnostic* was never given a very clear definition. A discussion of the Book of John called the "gnostic level" "a plane of knowledge and spirit and energy which can be penetrated in moments of powerful prayer and which, in turn, can pierce down through to the earth plane and make contact with an open mind in the form of thought and idea." The description then went on to say that for people who are in touch with the unconscious, "there are documented instances of 'presences' being manifested in material or auditory form."[37] The clear implication of these two statements is that "presences" conjured up through the unconscious actually come from the gnostic plane."[38] Not only was the gnostic plane the source of individual insight, it also controlled the grand schemes of time. Creative Initiative believed that gnostic time occurred in thousand-year units: it was a thousand years from Abraham to David, from David to Jesus, from Jesus to the Norman Conquest, and it would be a thousand years from the Norman Conquest to the New Age, in the year 2000.[39]

Not only was Creative Initiative literally millennial, dealing with thousand-year blocks of time, but it was also religiously millennial, predicting that the turn of the century, which would also be the turn of the millennium, was destined to be a new watershed for the human race. One course claimed that all the great art and music had already been written and, curiously for a group headquartered in Silicon Valley, that all the great technologies had already been invented. Therefore the new focus of people's effort had to be to "perfect the human instrument." The way to accomplish this goal was to have, by the year 2000, one thousand people "deconditioned, educated in truth, and totally committed to service of the gnostic plane." The course ended with a claim that explained how the concept of the community as a collective messiah would work: "When we accomplish the mission of the 1000 whole persons, we will have accomplished the mission of the 4th millennium. . . . When we do this, we will have safeguarded the gains of past ages, and insured the future."[40] The exact mechanism to be used by the thousand people in the year 2000 was not specified because it was unknown. "When the time comes when we have the thousand, and if we have done our job," they believed, "we will find out what we are supposed to do then."[41]

In Emilia's mind, at least, the numerological millennialism of a thousand people in the year 2000 was the way to inaugurate the third age. It was not merely symbolic for her, it was mystical, almost magical. Speaking before admiring audiences, as they almost always were, Emilia tended to wax hyperbolic. When pressed about her more extreme statements made in the heat of the moment, she would usually explain that she was speaking symbolically and did not mean to be taken literally. The consistency and volume of Emilia's statements lead, nevertheless, to the inescapable conclusion that both she and her followers certainly believed they knew the truth. So there is no reason not to take it literally when Emilia told the participants at an "A" seminar that the thousand people would "have a channel that is sufficiently powerful to counteract the negative psychology, psyche, fields that are created by people's psyche. You can only do that by a thousand clean, pure, absolutely complete people. Plus—if you can produce a thousand people, you have established the new species."[42]

The most common device for trying to make contact with the supranatural was meditation. "We have to leap into the irrational through the rational," Emilia said. The "communication from God" was irrational, but she believed in it nevertheless.[43] Borrowing from the work of Gerald Heard, who was heavily influenced by Asian meditative practices, the movement distinguished between vocal prayer and meditation. Praying aloud was considered a lower form of devotion but still a useful one for verbalizing feelings and overcoming inhibitions about dealing with God. Much more common were "guided meditations" in which people were told to imagine a short scenario. They believed meditation helped people understand their inner selves and, when done together, unified "the group so that the force of God's power may be experienced."[44]

The group never engaged in intercessory prayers of the type traditionally addressed to a personal God. Prayer and meditation were devices aimed less at God than at the person praying. According to an early course, prayer would produce "1. right psychic being, 2. right knowledge, 3. right doing, and 4. right physical body." Prayer was an action that integrated, motivated, emancipated, and transformed the person praying. Yet above all, prayer was a way to get in touch with the "abstract spirit, abstract idea, abstract truth, which exists in the gnostic plane." Prayer was the conduit to the supranatural. They believed that "a praying human is in active relationship to the gnostic plane (noosphere, new sphere, heaven), receiving, understanding, and carrying out orders—step by step."[45]

The very process of meditation was extrarational. The meditations were exercises with the express purposes of taking the movement beyond what they saw as the masculine world of systematic thinking into the feminine realm of the intuitive. Although they sometimes used a mantra to induce a more traditional eastern kind of meditative state, they usually employed the meditative process as a way to personally experience the suprarational. The meditations had the additional effect of investing the group's philosophic doctrines with an aura of mystical legitimacy. Their style of meditation was not so much a device designed to achieve the monistic goal of sensing unity with all creation as a prayerlike method of visualizing the duality and conflicts of the world and marshaling personal strength to do God's will: "At this moment / You and I / and all humankind / are standing at the crossroads of time. / Together / we are standing / on the razor's edge of two cataclysmic forces. / On the one side / are the forces of decay, / destruction / and death for all humanity. . . . We believe / if we join together / as One Earth, One humanity, One spirit / we can tip the balance / toward new life."[46]

Living in the Kingdom of God: The Individual and the Community

The future that Creative Initiative hoped to insure as a collective messiah with a thousand "whole" people gathered by the turn of the millennium, was, of course, the Kingdom of God. "Man has always dreamed of an ideal world in which all his needs and desires would be met," wrote Harry in 1975, "a world in which he would exist in an imagined state of bliss. There would be no war, no violence, no unpleasant conflict among people, no crime, no poverty and everyone would be loving and cooperative." Harry did not deny that such a world might be possible but insisted that to bring it about people had to be responsible for one another and for the world as a whole. In other words, the Kingdom of God on earth would be created by human beings: "There is no magic. The outcome is up to man." There would be no second coming of a messiah to save the world in "one radical or cataclysmic happening"; rather the "worldwide Kingdom of God is the product of a process which takes time and man's growth in consciousness and responsibility."[47]

Written material for a basic seminar in 1968 contained a description of life on earth when all people had been converted to the new way of thinking. Although it did not label the ideal world the Kingdom of

God, the course material is the closest to a description of Creative Initiative's ideal world that we have. The course described four aspects of life that would be improved in the utopia the movement was trying to build. First, in the economic sphere, there would be "adequate provision for the material, physical needs of every person on the planet." Second, politically, there would be a "world government with world law to function until all people shall have transcended the need for legal controls." Third, the environment would be aesthetically pleasing because nature would be preserved and "man-made ugliness" would be banished. Finally, people would interact spiritually out of "loving concern for one another in order that the continued evolution of each individual shall be most effectively nurtured."[48]

In the Jesus as Teacher course, which was the capstone of the Creative Initiative program of study, Jesus' ideas about the Kingdom of God were explained in some detail. The course began with the historical background of the various Jewish interpretations of the Kingdom of God in the time of Jesus. It explained that some Jews expected a political messiah who would establish a Jewish kingdom on earth ruled by a man anointed by God. Other Jews looked for an apocalyptic messiah who would come to judge human beings and sort the saved from the damned. It was important to Creative Initiative to demonstrate that these were false expectations rejected by Jesus, because it was that understanding that led them to reject political action as a means of saving the world, while at the same time denying that God would again intervene with an anointed leader who would lead the human race to salvation.[49] In addition, Creative Initiative claimed that Jesus rejected "economic messianism" when he said "Man does not live by bread alone," by which he meant "economic emancipation does not give meaning to a person's life."[50] This interpretation, too, was designed to show the parallel between the teachings of Jesus and the movement's strong rejection of materialism as a goal of life. Instead of using political action or awaiting a great leader, Creative Initiative believed that Jesus told his followers they could, by following his teachings, become the Kingdom of God.

To explain explicitly what Jesus meant, Creative Initiative turned to the parables, giving each an interpretation that strongly supported the values and actions of the movement. The parable of the mustard seed was said to make the point "that the society of people who make up the Kingdom of God has a very small beginning," a comforting thought to the modestly sized group. Similarly the story of the leaven in the meal was said to show how "a growing 'creative minority' makes progressive changes that affect the whole society." The wheat and tares parable meant that the Kingdom of God and the kingdom of the devil could coexist in the world "so long as there are people who have not entered the Kingdom of God." The parable of the growing seed was said to show not only that the group would grow, but also that "anyone who has experienced the values of 'citizenship' in the Kingdom of God 'can do no other' than recruit others for membership. The impulse is irresistible to share those values." Finally, the parable of the sower whose seeds fell on both rich and fallow ground meant that not everybody who heard the message would seek the kingdom—or join the movement.[51]

The homocentric approach that found justification in Jesus' rejection of political and apocalyptic messianism began with the elemental root of society, the single person. Creative Initiative recognized that changes could be forced on people through political coercion but argued that "any change in social structure which does not have a change in attitude as its basis is superficial."[52] The movement likened the individual to a single cell in a greater organism in which the parts worked for the good of the whole and the whole worked for the good of the parts. The chain of responsibility started with the person, then extended to the marriage, the family, the neighborhood, and so on up the line until at last it reached the nation, the continent, and the entire world.[53]

Even though all change had to start with the individual, it was the collective through which the most effective change was implemented. "We are a community of teaching and a demonstration of what we teach," claimed a "Statement on Goals"; "We believe that the message and the messenger must be one."[54] The central concept of cooperation obviously presupposed that the process involved more than one person. The act of transformation was not a private one between a person and his or her God but rather a first step toward the ultimate goal of "cooperation of first the religions, then the races, and finally the nations of the world."[55] Only by cooperating together in a community could the validity of the individual transformation be demonstrated.

Their idea was to create in their own community a model of how the Kingdom of God on earth would function. It was possible, they insisted:

It is a conscious decision to be made by the most developed persons of destiny. These will constitute the prototype community of the future. There will be new customs, conventions, and institutions. There will be a naturalness, spontaneity, freedom in the person which springs from the intuition. There will be cooperation, peace, harmlessness—absence of violence and fear. There will be a new way to deal with conflicts because truth will be objective.[56]

Surrendering to the Authority of God's Will

Just as the belief in continuing evolution was the cornerstone of Creative Initiative's understanding of the external world, surrendering to the authority of God's will was the basic internal act that the individual had to take in order to participate in the furtherance of evolution.

The idea that the individual had to give up his or her own egocentric will and submit wholly to the will of God was a tenet whose roots could be traced back to the earliest work of Henry B. Sharman. Sharman had been adamant about the necessity of obeying the will of God but very vague about just what it was that God willed people to do.[57] Through the use of the concept of continued evolution, which the Rathbuns appended to Sharman's doctrine, they were able to give their followers much more direction than Sharman ever had. Like Sharman, nevertheless, the Rathbuns' discussions of God's will could be extremely imprecise. When he was attempting to formalize the philosophy of the movement in a book, Harry described the process thus:

Total commitment to God's will, to the undivided love of God, means to be doing what is right all the time, not just some of the time, in every situation, not just when it is convenient. What is right, to repeat, is what works toward, rather than against, the best outcomes for all, what makes for the continuance of the evolution of consciousness, and the well-being of our entire planet.[58]

If one were inclined to ask how one could know what was right, one answer was, "All of us who are normal know what that is."[59]

Because Creative Initiative believed that God was everything and everything was God, almost any point they wished to make could, and usually was, couched in terms relating it to authority (God). Material from both the Old and New Testaments was easily interpreted in ways that were consistent with their broad definition of God as authority. They taught that "God's authority is expressed through Jesus, who verbalized for Him."[60] By holding up Jesus as the model of a person who surrendered his will to the authority of God, the group was emphasizing the benign nature of that authority. There were two kinds of authority, they explained, authoritative and authoritarian. Authoritarian authority was said to be overprotective, manipulative, subjective, and arbitrary. But the authority of God and Jesus—and those who align themselves with God's will—was "enlightened authority that loves, guides, shares and is aware of another."[61]

Creative Initiative taught that it was not enough simply to obey the will of God; one had to *surrender* to the will of God. As in Sharman's day, the operant text continued to be, "Whosoever shall lose his life shall save it." "Losing life" meant giving up the individual will, the ego, and making all life decisions according to God's will.

The ego-driven person was the corrupt tree that bore evil fruit: "resistance, hate, rigidity, stoppage, alienation, slavery, death. *You are a walking devil.*" Those aligned with the will of God were like good trees that brought forth good fruit: "acceptance, response, love, mobility, flow, at-one-ment, freedom, life. *You are a walking God.*"[62] A person was either one or the other. There was no middle ground, no compromise, no halfway covenant. God had to become the total focus of one's life. Emilia told members that "God does not tolerate a rival." If a person said, before I give myself to God "I am going to give to my children, my family or pursue my own interests," then that person was creating a rival for God and would not find the peace and love that came with total surrender.[63] Even a woman's maternal instinct had to be surrendered to something bigger and more important. "Mothering, and the religious life," said Emilia, "are mutually exclusive."[64] These last two statements were probably not meant to be taken literally; rather, the group would have explained that a person could be a better spouse and parent when he or she had surrendered the egocentricity and aligned with God's will. The fact that Emilia could speak in such extreme terms was, nevertheless, indicative of the depth of commitment she believed was necessary to achieve totality, that is, detachment and obedience to the will of God.

In the Creative Initiative system of belief, surrender was an essential part of love. The way to love was to surrender to the love object and, since God was the most infinitely loveable object conceivable, God was also worthy of the greatest love.[65] The movement expected that mature, loving people would manifest their love by living in benign relationship with others and the world. Harry discussed the worldy application of love in terms of the three categories described by Jesus: enemies, neighbors, and brothers. When Jesus said love your enemies and pray for them, Harry explained that meant people should try to "surround and envelop your erstwhile enemy with a positive field, an atmosphere of good will, within which he has a better chance of illumination than without it." In that case, said Harry, "you are, at the very least, doing no harm to the subject of your concern."[66] This desire to be harmless in the world appears to have been a belief the group took very seriously and explains their gentle demeanor, which outsiders frequently had trouble accepting as genuine. They almost never confronted or replied to critics or enemies and, in the one situation in which they did have a direct confrontation with another group, they bent over backward to resolve the differences amicably. In that case—a dispute over the Ben Lomond property they controlled jointly with the Quakers—a local Quaker historian has concluded that the Creative Initiative acted more like Friends than the Friends.[67]

"Your neighbor," said Harry, "is defined as anyone you encounter who has a real need that you can fulfill, irrespective of his race, color, nationality, creed, or economic or social status." The parable of the Good Samaritan was the model for loving all people, even those who were culturally distinct from you.[68] Finally, *brother* was defined as "one who is committed to the same goal as yours, namely, to 'doing the Will of God.' " Within this context love took on a more complex meaning than in the previous two cases. Love of an enemy could mean just wishing the enemy well. Love of a neighbor meant helping the person. But love of a brother included both of the above plus the obligation to rebuke a brother who sins because "that gives him an opportunity and responsibility to mend his ways."[69] As we shall see below, this interpretation of love as criticism was also taken quite seriously by the group.

If surrendering to the will of God, which was the same thing as loving God, was the only proper goal of life, then, as far as the movement was concerned, free will meant only that human beings had the freedom to give up their own wills and obey the will of God.[70] By making the great paradox so basic to their philosophy, Creative Initiative created an intellectual structure that required members to accept a logical contradiction from the very beginning of their association with the group. People could be free only if they enslaved themselves to the will of God. Time and again in their lectures and their courses they would repeat the same litany: "There is no freedom," and "We can command nature only by obeying it." If people had no freedom but to obey nature, if evolution were the method through which nature (God) carried out its intention, if the community of Creative Initiative was an integral part of the next evolutionary stage of history, and if the individual wished to be part of the new third age, then it followed that people had no choice, no freedom, to do anything but dedicate themselves totally to the will of God and the work of Creative Initiative.

Psychological Techniques for Surrendering to the Will of God

Explicit psychological techniques were used by Creative Initiative, both to prepare people to surrender their wills to God and to "live the life" once they had become "identified" (i.e., initiated) members of the community. The use of psychological counseling and personal growth techniques had been introduced during the Sequoia Seminar period and continued uninterrupted through the Creative Initiative era. In the latter period, however, psychology became at once more central and more instrumental to the overall functioning of the movement. All active members participated in the self-discovery and conversion process and, for many, the preparation for the surrender of self was their most important single experience in the movement. However, the mutual criticism sessions among members which followed the personal transformation were just as frequently cited by people as the most negative aspect of their participation.

Stripped of its context, which makes the whole process appear more manipulative and calculated than it probably was, interaction at formal meetings moved from unconditionally given love and support at the beginning of membership to grudging approval doled out parsimoniously and perhaps even arbitrarily to the fully initiated. Members who had been initially inundated with flattery and support during their first year with the group might get nothing but demands for time and effort, accompanied by critiques of their style and attitude, after they had been in for several years.

From the philosophical perspective of Creative Initiative this switch in approach was both humane and logical. Initially the new people needed to be supported and reassured of their own importance as human beings—while, of course, feeling very attracted to this group that was supplying all the positive feedback. Once the neophytes had developed sufficient ego strength to be objective about themselves they could begin the process of investigating their own psychological strengths and weaknesses—admittedly a more painful process, but one which frequently led to tremendous personal insight and growing appreciation for the group providing the guidance. Finally, after surrendering their wills to the will of God, fully identified members were assumed to be acting from a totally new evolutionary perspective (as a new species) in which right behavior was its own reward. Hence, lack of praise and loving criticism would not be hurtful to them—and indeed might have the unrecognized effect of making the person work harder, trying somehow to recapture the psychological support that had drawn them into the group in the first place.

First contacts with prospective members were designed not only to introduce the Creative Initiative philosophy in general terms but also to make the new person feel accepted and important. Most of the psychological support during this early stage was informal or incidental to courses that focused on ideas, yet there were also more structured ways of accomplishing the same purpose. A brief introductory course called "Positive Self-Assessment," for example, stated that its purpose was "to affirm the positive qualities in ourselves in a way that gives us a realistic picture of the way we are."[71]

Once people had become more deeply involved in the movement and had accepted the basic system of beliefs taught in the first series of courses, the time came for them to begin preparing themselves for the crucial psychological step of surrender. The first step in this process was called the "A seminar." The name, specific content, and methodology varied, but the basic purpose remained consistent.[72] The A seminar was designed to help people examine their past interpersonal relationships, particularly with their parents, and in so doing to begin the process that Creative Initiative called "deconditioning," the necessary preparation for surrender to the will of God.[73]

The seminars, which at times lasted longer than five days, guided the participants through some extremely focused examinations of the relationships that had molded them. They tried to get people to look at themselves and reach their own conclusions. Leaders were warned that they could not make decisions for the participants and, in fact, that it was inappropriate for them to even give advice. In theory, their role was to ask questions and be supportive, nothing more.[74] In practice, the leaders could become quite dominating. One man reported that the leaders in his A seminar acted like parents while the participants "reacted as the dutiful, spoiled or resistant child," a technique that he felt was dishonest and manipulative.[75]

Because the process took place within the supportive environment of the seminar, isolated from the real world (usually at the group's beautiful mountain retreat in Ben Lomond), people identified strongly with the movement both as the instigator of their psychological insights and as the support network for their continued personal growth. Participants reported that they went through some of the most searing emotional periods of their entire lives at the A seminars. "The purging of my hatred caused a feeling of euphoria which I think about often," wrote one man, "wondering if that was the high a *totally* loving person feels."[76] A woman who attended one of the seminars described how she shared "something very personal" about her childhood with one of the leaders and that the leader "was very understanding and accepting." That night, the woman reported, "I had a dream that all the stars in the universe had shifted and changed their patterns. I began to trust at a much deeper level."[77]

Most of the Creative Initiative members who wrote about their A seminar experiences in our questionnaires linked the insight they had obtained in the seminar with a fundamental shift in attitude. Because the people who responded to the questionnaire were long-time members who had deeply internalized the group's philosophy, they almost always described that attitudinal shift in religious terms. "I knew answers were available for every need—all I had to do was learn to ask, seek, believe, knock," explained a participant, "so, I was gaining TRUST IN GOD and learning more & more what that meant."[78] Similarly a man who confronted his own anger at his mother and felt compelled to "go out into the woods and beat the ground and release torrents of absolute, uninhibited rage," came to the realization that he could no longer "trust my own rational thought processes." Instead he "decided, not that clearly at first but more and more clearly over time, to have faith that God existed and to put my faith in God."[79]

That shift to trusting God was, of course, the ultimate purpose of the entire process. The real purpose of the A seminar in terms of the Creative Initiative process was to free individuals from the psychological fetters that kept them bound to their parents, liberating them to transfer their emotional allegiance from the authority figures of their past to the authority of God. In the last years of Creative Initiative the A seminar experimented with the "STAR" technique in which feelings of resentment and anger were expressed in screaming and hitting with newspapers and pillows. "I will forever remember the incredible atmosphere inside," wrote a participant, "2 dozen people beating newspapers, screaming yelling—dust flying all over . . . trying to 'kill' our parents!!! The ones who got finished early were surrounding the slower ones &

coaxing them & screaming. . . . It was wild!"[80] When the people had "killed" the parents of their childhood, they were then able to be obedient to God. Because they felt it did not promote group bonding, and because the group was undergoing the transition into Beyond War, the STAR technique was dropped after one year.

Creative Initiative believed that "we are born with an inherent potential to see reality clearly," which was their way of saying that humans are inherently good. Because the environment is imperfect, however, all people develop defense and survival mechanisms that protect them from the "traumas and hurts we encounter in the early years of our helplessness and dependency." These psychological defense mechanisms, or conditioning, not only screened and distorted people's perception of reality; they also created for each individual a particular and personal "frame of reference." The effect of this, they said, was enormous. Nothing less than "the problems of the world" were caused by people who functioned "from a restricted, private point of view" because they think "more of themselves and their way than what is good for the other person or the world."[81] Thus, the A seminar was designed to begin the process of "deconditioning."

The first step a person had to take in deconditioning was to recognize that he or she could not change what was at any given moment. "The essential attitude is *acceptance,* neither resistance to nor rebellion against reality," wrote Harry.[82] By acknowledging that there was no point in railing against what was, the individual would be purged of nonproductive anger and be open to taking action—creative initiative—to make changes in accordance with God's will.[83] Thus, in the tradition of New Thought and New Age philosophies that have been so attractive to middle-class Americans since the nineteenth century, the battle against "resistance" sometimes took on a strong flavor of salvation-through-positive-thinking.

Somehow the conditioned self had to be "destroyed," the personal frame of reference broken, the resistance to reality replaced by response. According to Creative Initiative that was what Jesus was doing when he was baptized. It was at that point that he "let go of himself" without reservation to seek and obey the Will of God."[84] Indeed, there was no end of metaphors used by the group to describe this deconditioning process. It was, said Harry, "the night before the dawn, winter before spring, death before rebirth, crucifixion before resurrection."[85] "If a pitcher is full of water, it must be emptied first, in order to fill it with milk," explained a course; "the conditioned self cannot perceive, know or experience the unconditioned." "You must 'sell *all*' that you have," continued the course material, "you must empty yourself *totally*. Then you will be transparent."[86]

Since the Creative Initiative process of transformation was expected to take up to five years and was based on an educational model, there was no expectation that the change or conversion to "transparency," would occur suddenly. Nevertheless, the process was set up so that participants would spend the one-week "B" seminar taken at the end of their second year concentrating on the deconditioning experience. People could have dramatic insights into their own psychological problems at the A and B seminars, but the assumption appears to have been that the movement from resistance to response would probably occur slowly over time, as a cumulative result of the breaking-down process of deconditioning and the subsequent building-up process of education in the teachings of Jesus.

Besides the general introspection that accompanied the psychological seminars, there was one specific process that Emilia introduced from her own experience which formed a somewhat unexpected link with the early history of the Rathbuns—confession. Confession was perceived as a kind of moral emetic, the use of which cleansed the system of poisons and opened it to healthy new food. "The process of 'emptying' and 'cleansing' is possible through a one-time, all-at-once confession of all the negative things you have done in your lifetime," leaders told participants in the seminars.[87] One seminar described "the first stage in the religious process as *purgation,* that is cleansing the self so that it does not project subjectivity on reality."[88] The term *purgation* was repeated frequently in Creative Initiative documents.

Participants were asked to scour their memories and write down every negative thing they had done that caused them "guilt, blame, shame, feeling of unworthiness, pride, jealousy, etc." Simply writing it down was not sufficient, however. As in the Oxford Group from which Emilia drew this process, the sins then had to be shared. In the Oxford Group they were shared with a single "confessor," but in Creative Initiative, collective ideology dictated that they be shared with the group. "It is not enough to acknowledge it by yourself," the leaders continued; people also had to read their lists at a meeting where the other participants listened but did not comment.[89]

To assist them in the confession process, Creative Initiative supplied seminar participants with copies of the "four absolutes" that had been the central tenets of the Oxford Group. Frank Buchman had taught his followers that they had to follow lives of absolute honesty, absolute purity, absolute unselfishness, and absolute love.[90] A Creative Initiative information sheet on the four absolutes defined each of the admonitions. Absolute honesty meant confessing all sources of guilt and shame (they never used the term "sin"). Absolute purity referred to sex, requiring the confession of masturbation, incest, childhood sexuality, premarital sex, unnatural sex, pornography, adultery, and fornication. Absolute unselfishness applied to all aspects of life including time, money, possessions, skills, and so forth. Finally, absolute love, the goal of life, was discussed in terms of God and the model of Jesus.[91]

There was no sense of antinomianism in the movement. Having surrendered to the will of God did not mean that people automatically knew the will of God or that they could have the absolute knowledge that what they did was the will of God. Once more the problem that had plagued Sharman's students came to the fore. Even when one surrendered one's will, how could one know just what it was that God wanted one to do? Whereas Sharman had supplied no answer, Creative Initiative, by implication, did. Although they made no claims to infallibility, Creative Initiative appeared to believe that the collective could be trusted to know the true road more often than the individual, and that once a person had passed over into the identified state, he or she needed to be open to guidance from other identified people. Jesus said, "If your brother sins, rebuke him." To Creative Initiative, "brothers" were people who were together in the Kingdom of God. By sharing their perceptions of one another's faults, brothers and sisters in the kingdom gave one another the "opportunity and responsibility" to mend their ways or, if the rebuker were incorrect, to turn the criticism back on the originator.[92]

On the one hand, mutual criticism was sometimes described in gentle terms, as when a course told students that "the truly open mind will welcome a reminder that one seems to be defensive about a position held," or when a personal notebook revealed the belief that people should "receive & be grateful for gifts from others (confrontation)."[93] On the other hand, it could be presented in much harsher terms, usually by Emilia, who liked to leave the bark on. It was apparently she who told a group in 1967 that it was "necessary both to help each individual ferret out the shoddy egocentric motivation that became mixed in with his goodwill, and to give him love and support while he swallows his pride and risks himself to the next encounter."[94] And it was definitely she who told another group more than a decade later, "In CIF you will not only not get paid or thanked, but actually you'll only get criticized and straightened out."[95]

The reality appears to have been much closer to the harsh than the gentle. "The constant focus on what was wrong—constant criticism" was the worst aspect of her affiliation with the group, reported a member, "it bred hurt and resentment—lots of hurt. Much of the confrontation was done through *public* humiliation. Many people felt very bad about themselves for years. Our common bond tended to be around our mutual hurt over being humiliated in front of our peers."[96] Another person reported that the confrontations made her feel "shattered—physically ill, reduced to constant crying for weeks"; and "after one relentless year," a ten year veteran of the movement said, "I had to go to a therapist for 6 months just to regain some self-confidence."[97] They were, wrote a man, "bloodbaths . . . replays of the abusive harassment the Army put me through in basic training."[98] Despite the terrible personal stress created by the criticism, some people did feel that it helped expose problems, but, as one woman wondered, "the only question I often ask is did it have to be so very painful?"[99]

Much of the criticism of the confrontational approach focused on the attitude of the leadership toward others. The process of appointing people to leadership positions was informal and dominated by the "hub" group. There was a "power drive among the 'top' people," wrote one respondent and "dominant and aggressive women became 'the authority.' "[100] Those who were not among the chosen leaders sometimes complained that the leaders felt they knew what was right for others because they were more religious. Although some complained, others appear to have been content to accept criticism and guidance from the leadership because they in fact did believe that the leaders had some special religious authority. Even the man who called the mass confrontations unwarranted "bloodbaths," nevertheless recalled his one-on-one confrontations with Emilia as vital to his growth and concluded, "her focused power, combined with a perceptiveness that enabled her to penetrate a person's thoughts and attitudes, was overwhelming."[101] One woman characterized Emilia as "a well spring, forever giving, of her knowledge of the religious life. We have been the receivers of her gifts." Obviously such a person would feel no resentment at having her faults exposed by such a leader. In fact, this woman summed up her feelings about the Rathbuns by saying, "Emilia and

Harry have been my experience of God in persons, a demonstration of what a person can become."[102]

Those unwilling to undergo the episodes of humiliation simply dropped out, and those who remained could view the defection of those who left as evidence that they had not truly made the transition into the new evolutionary state of being. For the people who did stay, the confrontations may have strengthened their commitment on several levels. First, many found them useful in gaining personal insight and were thankful for the opportunity. Second, since by normal social standards subjecting themselves to public criticism was not behavior they should have endured, they had to reason that whatever it was that caused them to suffer must have been very important to justify their paying so high a price. It was a classic case of cognitive dissonance— that is, conflict between what one believes and how one is acting. Cognitive dissonance can be resolved either by changing beliefs or by changing actions so that the two are once more consonant.[103] Those who left the movement resolved the conflict by eliminating its source. Among those who stayed, some people lessened the tension by coming to believe that there was truly something useful in the process of mutual criticism. Others simply accepted the dissonance by admitting that the mutual criticism was distasteful, but saying it was compensated for by the many other benefits derived from membership.

In addition to the increased depth of personal commitment that such rationalizations encouraged, the raw power of mutual criticism also had the effect of promoting commitment on another level. It was surely intimidating to have everybody in the group upon which the member was totally dependent for social and psychological validation, gang up on a member and accuse him or her of doing something wrong, and Creative Initiative people had few if any friends outside the movement. People found that they not only quickly changed the "offensive" behavior, but much more importantly, they constantly checked themselves to make sure that they were not doing anything that might trigger another critical confrontation. One particularly perceptive respondent wrote, "Even short of damage, the confrontational style affected nearly everyone. It was reflected in a tendency to be on the alert for how one appears to others, especially in group meetings, and led to a conformity and uniformity of speech and behavior."[104] Others said the same thing, blaming the criticism for the homogeneity of thought and personal style that so struck everyone who came in contact with the movement.[105]

Theodicy and the Apocalypse

Confession and confrontation were complementary methods of dealing with the same issue: what in traditional religion is called "sin" or "evil." If, as Creative Initiative believed, God and nature were one and if natural laws were an expression of the truth that was God, then how did one deal with the problem of evil? Evil does not fit easily into a monistic world view. Rather than choosing to minimize evil to keep the monistic philosophy intact, Creative Initiative developed a structure that allowed monism and dualism to exist side by side. The educational process taught members to appreciate the unity of creation while at the same time stressing that there was an absolute distinction between good and bad.

The operant text was Matthew 5:39, which Creative Initiative usually rendered as, "resist not evil." Their interpretation of this message was somewhat in the tradition of late nineteenth-century New Thought religion, which held that the world was good, or at least neutral, and that wrong thoughts in the individual created the external evil. Taken to its logical extreme, as in Christian Science, this idea suggests that all apparent evil, including biological disease, can be eliminated through positive thought. Creative Initiative never went that far, but it did insist that *"the problem of evil is internal and never external."*[106] "No external event is evil as such," explained an early position paper, "but only as man at an inner, unconscious level projects outward the interpretation of evil upon it."[107] In another end-run around the issue, several courses dealt with what was really the issue of evil but was always referred to as "violence." Thus, they defined violence as "that which violates the true nature of anything." Using this definition, not only actions but feelings and attitudes could also be violent and lead to negative (evil) consequences. They taught that "violence is leading us to death; it is all around us and consuming us," and that only individual reform could control it.[108]

Harry tried to explain the Creative Initiative interpretation of evil in moderate terms. When Jesus told his followers not to resist evil, Harry said Jesus was telling them to face reality and not to deny that there were things that they did not like, because not until the difficulties were acknowledged could people take creative action to improve them.[109] Emilia's explanations of evil were characteristically more blunt and enigmatic. "Our birthright," she told members of an advanced seminar on the Book of John, "is to become co-creators with The Creator, to be co-determiners of the destiny of the planet, to know truth and express good will, to be reflectors of reality, to be wayshowers, to be lights to the world." There was no other choice she argued, "there is no half and half. There is only totality. You are totally a 'walking God,' or totally a 'walking devil.' "[110] By using the traditional term "devil," Emilia appeared to be setting up a Manichaean duality and thus contradicting the fundamental assumption about the overall goodness of the universe. But the devil she envisioned was only partially outside of the individual. The devil, she said, was "the self will of the human being."[111]

By setting up the dichotomy between good and evil so starkly, Emilia was expressing a world view that underlay much Creative Initiative thought. The world, they believed, would be destroyed by its inhabitants unless they changed their thinking. It would be destroyed by people who continued to view it from their own selfish, conditioned perspectives. Although the group avoided the antinomian belief that everything done by the converted was good, they sometimes seemed to subscribe to the converse proposition: everything done by the unconverted was evil. "When a person will not die an ego death or drop his resistance to taking in truth," Emilia told a Jesus seminar, "the resulting action is evil. When a person knows that what he is thinking or doing in a moment of resistance is not right, he is enacting evil."[112]

The traditional Christian view of humans as sinners survived in Creative Initiative in only slightly altered form. Although the word "sin" was never used, the concept of individual culpability for breaking God's law was inherent in their concept of evil—in fact, it *was* their concept of evil. The excessive desire for "food, drink, drugs, sex, comfort, pleasure, entertainment, sports, possessions, home, car, money in the bank, profession, job, family, position, prestige, popularity, power, reputation," were all violations of the first commandment according to Creative Initiative, because they constituted "other gods" put before the God.[113] In an "authority seminar," leaders wrote the following words on the board: "alcohol, drugs, tobacco, perverted sex, pornography, adultery, premarital sex, dishonesty, violence, greed, power." The participants were then told to come up with a code of conduct in relationship to these items. The course instructions noted that some people would "not want to choose to live that way, but it is the only way that a religious community will live."[114]

In Creative Initiative's philosophy the idea of "sin" was subsumed in the word *greed*. There were, they said, four forms of greed: addictions, possessions, pretensions, and personal relationships. Each of them interfered with a person's doing the will of God because each of them put the individual first. Addictions were all "things of the flesh." Possessions were all material goods. Pretensions were the desire to be recognized by others as good, successful, or important. Finally, greed in personal relationships was defined as the demand that others love or support you.[115] No seventeenth-century American Puritan could have been more severe in his condemnation of the worldly distractions that might divert the faithful from living a godly life.

Their formulation of God combined two disparate, even contradictory characteristics. On the one hand, they perceived God as the remote first cause of a monistic universe. On the other hand, they combined this with an almost pietistic sense of God's immediacy to produce an intense moral rigorism. The dictum that people had to obey the will of God as represented by their interpretation of natural law resulted in a de facto situation similar to that of traditional Puritanism. Like the Puritans they believed that God had created people to glorify Him through work and worship and that God's plan for the human race was immutable. Creative Initiative believed that those who lived their lives in glorification of God were, to use the traditional labels, "saved" and those who violated it were "damned": "You can say 'yes' or 'no.' 'Yes' equals Life, 'no' equals death, and no middle."[116]

Thus, lurking at the heart of their gentle, New Thought, New Age, monism was a very old-fashioned dualism. Over and over again their courses presented participants with the choice between "100% life" and "100% death." It was a choice without compromise that each person had to make. "How do you feel about classifying things as black or white?" participants were asked, "Why is it important to see things black or white and not grey?"[117] In 1984, one of the very last courses prepared in the style of Creative Initiative explained that "the Great Paradox is a binary decision." "There are only two ways to live one's life," the course declared. One was to be 100 percent loving and enter the Kingdom of God. The other was to be anything up to 99.9% loving and remain trapped in the Kingdom of Man.[118]

Dick Anthony and Thomas Robbins have suggested that most new American religious movements can be categorized either as monistic or dualistic. These new religious movements, they argue, are responses to the destruction of the traditional moral framework over the last fifty years. Prior to the New Deal, Anthony and Robbins claim that Americans balanced economic individualism with a very strict but limited code of moral conduct. Thus any behavior not explicitly proscribed was considered legitimate in the pursuit of private wealth, and people who failed in that pursuit were individually responsible for their own fates. During the last half-century, however, an increasingly bureaucratized economy has undercut both entrepreneurial opportunity and individual responsibility. Furthermore, according to Anthony and Robbins, an increasing acceptance of "hedonistic, leisure-oriented, 'permissive'" culture has destroyed the limited but very powerful traditional sanctions for deviant personal behavior.[119]

Anthony and Robbins suggest that people searching for something to replace the destroyed civil religion frequently join movements that either reconstruct a traditional dualism between right and wrong or seek a new synthesis in a monistic world view that sees everything as interconnected and good. The dualistic groups, which include both the right-wing Unification Church ("Moonies") and the left wing People's Temple, see themselves as models for and precursors of a nationwide or even worldwide, revolution against evil forces. The monistic groups, such as the Meher Baba movement or almost any other New Age group, try to find an ideology that moves beyond ideology. That is, they point to the underlying unity of all people, or all things in the universe, no matter what their apparent physical, cultural, or ideological differences. Thus, the dualistic groups reconstruct a structure based on rigid exclusive categories while the monists reconstruct it on an inclusive whole.[120]

Creative Initiative would appear to be the exception to the Anthony and Robbins model by incorporating both monism and dualism into the same movement. Their New Age monism that viewed all people and, indeed, all creation as integrally unified, gave the movement its humane, politically liberal outlook. But their dualistic interpretation of individual behavior allowed them to make strict demands on personal conduct. At least within their own community, they managed to recreate the lost Puritan synthesis by providing a rationale for generalized love in conjunction with being individually judgmental. Within Creative Initiative, traditional Protestant liberalism and traditional Protestant moralism once again went hand in hand with traditional Protestant economic success.

The ambivalent attitude toward materialism that characterized all of Creative Initiative thought was also essentially Puritan. They viewed wealth and material possessions not as evil per se but as dangerous when acquiring them became the object of life, when they became "other gods." A "Responsibility Inventory" asked people about their jobs: "Do you run it or does it run you?" "Is it a means or an end?"[121] Living the life of God through hard work and community were the central tenets of both Creative Initiative and traditional Protestantism, and worldly success, if it followed, was incidental. Creative Initiative and its neo-Protestant ethic appealed, after the fact, to precisely those people who had made it within the capitalist system. The New Religion did not view economic success as a sign of God's approval, but neither did it condemn wealth per se. Within their new religion they, like their Puritan antecedents, could maintain a very comfortable life style so long as pursuit of that life style did not become an end in itself.

Just because evil grew out of individual misperceptions of reality did not mean that the consequences were limited to the individual. Creative Initiative not only recognized but even emphasized that the collective impact of wrong perception (evil) was powerful enough to destroy life on earth. In fact, they predicted that the sole alternative to the millennium created by the continued evolution of humans was the apocalypse created by humans who refused to change. The apocalypse was near, they said, and it was humankind's unwillingness to obey the law of cause and effect that was bringing it on. Just as health and sickness were the result of cause and effect in the right functioning of the body, they argued that "the same can be said for a family, a city, a nation, or a planet. It is sick or it is healthy." It was a simple dualistic choice: people could remain ignorant, evil, alienated, unfocused on a single goal and bring sure death to the world, or they could move over the line to "hold all advances made to date, keep beauty and increase it in the world, advance education, ecology, population control, be a human race living in harmony cooperation and love," and bring sure life—the Kindgom of God.[122]

By constantly holding up an apocalyptic vision to its members and prospective members, Creative Initiative sought to frighten them into changing their lives, for it was only by changing their lives that the millennium could be substituted for the apocalypse. The script for a public slide show from 1967 summed up both the problem and the solution when it warned, "Either man will guide and shape the rapidly accelerating forces of change in the world—guide them consciously toward the goals of survival, cooperation, and fulfillment for all men—or he will be swallowed up in a cataclysm the likes of which the world has never known."[123]

The Cycle of Courses

Because Creative Initiative firmly believed that "the message and the messenger are one," the process of learning the philosophy was also a process of learning to live it. The vast majority of members were white, well-to-do, college-educated, married suburbanites. It is reasonable to assume that at the point at which they entered the movement they shared the religious beliefs and values of their peers. If they stayed in the group and rose through the ranks to a level of higher leadership, they did so only because they were willing to alter significantly those values and the lifestyle connected with them. The persons who emerged from the four-year process were supposed to be profoundly changed; they were a new species. The cycle of courses that brought about this transformation was no haphazard collection of do-it-yourself adult education classes, but a carefully developed and constantly refined process that paralleled the college education almost all the participants had experienced. Yet, for many of them it had the effect of nullifying the relativism that is so often the result of higher education.

The overall process was so complex as almost to defy description. New members were attracted by word of mouth, community presentations, or invitational meetings. From there they attended a course called "Challenge to Change" at which the basic philosophical positions of the movement were described, but in rather vague, nonreligious terms. If they decided to move on, their next step was to take additional low-level courses, like "Challenge of Time," to receive first-level leadership training, and then to lead their own invitational meeting.

There were always lots of courses and presentations to work on and, as people demonstrated ability and commitment, they were given additional leadership training and permitted (expected) to lead other courses including "Challenge to Change" and second- and third-step programs. The real heart of the educational process, however, was the seminars. Each of these was approximately one week long and usually held at the group's retreat center in Ben Lomond. Because they were presented in the summer when people were on vacation, members usually took one new seminar each year after having made a formal decision to move on from the previous level of involvement. The intervening time between seminars was used to work on other Creative Initiative projects and to test the depth of commitment reached at the previous one.

The initial A seminar, as noted earlier, was designed to help new members explore the meaning of authority, especially parental authority, in their lives. Having severed the immature bonds that tied one to other authority figures, the participants were then free to move on to the B seminar, also designated a "psychological seminar," where the process of "purgation" could take place. After the B seminar, they were expected to make a commitment "to the marriage forever" and to continue "the process of purgation until it is completed."[124] People who entered the third or "C" seminar were presumed to have internalized a concept of God, resolved problematic relationships and traumatic life experiences, gained a positive self-image, and adopted a giving, spontaneous attitude that led them to live life "with a sense of gratitude."[125] C seminars were explicitly described as "transitional" from the psychological to the religious, devoted to exploring the meaning of certain Old Testament stories, always called "myths" in Creative Initiative nomenclature. Having come to grips with the self or "I" in the first two seminars, the third was the opportunity to begin to explore the "Thou," and other-than-self. "To pursue this goal means to leave behind the narrow perspective of an individual point of view," the course said, "and move toward and into the Universal Frame: the all-encompassing, eternal dimension we call God."[126] It was as a result of this third seminar that people were expected to achieve what Creative Initiative called the "pass over," that is, the passing over from the egocentric world view of the personal will to the universal loving outlook of God's will.[127]

Finally, at the end of the fourth year, people were allowed to take the "D" seminar, the Jesus as Teacher or Records seminar. This seminar, based on the books and method of Henry B. Sharman, was the single most important carry-over from the Camp Minnesing era. Now, however, what had once been the first and only course in the movement had become the "senior seminar," available only to those who had persevered through three years and demonstrated their ability and commitment to the cause. As it had been in the Sharman days, the purpose continued to be "a religious seminar where a person can understand and adopt for himself the model for spiritual man as lived out by Jesus of Nazareth."[128]

Almost immediately after Emilia had her revelation and gathered the first ten women to launch the New Religion, the group began developing course material to explicate the new system of beliefs. The basic pedagogic approach involved the use of seven principles or seven steps. These were first formulated in 1963 and taught for four years as the

"Seven Steps to Reality."[129] In 1967 they were developed into a seven-week course called "Challenge to Change," which itself became part of a four-course introduction to the ideas of Creative Initiative entitled "Quest for Meaning." This was the prerequisite, in turn, for a course called "Preparation for the New Religion," and so on in an apparently infinite variety of ways that allowed people to keep busy studying or teaching aspects of the work.[130] The Challenge to Change course was designed as an introduction to the ideas of the movement. If, after discussing the seven steps, people were still interested, they would be invited to move on to the next level.[131]

Old Testament Myths and New Testament Models

The philosophical positions first presented to people in Challenge to Change would continue to be developed through courses and seminars over the years a person remained active.[132] After the A and B seminars in which they freed themselves of the psychological baggage that prevented people from reorienting themselves to do God's will, people moved on to the third, or C, seminar, in which the purely religious aspects of the work moved to the fore. At this level almost all biblical study was conducted under the rubric of "myth," and the myths of the Old Testament were invariably used to illustrate, demonstrate, justify, and "prove" the ideas introduced in Challenge to Change and other lower-level courses.

Using a combination of ideas from Rollo May, Jung, and P. W. Martin's interpretation of Jung, Creative Initiative justified the study of myth as a legitimate method of exploring the "intuitive aspect of the mind."[133] The movement claimed that the myths of the Old Testament contained "the most advanced and thorough symbolic history of the development of the three levels of existence," and that they expressed "in a dramatic form, a psychological truth, and often a wisdom, which otherwise would be inaccessible to our understanding."[134] The language of their analysis, which contained references to symbols and archetypes, was obviously drawn from Jung, who described myths and their archetypes as expressions of a human collective unconscious.[135] Theirs, however, was not an attempt to use Jung in any systematic way to analyze the Old Testament myths. He was barely mentioned. Rather,

Creative Initiative took a few fundamental concepts and constructed their own entirely original interpretations. In addition, they apparently hoped that by demonstrating the legitimacy of these old myths, they would, at the same time, be justifying their own symbols and stories, or what they referred to as the "living myth."

Their interpretations of the Old Testament were a long way from the close textual analysis that characterized their standard method of exploring the teachings of Jesus in the gospels. There, following the model of Henry B. Sharman, each phrase was explored for its meaning. In the case of the Old Testament, the group (in fact, Emilia) had come up with its own official interpretation of each story, and the process was to understand how the Old Testament myths fit the Creative Initiative view of the world, not to examine them in any fresh analytic way. Creative Initiative believed that "the basic steps of the religious life" were contained in those stories, and participants were told, "In the Old Testament we will see the unfolding of the psychic journey of mankind. The Old Testament is a story of the evolution of consciousness."[136] In other words, the Old Testament was a widely respected text that could be used to legitimize their own uses of myth and symbol.

Each Old Testament myth had its own particular interpretation. The most frequently studied was the story of Moses, and it can be used as an example of the group's approach. The Old Testament was, for Creative Initiative, the "history of man's experience in the domain of the opposites" and the expression of the first dispensation, and Moses was "the symbol of the Old Testament."[137] Over the years, Creative Initiative used at least five different interpretations of the Moses myths. Each of them had unique aspects, mostly having to do with the elaborate decoding of symbols, and some of them directly contradicted one another. For example, according to a 1968 commentary on the burning bush, "Fire is in nature. Man is nature. Fire in man is a generator of energy."[138] But a later version from 1974 stated, "Burning bush, not consumed. Not natural, not of nature. Refers to another dimension."[139] The 1974 version of the story specified the meaning of thirty-seven different symbols ranging from the major figures in the story to "shoes," "stone," and the numbers three, seven, and forty.[140]

The Creative Initiative gloss made Moses into a personification of every major philosophical position held by the group. When his mother put Moses in a basket in the river, they interpreted it as symbolic of a son's necessary detachment from his mother so that he would be free to pursue his destiny. When Pharoah's daughter saved him it was to show that the "masculine [is] safe when in touch with the right feminine." Moses killing the Egyptian was his "first act of totality" but was also meeting violence with violence and therefore made him unworthy to lead the Hebrews into the promised land. Every incident, from the well where Moses meets Zipporah, to the wandering in the desert, was linked to a Creative Initiative idea: dawn, archetypes, third dispensation, new role of women, life of the spirit, new identity, obedience to God's will, conscious and unconscious mind, mysticism, and so forth.[141] The seminar questions used in conjunction with the study of the Moses myth, like the interpretations of the myth itself, were designed less to explore the meaning of the story than to use the story for specific didactic purposes. The first three questions, for example, asked participants to explore their own relationships with their mothers.

Because Creative Initiative saw the Old Testament stories as mythical analogs of the spiritual history of both humankind and individuals, their study was supposed to help people make the personal transition from the state of psychological freedom obtained in the first two seminars to one of spiritual growth and commitment. They believed that, like Judaism itself, the study of the Jewish Bible was transitional. In the Old Testament God exercised his authority through the law, and the result was a Pharisaic culture of righteous moralism unable to reconcile all aspects of the human condition. The New Testament, using the example of Jesus, resolved the unanswered questions left by the Old Testament. Thus, the next step in an individual's development would be to study the documents of the second dispensation to discover the way love could triumph over law.[142] There were plans for a final, systematic study of how to apply the rules of the second dispensation in the third dispensation—that is, in the New Religion of the Third Age (Creative Initiative)—but they were never fully implemented.

Studying the New Testament meant studying the life and teachings of Jesus. Here Emilia's freedom to impose a Creative Initiative dogma on the biblical text was somewhat more constrained because of the tradition of gospel study inherited from Sharman and carried on, albeit in a very modified form, by Harry Rathbun. Creative Initiative was, nevertheless, willing and able to be much more specific about the meaning of what Jesus said than Henry B. Sharman would have been. At its most extreme, the deviation from the Sharman pattern abandoned objective study of the gospels and instead used the teachings of Jesus as post hoc justification for other ideas. Such an instance occurred in the late 1960s when a course called "Life of the Spirit" used Sharman's material to illustrate directly the

seven steps usually taught in Challenge to Change. Like the Old Testament courses, but unlike the Sharman gospel study, this course laid out
the interpretations for the participants and did not expect or even allow
them to come to any of their own conclusions. Whereas the Sharman
technique had begun with the teachings of Jesus and then asked the
students to derive their own meaning from the text, Life of the Spirit
began with the seven steps and used the teachings of Jesus to validate
them.

Although there was no reluctance to use Jesus as an example for
specific principles, the Sharman texts and a modified Sharman method
remained the major way to study the gospels until all religious elements
were dropped from the group after 1982.[143] Sharman had assumed that
each person would come to a truly personal conclusion about the
proper way to obey the will of God. Creative Initiative assumed that
people would come to the conclusion that obeying the will of God
meant working through the movement. By placing the study of the
gospels at the end of a four-year program of philosophical and psychological development, the participants were primed to look for very
different kinds of conclusions than had been reached in Sharman's day
and during the Sequoia Seminar period. It would appear that Creative
Initiative had decided that the study of the teachings of Jesus was so
powerful that it could be undertaken only after people had been taught
how to place it in the correct ideological context.

The Jesus as Teacher seminar began with a brief presentation of the
historical background of Jesus in his time as a way of establishing the
messianic tradition of the Jews. It then proceeded through the life of
Jesus, focusing on the baptism, the wilderness experience, the two great
commandments, the meaning of the Kingdom of God, the meaning of
the will of God, and the Sermon on the Mount. Each of these subjects
was explored using the Sharman books, but they were also supplemented with techniques that had been developed by Creative Initiative
and designed to elicit responses in line with Creative Initiative philosophy. Among those that had no precedent in the work of Sharman were
interpretations of dreams, writings about personal feelings, group
prayers, outside readings unrelated to the gospels, and drawing.[144]

By continuing to use the Sharman books and the original Sharman
rationale, Harry and Emilia were maintaining the connection with their
own religious history. Sharman was held up as the founding father, the
scholar who had the original insight now carried on through the work of
Harry Rathbun and the Records study activities of Creative Initiative.

Sharman and Harry were the Jungian archetypes of the wise old man, and they gave a cache of scholarly legitimacy to what in fact had become a spiritual movement. The three years of courses that preceded the final Jesus seminar made the study of the gospels a methodology to cement commitment to the will of God, as they had always been since the days of Sharman. But now the will of God had become coterminous with Creative Initiative and its system of beliefs. Jesus was the model of the perfect person in an age of individualism that had rejected him. Creative Initiative believed it was the collective second coming that would lead the world to implement the ideas they studied in the Jesus as Teacher seminar.

Dualism and the Educational Process

Although they had added a large, perhaps even dominant, spiritual–mystical component to the work, Creative Initiative continued to stress and believe that theirs was a rational process that would appeal to modern, educated men and women. The very structure of their work, similar to the organization and style of college courses, was designed to further this image. Certainly the vast majority of the people who became involved in the movement were educated at the finest universities in the country, usually in scientific and technical disciplines, and many had advanced degrees. Clearly then, the system of beliefs constructed by Creative Initiative, and the process for teaching them, had tremendous attraction for one sector of America's educated elite.

We would argue, as suggested earlier in this chapter, that a major reason for the attractiveness of the Creative Initiative belief system was its replication of a traditional Protestant philosophy. Under the broad monistic umbrella that gave the movement its gentle New Age air and liberal social views, it was able to construct a very old-fashioned dualistic religion that supported traditional family values, condemned indulgences of the flesh and excessive materialism, and thus set up a clear-cut dichotomy between right and wrong without ever violating its own rule of posing no enemies. We do not know why certain individuals and not others found the combination of monism and dualism in Creative Initiative so compelling. The fact, however, that Creative Initiative always downplayed, or even hid, their religious aspect during initial contacts with potential recruits indicates that they believed they had to educate people into accepting the extrarational aspects of their teachings. In a very real sense, the method of teaching people to accept the religious absolutes was a reversal of the educational process that William G. Perry, Jr., has suggested takes place in college. If one accepts Perry's model as appropriate, then Creative Initiative in fact ran a program of *re*-education.

Perry has argued that college students undergo a process of cognitive and ethical growth. They begin from a position of simplistic dualism in which they believe that authority will be able to supply right, as opposed to wrong, answers to life's questions. Eventually they move through eight stages to a position of committed relativism in which they understand that there are no totally right answers but that people can take strong stands based on their own ethical positions while knowing that those positions are not absolute.[145] If we assume that many of the people who joined Creative Initiative had reached the final positions in Perry's nine-point scale, then Creative Initiative had to somehow move them back through a re-educational process to a position in which they were once more comfortable with absolutes.

It is, of course, possible that Creative Initiative appealed to people who had never moved beyond the dualistic stages of personal development and were delighted to discover that Creative Initiative provided them with a spiritual rationalization for an already-held position. The fact that the movement appealed to scientific and technical people, who may have been less tolerant of ambiguity than social scientists and humanists, tends to support this possibility. In any case, however, it was desirable for the movement to put people through a process of education, or re-education, to get them to confirm their commitment. If, on the one hand, the recruits had moved through the whole Perry scale to a position of committed relativism, then Creative Initiative had to convince them that dualism was a morally and intellectually legitimate position to hold. On the other hand, if the potential members, despite the best efforts of their college professors, still retained a dualistic world view, then Creative Initiative needed to reassure them that such a view was legitimate and that they had been right to resist the authority of their professors but that they should now surrender to the authority of God.

Although not a perfect inversion of the Perry scheme, the educational process of Creative Initiative did try to achieve his last category, commitment, by moving people to the first one, dualism. The initial introduction to the work was made in terms of science, but science at a very elementary level. Creative Initiative's science was dualistic. Things were either right or wrong, true or false. There could be neither multiplicity nor relativism in the scientific world of Creative Initiative. Science was the authority that everybody had to obey. That, essentially, was the message of the first courses, especially Challenge to Change, that led up to the first seminar.

Having set up the dualistic model, Creative Initiative then proceeded to systematically and deliberately destroy any competing sources of authority. The first two seminars were designed to purge the individual of previous authority figures. Parents were singled out, but the implication was clear that they were only the prime, not the sole, authority figures who had to be confronted. The express purpose of the first two years of work in Creative Initiative was to liberate people from the negative emotional ties of their past and to purge the "frames of reference" from which they had previously viewed the world. At the end of the second year, a person was supposed to be in a state of openness, ready to begin a move to commitment. Although not exactly a position of newly discovered relativism (which would be the middle, or transitional, point in the Perry scheme), the people in the Creative Initiative process were supposed to have moved from a position in which they had been their own authorities (albeit conditioned by their own pasts) to one in which they recognized that they could never be first, they could never be egocentric, but that real authority lay elsewhere.

The third and fourth years of the Creative Initiative educational process were devoted to describing how the scientific dualism established as a philosophical standard during the first year could be extended to the religious sphere: God was equated with natural law. The end result was supposed to be people who saw all human action, not just science, as being either right or wrong based on the authority of God. Whereas they were politically and personally tolerant of those who did not agree with them, most members of Creative Initiative appear to have been intellectually and ethically sure of their absolute rightness and of the absolute wrongness of others, a position very close to the most elementary dualism described by Perry.

Indeed, it would appear that such a dualistic position is necessary for the formation of a sect. It is only by distinguishing insiders who are "right" from outsiders who are "wrong" that a group creates the distance necessary to separate itself from society as a whole. It is just that distinction that makes joining a sect a high-cost proposition and that, in turn, forces the group to provide a variety of rewards to offset those costs. The exclusivity created by a dualistic ideology insures that a group will retain its distinctiveness and not be diluted to death by being promiscuously inclusive. It took four years, four seminars, numerous courses, teaching, working, socializing, and sometimes living with other members of the community, but for those who saw it through, the process was successful in taking people who well may have been independent relativists and transforming them into tightly knit dualists. Those thus reborn into the movement believed that their sect was the New Religion of the Third Age, that their community was a collective messiah that would usher in that age by instigating the next step in human evolution, and that if they could only spread the word to the rest of humanity, the whole world could become the Kingdom of God. If they failed, the whole world would surely destroy itself.

5

Men, Women, and Children

Creative Initiative argued that the paradox of Jesus actually contained the essential scientific truth of creation: people were free only to obey the laws of nature and the will of God. Thus, they had to give up their egocentric wills and become slaves of God and God's order before they could achieve real freedom. Indeed, integrating apparent opposites was a continuing theme in all of Creative Initiative's work. They hoped to achieve sociocentric ends through homocentric means; they perceived a monistic universe and populated it with dualistic human beings; and they built a movement on science and Socratic inquiry and then linked it to a religion based on mystical revelation and philosophic dogma. None of these paradoxes was more complex, however, than the one by which a religion, started and led by women determined to save the earth from men, was transformed into a sect that promoted the traditional roles of wife and mother and expected women to eventually relinquish their major leadership role to men.

Masculine and Feminine

Creative Initiative believed that the transition from female to male leadership could take place because the men would have undergone the transformation process and in doing so would have acquired the necessary female characteristics. Only someone who had gone through the transformation process would be able to act as both the feminine and the masculine because he then would have "brought into perfect balance the masculine and feminine components which are present in every human being." The model for this perfect combination of the two genders was Jesus who "demonstrated and exemplified this perfect balance."[1]

Creative Initiative borrowed the idea that a mature adult combined both masculine and feminine elements from the work of C. G. Jung. Jung contended that both men and women were born with a latent image of the opposite sex. He called the feminine aspect of men the "anima" and the masculine aspect of women the "animus." He thought people developed these images through their contacts with members of the opposite sex, reaching genuine maturity only when they had learned to use the qualities of the anima and animus appropriately.[2]

In Creative Initiative work the masculine and feminine principles, as they were usually called, were vital concepts in describing appropriate behavior for members. In theory Creative Initiative believed that each person had to cultivate those properties usually associated with the opposite sex in order to become whole. Their material, however, stressed gender distinctions so aggressively that it was easy to forget that the ultimate goal was gender synthesis. For example, a part of the A seminar in 1973 described male and female personality characteristics as sexual analogs. According to the course, "Even the genitals bear this out. Woman is inner—the male is outer. Because the feminine is subjective and the masculine objective, we can also say that the feminine is passive, a receiver, and the masculine is active, a doer." The material went on to say that women's "passive, subjective nature allows her to receive and to let the creative birth process take place within her," but men, deprived of this biological opportunity to create life, created in the world. That, said the course, was why the great music, art, poetry, design, and even cooking had been produced by men.[3] The categorization of masculine and feminine characteristics in course material was extensive and often included elaborate charts in which the various traits were lined up in columns, sometimes with the "given" trait paired with its "misuse." For example, the "given" feminine trait of "nurturing" was paired to its "misuse" as "smothering." This pair in turn was contrasted with the "given" masculine trait of "aggressiveness" and its negative counterpart, "domination."[4]

Yet in Creative Initiative the ideal was some kind of synthesis of the masculine and feminine. They did not mean, however, that the mature person was an equal balance of the two. When it was properly struck, the balance was always within the boundaries set by traditional gender roles. On the one hand, "A woman who is too unbalanced on the feminine side," explained a course curriculum, "could be very passive, sweet, helpless, dependent [and] would probably have a hard time standing on her own two feet." On the other hand, "If she denied her femininity and functioned mainly out of her masculine side, she would probably be one of those bossy, domineering, aggressive kind of women of which we all know at least one."[5] Women had to somehow be feminine but not too feminine, and at the same time be masculine but not too masculine. The same course curriculum ended by saying:

And as for women, there are times when she must use her animus nature. There are times when it's appropriate to lead out and be aggressive. There are times when she needs to think logically and rationally. In fact, this is exactly what women must do today—be willing to be actively involved in the objective world—to use their minds and their strength. But the catch is, she must do it in a feminine way, motivated by her deepest feminine instinct—caring.[6]

This basically Jungian view of human nature had a profound effect on Emilia and, through her, on the entire movement.[7] She tended to see individuals within the movement in terms of Jungian types and based much of the underlying ideology of Creative Initiative on gender role models legitimated by, if not actually derived from, a Jungian world view. As we noted earlier, Emilia explained to an advanced seminar in 1978 that Harry was the Jungian archetype of the wise old man. He was not, however, the dominant male—that role, she said, was played in one generation by another leader, Jim Burch, and in the next generation by her son Richard. She told the group that "since Harry was not the dominant male, I had to move into position and function as if I were a dominant male until the transition to Community could take place."[8] But once that transition had occurred, Emilia explained, she and the women who had founded and led the New Religion movement during its first decade had to step aside. Men had been stymied because they had limited their dominance to war and science, but the time had come for "the Dominant Male archetype [to] move beyond the physical and mental dimensions to become the Spiritual Warrior, or we've had it." "The women cannot finish this mission," she explained, "because we don't carry this archetype of Spiritual Warrior. In the world, a man must manifest it."[9]

Because they equated the receptive with women and the feminine and the active with men and the masculine, Creative Initiative philosophy taught that women had almost always been first to understand new ideas in the history of humankind. Indeed, Emilia liked to claim that "the very first, most primitive cells were feminine in function and form," and in a grand leap of logic, she concluded, "that gives us some reasons as to why girls develop earlier than boys and we are considered older and wiser."[10] From Eve who tempted Adam, to Emilia and the first ten women in the New Religion, it was the feminine principle that was open to receive change, but it was the masculine that actually acted to bring that change about.[11]

Emilia developed a fairly elaborate theory about the female life-cycle, much of which appears to have been based on her own personal history. This theory dominated her ideas about the proper role of women through the mid-1970s and was a vital component in the overall philosophical structure of Creative Initiative. According to Emilia's theory, the first stage an adult woman entered was that of "lover." In this stage she surrendered the independence she had enjoyed as an unmarried woman and devoted herself completely to her husband from whom, in return, she expected reciprocal dedication. The key element in the first stage was the woman's willingness to give up herself for her husband—to "capitulate." The second stage was motherhood, in which the woman learned to love life through the life she had created. It was also in her role as mother that a woman cultivated "her certain talents, innate talents, on how to civilize and humanize the race so that [it] no longer will kill life but will be for life."[12]

It was, however, the third stage that was the key to the unique role of women in the transition to the third age and the salvation of the human race. In the third stage, said Emilia, the woman had to detach herself from the bonds she had forged in the first two stages: "She must detach herself from any demands of being loved by the lover. . . . She must surrender that, releasing the man so that he can help heal the planet. She must release her attachment to her children." In the third stage the woman had a new function, one that had been "predestined from the beginning of time," which was "releasing totally and aligning herself with everything that is for life."[13] The third-stage woman would transfer "her dependency on man to a dependency on a supra power, intelligence, will." The relationship she had once had with a man she would then have with "a power higher than man," who would become "the great love of her life."[14]

So profound was this transition to the third stage that it required new nomenclature. If one broke down the word *woman* into its componant parts (a favorite Creative Initiative explicatory device, sometimes employed, as here, in a way that had nothing to do with the actual etymology of the word), one got "wo[e]-man." But the third-stage woman, the Third Age woman, would not bring woe to men but would be a source of blessings and therefore needed a new name. Creative Initiative called her Blessman. "To be the Blessman," they explained, "has a different ring to it from being the WO-man. To be the Blessman would be to embrace and become one with the living myth."[15] In fact, the word *Blessman* was used for a number of years as the complimentary closing in movement correspondence.

Yet once more the ambivalence that marked so much of Emilia's life expressed itself in her definition of Blessman. She was a charismatic and socially dynamic woman who had married a somewhat shy and introspective man; believing that woman should play a traditional role in the family, her entire adult life had been an attempt to reconcile emotionally and intellectually the clash between her assumptions and her reality. Carried away by the vision of women as the avant-garde of the New Religion and the new evolutionary stage, Emilia painted a picture of women who had moved beyond their husbands and families to devote all their energy to God's will. When it actually came to defining how this new woman, the Blessman, would act, however, the extreme rhetoric translated into a much more traditional reality.

According to Creative Initiative, the Blessman would use her special female gifts of nurturing and caring for life to nourish her relationships with others, especially her family; she would not blame others for family problems but would look to "her own state of mind to discover what is going on with her."[16] She would be aware that she was "the servant, the giver." That is, she would give without expecting to be appreciated. She would give because she knew there was a need: "A good servant gives and gives freely to whatever is needed. She is not preoccupied with the question: Will I be appreciated, recognized, or thanked?" This position was a variant of the surrender theme that characterized surrendering the individual will to the will of God. By accepting the needs of her family as legitimate in and of themselves and by finding satisfaction in fulfilling them, the new woman was practicing an analog of her relationship with God. She was, however, at the same time freeing herself from her dependency on her husband. No longer doing things for his approval, the Blessman was freer to express her feelings of both love and anger toward him.[17]

Although they never quoted the poem, Creative Initiative certainly embraced the theory of William Ross Wallace who wrote, "The hand that rocks the cradle is the hand that rules the world." The poet whom they did quote frequently was Wallace's Victorian contemporary, Matthew Arnold, who predicted, "If ever the world sees a time when women shall come together purely and simply for the benefit and good of mankind, it will be a power such as the world has never known."[18] The sentiments of Victorian aesthetes were congenial to Creative Initiative's view of women because the movement had a basically Victorian conception of sex, sex roles, and the family. Much of Creative Initiative's views of women appears to have been a projection of Emilia's personal history and ideals, which were in fact of Victorian origins. She had been born and reared just after the turn of the century in an aristocratic Mexican environment, although an American father and schooling in the United States enabled her to escape the most extreme elements of that machismo culture. As a powerful and magnetic woman and a natural leader she had, nevertheless, to create for herself, and by herself, an environment in which to exercise her abilities and still be true to the values of her past.

Emilia found her solution within the New Religion as a spiritual leader. Like Victorian women who also made virtues out of necessities, the new religion acknowledged the secondary role of women in the world and their primary role in the home and then sought to show how they could exploit their positions to bring about the desired end. "It may be a long time yet before we shall be permitted to share temporal leadership and policy making at all levels," she wrote, "but spiritual leadership and power is ours for the taking at all levels, and we must assume it while we can still hope to turn the tide."[19] Emilia was able to attract other women to her new vision because they shared many of her life experiences, had similar problems, and sought similar answers. In the early 1960s, before real economic opportunities were open to women, and for women who had been raised to value being wives and mothers, becoming part of Creative Initiative both justified their preexisting beliefs and gave them a sense that they could move forward to work for the betterment of all humankind.

The women Emilia rallied to her cause may not have had power, but they did have a lot of discretionary time they could devote to the work. "As economically emancipated housewives, living in a time of frozen foods and gadgetry, we know that conditions in the world must be changed and that it is our obligation to effect that change," announced a flyer for an early seminar.[20] Creative Initiative always worked on the assumption that the women in the movement would be free to devote all their nonfamily time to the work. Indeed, theirs was a movement by and for women who did not work. For the first dozen years or so after Emilia's revelation in 1962, the group was completely dominated by women. "Men," as one participant remembers, "were almost incidental." Most of their meetings were held during the day, which made it extremely difficult for any interested working woman to participate. Moreover, as the same woman wrote, "a great deal of pressure was placed to reevaluate why a woman was working and to quit."[21] A workshop series put on especially for young mothers assured them that "the crisis in the world today is a result of the breakdown of relationships—the traditional role of mother" and urged them to resist the temptation to betray their true natures by looking for a place of prestige and power in the business world.[22]

Although the movement was never comfortable with working women, and working women (there were some) were never very comfortable in the movement, by the mid-1970s the women's movement had changed public attitudes sufficiently to make some concessions necessary. A speech to a women's gathering in 1974 acknowledged that women had moved out into areas once dominated by men, but "in the process [the woman] has abandoned or devalued her place of natural functioning." The speaker did go on to assure her audience, "this is not to say that woman must return to being tied to the home, stuck in roles in which she feels unfulfilled, but simply that woman must claim her feminine side, her natural side and make it conscious."[23] As late as 1977, nevertheless, they were using a guided meditation called "Arriving Home" which asked the man to "imagine in your mind's eye that you are driving home from work" but told the woman, "picture yourself in the house. It is late afternoon . . . You remember that your husband will be home shortly."[24]

The group built their theory of a special female strength using standard Victorian ideas about the nature of women. First, women bore children. "Every woman's task is to be a priestess to the flow of life," said an early paper, "to procreate, nurture, and fan the fires of creation."[25] From that undeniable biological fact they then deduced that women had a special aptitude for love. The narrator of a 1966 program told her audience that love "has been given to us as a gift that accompanies our role of giving birth to the race of man."[26] Love was defined not as doing but as giving, as a form of self-sacrifice: "Woman's basic self derives from her basic function: to love, to give of herself, and through giving, realize herself."[27]

There was a curiously contradictory element to Creative Initiative's ideas about married love. They were quite sure that the family was a model for the world and that the love between spouses was analogous to the love of the individual for God, but they were not sure whether individuals developed a love for God by experiencing love for people or if a love for others followed from the love of God. "We learn to love God through the workout of learning to love people," said the syllabus to a 1982 marriage course, "therefore marriage is the perfect workshop for learning to love with totality."[28] But Emilia told people that real love between spouses occurred "only when both partners are committed to loving God first. You relate as 'sons' of God, 'brothers' committed to the same goal."[29]

The love a woman felt toward her husband was defined as a "passive love" that taught her how to give; the love she felt toward her children taught her "pure love."[30] Women were told that just as they all had given love to their husbands and children they now had to give love to the whole world, to "give totally to a self-transcending cause." The group taught that giving love was the process of "civilizing."[31] "The only two things women can do better than men," wrote one leader in her personal notes, "is to bear children and civilize."[32] "Civilization" was used as a contrast to materialism and war, considered male in origin. A speaker at a 1969 women's meeting illustrated this point with an anecdote about her own children. Her sons had built a fort in the backyard, and one day her daughter went out and put curtains in the fort's windows, much to the disgust of the boys. "She was," said her mother, "trying to civilize at that early age."[33]

Putting curtains on the windows of the fort was a particularly apt example for women in Creative Initiative because one of the qualities that women were supposed to have to a greater degree than men was an appreciation of beauty. Beauty could have a functional role in helping people appreciate the mystical, or it could be seen as an important part in creating the right atmosphere for recruiting, but beauty could also be an expression of the woman's sense of self. In making the move toward taking responsibility for herself and for the work, one woman explained that the first thing she did was to "look at how I appeared." "It was quite a blow," she admitted, "20 pounds too heavy, no lipstick, very comfortable with 'Plain-Jane-Me.' "[34] Such an aesthetic self-assessment was not incidental but part and parcel of the process by which women discovered their special abilities. Women were told to evaluate all the visual aspects of themselves and their environment, "home decor— color, objects, dress, make-up, attitude, walk, stance," and others in the group were urged to share with a new woman their views on her appearance.[35] It is hardly surprising then that a newspaper reporter described one spokeswoman as "wearing a chic lime green frock and looking more like a fashion model than a crusader."[36]

The beauty that women could create contrasted with the ugliness that was so often the product of male activities. In Emilia's mind there was no doubt that men were in fact the source of most of the world's problems. "This is the century of women," she wrote in a personal reflection. Man, she continued, had been "emancipated from the child bearing function and been allowed to develop his psychic spiritual function," but he had not done a very good job of it. "On the whole, except for rare individuals," she wrote, "men have rejected the prototypes of excellence in the domain of human nature. For the most part they are arrogant, violent destructive beasts." The time had come for women to "move into enlightenment and to declare to men what God wills, or they, men, will destroy the earth." She wrote that men had been poor stewards of the earth and should no longer be the "rulers, priests and guides of life."[37] Although such powerfully antimale sentiments never made their way into any of the movement's course material, they do reflect a profound ambivalence in Emilia's feelings toward men. On the surface, she and the other women in the movement were always loving and supportive of their spouses, but underlying that was the explicit belief that women were morally superior. There were two kinds of ethics, a movement spokeswoman told a reporter in 1975, and Creative Initiative had developed a "new feminism based on the need to stop acting on male ethics based on greed, power and war, and form new female ethics."[38]

Dramatic readings at an early presentation designed to recruit new women into the movement captured the richly female-centered nature of the work. The audience was told that women contained "those watching, waiting, loving characteristics of awareness that know intuitively the needs, the conditions, the relationships for beauty, harmony, joy, movement, well-being—the climb toward God," and that each woman had those qualities because she had "built into her body . . . the chalice, the response to sunlight, the living well of water filled to overflowing."[39] Creative Initiative truly believed that anatomy was destiny, not merely for the individual woman but for the whole world. Through their use of Victorian gender stereotypes, however, the women of Creative Initiative were not locking themselves into the limited domestic sphere. They were saying instead that the whole world was their domestic sphere and that just as they could bring peace and love to their own families, they could do the same for all humankind.

Marriage

In 1952, almost a full decade before her vision, Emilia articulated a model of male–female relationships that remained constant throughout the history of the movement. Speaking to a continuation seminar (in that period, a seminar that followed Jesus as Teacher), she said that boys should be reared to have a "code of responsibility" toward women, and that girls should not be taught to think of themselves as sex objects. Girls' self-image, she said, "should be that of the saint, as in bygone days, so that man will do anything, slay all dragons, to get the worthy woman!" The most important thing, she added, was for girls "to be educated into the art of being good homemakers and how to handle men rightly; they ought to be educated to be feminine."[40] They were to be, in other words, traditional wives and mothers.

Creative Initiative believed that the family was the paradigm for the world: it was primarily the woman's job to make the family work, just as it was primarily women who would launch the third age for all people. "If we as women want a better world we had better start with ourselves," they were told. "We can change the atmosphere affecting first our family situation and then moving out into the world. What is going on at home, is going on in the world." Their language seemed to leave little hope that the unmarried would be able to achieve wholeness as human beings because, as they explained, "to learn to love reality and our fellow man is the created purpose of a human, and the marriage is key in promoting this discovery."[41] For obvious reasons, then, single people frequently did not feel welcome or comfortable within the group. The movement considered single people, especially single women, incomplete, and at various points in their history Creative Initiative either excluded unmarried people altogether or relegated them to special singles groups.[42] This practice was particularly hard on those who wanted to participate in the various ceremonies usually carried on in families, or by groups of families. One such woman remembers "having to invite myself to dinner" so that she could celebrate the Sunday ritual.[43]

Like so much else in Creative Initiative's program, the stress on the importance of uninterrupted marriage appears to have been a projection of Emilia's personal experience that struck a responsive chord in other women. She had always taken a personal interest in helping couples avoid divorce and, as the movement grew and became increasingly institutionalized, more formalized methods were developed to help preserve and strengthen marriages. Making a "lifetime commitment" to marriage became one of the milestones in the Creative Initiative involvement process. The stress on lifetime monogamy must have been especially appealing to Creative Initiative women, not only because it reinforced traditional social values but because many of them had given up the opportunity for outside employment and were therefore economically dependent on their husbands. By making marriage a core value, Creative Initiative was, in effect, rewarding its women members for the economic opportunities they had foregone.

In order to help couples build the kind of "responsible" marriage that would allow the wives, and eventually the husbands, to participate actively in the work of the movement, Creative Initiative conducted numerous marriage courses. Like the various self-assessment courses, these experiences were designed to get people to look at themselves and their relationships honestly, build communication, and strengthen commitment—to the marriage, to the community, and to the will of God. Some of the courses were offered at a beginning level and were actually recruiting devices. Others were longer, more complex, and designed to complement the married couples' education in other Creative Initiative beliefs. In all cases they emphasized the importance of giving over getting.

Like all other Creative Initiative programs, the marriage courses were constantly undergoing revision, but for the most part they followed a series of steps that sought to help the participants move through a process of insight and renewed commitment. The courses usually began with an introspective session in which both partners sought to identify "areas of resentment, dependency, hurt, conflict, guilt, non-giving, patterned behavior, and all other manifestations of hate." This was followed by a lesson in conflict resolution in which the individuals were taught to see that their anger at their partner was their own problem, to look for the sources of that anger in their own psyches, and then to resolve both the feelings and the issue that had caused them.

Next, the courses tried to help people to recognize the frame of reference, based on personal history or "conditioning," that each person had in the marriage. Finally, they were guided to find what was "unique and precious" about their marriage and hopefully to realize that the marriage was "a training ground for living the Life of the Spirit."[44]

The material from the marriage courses stressed the importance of communication, sharing, and conflict resolution. From all appearances such techniques were gender-neutral and placed no special obligation on either spouse to fulfill a particular role or make any concession to the other based on sex. Participants were always instructed to come to their own conclusions on such potentially gender-related issues as housework and child rearing. The even-handed approach of the marriage courses is somewhat surprising in light of the group's outspoken support of gender-linked character traits that were supposed to express themselves in specific behavior patterns. There was nothing in the marriage courses that would have prevented a very traditional division of labor between husband and wife, but there was also very little that seemed to advocate it. Other evidence, however, indicates that this neutral appearance did not in fact reflect reality. As might be expected from the group's beliefs about masculine and feminine characteristics, women were frequently advised to take a passive but controlling position within the marriage.

In various courses that involved only women, participants were told that women were the ones who actually set the conditions that determined whether or not a marriage would succeed and therefore they had to take on the responsibility to make it a "creative marriage." There were no "Prince Charmings" to rescue them from their problems, just as there were no great leaders or messiahs to rescue the world. Women had to shoulder the burden.[45] Their control of the marriage was not, however, straightforward. Handwritten notes, evidently taken by one of the participants in a marriage course, indicate that loving a husband was the same thing as "training" him to be good, "encouraging" him to seek enlightenment, and "pushing" him into the Kingdom.[46] The same tone can be found in another set of participant notes that seem to say that a woman could (should?) use sex as a reward or punishment for her husband's behavior. This second set of notes observed that consent is necessary for sex, therefore, the woman "can get the man to do practically anything you want, so want the highest for him."[47]

The use of affection as a device to control men, even for their own good, does not appear to have been either widely advocated or used (although the fact that it turned up in two sets of notes is suggestive).

Much more common was the advice that a woman capitulate to her husband's demands if she were otherwise unable to reach an agreement with him. The admonition "resist not evil," was interpreted within marriage to mean "resist not, period!" "We violate the laws of relationship when we resist," members were told. "For example, if you've a very egocentric husband, something has to give, and it will have to be you."[48]

Although men may have been advised to capitulate to their wives, we found no evidence of such in the historical record. All the examples we found consisted of women surrendering their resistance to their husbands. When they did so, they were often quite pleased with the act and the consequences. In a talk to a low-level course, one Creative Initiative leader told her audience of women how she dealt with a situation in which she wanted to go out to the movies but her husband wanted to stay home. "I would," she said, "respond by staying home with him—fixing something special for dinner and just relaxing with him." If she really had a need to go to the movie, she said, she would make arrangements to go see it with a friend during a matinee in the middle of the week.[49]

Not all women responded to the Creative Initiative philosophy by capitulating. Some seemed to find that the teachings gave them a sense of independent legitimacy that allowed them to claim their own feelings, although those feelings were often expressed in doing traditional woman's work around the home for its own sake, not because they expected some kind of reward from others. It may be that this also involved capitulation, if not to one's husband, then at least to the role of wife.[50] Just as the family was a paradigm for the world, the role of wife within the family was a paradigm for individual behavior in the world. The woman's special feminine qualities were given their primary arena for expression in the family. By bringing love, beauty, and morality to her family the wife could take the first step toward bringing them to the world. By learning to capitulate, both to others and to her role, she could rehearse and prepare herself for the necessity of capitulating to the will of God.

Sexuality

The paradoxical concept of victory through capitulation extended even into the bedroom. For a number of years Creative Initiative used a book by Dr. Marie N. Robinson called *The Power of Sexual Surrender*. Like the group, Robinson placed great stress on women fulfilling their natural feminine role—the crux of her book on how women could overcome problems of frigidity. Robinson, for example, talked about a "masculine woman" who held an important position in business, earned three times as much as her husband, and was incapable of a "normal" vaginal orgasm.[51] Robinson said that the secret to achieving a mature orgasm was learning how to surrender. She believed that sexual relations were a reflection of the greater world, reminding her reader that "in sexual intercourse, as in life, man is the actor, woman the passive one, the receiver, the acted upon." By accepting that reality and surrendering to it body and soul, Robinson said that a woman could achieve the psychological freedom necessary to respond physically to the act of love.[52]

The movement used Robinson's book because it reflected their own view of women. Women could achieve what they wanted not by fighting for it but by surrendering. In an important sense, however, it is misleading to judge Creative Initiative's attitudes by their use of Robinson's book because Robinson stressed sexual satisfaction as a positive goal much more than did the movement. Creative Initiative's neo-Victorian model of feminine behavior included an inherently ambivalent attitude toward sexuality. Most course references to sex were fairly straightforward, advising that the couples look at their expectations and assumptions about sex and try to consider the other person's feelings instead of merely their own. Yet underlying this reasonable advice, there was a subtext that defined appropriate sexual practices very narrowly and implied that sex itself, it not actually bad, was a temporary desire that would be left behind as people moved higher up the evolutionary ladder.

Creative Initiative strongly rejected the unbridled behavior that grew out of the sexual revolution, and leaders of marriage courses were told to "present the community stand on marriage and sex clearly and firmly," and informed participants, that "our stand is not today's norm for the rest of the world."[53] Creative Initiative believed that sex achieved a special role only within the context of a monogamous marriage. When each person in a monogamous relationship was limited to one other sexual partner, something special was constructed from something universal. They claimed that fornication and adultery were wrong because they detracted from this uniqueness and substituted breadth of experience for depth of experience: "How many instruments can one learn to play in a lifetime?"[54]

The clearest evidence of their position on female sexuality was their use of Dr. Melvin Anchell's book, *Understanding Your Sexual Needs*.[55] Creative Initiative admitted that the book was controversial and cautioned that they did not subscribe to everything in it. They did, however, particularly recommend chapter 2.[56] They suggested the book in many of their classes and received permission from the publisher to reproduce and distribute the favored chapter in their courses. Couched in the folksy, anecdotal style so popular in mass-market self-improvement books, chapter 2 related the story of Patty and Bob, an "average young couple." The couple was having problems because after seven years of marriage and four children, Patty had lost interest in sex. Anchell explained that the couple's problems lay in the fact that they had accepted the popular notion that women were as sexually responsive as men, when in fact they were not. There is a "natural female indifference to the sex act," Anchell explained. On the average, he continued, men are capable of three orgasms per week after age thirteen. Women, however, cannot even have a "genuine orgasm" until their mid-twenties. Between their mid-twenties and menopause, Anchell wrote, most women are capable of a maximum of two orgasms per month, whereas after menopause a woman "gradually returns to a neutral or passive attitude."[57]

In other chapters in his book, Anchell railed against "sexpert professors" who claimed that women had libidos as active as men's, he attacked premarital sex, denounced the sexual revolution in general and "free-love hippies" in particular, and referred to oral sex as a "perversion." He implied quite strongly that a woman with a job could not have either a satisfactory family life or a normal sex life. Anchell blamed most of society's sexual problems on the media, which glorified female sexuality and thus misled both men and women into false expectations.[58] It would be difficult to imagine a book on sexuality more at odds with the trends of the time in which it was written—or more in tune with the basic beliefs of Creative Initiative.

As the use of Anchell's book implies, Creative Initiative did not equate sexuality with marital happiness. They considered sex between spouses a legitimate expression of marital love so long as it did not venture into excess, but sexual pleasure was not a goal to be sought of and for itself. Seeking sexual pleasure per se was considered "lust," one of the most frequently condemned human passions. "Lust is an experience of aberrated sexual energy," they believed. "It is a dead end and connected to a powerful pleasure complex," which, if left unchecked, "would become obsessive and destroy the individual."[59] Their writings often referred to sexuality as "the procreative drive," implying that the primary purpose of sex was reproduction. In a discussion of the Old Testament myths, the group explained that Sodom was destroyed because "its name became synonymous with aberrated sex," and that "homosexuality is a violation of correct functioning because it produces no offspring."[60]

In a general sense, it is probably accurate to say that Creative Initiative understood reproduction to be the primary purpose of sex, although it also had its place as an expression of love. Yet the movement never took the Roman Catholic view that each act of sexual intercourse had to carry with it the possibility of conception. Quite the contrary. Not only was nonprocreative sex never condemned but, in fact, the movement placed great stress on the efficacy of birth control and abortion as a means of controlling world population. As an ecologically oriented group, they appear to have been heavily influenced by the zero population growth movement of the early 1970s, and a draft document from that period recommended universal voluntary birth control, to be achieved by "massive education, tax penalties for more than two children, free sterilization, intensified research on safe and convenient contraceptives, and unconditional abortion."[61]

The most direct formal confrontation with the group's ideas about sex came in the C seminar when participants used the "four absolutes" of the Oxford Group to confess their transgressions. The second of these four was "absolute purity," which was "to be looked at with reference to sex." They taught that cultural taboos existed in order to impose some control on sex; otherwise it might get out of hand because "man does not seem to be naturally monogamous." This comment implies that in the area of sex Creative Initiative inverted its basic philosophical assumption that nature was good and that people had only to discover the reality of human nature to know how to act. It would seem that Emilia believed (since the four absolutes came into the movement through her) that people were "naturally" inclined to unacceptable sexual behavior on which the group had to impose a strict code of conduct. To help people discover and confess sexual behavior that might have produced guilt or shame, the group listed seven problem areas: (1) masturbation; (2) incest; (3) childhood sex play; (4) premarital sex; (5) "sexual abnormalities," including, but not limited to, oral sex, anal sex, homosexuality, and lesbianism; (6) pornography; (7) adultery and fornication.[62]

Thus, Creative Initiative tried to confine sexual expression to the narrowest possible area and held out the possibility that members might eventually transcend it altogether. After marriage "normal" sexual relations between spouses were acceptable, but any action that seemed to expand the boundaries of sexual expression and thereby treat sex as an area of human creativity was discouraged. Sex was not to be banned, as for Catholic religious; nor was it to be used in a way open to the possibility of procreation, as for the Catholic laity; rather it was to be accepted as a necessary part of the natural order, good only so long as it was kept under control. The excessive pursuit of sex, like the excessive pursuit of beauty or material goods, could lead a person away from doing God's will by becoming a god itself.

The deemphasis on sex seems to have been linked to the movement's version of the Freudian notion that sublimated sexual energy could express itself through creativity. In one course on the teachings of Jesus there was a long section addressing the issue of lust. Among the questions posed for discussion was: "For the person who had decided to lead the religious life, what is the highest use of the procreative energy?" The desired answer was to "direct these energies toward creative action that benefits all life. This can only be done by loving other people and all life more than desiring our own immediate pleasures and self-interested pursuits."[63] The trick, however, was not to try to suppress the sexual drive—that, said Emilia, would only "reinforce the unconscious and focus attention there." She told the people in the movement that if they redirected their energy, the sex drive would eventually atrophy.[64]

The idea that libido would decrease by itself was borrowed from Gerald Heard who viewed sex and pain as manifestations of redirected psychic energy that would diminish as people moved up the evolutionary ladder and became more spiritual.[65] The sexual drive decreased as the level of psychic awareness increased. One did not achieve a higher spiritual level by repressing sex; rather one worked to fulfill the will of God and the diminution of the sexual drive was seen as a result, not a cause, of leading a successful religious life. Some people in the movement whispered about high leaders in the "hub" group sleeping in separate beds and, although it was not a topic of formal discussion, assumed that they had little if any sex.[66] A young woman who had grown up as a teenager in Creative Initiative wrote, "everybody knew . . . if you were truly a member of CIF (3rd seminar level plus commitment) then you would not engage in oral sex with your spouse."[67] Because there was the widespread belief that the leaders were "better," in the sense that they had achieved greater "totality" in dedicating their entire lives to the will of God, what they did was presumed to be the appropriate model for others. These leaders not only believed that sex was inversely proportional to spirituality, they lived it ("the message and the messenger are one"). The result was, according to one member, that many of the people in the movement suffered from "severe sexual hangups."

The downplaying of sex, even within marriage, and the apparent lack of sexual contact among members not married to each other, had the very functional effect of focusing more of the participants' energy on the movement. Raymond Trevor Bradley has argued that in communes with charismatic leaders particularized relationships are usually suppressed while generalized love is promoted. This could be promoted either through celibacy or nonexclusive sexual relationships.[68] Given Creative Initiative's strong family orientation and moral rigorism, sexual promiscuity was obviously out of the question. Pure celibacy was equally untenable for a group that stressed marriage and children. Thus, they promoted celibacy for the unmarried and looked forward to refocusing their sexual energies as they became increasingly involved in the spirituality of the third age.

Men

Not surprisingly, given the distinctly feminine focus of the Creative Initiative movement, there was comparatively little attention paid to men. There were many fewer courses, many fewer special meetings, and generally less philosophical attention paid to the husbands until quite late in the 1970s when the second generation took over and eventually led the group into secularization.[69] As noted earlier, the women who formed the religious center of the movement appear to have had a profoundly ambivalent attitude toward men. On the one hand, they acknowledged men as the people with the greatest intellectual, economic, and political power, but on the other hand, they blamed most of the world's troubles on that power. They did not believe that they as women could lead the movement into the third age, but at the same time they believed they had to get it started on the right path and educate enough men so that the males could eventually complete the journey. Thus men were both the root cause of the world's problems and its ultimate saviors. It was the women who had to change them from one to the other.

Men in the third dispensation were something like Eve; they came second and were produced out of the body of the women's religion. Their pledges and ceremonies were masculinized versions of the women's, and their courses and ceremonies were often afterthoughts. In addition to the philosophical reasons for the secondary male role in the movement, there was also the practical consideration of time. Creative Initiative women were not employed outside the home; their husbands were. Men had less time, less energy, and generally less inclination to become involved in unconventional spiritual enterprises, a fact that was recognized by the movement, which almost always aimed its recruiting material at wives.

Men never adopted a new name similar to Blessman, but they expected that through prayer, dropping resistance and hatred, mutual criticism, and following the example of Jesus of Nazareth, they would develop the character necessary to take up the burden of leadership. This army would emerge "made up of men who claim their destiny as men, exercising their masculine qualities of aggressive, courageous initiative at the highest level while coming to terms with their feminine components in such a way as to be integrated, resourceful, creative, effective human beings."[70]

The incessant use of the military metaphor to describe the activity of the men was necessary to integrate the Jungian concept of masculine traits with the movement's monistic world view. Because they believed that men were naturally aggressive, they frequently used martial language and symbols (the flaming sword) to express their desire to bring about a peaceful, unified world. Reading the men's material, one gets the distinct feeling that somehow Creative Initiative males were afraid that they would be considered unmasculine if they simply declared their support for peace, love, and unity, a feeling that may have been strengthened by their belief that men had to be shown the way by women and had to develop their own feminine characteristics (their anima) if they were to be successful. By adopting a martial posture, the men were able to dress these "feminine" values in traditional masculine garb and thus integrate the various roles they were supposed to play.

Children: The Second Generation

Creative Initiative taught that "the purpose of the family from the beginning has been to educate the young on how to survive" and that "what is needed now, more than ever before, is for parents to take back the power and responsibility for training their young in what it means to be in right relationship to themselves, other people and the environment."[71] Just as a person needed a spouse to experience one of the steps toward total love, so children gave parents an opportunity to expand their love. For a family to be a true model for the world, it needed two generations so that the older could train the younger to be part of the new age. Having children, however, as virtually all of the members did, not only generated the usual parent–child conflicts but two special problems that stemmed directly from the sect and its teachings.

The first problem might be called the issue of loyalty. Creative Initiative stressed that the family was the paramount social institution and structured most of its rituals around the nuclear family. So one's primary loyalty would seem to belong to the family. Yet the group also believed that the family was only a second step (the individual was the first) toward the ultimate goal of changing the world, and the instrument for that final purpose was the community. For many years, subgroups of cooperating people in the movement were called "family groups" and people in these larger "families" were expected to treat one another like family members, which they in fact seem to have done. So individuals were expected to be loyal to their blood families, to their movement families and, of course, to the movement itself. Loyalty to the movement or commitment to the cause was a measure of "totality," of having surrendered the individual ego for obedience to the will of God. Practically, however, given the limited resources of time, money, and energy, totality as an attitude could not be translated into giving totally in all places. Somehow a way to explain the lack of totality in some areas had to be found.

Second, there was a conflict between the desire of members to make their children active participants in the movement and their realistic recognition that they could not force their children to believe anything. Unlike their parents, the children did not have to go through a process of transformation, nor did they make a conscious decision to commit themselves to the movement. Because they had joined the movement of their own free will and had paid the personal costs of being members of an unconventional religion, the parents were highly motivated. The children, however, were born into the New Religion and for many, establishing independence meant rejecting their parents' religious beliefs, at least for a while. If adults could not force their children to believe, at least they might try to have their children behave according to the Creative Initiative code of values. But their children were growing up in an era of political radicalism, sexual liberation, and drug use. It proved to be even more difficult to get their children to act the way they wanted than to get them to think the way they wanted, although in the end Creative Initiative members appear to have had at least as much success as other parents—perhaps more.

In theory, Creative Initiative took a relaxed view toward parenting; the term they used was "detachment." Their entire childrearing philosophy was based on the presumption that children were not, and could not be, their parent's possessions: "Our children are not our children but the sons and daughters of life. . . . And although they are with us they don't belong to us." All parents could do, all parents should do, was to remember that the message and the messenger were one and lead their lives accordingly. If parents were sure about their own journey, the group said, then the children would be able to see what was the right path for themselves.[72]

Drawing on the work of Erikson, Piaget, Maslow, and other psychologists, the group saw childhood as a series of distinct stages, each with its own characteristics and needs. Creative Initiative explained that children, by the time they entered school, were beginning to look to people outside the family for friendship and models, and they emphasized the necessity of allowing children to develop independence. Although they did not say it in so many words, the group appears to have been trying to minimize the kind of authoritarian parental control that had created "authority problems" for many in the movement. The message seemed to be that if they could raise their children to be as free as possible of destructive parental control, then the children would find it that much easier to discover the will of God on their own.[73] If children were to find authority and support outside the family, however, then it was crucial that those outside authorities be supportive of the ultimate goal of following God's will. Thus, it was obviously best if Creative Initiative children found their closest friends within the movement, and most of them did. It was also important that they saw the movement itself as an extended family to whom they could look for support.

In addition to this religious justification for seeking a detached style of childrearing, there was also the practical matter of parents dividing their time between children and the work. Although there was a continuous series of child-centered activities through the history of the movement, and detachment did not mean laissez-faire, there was also a sense that if parents could realize that their children were independent persons who had to find their own way with the help of people outside the family, then parents would feel less guilty about putting time into the movement and not into their nuclear family. "Do you have a *private* life of fun and work and relationship with your kids?" Emilia asked a group of seminar participants.[74] "Yes" was the wrong response.

People were supposed to give their first loyalty to the group. The sense of community had to be built among adults and between the adults and *all* the children, not just their own. The essential tasks of parents included "caring, concern, honesty, direct encounters, establishing trust, [and] demonstrating and communicating right attitudes and right conduct" to all the children in the community.[75] One of the most frequent comments to appear on our questionnaires from movement children was how much they appreciated the genuine closeness, love, and support they received from adults other than their parents. "Every father was your father," wrote one young man.[76] One of their most frequent complaints, however, was how much time their parents had spent on movement work to the neglect of the family. This view was also shared by some parents, one of whom told us, "I feel the time commitment was out of proportion and caused many parents to neglect their children. People (myself included) were made to feel guilty if they didn't attend meetings, seminars, etc., and were told they were too 'attached' to their children."[77]

Since the movement had always defined its end as transforming the individual and its means as education, the education of children became a central concern. The fullest development of their educational philosophy came in 1972 when they took the logical but short-lived step of creating their own elementary school, called Escuela de Luz, which taught only kindergarten through grade three and enrolled approximately fifty children. When they discovered halfway through the first year that the open classroom format they had begun with was not working, they switched to a more structured and disciplined style. They concluded from this experience: "We saw once again the freeing effect on the children of knowing exactly where the limits are, rather than operating from a personal base."[78] Thus, they interpreted the educational experience of their children as another example of the great paradox—obedience is freedom. The Escuela de Luz experiment lasted only two years. It was shut down because it demanded too much time and effort that the group thought should be going into projects to educate adults, which was, after all, their main purpose.[79]

Most of the Creative Initiative childrens' programs were of a less formal nature. Afterschool, weekend, and summer programs led by teenagers and parents were the most prevalent form for communicating the group's ideas to their children. The education program for children had originally begun as a direct response to the needs of young parents who, by the late 1950s, made up the overwhelming majority of participants. If these people were to take the necessary seminars to deepen their commitment, something had to be done to accommodate their special needs. For these young adults a stay of two weeks (or even one week) at Ben Lomond was a near impossibility since there was no practical way either to take their children to the camp or to leave them for that length of time with somebody else. So, in 1960, Sequoia Seminar ran an experimental "family camp" that included a day camp for the children of adult participants. It was sufficiently successful for Harry to announce that there would be additional family camps in the future. At first, the children's camps were mainly day care with no attempt to achieve an educational function of their own. "It is the experience of the adults which is the really important factor," Harry declared. "If the parents achieve the change which the seminar envisages, the children will be direct beneficiaries for the rest of their lives."[80] By 1969 the summer camp program had expanded to accommodate the children of many of the adults attending "continuation" seminars. Although the prime purpose was still to keep the children occupied while the adults participated in the seminars, Creative Initiative did promise that they would "give the children a good growing experience."[81]

Finally, during the mid-1970s, the camp program reached a highly developed form. Most of the children of members attended camp as campers or counselors or both, and many remember their experiences with great fondness. The camps now had names, Aurora for the girls, Arriba for the boys. In 1973, more than forty adults and fifty teenage counselors cared for over two hundred children, with a budget of more than fourteen thousand dollars. More important than size, however, was the new purpose of the summer camps. No longer content to provide merely a safe place for children, or a "growing experience," the camps were now invested with a full educational and religious purpose.

The camp prospectus for 1973 stated that they wanted campers to learn about the outdoors, "new ways to behave, relate to others, a sense of wonder, and a feeling of belonging to this Community."[82]

An overview of youth activities in 1980 gives some idea of the extensive variety of services that Creative Initiative organized for children. It is also indicative of the kind of services that the group provided for members in its functioning as a sect. Twenty-five of the fifty youngest children, all under age eight, were taken to a camp out of the county to avoid the helicopter spraying of pesticides for the Mediterranean fruit fly that infested Santa Clara and surrounding counties that summer. The fifty children of elementary-school age were involved with various family-centered youth programs, had special seasonal celebrations led by teenage counselors, and could attend either the boys or girls summer camp. Thirty-one junior high schoolers had young-teen groups, Aguilas for the boys, Jovencitas for the girls. They could attend boys' or girls' summer programs, and there were several ceremonies for those young people who had already gone through their Eagle or Spring Maiden rite. High school students (and there were ninety of them in 1980, more than any other age group) were offered a communication course, an organized youth center with lectures and social events, an opportunity to begin studying the Records, and the chance to become counselors in the summer camps. That year they could also participate in the Youth Conservation Corps, a community action program. Finally, the seventy college-age students could participate in two experimental live-in cooperatives, attend special discussion groups with high-level leaders, or supervise the Youth Conservation Corps.[83]

As indicated by the creation of separate boys' and girls' summer camps and other sex-segregated activities, the strong sense of gender distinction that marked the movement's adult philosophy was played out fully at the children's level as well. In fact, the group made a point of promoting parent–child activities that were almost always structured along traditional gender role lines. A particularly telling example of this traditional division of roles can be found in an outline for a series of meetings for teens and their parents. The first day was to begin with "informal discussion while breakfast is being prepared by women." On the second day "girls help get breakfast"; this meal was to be more formal, so participants were instructed, "Men seat wives." After breakfast, leaders were told to "ask girls to clean off the table and the boys to do some task (You might ask them to go out and find a rock.)." The third day's breakfast had no specification as to who should prepare it because it was a cookout, but girls were once more asked to help the women with the fourth day's breakfast while the boys and men met together to "discuss how they could show the girls appreciation of breakfast."[84] There were numerous projects in which boys and girls, especially in their teens, worked together, but there were even more programs that divided children by sex in order to imbue them with what were considered gender-appropriate values.

For boys, the group proposed a complete cycle of activities beginning when they were seven and ending when they were fifteen. Although this plan was not always followed to the letter, the general structure was instituted and for many years was an excellent example of the kind of practical benefits that Creative Initiative provided members of the sect. Each of the activities was designed to help the boys become more independent and self-confident and to give them a sense of their maleness. Boys could not participate in the program unless their fathers did too. Not only did the group believe that the fathers had to be present to be models for the boys, but the activities were thought to benefit the father as well as the son, specifically his "masculinity and identity will be strengthened when he consciously puts himself in the position of leading boys."[85]

The most elaborately developed of the childhood activities for boys was the "Eagle" ceremony. "Eagle" was later changed to the Spanish *aguila* in line with the widespread use of Spanish in community activities, especially those for the children. The ceremony, which took place after the boy had turned thirteen, was consciously designed to be a rite of passage from boyhood to young manhood and, unlike most of the other activities, was overtly and almost exclusively religious in nature. It was intended to be the "high point in [the] entire Boy's Program."[86] Candidates for the ceremony were told that "throughout history, men have recognized the passage of their sons into young manhood with special rites and ceremony." By participating in the ceremony of Las Aguilas, the boys were demonstrating their "acceptance of responsibility of manhood and a willingness to cherish and preserve our religious tradition."[87]

Participation in the ceremony was not automatic. Like all other steps in the Creative Initiative program it was voluntary and, like most others, it also needed the approval of the community. Candidates for the Eagle ceremony and their parents had to demonstrate a high degree of commitment. The parents were required to have reached a point where they were participating in advanced-level seminars, which meant that they had to have been in the program for at least three years. All those concerned, sons and fathers, met for counseling and instruction with peers who had previously gone through the ceremony.[88] The actual plans for the ceremony were approved by "elders in Region to insure quality and appropriateness of Blessing: content, tone, size."[89] And finally, the candidate went through a two-month period of intense religious training in preparation for the ritual, in which he received instruction in the beliefs, ceremonies, and obligations of Creative Initiative.

The Eagle ceremony was intended to be more than a symbolic rite of passage. Within the belief system of the movement, those who went through the Eagle ceremony were seen as separating from their parents, freeing themselves in preparation for commitment to God. The boy's father was told to take "initiative out of internal motivation to pass on what is of value to his son." Although the exact meaning of that rather opaque phrase is not obvious, the implication appears to be that the father would pass on to his son the right and the ability to make decisions for himself. More explicitly, the ceremony was said to "mark the 'first cut' from the family, a move from the family into the brotherhood of peers." In the process the son was transferring his concept of authority "from the family and father to the clan, represented by men other than the father."[90]

This last aspect was formalized by the boy choosing a new "spiritual father" from among the other adult males in the movement. Girls also chose a spiritual mother for their equivalent ceremony. The use of spiritual parents actually worked two ways. For the spiritual children there was a sense of independence from the nuclear family, and for the spiritual parents there was formalization of the communal ideal that the adults were parents to all the children and youngsters children to all the adults. This ceremony confirmed both the young person's progress on the path toward enlightenment, moving away from parents as authority figures, and also reinforced the sense of mutual support and caring so crucial to the operation of the community as a sect. Several Creative Initiative children whom we interviewed or who answered our questionnaire expressed special fondness for their spiritual parents.

There appear to have been many fewer structured opportunities for women to engage in activities with their daughters, but those for which we have records were, like the boys' programs, designed to reinforce the sense of the child as a member of a gender with very specific sex-linked skills. A program to recruit girls to take care of the babies of people attending seminars required that both mothers and daughters agree to be a team, with the mother acting as advisor and emergency backup for her daughter. The girls were told that the experience was worthwhile not only because they would be paid but also because it would give them "the opportunity to prepare for your own motherhood by having a baby to 'practice' on."[91] But for the girls, as for the boys, the highlight of the formal youth programs was the rite of passage into young adulthood—the "Spring Maiden" ceremony.

The Spring Maiden ceremony was an analog of the Eagle ceremony. Like the Eagle ceremony, it was an act of commitment not only by the child but also by the same-sex parent. "Because our work is mystical in nature, this program evolved as a way for mothers to pass on this spiritual heritage to their daughters," said the ceremony announcement. It went on to explain that before her daughter could participate in the program, "each mother must first decide that this work is the focus for her life."[92] The ceremony itself was designed to affirm the "maiden's" "femininity and her uniqueness." The decorations were quintessentially feminine: pink and yellow roses with butterflies symbolizing the metamorphosis of the girl into womanhood. The girls also went through a preparation for the ceremony which at times included learning female crafts like crocheting, candle-making, and flower arranging. They were given lessons on the meaning of the ceremony and on problems faced by teenagers such as drugs and sex. There was also a session on choosing a college (which seems a bit premature for thirteen year olds) and, interestingly, a session on careers. Creative Initiative mothers apparently assumed that their daughters would not only go to college, but would also have careers, even though they themselves did not work or had left their jobs to work in the movement.[93]

Teenagers: Living (And Not Living) The Life

The preparations for the Eagle and Spring Maiden initiation ceremonies were the most formally structured religious instruction given to Creative Initiative children. It was assumed that by the time the children reached their teen years, they would have absorbed the basic principles of the movement, and therefore most of the teen-focused activity was directed at showing the young people how to apply their beliefs, how to "live the life."

The movement mounted two particularly ambitious programs to allow teenagers to put their values into action, one for young men and the other for young women. The men's project began first, in 1979. Nineteen young men, ranging in age from sixteen to twenty-two, were given a six-month training course and sent to work for three months in Nepal. Richard Rathbun, Harry and Emilia's son, had spent three years in the Peace Corps in Nepal and acted as the project supervisor. After their work in the Nepalese villages the participants returned home and, except for high schoolers, decided not to go back to school immediately. Instead, they created an organization called YES (Youth Evolving Solutions). Until they all returned to college in the fall of 1980, the young men in YES lived together and participated in a series of ecology projects designed to get people to use less fuel by riding public transportation, bicycles, and carpooling. Participants lived in a house in Palo Alto that they ran as a cooperative. It was during this project that YES first used a slogan that would be resurrected in 1987 by Beyond War, "Think Globally, Act Locally."[94]

Admittedly jealous that the boys had had an opportunity to do something denied to them, a group of movement girls asked if they could set up a similar project. So for a year, from July 1981 to June 1982, about a dozen young women also lived cooperatively in a house in Palo Alto, creating and running their own community service projects. They called the one-year program "Salvatierra" (save the earth) and, unlike the boys' project, Salvatierra had a very strong religious element. Initially the girls were employed at a variety of jobs, including work on the line in a San Francisco factory and field work on farms in Fresno. Most of their time, however, was spent in religious training, self-improvement, and preparing to teach three one-hour units to elementary school children.[95] A particularly difficult aspect of Salvatierra was the problem that the young women had dealing with adult expectations. One participant had two nervous breakdowns trying to cope with the demands placed on her in that intense living environment.[96]

Although Creative Initiative did promote a process of freeing children from their parents' authority, in no sense did it give the young people carte blanche to explore freely in the world to find their own truths. In place of the parents' authority the movement substituted the authority of the community, usually described as an expression of the will of God. So long as they were living at home, children could rebel against their parents, but when they were living away, among their peers, a more oppressive kind of authority exerted itself because rebelling against one's peers meant risking alienation from friends and community.

Emilia had crystallized her opposition to drinking, smoking, and even dancing as early as 1952 when she spoke out against them at a Sequoia Seminar continuation seminar.[97] Although the opposition to dancing did not survive, smoking and drinking continued to be anathema to Creative Initiative. There was tremendous pressure on the children not to engage in these forbidden practices, to the extent that teenagers were requested to sign contracts agreeing not to smoke or drink alcohol.[98] Although nobody was "forced" to sign such a contract, the teenagers realized that refusing to do so was tantamount to rejecting the movement's core demand for "totality."

The single most common complaint from Creative Initiative children who answered our questionnaire was the criticism and guilt they suffered for not being able to live up to the ideal of totality. In this sense they were no different from their parents who also found the demands for perfection and the confrontations that resulted from their presumed failures the most difficult aspect of their participation. Unlike the adults, however, the children did not have the option of dropping out of the movement. All their parents' friends and, in many cases, most of their own close friends were in the movement, and the costs of rebelling were extremely high. As one respondent told us, "I saw my [non-Creative Initiative] school friends as having lower standards, so I kept many of them at a distance."[99]

The responses to our questionnaire give the impression that Creative Initiative teenagers were more rebellious than other young people of their age and status, but that impression may well be misleading. Because of the strict standards to which they were held, behavior that would have been seen as normal or experimental among their peers was labeled "rebellion" by both the Creative Initiative children and their parents. And, within the context of the movement's demands, it *was* more rebellious than the same action would have been in the "outside" world.

Young men and women who violated the movement's values were made the objects of the same kind of peer criticism that adults experienced. Groups of teens were brought together, one young man reported, "and forced to accuse one another."[100] Although most of the mutual criticism seems to have been directed at personal behavior involving sex, alcohol, and drugs, other aspects of the community's values were also considered fair game. Another young man who remembered being critiziced for being insufficiently masculine (an apparently chronic fear among Creative Initiative men) said, "It was hard to feel good about yourself, but the criticism kept coming in the hope you would become a better person because of it."[101] This process could begin when the children were as young as twelve. The effect was to seriously weaken the self-confidence of some who experienced this group criticism, thus undermining the very sense of self-worth and ego strength that the movement was trying to impart.

As a result of the demand for "totality," many Creative Initiative children reported that they developed a curious combination of hypocrisy and snobbery. Sometimes individually and sometimes as groups, they broke the rules, but they lied about it both to the adults and to some of their peers within the movement. They pretended that they were upholding the standards while leading a secret life.[102] Yet, despite the reports of widespread violations of community standards by teenagers, our respondents also wrote that there was a strong sense of moral elitism among the children. In one sense this is not surprising since it reflects a similar feeling among the adults, but, from all evidence, the adults lived up to their own values and were perhaps justified in feeling superior to ordinary folks; many of the children did not.[103]

Despite their willingness to break the rules of the movement, most of the children who answered our questionnaire ultimately valued their childhoods in Creative Initiative. Many mentioned the benefits of having parents who adhered to a strict moral code and who had worked out the problems in their marriages. Even more important, most were thankful for the values they had learned—even if they had, on occasion, wandered from the strait and narrow. The second-generation respondents tended to be positively disposed toward the movement, and many were active in Beyond War. Yet even those children who did not stay involved with the movement as they grew older usually expressed appreciation for the strong sense of right and wrong and the concept of unity with the world that they had learned from it. In addition, of course, there were those teens who never did rebel and who were able to operate in a world of drugs and casual sexuality without ever being touched by either because of their Creative Initiative training.

Creative Initiative never actually addressed the second-generation problem per se, although they discussed the unique problem presented by children who, unlike their parents, had never made a decision to join the movement. There seem to have been two reasons for this. First, the sect was very new. Every member was a convert and imbued with the fervor of people who had deliberately rejected one value system for another. Although the group had some structure, including an informal hierarchy, ceremonies, and a body of written dogma, it did not have a standard churchlike organization. This meant that children did not have to be formally inducted into membership. Second, as a millenarian movement, Creative Initiative hoped it would be able to change the direction in which the world was moving. No dates or predictions were ever made, but one gets the sense from the group's materials that they thought the balance could be tipped during their lifetimes—some early works made vague references to the year 2000 as a kind of deadline. Given that assumption, the principal effort was always directed at educating other adults. Children's training was not ignored, but growth of the movement was linked to rational decision making by mature adults, and the assumption seemed to be that the children would make their own choice to join or not in the course of their own lives.

Gender and Paradox

The unifying theme in Creative Initiative's approach to men, women, and children in the family was an attempt to integrate opposites. Their dualistic view of human nature made them see human behavior as similarly bifurcated. Some things were either good or bad and thus could be dealt with in a straightforward fashion. Other dualities were more complex. Men and women were seen as opposites but not as good or bad. Likewise, sexuality and celibacy were two ends of a continuum on which they sought a middle ground. Finally, Creative Initiative tried to find a way to reconcile the conflicting demands of family and children on one side and of religious community on the other. In the area of family and gender relationships, Creative Initiative took the same course it did in other areas of awkward dualism. Rather than choosing between what seemed to be opposites, Creative Initiative wove the opposites together in a way that allowed them to explain the apparent contradictions in their beliefs.

For the women, the movement provided a sense of purpose within the traditional woman's role. Raised in an era when it was assumed that women would become wives and mothers and nothing more, these educated women found in Creative Initiative something better, but something that did not compete with their preexisting beliefs about what women should do. The movement assured them that being a good wife and mother was not only their most important task but, when done right, would make their families models for a new world. Working for Creative Initiative was voluntary and, therefore, considered appropriate for housewives. Yet, Creative Initiative demanded more time than would have been acceptable to most traditional-minded women, so it developed both child-care institutions and a philosophy that allowed the women to spend less time with their families and more working for the movement.

Unable to take over leadership until they had changed sufficiently to be trusted with the fate of the earth, men played a less central role in the early history of the sect. Unlike women who were assumed to have a natural understanding of what needed to be done to prevent the apocalypse, men were assumed to have a natural inclination to bring it on. Women had to develop their leadership skills to spread the word to other women and eventually to men. Men had to sensitize themselves to the message being brought by women. For the most part, male activity was an imitation of female activity adjusted for what the group considered appropriate male characteristics. The martial style and language of much of the male activity appears to reflect both the assumption of male aggressiveness and a deep suspicion that somehow either the group or its message was unmasculine, a doubt that had to be countered at every turn.

Whether they were men, women, or children, the people who lived their lives in Creative Initiative participated in a totally integrated religious experience. For them, religion was not a Sunday thing, not an afterthought, not even a separate philosophical entity. Religion was the warp and woof of their existence. It informed all their thoughts and all their actions. It defined their gender identity, their marital relations, and the interaction between parents and children. The family was the first level of collective expression of their religious ideals. The community was the second.

6

Creating a Community of Believers

The Creative Initiative movement adhered to a homocentric approach to reform in which their work always focused on the individual rather than on the society. Personal conversion, not external coercion, was both the starting point and the sine qua non of the group's work. Yet unlike many traditional Christian denominations and Christian fundamentalist sects, Creative Initiative never believed that personal conversion and salvation were ends in themselves. It was not souls that needed saving but the earth and everything on it. Although Creative Initiative sincerely believed that the earth would be saved more or less automatically when enough individuals had dedicated their lives to the will of God, they were not averse to demonstrating on the more limited scale of the community just how such a process would operate.

And if their ideology was certainly important in keeping people in the movement, the sense of community that people found in the group was equally significant. Members frequently remarked that they had a feeling of "coming home" when they first joined the movement. Obviously then, other social organizations and institutions had not provided them with the sense of centeredness that they found in Creative Initiative. The movement successfully integrated social support and philosophical purpose for its members by starting with individual conversion and then making the community of believers the instrument through which the converted person would affect the world: "In a true community the effect of the whole exceeds the sum of the parts just as you as a human being are more than the sum of your physiological parts."[1]

Creative Initiative eliminated the distinction between the person and the group and, at least on the local level, resolved the tension between homocentric and sociocentric methods of change.

Creative Initiative had another purpose for creating a structured community of believers. Emilia and the other women who began the New Religion had embarked on a process of sect-building. By definition, a sect demands strong commitment from its members and provides them, in return, with valuable services—practical, psychological, and spiritual. If it were going to call for a total dedication to the group, then the group had to be organized to provide the necessary rewards. As a community that believed it was part of the Kingdom of God on earth and an example to those who were as yet unconverted, Creative Initiative had to evolve into a carefully organized "city on a hill."

The term "community" was ubiquitous in Creative Initiative literature. Sometimes it was put in quotation marks, sometimes it was prefaced with "new," but always it was there, standing for a sense of collectivity and cooperation that would eventually grow to encompass all humanity. When referring to themselves Creative Initiative sometimes seemed to have a distinct geographic community in mind, but more often they were alluding to a group that was differentiated from the rest of society in attitude and outlook. Like the family, the community of believers was a laboratory for the movement's ideas. If they could demonstrate that their vision was practical for their own educated, professional, and affluent members then they could take the next step. Beyond the community of believers were the civic community, the state, the nation, and the world.

The Community at Ben Lomond

Although the Rathbuns and most of the inner circle of members lived in the Palo Alto area, the spiritual center of Creative Initiative was in the Santa Cruz Mountains at their retreat center in Ben Lomond. The center grew steadily over the years until it encompassed more than 230 acres of beautiful redwood forest land commanding impressive views of the fog-shrouded mountains. To this idyllic setting came the weekend courses, the summer seminars, and eventually, as

Creative Initiative grew and became Beyond War, the large regional meetings.

There still remained the original dream that Harry and Emilia had first articulated in 1945 during the great Camp Minnesing debate, the dream of a center like Gerald Heard's Trabuco College where people could live the life as well as study it. Harry was not content to use Ben Lomond just to carry on a few basic seminars. In 1961, he told the group that with their help, "the Ben Lomond camp can become a center of light to which people who have the capacity—the natural endowment—can come from all over the United States and ultimately the world to light their torches and carry the light back to their own respective centers, there to light other torches."[2] He said Sequoia Seminar was nothing less than "an instrument of God's will, committed to the discovery and carrying out of His purpose for the seminar and those associated with it."[3] And Ben Lomond, as the place where the members gathered to live temporarily and learn, was both the geographic and spiritual center of the community.

Until 1970, all financial and manpower efforts of Creative Initiative went into developing the Ben Lomond property, and even after that they continued to solicit money to expand the retreat. Available financial data are fragmentary, but there is a consistent pattern of the group spending virtually its entire income on Ben Lomond and augmenting that with extensive volunteer labor. Approximately one-third of the operating budget was donated by members, and the rest came from fees charged for the courses and seminars and from the sale of educational materials. Considering the size of the operation—more than two thousand people ate, slept, and studied at Ben Lomond each year—the budgets, which ranged from $78,000 in 1962 to $180,000 in 1973, were relatively modest. Loans were taken out to cover some capital expenses, but they too were modest and quickly repaid.[4]

In 1968 a reporter for a left-wing alternative newspaper speculated that Sequoia Seminar had an income of more than one hundred thousand dollars a year, which was probably very close to the actual figure.[5] The implication, however, that somehow Sequoia Seminar was a very wealthy organization does not seem warranted. The average annual donation at that time was probably in the neighborhood of two to three hundred dollars a year per family, or about five dollars a week, certainly not an unreasonable donation for successful people to be making to what was in effect their church. Some people, of course, gave more.

One exaffiliated couple reported that they gave as much as fifteen hundred dollars a year, but they, and other ex-members, agreed that there was never any pressure to donate, and people gave only what they wanted to.[6]

At no time was there ever any hint that anybody was profiting from their association with Creative Initiative. On the contrary, the leaders appear to have sacrificed more time, effort, money, and economic opportunity than the rank and file, a fact that sometimes seemed to rankle a bit when members were not as willing as leaders to sacrifice for the cause. As early as 1961 Harry remarked, "We have probably not asked enough from the beneficiaries of our efforts." He admitted that what the leadership gave, it gave freely, but added, "for mental and spiritual health it is necessary for one to want to *give*," and suggested that a "tithe" of 4 percent of gross income would be a good guideline for giving.[7]

The Meaning of Community

According to the economic model of church and sect, the greater the demands for sacrifice (of time, money, prestige, opportunity, or any other secular benefit) that a group makes on its members, the closer it is to the sect end of the continuum. Creative Initiative never made the kinds of extreme demands usually associated with groups referred to as "cults." Members were not expected to give up all their worldly goods to the movement, change their names, wear distinctive dress, or move to a commune. Yet, Creative Initiative obviously wanted a lot more from its members than the run-of-the-mill mainline church. In some areas the requirements of membership could be met by participants at relatively low cost. For example, the process of individual transformation may have required a major expenditure of psychic energy, but there was little cost to the person in terms of secular benefits. Similarly, the approved modes of family relations advocated by Creative Initiative were generally consonant with middle-class expectations about the nature of marital and parent–child relations.

Community relationships came at a higher cost. A 1969 outline entitled, with some circularity, "Identity the Basis of Community. Identification with 'the Community' the basis for Identity," began by defining the community of believers as a group that existed beyond alliances with "family, race, nation, vocation, profession, class, denomination." This community of believers was the true basis for personal identity. The outline emphasized the cooperative nature of the community, stating that there should be "no competition, no power drive, no private advantage." Although the "privacy of all related to the individual, his own job, house, children (his responsibility to care for and educate), [and] marriage," were recognized, the paper also stressed the "commonality of all that was related to the work, Ben Lomond, office facilities, contributions of money." It ended by advocating the importance of "subordination of private interest to the whole" and emphasized, *"the more you give, the more is given to you!"*[8] The sacrifices of joining would be rewarded by benefits of membership.

The paper mentioned Ben Lomond as a focus of common concern because it was still the spiritual center in 1969, but it could not be the center of a living community. If, to paraphrase William James's remark about the Unitarians, Creative Initiative believed in the fatherhood of God, the brotherhood of man, and the neighborhood of Palo Alto, then Ben Lomond, a hard hour's drive across the mountains, was just too far away. That same year, however, Creative Initiative would finally begin to create a model living community, moving closer toward, if not exactly fulfilling, Harry and Emilia's twenty-five-year-old dream of an actual, physical community of believers. From the fall of 1969 through the spring of 1970, Creative Initiative underwent one of its occasional bouts of introspection, triggered this time by the end of an experiment in national voluntary service. One of the ideas to emerge from this period of unstructured "brainstorming" was the plan for a "new community" where members could live in a life style more appropriate for the third age.

Creative Initiative had a pattern of beginning new projects with no-holds-barred "brainstorming" sessions that frequently generated initial plans that were admittedly unrealistic, grandiose, and ideologically pure—that is, terribly impractical. One such "working paper" (actually an outline) circulated in June 1970 dealt with the internal political structure and the external public relations of the new group. The outline suggested that clarification was needed in such shared aspects of living as: cooperative food buying, home payment pool, carpools, and internal governance (the Quaker model of consensus democracy was proposed). The author of the document was also concerned with how this *imperium in imperio* would relate to external authorities. Although not stated explicitly, the implication was clear that some people were envisioning the new community as a "city on a hill," a model for the rest of the world.[9]

Communities to Live in

Although the reality never matched the elaborate vision of the planning documents, Creative Initiative did involve twenty-four families in a summer communal-living experiment, that, in turn, spawned a very small permanent new community occupied by ten of the most senior and influential families, including the Rathbuns.

"The New Community Experiment Group," as it was called, met in September 1969 to discuss the possibility of setting up a temporary, experimental community as the first step toward something more permanent. This initial move became possible when Stanford University told them they could use a campus mobile-home park if they could get departmental sponsorship. The mechanical engineering department was enlisted to study the impact of the physical environment on group living and, in March of 1970, an invitation went out to continuation members to volunteer as part of the experiment in group living.[10] Although they had some trouble renting their own homes so that they could afford to move into the trailers, eventually twenty-four families participated in the summer project. From June 21 to September 4, forty-eight adults and fifty-one children lived together, bought, cooked, and ate their food together, took care of one another's children, and tried to help one another practice the kind of cooperative, loving, ecologically sound life style they had come to believe in.

The results were mixed. The participants claimed that they learned a great deal about the problems of organizing group meals, economics, and activities—despite their own assessment of the summer as "wandering, inconsistent and disorganized." They attributed the problems to a lack of strong leadership (hardly surprising in a group that was committed to governance by consensus), lack of experience, and a desire to try many different things. Perhaps the biggest failings were the absence of any discernible spiritual benefits or clear example of how their experiment could be a model for the outside world. They recognized that since the project had been "conceived, designed and carried out by a very select group who have a common religious goal," what they were able to do (and not do) was not necessarily applicable to less motivated people.[11]

The trailer-park experiment fueled a period of intensive interest in and examination of the meaning of the term *community*, which culminated when they paid a hundred thousand dollars for six acres in Portola Valley, a semirural annex of Palo Alto that is one of the wealthiest suburbs in the United States.[12] Although local zoning required one acre per house, Creative Initiative got a variance to build ten houses on their six acres on the strength of their promise to give special consideration to ecological matters and to maintain the common property, which included a charming tudor-style home built in the 1930s.[13] The projected costs for the project ran so far ahead of expectations that the whole plan was temporarily abandoned in March of 1973 when the group briefly considered buying a Catholic convent where the families would live in a single building and have a school, administrative offices, and an auditorium on the same premises.[14] Eventually, however, the costs were controlled, the homes were built, and the ten families moved to Portola Green (as the cluster was called). It is an indication of their high socioecomonic status that this move to custom-designed four-bedroom homes, nestled in a wooded hillside in one of the Bay Area's most exclusive towns, was considered a demonstration of simplicity and moderation and a step down by many of the residents. Their communal life style never quite amounted to the joint ownership of wealth sometimes talked about after the Stanford experiment, but they did make some effort to sustain a cooperative existence. Common grounds and gardens were worked on by all residents. For a number of years evening meals were cooked and eaten in three subgroups, even though each of the houses had its own kitchen. The homes were built without family rooms (but with living rooms) to promote the common use of the old central home that they named "Four Winds." Four Winds also served as a gathering place for more general meetings of the Creative Initiative community, thus giving nonresidents some connection to the Portola Green neighborhood.[15]

In 1977, after only two years at Portola Green, four of the older families, including the Rathbuns and architect William Busse who designed the enclave, decided that because their children had grown and left home they no longer needed the country life-style. They also discovered that living out in Portola Valley removed them from the day-to-day activity of the movement. They sold their homes to younger members and moved into a cluster of five houses in downtown Palo Alto close to

Creative Initiative headquarters.[16] In addition to Portola Green and the five contiguous houses in Palo Alto, there was another group of Creative Initiative members who lived in an apartment complex in Santa Clara about fifteen miles away. Although these small neighborhoods of believers provided an opportunity for cooperation and mutual support, they never became either the demonstration model "new towns" that some people hoped for or the Rathbuns' old dream of a Trabuco-like center for living and teaching. Creative Initiative remained, like most religious movements, a community of spirit and not geography.

Economic Theory and Practice

The attempts to establish cooperative communities were motivated by the desire of members to live their values in a collective environment. The cooperative aspect of the experiments had economic as well as social and spiritual implications. When, in another of the many draft documents, police were rejected as unnecessary, that conclusion was based on the assumption that police usually protected property but that all possessions in the Creative Initiative community would be "active and useful, so they don't need protection."[17] Although in practical terms such a statement may not have made much sense, philosophically it was a powerful expression of a streak of antimaterialism that sometimes seemed to border on Christian socialism. Another draft document from 1970 explained, "The transition from the old to the new will involve the destruction and dissipation of economic power as we now know it." The statement concluded that "man no longer has the absolute right to do as he pleases with his 'property.' Our survival will now depend on our ability to cooperate, instead of our ability to compete."[18]

In 1967, during a period when the men in the movement were trying to define their role in the practical (i.e., nonmystical) aspects of the work, there were a number of meetings on what was called "econolution." The term itself was a catch phrase for the role of economics in the movement and referred both to personal activity and to a broader theoretical perspective. On an immediate level, it addressed the issue of how individuals and the community of believers should raise and spend money. On a higher level, in what they themselves called "the vision," it had as its goal "to feed, clothe and house the world!"[19]

In accord with fundamental Creative Initiative philosophy, however, their vision of feeding and clothing the world was quickly personalized: "Before we can, individually or collectively, move out to solve the problems 'out there,' the necessity remains to move through the issue of economics individually."[20] The issue, they believed, was not constructing a new economic theory—"these programs have been developed in multitudes by experts"—instead, they explained, "economics must be brought to the personal level of values."[21]

The econolution discussion set the tone for continuing concern about economics. Although the Creative Initiative movement never constructed an alternative economic theory, their beliefs that one should not pose an enemy, that all people should be united in their humanity, and that cooperation rather than competition was the way to live did lead them to an undefined position critical of the way the current economy operated. Although at no point did any of these people, most of whom made very comfortable livings in the private sector, suggest the end of market capitalism, they were not reluctant to pass harsh judgment on its effects. A key document from this period summed up their criticism thus: "We are conditioned to things, more things; we are conditioned to money, more money; we are conditioned to profits, greater profits; and we are conditioned to success, and more success, based upon things, money, profits and their achievement. We all know that as ultimate goals these are death. We must find a way to move through this conditioning and move to a new level."[22]

The core of the economic position was moderation. On the one hand, there was no suggestion that people give up a comfortable middle-class life style or sacrifice the education of their children on the altar of the third age; on the other hand, they were quite sincere in their willingness to propose some significant reduction in unnecessary consumption of material goods. One (unimplemented) suggestion in 1975 called for members to put a voluntary twelve thousand dollar cap on their expenditures but not on their incomes. They would do this by pledging to donate one dollar to the foundation for every dollar over twelve thousand that they spent. The hope was that the new life style that would result from this moderate spending pattern would act as a model for people outside of Creative Initiative, inspiring them to pursue a more restrained life style and thus preserving America's natural resources.[23] Although the idea did not appear to have widespread support, there were even suggestions for a "communal life on permanent basis where all money was put in a pot and shared equally."[24] But what the group regularly returned to was the notion that materialism bred competition and competition bred exploitation of people and natural resources. By cutting back on their desire for possessions, people could compete less, cooperate more, and preserve the environment.

Structuring the Community of Believers

As the group grew beyond its Palo Alto origins (and it had always had some members who lived in other parts of California and even other states), it became increasingly necessary to develop some administrative structure to coordinate the educational and religious activities that were the purpose of Creative Initiative. Because of their complexity and mutability, it is difficult, and probably not very productive, to dwell on the organizational details of Creative Initiative. In 1971, for example, there were thirty-eight committees dealing with all facets of the work from scheduling courses at Ben Lomond to reviewing the kind of music played at group functions.[25] The movement prided itself on its flexibility and willingness to change form and structure, and the most elaborate plans could be, and frequently were, dropped if they did not seem to be working as anticipated or if something more interesting caught the attention of the leadership. A note on the bottom of a 1966 organization chart sums up their attitude nicely: "This is not a rigid chart. It is open, flexible and subject to instant change."[26]

Like all small groups with a desire to grow, Creative Initiative had always been fascinated with what might be called the fallacy of geometric progression. Mathematically accurate but socially unrealistic, the theory was that if each member could recruit x number of new people each year (ten was a favorite number in Creative Initiative), then in just a few years of exponential growth the group would have millions of members. Starting with the first ten women, Creative Initiative adhered to a decimal model through most of the 1970s. Ten individuals formed a group; ten groups formed an area; ten areas formed a section; and although there was no designation for ten sections, the ultimate object remained the same. A memo in 1966 reminded members, "Our goal is the world—exactly 7 steps out from the individual." This idea was illustrated as concentric rings moving outward from the individual through group, area, and section, and concluding with state, nation, and world.[27]

For an organization that consistently projected its growth as potentially national and even international, Creative Initiative found it surprisingly difficult to maintain a consistent organizational structure at the local level. The sizes and names of the hierarchical units changed constantly, as did the names and functions of the organizations to which these units belonged. From 1962, when Emilia first shared her vision of the new age, until 1965, the group did not have any umbrella designation other than Sequoia Seminar, which was the legal corporation that owned the Ben Lomond property as well as the name of the summer meetings that studied the synoptic gospels. People who were active in the New Religion aspect of the movement would refer generically to "the community," or somewhat more specifically to "the women's work" and "the men's work." In 1965 when the women of the movement decided to go public with their message they needed a more specific appellation, so they chose "New Sphere."[28]

Two years later, in 1967, the women's group dropped the New Sphere name and adopted the highly descriptive but completely unmanageable title "Woman to Woman Building the Earth for the Children's Sake." At various times this was shortened to "Woman to Woman," then to "For the Children's Sake," and finally to "Build the Earth." The name "Build the Earth" continued to be used until 1977. In the meantime, however, several other terms emerged to refer to different aspects of the movement's work (not counting ad hoc, highly focused subgroups, each of which had its own name, and which will be discussed in the next chapter). The men, who were less public than the women, did not adopt a name until 1968, when in conjunction with a drive for voluntary national service, they started to use the name "National Service Foundation," which they soon changed to "National Initiative Foundation."

National Initiative Foundation became the de facto designation for all of the activities that dealt with the public. It was incorporated as a nonprofit organization to conduct educational programs. It did the initial recruiting and ran the first- and second-year seminars. People who wished to go on for advanced work moved into the Sequoia Seminar program. In 1971 the National Initiative Foundation legally changed its name to the Creative Initiative Foundation, although its function remained the same. It eventually expanded to absorb the women's work under the same name after 1977. Finally, in 1983, the group adopted the name Beyond War to designate its new focus on antiwar activity. Both

Sequoia Seminar and Creative Initiative Foundation continued to exist for legal reasons, but for practical purposes all work of the movement was subsumed in the new Beyond War organization.

In theory, Creative Initiative was supposed to grow beyond the San Francisco Bay Area in geometric progressions of ten. The reality was much more limited. Because there was no actual card-carrying membership process and because the records are incomplete, it is impossible to give an exact longitudinal description of the fluctuations in the group's size. What evidence does exist, however, indicates the number of participants rose from 300 in 1965, the year the New Religion began recruiting in public, to a peak of 1,864 in 1975. Of those, approximately 15 percent were in what were called "outposts," beyond the Bay Area.[29]

The growth curve was inevitably limited by the protracted process for becoming a full-fledged member. The multiyear curriculum of courses and seminars served several purposes. First, a "probationary" period of several years allowed the existing members to see the potential members in a variety of situations and to evaluate whether or not they had a sincere interest in joining "the work." By the same token, it gave prospective members a lengthy period in which to become thoroughly familiar with the ideas and activities of Creative Initiative and to drop out if the group was not what they were seeking, which the vast majority of people did. Perhaps as important, the long introductory period allowed Creative Initiative to introduce their ideas slowly, because they learned from bitter experience that most educated, successful, middle-class people reacted negatively to the religious formulation of their ideas unless they had first been introduced to and accepted the psychological and social implications of the message. In other words, Creative Initiative inverted their own historical process, presenting the effects before the cause, the implications before the explanation.

Between 1962 and 1965, while Emilia and the original ten women were creating the structure of their New Religion of the Third Age, the issue of how to present their ideas to the public did not arise because they remained a private group that sought new members on a one-to-one basis. Then, in 1965, they decided to go public with their New Religion using the name "New Sphere." Taking a more public position raised the problem of how to present a set of new and highly unconventional religious beliefs to people who had no grounding in the Sharman method or the philosophy of Sequoia Seminar.

In an attempt to take their ideas to outside people and attract more women to the organization, members of the group organized a "Symposium for Women" at a local junior college auditorium that seated one thousand people. They worked for months through the winter of 1965 writing and rewriting their speeches because, for almost all women, it would be their first experience talking before a large audience. Then on March 21 they made their pitch to a full house. The fourteen women sat on high stools painted to match the rainbow colors of their dresses—rainbow-colored uniforms and color-coordinated accessories would become a trademark of Creative Initiative presentations.[30]

The language and tone of that Symposium for Women set a pattern that would continue in all of Creative Initiative's public presentations up through and including Beyond War. To outsiders unfamiliar with the movement's specialized language many terms must have seemed meaningless and many ideas equally vague. For example, the group repeatedly referred to itself as "an emerging dynamic community of women." They did not make at all clear just what they were emerging from, what they were doing to warrant the adjective dynamic, or what constituted their community. Only the fact that they were women seemed unambiguous.

The presentation itself began with the assertion that the group was not political, was not a peace movement, and was not a church. It was, they said, "a community of women who are concerned about the atmosphere of crisis in the world." We have notes from eleven of the women who gave talks (we have none for Emilia), and of those eleven not one mentioned religion, the teachings of Jesus, the Kingdom of God, or even individual transformation. Instead, they focused on the need for a good sense of self, for a strong family life, and for an understanding of the role of the individual in society, in space, and in time.[31] One hundred fifty women worked for months to prepare a presentation to a thousand other women concerning a philosophy that emerged both from the study of the Bible and from an experience ascribed to divine revelation from Christ, and yet there was no mention of God or religion. In fact, by stating at the outset that they were not a church, the women gave the distinct impression that they had no religious intent—which was accurate only technically since they, indeed, did not consider themselves a church.

The group's unwillingness to be open about its religious core led to an approach that many people through the years would consider duplicitous, amounting to an intellectual "bait and switch." In fact, to avoid discussing the religious basis of the movement with new members, Creative Initiative ultimately instituted a three-year "probationary" period during which the inner religious truth was withheld. This cautious approach to neophytes had the dual purpose of not scaring away prospective members and protecting actual members from possible social opprobrium. Harry explained the reason for this technique in a talk to the 1970 basic seminar. "We don't want to turn you off until you have found some truths," he told them, "and we couch them in language that is non-religious and which you might be able to take. The language of psychology, anthropology and science."[32] He admitted that they had discovered that they "turned people off too soon by using religious language," and that was the reason why, he told the participants, "you don't get promoted to Jesus until your third seminar."[33]

Within a year of its coming out into the public, New Sphere had created a body of courses that exceeded in number and complexity anything during the Sequoia Seminar period. Their 1966 catalog listed forty-six courses for the winter and spring. Open to all identified members, the curriculum included courses that ranged from the religious to the psychological to the secular. On the religious side were numerous courses on prayer, spirituality, and the clarification of New Sphere philosophy. Those who wanted to explore the psychological dimensions of the work could choose courses on "psychosynthesis" and "psychocybernetics," Jungian theory, group dynamics, and "Growth Through the Marriage Relationship." Finally, there were a whole series of courses designed to improve personal skills that would be useful in New Sphere work. These included public speaking, communications, and even "Atmosphere—Yourself and Your Home," which was described as "a series of six sessions, designed to help improve personal appearance and that of the home . . . it is particularly for those women who are aware that they really need help in this area."[34] All the courses were taught by members of the movement, most of whom do not appear to have had any professional expertise in the areas they were teaching. People who took the courses remember them as uneven but frequently useful.

The development of a complex set of courses served the same purpose in New Sphere as it had in the last stages of Sequoia Seminar. For those who were new to the work, it created an interesting set of educational hurdles that had to be cleared to move up in the informal hierarchy of the group. For those who were experienced it created a continuing menu of "something to do," either by taking new courses themselves, or by developing and teaching them to others. In the absence of regular religious services at which the members could gather to meet and reinforce one another's beliefs, the courses provided a necessary mechanism for promoting group solidarity and did so in a form that mirrored the college education of most of the members. In the years after 1966 the structure of courses became increasingly hierarchical, so that, like college, introductory courses became prerequisites for more advanced study. The net impact was to give the participants a feeling that they were pursuing their new religious values in a manner appropriate to their self-defined mission of education. Build the Earth remained the women's branch of the movement until 1977 and continued to hold both introductory programs to solicit new members and enrichment courses for identified women. But after 1968 the really high visibility shifted to the new organization originally created to promote the national voluntary service plan, the National Initiative Foundation. The national service plan lasted barely half a year. The National Initiative Foundation, however, continued.

Shorn of its founding mission, the National Initiative Foundation became the umbrella designation for the group. The name Build the Earth was reserved for exclusively female activities. Because it was run by men, and the movement believed that men were meant to be more aggressive in the public arena, it attempted on several occasions to broaden its scope beyond sponsoring courses. Even more so than the women, the men tended to downplay their religious roots when they operated in public. For example, the National Initiative Foundation devised a plan in 1969, called "A Model for Mass Community Involvement—The Motivated Community," that was the most fully developed example of this tendency to divorce the product from the source. The men applied to at least three different foundations for funding for a proposed program that focused on the concept of community, although as they used the word it applied to both the community of believers and to the civic community.

Their letter seeking support from President Nixon's consultant for voluntary action contained a number of examples of the ways in which Creative Initiative kept their public identity secular while they were privately functioning as a religious sect. In describing their origins, they mentioned Sequoia Seminar, the original ten women of 1962, and Build the Earth, but their discussion was limited to the observation that these groups experimented "with the educational problem of attitudinal change and motivation to work for the social good."[35] Proposals to other sources of potential support were hardly more illuminating. Their letter to the San Francisco Foundation began with the usual warning of the dire plight of humanity and then summed up their philosophy thus:

The thesis presented here assumes that the specific visible social problems we are now facing are a part of the fiber of all levels of our population and stem from a deep aspect of the human, namely the level of his most basic preconceptions, attitudes, values he holds and which his culture promotes, as well as his motivation toward healthy change.[36]

Syntax aside, it is difficult to imagine what the writers thought an outsider would make of that statement. Unwilling to come right out and explain their religious motivation, fearing that they would be dismissed out of hand, they disguised their ideas in a flurry of words that could only bewilder the uninitiated.

Unsuccessful in these and other attempts to obtain outside funding, the National Initiative Foundation dropped its plan for "The Motivated Community" in 1970. In 1971 it changed its name to the Creative Initiative Foundation. The name Sequoia Seminar, which had first been used in 1946, continued to be the designation for the Jesus as Teacher seminars through 1982, but Build the Earth was absorbed by Creative Initiative after 1977, and the latter was the name by which the group was best known during its period of civic community action in the 1970s. The new name, which had real significance for members, frequently puzzled outsiders. People had trouble remembering it because the words did not seem to mean anything in conjunction with each other. To the movement itself, however, each word had a very specific and important meaning, but one that made sense only in the context of their total philosophy. A recruiting brochure tried to clarify the name by explaining that "creative" meant "being able to use both sides of the brain—the rational and the intuitive," while "initiative" meant "taking charge, being a leader, accepting responsibility."[37] But even this explanation failed to convey the Jungian background of the first word and the element of commitment to the will of God that lay behind the second.

The decade of activity under the Creative Initiative label was essentially ten more years of the same thing. Introductory events designed to attract nonmembers were followed by a lengthy process of involvement that culminated in an initiation ceremony. The experiments in civic community activity begun under Build the Earth and the National Initiative Foundation continued. A project would begin with tremendous initial enthusiasm and work, followed by a brief period of activity, and then be changed or terminated as the group explored some new avenue of activity.[38]

Lying behind the decades of flux in names, courses, and programs, was the desire to expand the community of believers. To do this the group needed to communicate to potential members what they believed, what they were, and what they could mean for people who joined. None of these steps was as easy as it seemed because all of them involved coming to grips with the issue of presenting a new religion to the outside world and thereby risking being labeled a cult. If they came to be perceived as a cult they would find it more difficult to recruit new members and existing members would be forced to pay an even higher price for continued affiliation.

Statements of Belief and the Problem of Candor

Statements of belief posed a particular problem because the general population was likely to reject a creed that continued to be based on the conviction that the believers were instruments of God and members of a community that would be the salvation of the world. Yet, that was what everyone in the movement believed. Even Harry, who always prided himself on his more objective and rational approach to religious matters, was swept up in the vision of a new age. "All indications are that *this is the time*," he wrote to his son, Richard. "We are calling it the *Third Dispensation*." Like Emilia and most of the identified people, Harry believed that their mission was divinely inspired. "The work we are engaged in," he told Richard, "is a mystical work; it is directed from a plane of knowledge and intention far above that of the purely human (and that continues to be verified) so 'the sky is the limit!' "[39] In its own eyes the community was not a messianic movement, because rather than following a messiah, they were the messiah. In a letter Harry explained their thinking as follows:

We have talked about our being a community in which every member is a carrier of the message, a "messiah," and that the "second coming" dreamed of in traditional Christianity is thus corrected and realized in this *community* of people—not in a special individual (and certainly not in one who is a judge and executioner!)—who *have* the answer to the world's need, and who are demonstrating it in action.[40]

Public statements of belief had to be consistent with these millenarian–messianic sentiments, while at the same time soft-peddling them lest they put people off. For the first few years, while Emilia and the early followers were developing the New Religion, Sequoia Seminar continued using the statement of general principles it had developed through the 1950s, still based heavily on Sharman's ideas.[41] With the coming of New Sphere and Build the Earth, however, the movement entered what would be a prolonged period of conflicting styles, sometimes being so vague as to be misleading, and sometimes allowing their deep concern and commitment to overrule their caution so that they expressed their values directly.

There was real danger in frankness. In May of 1968 Build the Earth published a position paper entitled "This We Believe." In it appeared the statement: "Revolution is the key. Revolution in home, church, government, economics, education, sex, race, culture, art and science."[42] The quote was intended to make the point that society was undergoing revolution in all facets of life; it went on to explain that Build the Earth was also revolutionary because it wanted to bring about a new age of peace, freedom, and cooperation. However, that one passage was quoted several times out of context to brand the group as radical.[43]

At first during the early New Sphere period of 1965 and 1966 the group presented itself in a way that made it clear at the outset that they were a religiously oriented movement, if not a new religion. For example, in a 1966 sermon to the Unitarian Church of San Mateo, Harry explained that the third dispensation had arrived and mankind had to move beyond Christianity just as in the second dispensation Jesus had tried to move the Jews beyond Judaism. He called for new symbols for the new age and told the congregation that they were the second coming of the Christ who would save the world. Aware that these ideas might strike his audience as bizarre, he told them that they must be willing to "be called heretics, kooks, arrogant, blasphemous" because true leaders always suffered such accusations.[44]

In 1967, however, the group recognized that their candor was sometimes counterproductive, and a new curriculum was developed "in response to the need to communicate the religious concepts in nonreligious terminology." The new "Seven Steps to Reality" curriculum was the first in a long line of efforts to secularize the religious language without losing the religious message.[45] So long as the group had perceived itself as an extension of Sharman's work, that is to say, as long as it was just Sequoia Seminar, its sole stated purpose was to explore the teachings of Jesus, and those who did not want to do that did not join. Once it had transformed itself into the religion of the third age and the communal personification of the second coming of Christ, then it had an obligation to spread its ideas and, ironically, one of the ways it did so was to downplay the very religious message it was attempting to disseminate.[46] In 1971, when a reporter asked one of the leaders if Build the Earth were "a new answer to Christianity, the new religion?" the somewhat evasive answer was, "Well, in a way it is. But woman has never taken it seriously."[47]

Because they feared others would misunderstand their responses, evasiveness in the face of specific questions about the religious nature of the movement was explicit policy. One ex-member referred to it as "the Strategy," that is, to tell the truth, but not the whole truth.[48] When confronted head-on by a newspaper reporter, Richard Rathbun, who became president of Creative Initiative in 1976, avoided using the term "new religion" but did acknowledge that they followed the teachings of Jesus. He said that "religious words" tended to drive people away but that they never denied their religious foundations when asked.[49]

This unwillingness to be completely open invoked keen displeasure from some attendees at Creative Initiative activities who thought the events were one thing only to find out they were something else. One man, who spoke warmly about the benefits of the marriage seminar, went on to explain that he was "appalled at how an essentially sectarian group could so cleverly and brazenly disguise their religious intent."[50] Another charged the movement with being as dogmatic as any established religion, but unlike them unwilling to admit it. His response to the usual statement that the group's ideals were printed in the Challenge to Change course (itself not available to the public) was "Bullshit!" "Specifically," he charged, "the community has a closed mind and holds dogmatic positions in the areas of human sexuality, the roles of men and women, the meaning and significance of a certificate of marriage, etc."[51]

So deeply was the religious message buried during some periods that people were sometimes active for several years before they realized the psychological work was built on a religious foundation. One long-time member reported that it was two years before he understood that Creative Initiative was a religion, but by that time he "liked the movement enough to put up with the religion, eventually coming to really appreciate the Teachings of Jesus and finding it more valuable than anything else."[52] Yet even people who eventually accepted the religious basis of Creative Initiative and committed themselves to "living the life" were frequently uncomfortable with the initial lack of candor. One fourteen-year veteran said that while the group purported to be "straightforward and honest," it had "used very devious methods in order to attract new members" and thereby violated its own rule that the ends do not justify the means. He remembered being specifically "instructed to avoid mentioning [religion] to new people." They were told to answer the question honestly if it should arise but not to bring it up themselves.[53]

The Functioning of a Sect

Whatever their hesitation in publicly declaring themselves a new religion, privately the members of Creative Initiative functioned as a religious sect. Their religious philosophy and ceremonies were described in chapter 3, but their sect behavior was not merely a matter of belief and ritual but consisted also of the pattern of demands they made and rewards they provided for their members. Despite bland public statements that they had nothing really new to offer and were merely teaching the great religious truths of the ages, Creative Initiative did believe that it was a new religion and the precursor of the third age. Hoping at first to maintain some of their ties to the mainstream churches, the group tended to paint itself as an ecumenical movement during its New Sphere period. Indeed, in defining itself it stated, "We do not seek to build new political or religious organizations; instead we seek inspired human spirit to operate within and supplement these structures."[54] In 1966, apparently in this ecumenical spirit, they managed to attract half a dozen ministers from the Palo Alto area to a special ecumenical weekend.[55] A minister who did not attend later claimed that those who did were "tricked" into going and allowing their names to be used in New Sphere promotions under the guise of ecumenical activity.[56]

The minister's suspicion would appear well founded, because all evidence points toward Creative Initiative using the churches primarily as a recruiting ground, a practice they continued until at least 1972.[57] So long as there was only Sequoia Seminar, an uneasy alliance could exist between the churches and the movement, but as harbingers of the third age, members of Creative Initiative saw the churches as irrelevant at best and at worst as stumbling blocks on the road to continuing human evolution. There were reports that from the very beginning of the New Religion phase Emilia demanded that women choose between the movement and their churches.[58] In fact, almost all members of Creative Initiative had to give up their outside church affiliations by the time they went through the initiation ceremony. In one interesting case, a Presbyterian minister who joined in 1969 wrote about the intense pressure he felt to leave his congregation and church. Eventually he did leave, but only after the top Creative Initiative leadership had passed down the word for others to leave him alone. In addition, his decision to join Creative Initiative was substantially facilitated by his discovery that both his father and grandfather had studied Jesus through the works of Henry B. Sharman.[59]

Having gotten wind of the stories that people were being "forced" to leave their churches, *San Francisco Chronicle* religion columnist, Lester Kinsolving, wrote a very critical piece on the group that quoted someone (who sounds very much like Emilia) as saying, "Christianity has evolved to its highest level . . . New Sphere is the next level . . . Now that the church is out of it, nobody cares what side it takes," and cited examples of couples leaving their churches after they joined New Sphere.[60]

Kinsolving's column branded the movement a "cult" and complained that all his attempts to get straight answers about their ideals and values were met with vague generalities. Although he apparently did not know of Emilia's connection to the Oxford Group, he compared New Sphere to Moral Re-Armament because both groups seemed to focus their attention on "attractive and sophisticated young couples." Ex-members would sometimes use the pejorative term "cult" when discussing their experience with Creative Initiative. One such person described the "deconditioning" process—during which new members rid themselves of the effects of prior authority figures—not as preparation for accepting the will of God but as preparation for accepting the authority of the group.[61] A three-part series that ran in the *Oakland Tribune* in 1976 included the following headlines and comments: "CIF: Cult or Way of Life?" "The CIF: Atomic Age Zealots," "a mystical cult," and "a movement of 'middle-class Moonies.' "[62] Although the content of the articles did not live up to the sensational headlines, they were the kind of publicity that perpetuated the idea that Creative Initiative was a cult.

The label "cult" was, however, clearly inaccurate. As highly educated and reasonably sophisticated adults, the members of Creative Initiative worked hard to avoid the cult label, and the continued success of the movement clearly depended upon the members reassuring themselves that they were there of their own free will and by virtue of reasoned judgment. A long-time member reported, "My experience of early CIF has enabled me to see how cults like Moonies and Jim Jones could take over people's thinking for them." The saving grace, he said, was that "people were always free to leave, which they did."[63] The leadership, too, was acutely conscious that it was constantly in danger of becoming dogmatic, which would have been a violation of their claims to scientific objectivity. "The community itself must avoid becoming another orthodoxy which prescribes for its members exactly what they should do," warned an early description of New Sphere.[64] "We are constantly aware of the possibility of errors and aberrations," admitted the author of another early position paper. "We know of failures of other groups with utopian aims. Ignorance, naiveté, selfishness, fanaticism, organization, infiltration . . . all are dangers which we must guard against."[65]

The role of the leadership was particularly problematic for many members who took the analytic approach at face value. There was a reluctance, perhaps inevitable, on the part of the inner leadership to share their authority with newcomers even though Creative Initiative assumed that it would spread by training new leaders who would, in turn, train new leaders, ad infinitum. In actual practice, not only did the leaders relinquish power slowly, but there was some feeling that they also cultivated what one member called "a cult-like leader dependency."[66] This analysis could be somewhat misleading, however. It must be remembered that most of the complaints were aimed at a relatively large group of Palo Alto–based leaders, not specifically at a single prophet figure. Harry simply did not have the personality to be a cult figure. Emilia, by contrast, could easily have stepped over the line from leader to prophet. She was aware, however, of the tendency of women in particular to endow her with supernatural insight, and she usually refrained from demanding personal loyalty. Indeed, she was primarily responsible for preventing the formation of a cult around her by her insistence on sharing insight and responsibility among the group. Although she was usually the spark plug for change, she was careful to provide the membership with an opportunity to criticize and confirm her ideas. Whereas Emilia's propensity for brusque critical confrontations with members in whom she perceived faults was a problem for some, most members found her to be an inspiring spiritual leader, a helpful counselor and confidant, and a role model.

To the outside world, the group always described itself as leaderless. None of the group's presentations or publications carried any credits (except Harry's book, *Creative Initiative*), and the dedication to anonymity was explained as an expression of the collective dynamic of their movement. In an early speech, one of the long-time leaders denied there was any "hierarchy of human authority." He said that nobody was in charge and that everybody took responsibility.[67] In fact, of course, there was a clear and universally recognized hierarchy within the movement with Emilia and Harry at the top, a handful of old allies from the Sequoia Seminar days under them, and then a slightly larger number of inner-core people completing what was usually referred to as the "hub." In an early draft of his book, Harry presented an unexpectedly candid rationale for this structure. Having just defined the group as a "province" of the Kingdom of God, he then explained that within the province there would be a hierarchical leadership headed by an "elite." Membership in the elite would "be based on such qualities as wisdom, breadth of experience, natural and developed gifts of leadership and initiative, and the ability to evoke the loyalty and cooperation which the religious commitment calls for."[68] That particular explanation never made it to the final version, but it accurately describes the structure and probably the attitudes of the leadership.

The perceived abuses of power were not the cultlike excesses of a prophet but the more sectlike problem of an inner core of administrators, most of whom had roots in the Sequoia Seminar period, and who were reluctant to entrust their movement to newcomers who might not share their commitment and who certainly did not share their history. In theory, and to some extent in practice, the movement held that "the full and equal worth of every human being is a basic fact to be recognized," and, therefore, the "consent of the governed: that is, of the entire group, needs to be obtained before important policies initiated by the leadership and affecting all are put into operation."[69] But the consent of the governed was often sought only after the self-appointed governors had already made the basic decisions.

The opportunity to lead was the reward for commitment as defined and interpreted by the existing leadership. "People who were in leadership were the very important ones and really could do nothing wrong," one member wrote, "while the rest of the people were around to get confronted and do the grunt work. People vied for the leadership and the status that went with it."[70] Just what individuals or couples had to do to become leaders was not always clear to the members. Several respondents to our questionnaire used the same phrase (clearly Emilia's): People either "have it" or "do not have it," but "it" was never defined. If, however, you were deemed to "have it," you not only could lead your own study groups, you could also become part of the informal hub leadership group, referred to by some as "the elders," and it was they who tried to insure that members toed the mark in "living the life."

Because they had few other sources of affirmation, many women were particularly hurt when they were found wanting and denied the opportunity to lead and, in turn, resented the "dominant and aggressive, left-brained, masculine" women who held authority.[71] A woman who joined the group in the mid-1970s reported that on one occasion her son was questioned in front of her as to whether she "was *really* living a religious life." In retrospect, she was not sure why she "put up with it" but felt that the "leadership took liberties with peoples' lives that were beyond what was appropriate." She did not approve even at the time but acquiesced, she said, because if she had said anything "it would be turned into MY problem . . . it always was . . . and I would be OUT of an organization which had important goals."[72]

Although there was no formal process by which nonconforming members were tried and banished, those with an "attitude problem" were asked to reflect on whether they might not be happier in some other situation. The tight homogeneous structure of Creative Initiative insured that people either changed or left. If anything, the group bent over backward to avoid attracting and keeping people who did not share their philosophy, and it was this tendency to be exclusive rather than inclusive that differentiated them from the more heterogeneous "cults." Even critics pointed out that the movement was not rigidly structured and did not try to trick people into joining or overwhelm them emotionally (brainwash them) to get them to stay. Quite the contrary, the formal governing structure was loose, and numerous "escape hatches" were built into the involving process to permit people to leave gracefully if they discovered that they were uncomfortable with the group.[73] For example, leaders of an introductory course followup were reminded that the meeting was not only a way to attract new members, it was also a way to screen them. "No one who decides to continue," said the instructions, "should be able to say that he didn't know he was expected to 'do' anything." And people who were judged not ready to take on the commitment of action were to be discouraged from going on.[74]

Clearly, then, Creative Initiative never attempted to cast a wide net. The selectivity, even exclusivity, of the movement was one of its main attractions to those who could qualify. Furthermore, unlike the better-known religious "cults," Creative Initiative never tried deliberately to manipulate people into psychological or financial dependence on the group. Nevertheless, if we substitute the more neutral word *sect* for the pejorative term *cult,* then Creative Initiative's exclusiveness was certainly an important component of sect formation. Participants who completed the first-level A seminar were asked, among other things, "Do you feel at one with every individual in this group?" They were told, "Each A Seminarian must see himself contributing money, time (two nights a week), energy (two work camps a year)."[75] In a first draft of his codification of Creative Initiative philosophy, Harry included the passage, "If you were to apply for training for membership, how would you catalog for yourself the assets you could contribute to the community and the mission?" and the first two he listed were "financial and material."[76] Significantly, this section was left out of the final version, presumably because the expectation of commitment, like the religious nature of the movement, had to be introduced slowly.

Certainly if the critics who called Creative Initiative a cult had seen the statements of purpose that circulated during the late 1960s and 1970s they would have been more convinced than ever that the level of commitment demanded from members went well beyond anything required by mainline churches. One such statement, a pledge for men in the New Sphere period, which may not actually have been used, began with a doomsday preface: "People are consumed in war, riot, racial hatred, and moral decadence. We crouch in isolation, fearing in others the murderous impulses we ourselves possess. I must begin now to change the world or we will continue our downward plunge, until death."[77] Acknowledging that a new age was coming, the signer of the document promised to dedicate his "total life and energy" to fulfilling the work. He promised to "rise above desire for power for myself, my group, or my nation" and further pledged to rise above the desire for wealth and possessions, the desire to escape his obligation through recreation, to forego charitable work in outside organizations, and to "rise above desire for indulgence of bodily appetites."[78]

As this pledge and similar ones used later indicate, most of the members' free time was dedicated to working for the group—for women who were pressured to give up outside employment, this meant virtual full-time work for Creative Initiative.[79] Eventually a significant number of men either retired early or took sabbaticals to devote themselves full time to working for the movement. Just as they divorced themselves from other churches, most group members appear to have divested themselves of outside friends. It was not that they were in any sense "forbidden" to have friends who weren't in the movement but that total commitment left them no time for anything else, and so friendships naturally revolved around the activities of Creative Initiative.[80]

The drift away from outside friends as couples became more deeply involved in Creative Initiative work was a natural consequence of the demands for time and commitment, and it took place without any pressure from the leadership. Friendships with couples who left the movement was another story. Ex-members rarely denounced the movement or its principles and thus continued to share a personal history and values with the friends who remained in Creative Initiative. Yet rather than allowing the bonds of friendship to dissolve slowly (as they almost certainly would have in most cases), couples who remained in the movement were told to sever all ties with those who left. One member used the term "shunned" to describe how defectors were treated. The leadership told members that the dropouts needed "space" and that leaving them alone was "the loving thing to do." There reportedly was a great deal of pain, however, on the part of those who left when they discovered they had given up not only the formal community of Creative Initiative but the personal friendships as well.[81]

The expectation of time, energy, and exclusiveness made by the group was one of the major reasons that people dropped out. In a letter of resignation, one couple explained that the "demands for total commitment to the life of the Community" made it impossible for the husband, who was involved in nuclear research, "to speak out as a qualified and independent scientist" and also made it impossible for them to continue their outside professional and church activities.[82] Harry confirmed the seriousness of this problem in a letter to Richard when he wrote, "We continue to lose people from involvement in the 'mission'—in the work in which we are engaged. And whatever the reason they assign, it almost invariably turns out that dedication to the mission proves to have more implications of demand as to what they have to do than they are willing to meet."[83] Interviews with six ex-members in 1979 revealed that all of them left because "the unending series of meetings often kept them out of the house for several nights in a row and away from their children."[84]

Creative Initiative leaders were sometimes willing to admit publicly that members were expected not to drink or smoke or be unfaithful to their spouses.[85] But neophytes who accepted the group's assurance that it had no dogma and did not dictate life style could be in for a rude awakening. One new member was surprised and distressed when he was told it would be "inappropriate" to serve wine that a guest had brought to an introductory dinner. He asked, "Does C.I.F. say 'Thou shalt not drink wine'? Does C.I.F. have *any* 'Thou shalt nots . . .'?"[86] There is no easy answer to the last question. Formally there were none. Informally there were a great number. Similarly, there was no formal dogma, but the philosophy codified in the courses and ritualized through the ceremonies became for all intents and purposes a dogma. What irritated neophytes and raised suspicion in outsiders was the group's unwillingness to admit that they were a religion that placed the same kinds of limits on thought and behavior as all other religions.

Obviously, then, there were high costs involved with being a member of Creative Initiative. Even if the pledges were not taken literally, and the evidence is that they were, people were making an explicit commitment of the strongest kind. They not only gave up their churches, their friends, their time and money, they also agreed to change their life style and reorient their goals from personal material aggrandizement to spiritual growth and concern for the commonweal. The group sought to strike a balance between the demands of individual life and the demands of the movement, and, once again, that balance kept it from going off the deep end and becoming an all-consuming "cult."

The high costs required high rewards. If they could not be the traditional rewards of private, middle-class, suburban family life, then they had to be something else. The economic model predicts that the higher the cost of joining a group (i.e., the most sectlike the group), the higher the rewards that people will require to remain active in it—and those rewards have to be practical as well as spiritual.

Long-term members of Creative Initiative continually cited the sense of community they found in the group as one of the important practical reasons for joining and remaining in the organization. Time after time in answering our questionnaire members spoke about the quality of people in Creative Initiative. They were described by one respondent as "dynamic, interesting, intelligent, *caring* and genuinely interested in others."[87] Another said he could not "recall any such effort [of cooperation] in my church, or on the job in my profession."[88] Moreover, because of the great stress on sexual probity and the integrity of family, the working relations between men and women within the group appear to have been marked by a singular lack of sexual tension. A psychotherapist member said he "had never encountered any organization, business, professional or religious, where there was not at some level, a pattern of sexual seductiveness or flirting going on among some of the members."

Yet in his eight years in Creative Initiative, he claims never to have encountered or heard of any, even in his capacity as a psychotherapist for certain group members.[89]

Ultimately, however, it was not simply the quality of the individual members but the quality of the community that held people in the group. "It was," said one woman, "an extended family." She knew that "if someone was ill, meals would be brought in, children would be taken care of, the house would be cleaned, etc." This was affirmed for her every Sunday when the family gathered to light their candles and repeat, "We are families of Light and we have come from the Place of Light."[90] She reported that the members of the family groups showed "a tender interest in one another, often pitching in to baby-sit and cook for members in difficult straits."[91] The support community, particularly among women, provided a sense of belonging and friendship that was both practically useful and psychologically fulfilling because it was based on the belief that their assistance to one another reflected a model of enlightened humanity that would save the earth.

Men, too, gave each other practical as well as moral support. During the 1974 economic slump in high-technology-oriented Santa Clara Valley, a special task force of men established a project that helped those out of work organize their search for new positions.[92] Although they deliberately avoided setting up a placement service, in fact a large group of men eventually found work at ROLM Corporation, a manufacturer of computerized communication equipment, one of whose founders, Gene Richeson, had retired to devote full-time service to the movement.[93]

For some, the sense of community could become stifling. People inside as well as outside the movement found that there was a tendency for everybody to begin looking and sounding alike. For women the pattern was obviously set by Emilia. Her style of dress, her pet phrases, even her voice inflections were picked up by others for whom she had become a role model. The source of male homogeneity is less obvious, but it was still there. Several members expressed relief that with the transition to Beyond War there was more variety in the membership and less informal pressure to conform to a community standard.[94]

The family was a vital component of Creative Initiative's concept of community, and virtually every person who responded to our questionnaire said their marriage was improved or even saved by having joined the movement. There was a strong sense that the courses they took gave them insight into their own problems, their spouses' problems, and a forum in which to talk out their mutual difficulties. Moreover, because of its assumption that both partners in a marriage would work in the movement, Creative Initiative gave couples a common interest beyond their home and children. Fairly typical was a comment from the evaluation of a woman who attended a 1975 seminar. She noted that "the most important factor leading us to seminar was a crisis in our relationship. We had reached the point of decision—either we get the relationship into shape, or we end it." She was a woman seeking a solution to a specific problem, and Creative Initiative was simply one of a number of "courses and experiences" she had tried.[95]

The practical benefits of being part of a loving community were recognized as extremely important by those who were members. Ultimately, however, those people who chose to stay with Creative Initiative did so because it fulfilled both their need for community and their spiritual needs and provided them with a sense of purpose in life. Community was not enough by itself. People also joined Creative Initiative for the same reason that they joined any movement that promised to answer life's larger questions—they had the questions but had not yet found the answers. Asked in 1979 why they had joined Creative Initiative in the first place, several ex-members included both community and a sense of spiritual purpose in their explanations. They wrote that "they were at turning points in their lives and they were looking for support, acceptance and sense of belonging."[96] "I felt the values of family life, of women taking their place in the world for the cause of 'saving the world,' were paramount in my life," reported a member. "It is wonderful to have a mission in life and CIF provided the right one for me," she concluded.[97] Not a few of the members were self-defined "seekers" who had tried a number of New Age and human potential movements (est was frequently mentioned) before finding what they were looking for in Creative Initiative. They spoke about "coming home" when they found Creative Initiative, but they found home only after knocking on a lot of doors of houses that looked very much alike.

Recruiting New Members

The ultimate purpose of the Rathbuns' work was to "bring the entire world of men under allegiance to God."[98] Central to the success of this monumental task was the belief in the geometric growth curve to be realized as each participant recruited a specific number of new members each year. Creative Initiative was a movement that legitimized itself in terms of its potential growth but whose real growth was limited by its desire, inherited from H. B. Sharman, to attract only successful, well-educated people. They wanted people, said Harry, "who can be motivated here to carry forth the torch—to spread the good news—to become motivated for the life that God desires, which means becoming infectious sources of inspiration to change, to action and to illumination for others."[99] In 1961 Harry drew up a list of the kinds of people he hoped to attract to the movement. They included business executives and leaders, teachers, college faculty and staff, graduate students, professionals such as doctors and lawyers, and church lay leaders (although ministers were pretty much discounted). Even as late as 1968, when discussing geographic expansion, university towns were preferred and church groups were targeted as excellent sources of recruits.[100]

The major thrust of recruiting, usually called "outreach," was through one-on-one contacts. A 1967 memo urging participants to recruit more actively was unequivocal: "There is no excuse," it said, "for each person or couple not getting at least 10 people to their homes to hear about this work."[101] Members were urged to use their own positive experiences as a basis for contacting friends, parents of their children's friends, colleagues, and fellow members of civic and church groups. Once contact was made, they were told to send the prospective members brochures (which were to be kept "in your coat pocket, purse, or desk for opportunistic use") and then to phone the person again. "Follow-up. Follow-up. FOLLOW-UP. We KNOW that personal follow-up does the job," said a 1966 recruiting memo.[102]

During the first few years after Emilia's religious vision, while the group still retained some of its ties to the established churches, they defined one of their tasks as "sorting out church member people for pulling together identified people in their churches to actually launch New Sphere."[103] The "people" referred to were invariably women. "*Lead off with the women*" advised a 1968 recruiting memo.[104] Women had more free time to devote to the movement and, since women were the ones who made most of the initial contacts, it was obviously easier for them to approach other women. In addition, of course, in its early years Creative Initiative was primarily a women's movement. Because of the heavy stress on the family, however, neither women alone nor men alone were satisfactory members. The movement wanted couples. Indeed, when initial contacts were made with either men or women, Creative Initiative found that the new people did not retain interest unless their spouses became involved. Special efforts were always made, therefore, to involve the husbands and wives of new recruits as soon as possible.[105]

The common thread that ran through all the recruiting techniques was food. Beginning with the student teas and dinners they held before the war when they were recruiting for Sharman's seminars, the Rathbuns always placed great store in the effectiveness of food as an attractant. The meals themselves provided additional opportunity to present the ideas of the work and to get a commitment for further participation.[106] With a long history of etiquette instruction dating back to her college days in the YWCA, Emilia and other leadership women undertook to teach hostesses about the proper food (butter rather than margarine), table linen (cloth rather than paper napkins, pink preferred), and decorations (fresh flowers). The instructions on proper form were not hard and fast, and were always presented as suggestions rather than requirements. Nevertheless they seem to have been universally followed.

In what might be called the "classical period" of Creative Initiative, the mid-1970s, when it achieved its most developed form, the recruiting process was raised to a highly structured art. Potential hosts for "introductory evenings" were given instructions at a special "recruitment preparation meeting." These preliminary meetings began by stressing the religious importance of attracting new people to the mission and by reminding them that Jesus also recruited.[107]

The second part of the preparation meeting, called "clarification," consisted of sample questions designed to get the recruiters to clarify their beliefs, and thereby their answers to issues that might be raised by recruits. There were twenty-one clarification questions indicating the kind of questions raised regularly. Along with general points about the history, methodology, and governance of the movement, the sample included questions about the religious aspects of Creative Initiative and its relationship to established churches, the lack of minorities, the emphasis on married couples, the upper-middle-class membership, the impact of membership on one's social life and children and, finally, questions as to what the members hoped to accomplish for themselves and for the world.[108] Although it may have taken some people several years to discover the religious nature of the work, these questions indicate that others frequently perceived the group as a sect of some sort and that the recruiters had to clarify the issues in their own minds before they attempted to attract others to the work.

The recruiters were carefully briefed on all aspects of the presentation. The location was usually someone's home, but sometimes a rented public space was used. The recruiting site was supposed to be "aesthetically pleasing," and the hosts were reminded to clean their homes because "a clean home helps set a positive atmosphere." The food, they were told, "should be simple, attractive, delicious and abundant," and they were reminded not to serve alcoholic drinks, "including wine." Decorations were to be kept simple. The hosts were to greet their guests with name tags ("attractive, Do not have children write them"), punch, and nuts. It was suggested that one of the two leadership couples at each dinner dress more formally and the other more casually, so that guests would feel comfortable whatever they chose to wear. Specific suggestions were given on how to run the predinner discussion, complete with sample questions, and the instructions ended with a last reminder to try to get checks for the seminar before the guests left and even to write checks for them if they had forgotten their checkbooks.[109]

Toward the end of the decade of the 1960s there appears to have been a turning away from the somewhat unrealistic expectation of rapid exponential growth toward a concentration on developing a dedicated core of leaders.[110] One obvious way to expand their leadership pool, and perhaps their membership as well, was to move beyond the Palo Alto region. Although there had always been small "outposts" in other cities, usually set up by Palo Alto people who had moved, they had never been systematically cultivated. Starting in 1968 and expanding through the 1970s, however, geographic expansion became a more consistent theme in the recruiting policy. Whereas in the Sequoia Seminar days the goal had been to generate autonomous units capable of leading seminars in the Records and perhaps creating their own offshoots in turn, in the sectarian operation of the 1970s, outposts were to be closely supervised by Palo Alto headquarters. An early plan to expand the outposts emphasized that Palo Alto was to "maintain close control from here over who does what, how many, leadership, etc." In addition, Palo Alto was to provide leaders for the outpost weekends, and continuation seminars were to be held only in Ben Lomond. It was even suggested that both Palo Alto and the outposts exchange tapes of important meetings so that each would know exactly what was going on at the other location.[111] Clearly the assumptions were long gone that any group could discover the will of God by studying the Records and that leadership was as simple as "see one, do one, teach one." As a sect with a highly organized philosophy, almost a dogma, and a complex ritual structure, consistency—even orthodoxy—had been imposed upon the individual search for truth.

Besides utilizing couples who had moved from the Palo Alto area to start new outposts, Creative Initiative considered two other techniques for geographic expansion. The first consisted of sending a team of people into a city for a brief but highly concentrated drive. The second, which eventually became the model followed into the Beyond War era, was to have a couple actually move from Palo Alto to live in the target city for a protracted period that might be as long as two years. Both techniques were de facto models of mainline missionary activity and were one more expression of the institutionalized new religion that Creative Initiative had become.

The short-term team method of setting up an outpost was used in an attempt to spread the work to Napa, a small city in California's wine country, about ninety miles north of Palo Alto. A team of nine men spent approximately a week there contacting the media and city officials to give the group "credibility" and to invite people to subsequent presentations by two teams of three and four couples each. The fourteen people in the second group arrived two months after the advance guard of men, approached the contacts established by the first group, and attempted to gather additional names of people to meet. The results of the three-week effort by two dozen people were meager. Only six people went to any meetings beyond the introductory ones. Assessing the meaning of the "Napa experience," the participants concluded that it had been a valuable learning episode for them because they had come to view themselves as a "team of 'priests'" and had developed "closer bonding to each other and the mission."[112]

Creative Initiative, however, was more concerned with expanding the membership than with reinforcing the missionaries' level of commitment. To that end, in 1972 the group drew up a comprehensive plan for overseeing outposts. Harry was very excited about the possibility that some hub leaders might be able to take a sabbatical from work to become full-time resident recruiters in a new area.[113] His idea was not pursued at that time because the group was still afraid that it might overextend itself. Instead the plan was to operate only with those active couples who found themselves in new locations and wished to start a local Creative Initiative group.[114] An outreach newsletter was created to keep everybody in touch, but there appear to have been only a couple of issues published, and they were rather casual. There were nine outposts or "outlying areas" (apparently areas with members but no formal recognition as an official outpost). They were Los Angeles, Sacramento, Santa Rosa, Monterey, and Santa Cruz in California. In addition there were active groups in

Portland, Oregon; Denver, Colorado; Seattle, Washington; and, vaguely, "the East Coast."[115]

The cautious attitude toward expansion reflected both the limited resources of Creative Initiative and their fear of growing too quickly and losing their identity. For a movement that spoke so freely about transforming the world, they were always extremely reluctant actually to plunge into the turbulent reality of a mass movement. In 1976, somebody prepared a plan to spread the movement aggressively by blitzing key cities in the nation with a team from Palo Alto and then following them up with a core of semipermanent couples who would build on the momentum established by the first group. Within a year each city was supposed to mount a similar assault on others in its area, which in turn would spread the movement to a third level.[116] Although this was another more grandiose version of the geometric progression concept, the basic plan outlined in this proposal was finally implemented in 1984 when Beyond War sent several full-time "missionary" couples and their children to live in cities in the midwest and east and set up what once would have been called outposts.

"Who We Are": The Demography of Creative Initiative

In 1965, when the movement was first presenting itself to the public, a New Sphere paper entitled "Who We Are" sought to describe the group. Although most of the statement addressed philosophical questions, it began with a demographic definition. "First," it said, "we are an emerging group of women of all ages and stages, backgrounds and talents, single women, wives, working women, grandmothers, women of various racial and religious backgrounds."[117] As a group whose ideology was founded on the assumption that all people were brothers and sisters and that God willed the unity of all nations, races, and religions, it was natural that they would try to present themselves as multiracial and ecumenical. The community, *their* community, was supposed to be a model for the world, and how could it be a model of the unity of humankind unless it contained all kinds of humans?

Except for several years in the mid-1960s, however, when they worked with two black churches in East Palo Alto, Creative Initiative had very little contact with minorities and even fewer minority members. From time to time there were a handful of blacks affiliated with the group and a smattering of Chinese and Japanese names appear on the membership lists over the years, but for all practical purposes the group was all-white and overwhelmingly Christian despite an ongoing interest in attracting Jewish members. Just as the group was ethnically homogeneous, so was it similar in terms of members' social, economic, and educational background.

There were several reasons for the remarkable homogeneity of Creative Initiative, some which may have been related to their philosophy and some which were the result of conscious choice on their part, even though such a choice could be interpreted as violating the spirit of their purpose. First, as a movement based on the teachings of Jesus it was inevitable that Jews would be reluctant to associate with Creative Initiative, even though Emilia insisted they were not Christians and they spoke only about Jesus' humanity and never his divinity.[118] Emilia had an ambivalent attitude toward Jews. On the one hand she shared most of the ethnic stereotypes of her generation, viewing them as exclusive, clannish, and paranoid—and others appear to have adopted her attitude. A handwritten note from the 1966 period states, "Jews have a tremendous vitality, aggressive, acquisitive, they are greedy for things, good money makers."[119] Emilia encouraged Jewish members to persevere but thought they had special ethnically linked barriers that they had to overcome before they could move into the third age. "They claim a Godhead and a clan that totally poses an enemy and will fight absolutely to the death for it," she told a seminar. "It is a total mind set. The mind is rigid. It is in the very genes of the Jew to hate, fear and pose the enemy of all 'others.' "[120] Furthermore she blamed Jews in the Stanford power structure for many of Harry's academic problems. On the other hand, the prominence of Jews among the kinds of professionals Creative Initiative sought to attract, and the group's self-professed goal of uniting all religions, made Jews a logical recruiting target. Although some Jews remained in Creative Initiative and rose to prominent leadership positions, most seem to have found the work too alien, too Christian, and did not stay long.

Second, by focusing on the conversion of the individual as a necessary precursor to the coming of the Kingdom of God to earth in the third age, the group did not address the immediate needs and concerns of poor people—and that was how they themselves frequently explained their failure to attract working-class members. From Creative Initiative's own point of view, the explanation was particularly attractive because it absolved them of any responsibility for their failure to attract minorities and the poor, most of whom, they argued, were preoccupied with surviving. They believed that those few poor who had some discretionary time to devote to reform would join movements that addressed the immediate issues of economic discrimination. This explanation appears fairly weak since Creative Initiative, as a millennial movement, might just as easily have attracted poor people who would have much more to gain from a new world and much less to lose in the destruction of the present one than the kind of people who did join Creative Initiative.

The third reason that Creative Initiative failed to attract a more diverse membership, and one which the members felt ambivalent about, was their own elitism. Although Emilia and Harry strayed from the narrow academic focus of Sharman, they adhered to his underlying logic that social change could be most efficiently effected by first changing society's leaders. For Sharman, the leaders were students and professors. For the Rathbuns, the leaders were adults who had achieved positions of prominence and respect. In fact, they believed that they could change the planet if they could motivate a "creative minority" of 8 percent.[121] Both Sharman's and the Rathbuns' models, however, excluded working-class people by default if not by intent. Indeed, the rhetoric about being a heterogeneous movement that accurately reflected the ethnic, religious, and economic spectrum of society was sporadic, and acknowledgments of the middle-class makeup of Creative Initiative began fairly soon after the movement went public. At the end of a statement of self-definition written in 1967, the leaders of New Sphere referred to themselves as "middle-class, affluent Americans, who by virtue of their education and privilege could . . . lead the way."[122]

By making a virtue of their exclusiveness the movement was able to give its members a sense of specialness while at the same time providing them with an opportunity to remake the world for everybody. If we use the traditional model of the volunteer social improvement association, including everything from the Junior League to the Kiwanis, then Creative Initiative can be seen as very much in the mainstream of middle-class reform. The organization itself is exclusive, applying criteria for membership that screen out socially unacceptable people and allow those people who are accepted to feel special. Yet the purpose of the organization is charitable, thus mitigating any guilt caused by the undemocratic selection process. "The people we seek have probably already achieved a certain degree of success: a good job, a nice house, marriage, children—the things we usually associate with the 'good life,' " explained a recruiting pamphlet, "Yet they know that something important is lacking."[123] Harry told Richard in a letter, "We are becoming increasingly effective in 'turning on' the middle-class grass-roots people . . . and they are the ones who are going to have to 'do it.' " Harry believed that the "frustrated underprivileged" were not ready to abandon their "exciting destructive 'kick,' " and that people of great wealth were too self-centered to care about the fate of the world.[124]

It was precisely this concern with doing good work that the group used to justify itself when outsiders accused it of being exclusive. Responding to a charge that "CIF has shown no interest in recruiting outside the class of the comfortable," Richard Rathbun countered, "We have always believed that it is imperative that those people who have achieved a certain degree of economic freedom take on the responsibility to use their time and resources for something more than just self-satisfaction."[125] The response, of course, did not address the charge. In fact, it tacitly acknowledged it. Richard was in effect saying, yes, we do only recruit among the middle class, but that is OK because we do good things for everybody, even those who are not members of our group.[126]

From its early days as Sequoia Seminar through its most recent incarnation as Beyond War, Creative Initiative has consistently made a point of advertising the high-status employment of its members. This policy became particularly obvious after 1965 when, as the self-proclaimed New Religion of the Third Age, the group risked being dismissed as a cult. A 1972 brochure designed to describe the Creative Initiative Foundation to the outside world, for example, had a list of seventy people on the back cover described as those "whose deep involvement and leadership help guide the Foundation's programs and direction." Of the seventy, only seven were women, and not one of them had a professional affiliation listed after her name. The names of every one of the remaining sixty-three men were followed by a profession and, in the cases of a dozen men, advanced degrees (Ph.D.'s and M.D.'s).[127]

Outsiders always voiced the impression that Creative Initiative was made up of highly educated, well-to-do, white people. All the evidence available confirms this impression. For example, the answers to a brief questionnaire aimed at those members of the leadership who were thinking about moving to Portola Green give us a very good idea of the life style of some of the people who were setting the pattern for the movement. Not counting the Rathbuns, who were retired with a very modest income and assets, four of the six returns reported earning over $22,000, enough to put them in the top 5 percent of families in the country in 1971.[128] Another batch of data, apparently personal information cards for a seminar in 1964, lists the birthdates, jobs, and education of eleven couples. None of the women worked outside the home. All the men except for one were in business or education, and all but one had degrees and/or jobs in science or engineering. Except for one couple, neither of whom had gone to college, all the other wives and husbands had college degrees. Most of them had graduated from prestigious schools (Stanford, Berkeley, MIT), and three of the men had Ph.D.'s.[129] Neither of these very limited sources of data is conclusive, but they both tend to confirm the impression given by the published lists of people and their jobs. Creative Initiative members were well educated and economically successful.

In order to try to develop a more accurate statistical picture of Creative Initiative as it existed prior to its dramatic expansion as Beyond War, we drew up a questionnaire that included questions about the personal, educational, and economic background of members who had been in the movement prior to 1982. Our sample was biased by several factors. First, of those people who had been active before 1982, we reached only those who were still active in 1986 when the questionnaire was distributed. Second, because the questionnaires were distributed by and through the communication network of Creative Initiative, it is possible that certain people were deliberately excluded—although we have no reason to believe this happened. More significantly, because we did not have control over the distribution process, we are not sure exactly how many questionnaires actually reached members so we do not know the kind of percentage of returns we received. It seems possible, perhaps even likely, that given the high level of achievement of most members, those who thought of themselves as below the norm either refused to or were more likely to forget to return the questionnaires to us.

We nevertheless received responses from more than four hundred long-term adult members (a separate questionnaire was answered by children who had grown up in the movement). They enable us to say with a high degree of assurance that those people who did answer represent the hard core of Creative Initiative members and that their social, economic, and personal situations are typical of people who remained active in the movement for extended periods.[130]

Over the years, numerous observers have commented on the "whiteness" of the Creative Initiative membership, and in fact more than 85 percent of the people who responded to the survey came from northern

European ethnic backgrounds and, concomitantly, more than two-thirds of them were from mainline Protestant backgrounds. In an area where more than a quarter of the people were Catholic, only about 15 percent of Creative Initiative members were Catholic, and about 6 percent were Jewish. Thus, despite their strong commitment to the ideal of unifying the races and religions, the liberal Protestant origins of the movement and the strong informal preference for high-status members biased the group toward a heavy WASP participation. The preponderance of people from white, mainline Protestant backgrounds is particularly notable given their location in the San Francisco Bay Area where there is a large Catholic population and where a focus on highly educated and successful people could have been expected to bring in a higher percentage of Jews.

Even in Sharman's day, of course, it had been a WASP movement. Sharman operated through the YMCA and YWCA and the Student Christian Movement, all mainline Protestant groups. Under the Rathbuns, however, the student focus had been dropped in favor of more mature members. Indeed, if the questionnaire is an accurate reflection, students were virtually eliminated from membership. Fully 70 percent of those who responded first joined Creative Initiative when they were between the ages of twenty-seven and forty. Given the group's strong emphasis on marriage and the family, couples with children at home who were experiencing the stresses of midlife were the prime candidates for membership. This is borne out by the fact that the mean age at joining was thirty-three for women and thirty-seven for men and almost half of those joining had two children. In fact none of the long-term members who answered the questionnaire had been younger than twenty-two when they joined, and only 15 percent had no children.

Although Harry and Emilia did not pursue the Sharman tradition of seeking members only from within the academy, their desire to attract high-status people and their stress on education, both as a method for spreading their idea and as a technique for understanding it, meant that people comfortable with the methodology and terminology of college education would respond to their appeal. Only 18 percent of the women and less than 6 percent of the men did not have a college degree. Not only did virtually all the men have college degrees, but more than half had advanced degrees, and 20 percent had doctorates or medical degrees. Fifteen percent of the women had advanced degrees, and another 10 percent had teaching credentials in addition to their bachelor's degrees. Not only did they have college and graduate degrees, but they were disproportionately from high-prestige universities. Forty percent of the men had graduated from Stanford, Berkeley, or one of the Ivy League schools, although the corresponding figure for the women was only 15 percent.

Neither Harry Rathbun nor Henry Sharman brought to the study of religion the analytic skills common to the humanities and the social sciences. The systematic application of historical, sociological, and theological analysis was extremely rare in the work of the Rathbuns, and their use of psychology was always psychotherapeutic rather than analytic. When elements of the humanities and social sciences were introduced, it was usually through use of popular rather than scholarly work, and more for the purpose of bolstering previously arrived-at conclusions than to examine any basic assumptions.

It is, therefore, not surprising that rather few people with formal training in the humanities and social sciences were attracted to the movement and that a solid majority of the membership was made up of men whose degrees were in technical fields: the sciences, engineering, and business. Fifty-eight percent of the men had degrees in one of those technical fields. The same was not true for the women who went to school at a time when there were virtually no women in business or engineering. Yet even here, given the constraints of the system, the bias was clearly toward the technical, with almost half the women getting degrees in the social sciences and virtually none in the humanities. The second largest group, 15 percent, majored in education.

From the beginning, Creative Initiative operated on volunteer labor, almost all of which was provided by the women. Almost 60 percent of the women respondents to the questionnaire did not work outside their homes at the time they joined the movement, and only a handful had professional occupations outside of education. They were mothers with young children who could put what free time they had into their Creative Initiative work. Almost 60 percent listed their occupation as full-time volunteer for Beyond War when they responded to the questionnaire in 1986.

As could be predicted by their education, most of the husbands went into technical and scientific occupations, or into the teaching of those skills. Seventeen percent identified themselves as scientists and engineers, and about half were in managerial or sales positions—but almost all in Silicon Valley's high-tech industries. Only about 10 percent were in education (which would undoubtedly have disappointed Sharman), and most of those taught technical subjects on the university level. They were extremely successful in those occupations. The average family income for respondents in 1986 was around seventy thousand dollars, and there were thirty-two families that made more than a hundred thousand dollars per year; and it should be remembered that these are, for the most part, single-income figures. At the other extreme, only ten families made less than twenty-nine thousand dollars per year. Obviously, the popular impression that members of Creative Initiative were well-educated and well-heeled was completely justified.

Demographically, Creative Initiative was made up of people who should have been members of a country club, or even a yacht club or polo club. Ethnically, educationally, and economically they were on the top rung of American society. Instead of joining with others like themselves in pursuit of pleasure, however, they joined a religious sect that advocated economic moderation, complete commitment to the movement, and living a life purged of the baser emotions. It was, moreover, a life style that incurred social cost because they aggressively rejected the competitive materialistic life of their peers. Although the highly structured community that Creative Initiative created tried not to advertise its unique religious position too blatantly, their many public activities and their instantly recognizable personal style made them the objects of curiosity and some suspicion.

People who became part of the community of believers made their participation in Creative Initiative the central involvement in their lives. The "totality" demanded by the group excluded the possibility of most other pursuits, and the great intimacy required of members meant that they recruited people from a very narrow slice of society. The tightly knit and homogeneous community that emerged in the 1960s and 1970s was a successful religious sect, but one that, in some important ways, contradicted its own principles. Creative Initiative preached the gospel of oneness but lived a life of de facto exclusivity. The overwhelmingly WASP, educated, well-to-do membership rationalized the makeup of their community by explaining that it was a model that would demonstrate how the Kingdom of God would operate and a training ground for leaders who would eventually spread out to bring the word to a broader spectrum of people—something they in fact began to do in 1983 when they became Beyond War.

So long as they functioned as a relatively small and geographically limited community of believers, Creative Initiative could be highly selective about the people it would accept as members. The process of attracting and involving new people required that they walk a very fine line between education and manipulation. The process in which individuals were freed from their ties to outside authorities and introduced to the group's concept of absolutes may be viewed as "re-education," but it was not brainwashing. Creative Initiative worked as a sect because it provided its members with a sense of community that was compatible with their established places in society. They continued to be the same successful business and professional families that they had always been. Their children went to school with outside children. They lived in their towns and interacted with their neighbors, clients, co-workers, and others without suffering acute conflict between what they were and what they believed. In other words, they were not cult figures who had to withdraw from the greater reality in order to preserve a new inner vision. Their new identity with the community of believers was based on an understanding of themselves and the world that left them free to be in it and of it, while, at the same time, giving them a sense of personal satisfaction and a new sense of purpose in life.

Henry B. Sharman, 1921

Emilia and Harry Rathbun at
Asilomar, 1948

Seminar group, Casa de Luz Lodge, Ben Lomond, 1960

Ecology and Population display, 1969

Scene from "Thirteen is a Mystical Number," 1972

March during Arab-Israeli War, San Francisco, 1973

Scene from "Blessman," 1973

Women's march as part of "Project Survival," Los Angeles, 1975

Women's demonstration about pesticides and toxics, San Jose, c. 1976

March in support of Irish women's peace movement, 1976

Women representing the races in "Blessman," 1976

"Global 2000" office, Palo Alto, 1980

Project headquarters for "Global 2000," Palo Alto, 1980

Emilia and Harry Rathbun, c. 1982

7

Public Presentations: Programs and Politics

As a collective messiah destined to save the earth from destruction, the Creative Initiative community felt a deep obligation to convert the population, or at least a "creative minority" of it, to their way of life. Proselytizing was not just a way to make their movement grow, it was a necessary step toward creating the new community that would rescue humankind from its headlong rush to calamity. To achieve this first goal, a large part of their missionary activity was designed to attract people who would be gradually initiated into the religious aspects of the work. A second effort, however, was aimed at spreading their ideas to the population at large, even when it was clear that most of those who heard the message would never actually go through the identification process. This was done both through "direct action" in the social sphere and through generalized public information programs.

There was a constant temptation to move out into the world and use their considerable talents to alleviate the numerous social ills that they saw around them. This tendency followed almost instinctively from their apocalyptic view of the world situation. Racism, pollution, waste of limited resources, overpopulation, crime and violence, drugs, pornography and promiscuity, and nuclear war were pictured as imminent threats that would destroy society. The ultimate solution was, of course, to convert enough people to the new attitudes of the third age, and the conversion of individuals was always Creative Initiative's first priority. Their unwavering commitment to a homocentric solution, however, was occasionally supplemented by an excursion into social action and by

235

a very regular set of purely informational activities designed to educate the public-at-large about the dangers that faced them and about the ideas and attitudes of the third age.

Dramatizing the Message

For ten years, from 1966 to 1976, Creative Initiative members used dramatic theatrical productions as a way of crystallizing their ideas and presenting them to the general public. The costume-and-drama approach was not taken only to the stage, it also spilled over into some of the group's public demonstrations, leaving outsiders somewhat puzzled but always impressed with their careful preparation and well-organized theatrics.

The precise genesis of the theatrical method of presenting their ideas is not clear, but it emerged soon after the group first went public in their New Sphere phase. In 1966 the women presented a program called "The Universal Song" in which a black man and a white woman, a Jew and a German, forgave one another and demonstrated the possibility of racial and religious cooperation. Obviously pleased with the success of their first effort, the show was reworked as "People, War & Destiny" and presented five more times at the end of the year and in early 1967.[1] The group perceived the presentations as recruiting vehicles, for each of the last three was followed by dinners and discussions in private homes—all for one dollar and fifty cents.[2]

The show itself consisted of dancers, singers, and individual speakers dressed in black, white, red, and yellow costumes to represent the four races. The action took place on a bare stage with a twelve-foot papier-mâché globe behind a couple of stools on which the individual speakers sat.[3] The message in this first show, as it would be in all others for the next decade, was a simple distillation of the basic philosophic premises of the movement: teleological evolution, a history of human conflict, and the need for humans to make a conscious choice to take the final step toward a new level of being. But it was all presented in nonreligious humanistic terms.

The most important extension of the theatrical tradition was "Blessman," first called "From Woman to Blessman" when it was presented in December 1971, and staged annually for all but one year until 1976. The first "Blessman" was created as a celebratory ritual to conclude the autumn study program for new women in 1971. The show not only marked the end of the first phase of the neophytes' introduction into the movement, but, as one participant explained, it also enabled them to "make some kind of positive, feminine response to what we saw happening in the world."[4] This first "Blessman" was written and produced entirely by women with an all-woman cast. With less than one month between conception and production, they did not even have time for a full dress rehearsal before the show was presented in San Francisco's two thousand seat Masonic Auditorium on December 10, United Nations Human Rights Day. We have no script, but according to a participant, "the finale featured a woman dressed in a beautiful rainbow cape to symbolize Woman's covenant with God. The women, dressed in golden blouses and long skirts, carrying crepe paper gold roses wrapped around hidden lights, processed down the aisles and up to the stage."[5]

"Blessman" was successful enough to be presented once again on United Nations Human Rights Day the following year. This time, however, there were three performances and men as well as women were involved. More than 500 people worked on the show, and there were 250 in the cast. Advance publicity stressed the U.N. connection, which the movement now adopted as the primary public rationale for the program. The name of the show was changed from "Blessman" to "Bless Man." "Blessman," of course, was the term coined by the group as a linguistic symbol of the new role of women in the third age. After the first year men became involved in the show, so the more conventional two-word spelling, which also fit the Human Rights Day theme, was used. The production, as it was presented for the next five years, was indeed impressive. By 1976 the cast had grown to more than 800, and the grand finale, in which the costumed chorus with the flags of 148 nations sang a "universal anthem," resembled a full-sized version of Disneyland's "Small World" exhibit.[6] Photographs of the pageant and beautifully produced, sixteen-page, full-color souvenir booklet, show magnificently costumed people carrying various banners, flags, and symbols. There is very little from the pictures that indicates the amateur status of the participants.[7] The massive publicity that accompanied the productions makes it clear that the primary purpose of the pageant was to spread the message, regardless of whether or not it attracted new members. The message was summed up, at least for the 1970s, in the motto, "We are one." That phrase, used prominently in the show, suddenly seemed to be ubiquitous and was Creative Initiative's way of promulgating its vision to the community at large. Bumper stickers with the rainbow logo and the slogan "We are one" appeared in large numbers in the Bay Area (in fact, they were so closely identified with Volvos that some people thought they were standard factory equipment). The cover of the Pacific Bell Telephone magazine for December 1973 was the "Bless Man" symbol surrounded by the message, "one earth, one humanity, one spirit."[8] This was also the theme of handsomely produced Christmas cards used by the group for several years in the mid-1970s, as it was of a two-page, full-color advertisement in the Sunday supplement magazine of the *San Francisco Examiner and Chronicle*.[9]

Producing the "Bless Man" pageant appears to have had a positive effect in two areas. First, the group obviously felt that the drama and its attendant publicity helped spread the philosophy of Creative Initiative to people in the Bay Area. Second, the intensive cooperative effort needed to produce a show as large as "Bless Man" was a powerful community-building experience. For a group with no regular ceremonial gathering, the shows became a ritual whose very production—even apart from its content—was symbolic of their beliefs and life style. A photograph from the 1972 performance shows several circles of costumed men standing backstage with their arms around one another's shoulders praying.[10] The printed program contained the narrative script but, because they did not want anybody to be thought of as a star, no names were listed. It was a community effort in which each contributor was important and necessary for the final product and in which the individual ego had to be subsumed in the work of the whole.[11]

Viewing the pageant as a ritual of community solidarity as well as a vehicle of public education explains why Creative Initiative decided to present a second show in 1972, entitled "Thirteen Is a Mystical Number." Like "Bless Man," "Thirteen" depended heavily on pageantry, although it had a clearer story line. Also like "Bless Man," "Thirteen" was a medium for presenting Creative Initiative's particular interpretation of the history of humanity. The press release announcing the show explained that the participants had worked to produce "a chorus, orchestra, script, 20 original songs, brilliant set designs, costumes and a solid team of actors, singers and dancers."[12] In keeping with the tradition of emphasizing the community over the individual, the four-color program accompanying the show listed the scenes and reproduced the song lyrics but did not contain a single name. A note on the back cover explained: "The creative, cooperative efforts of 1000 people have produced this play. . . . Our play is given anonymously as a gift of love, dedicated to the vision of what this planet could be if people were to turn their attention to the inner condition of man and bring about a rebirth of the spirit of goodness."[13]

The title of the play was based on the belief that the number twelve equaled humankind and that the number one equaled God, and that the two of them together were the unity of thirteen.[14] Like a medieval morality play, "Thirteen" was an expression of faith designed both to entertain and to educate the audience about religious values. The story of "Thirteen" takes place at the "Inn of the Universe" where the proprietor offers travelers on a journey through time a chance to play a card game. Three women in succession, Eve, Mary, and Dawn, accept the offer, and the symbols on the cards they draw describe the development of human nature. Incidental travelers in the play personify Jungian archetypes and the soul found in every person.[15]

In the first act, human consciousness is awakened and humankind is given the choice between good and evil. Evil prevails and leads to violence. The first player, Eve, who stands for "the unconscious feminine, receptive part of man's nature found in both men and women," is lured with the promise that she can have more of everything if she wins. Her cards are "Night," which represents the unconscious; "Masculine" and "Feminine," which are the two sides of human character as understood by Jung; "Life" and "Death"; and "Good" and "Evil." Told that she must discard either "Good" or "Evil," she asks what each stands for. The proprietor tells her "Evil" is "more"—more power, more things; however, Good is wisdom, which involves the expenditure of time, sweat, and discipline. Unable to make up her mind, she abdicates the decision and gives birth to both Cain and Abel, and they play out their terrible story of fratricide.[16]

Act Two introduced the next traveler to play the game, Mary, who represents feminine perfection. She is promised that if she wins the card game the whole planet will change. Mary is dealt cards that represent "Light," "Life," "Death," "Good," and "Evil." She discards "Evil," but the travelers who are with her at the inn reclaim it, saying they want a king, pomp and circumstance, power and position. They, in turn, discard the "Good" and "Female" cards and then go on to invent the diversity of religions, as well as science and technology, which all begin to quarrel with one another.[17]

In the final act the third female figure, Dawn, plays the game. Dawn is described as the "new level of consciousness, decision and action that comes when the opposites within men are reconciled."[18] But she is, of course, more than that. Dawn is the name of the women's initiation ceremony used by Creative Initiative and, although it is not made clear to the audience, it is obvious that she is also the organization presenting the play. The proprietor tells Dawn that the hand he deals her will be the last game, "All the chips are on the table. It's all or nothing this time. Power is destroying the world. The madness of possession is leading to wars. Rebellion is everywhere." Dawn tells the people they have become slaves to violence and materialism. A group of women accept their new role, embracing the masculine traits that will allow them to be whole and urging men to accept their feminine side and reject war. The men then forgive Cain and Judas. Dawn proceeds to replace the crown of thorns on a cross with a crown of roses and, in a final wedding scene, sky and earth, mind and soul, human and God are united.[19]

Members of the audience were witnessing, in addition to a musical theater version of Creative Initiative's philosophy, much of the group's initiation ceremony. "Thirteen" was in fact an extremely candid expression not only of Creative Initiative's secular ideas, but also of its psychological (masculine–feminine) and religious ideas. A preview article in the *San Francisco Chronicle* summarized the religious theme of the piece, as did a review in the *Palo Alto Times,* but neither article questioned what lay behind the organization that presented this rather unusual show. When the play was staged again in October, the *Times'* headline called it a "happy up-with-people thing" (appropriately, since Up With People was the singing group that grew out of Moral Re-Armament). A second *Times* reviewer managed to ignore the religious theme entirely. He spoke instead of love and "the aura of brotherhood which begins with the parking lot attendants and extends through to a finale that shouldn't be missed."[20]

The different interpretations of the reviewers would not have concerned the people in the movement at all. The play was supposed to be understood on several levels, and that one viewer saw it as more religious and another as more secular merely confirmed that it was functioning as intended. The play was a dramatic expression of what the movement referred to as their "living myth," further defined as a "force, a spirit which binds men together, motivating and inspiring them to strive toward a common goal, a higher destiny or potential." They believed that all ideologies and religions were "living myths," and they were adding their own to motivate people to "work toward the survival of this planet."[21]

In 1980 the children of Creative Initiative presented "Angel's Advice," their own theatrical version of the group's ideas. Their show, which, incidentally, broke with tradition and listed all 160 children's names on the program, contained the same fundamental elements: the beauty of nature, the unity of humankind, the necessity of decision, and the dangers of material temptation . . .

> We've got money!
> We've got status!
> We've got mansions!
> We've got quick cash!
>
> Quarter, Dimes, and Dollars,
> Spending more and more!
> I'm so nice that, for a price,
> I'll let you through my door!
>
> Got to have the very best . . .
> Rolls Royce, Mercedes Benz!
> Nothing has too high a price,
> It can even buy your friends![22]

Creative Initiative used two other media, films and radio, to educate the general public during the 1970s. The first films were put together as part of the 1968 meeting that announced the voluntary national service project. Although the volunteer national service project had a brief life, the use of films to communicate the movement's ideas lived on into Beyond War.[23] The group prepared scripts for five films, three of which were produced and used extensively before the Beyond War era. All the films were written by Emilia, although she never claimed public credit.[24] Like the theatrical productions, the films were intended to present Creative Initiative's basic ideas to a general audience in an easy-to-understand and nonthreatening way. The films, however, were much less overtly religious than the pageants, in part because they were designed to be used with people even further removed from the Creative Initiative sphere than those in the theaters. Generally, the films were a collage of quick-cut stills and short bits of action with classical background music and a narrative voice-over.

Besides being used in some of the introductory courses, the films were shown widely to the general community, to government groups, managerial conferences, and at public "fairs."[25] Thus, there was a strong emphasis on the secular rather than the religious message. Except for the title of the proposed fifth film, "Choose Your God," there were no explicit religious references in any of the scripts. Nevertheless, the themes of evolution, danger, and choice were as central to the films as they were to the pageants.

Certainly, the most unequivocally educational of all the dramatized messages were a series of forty one-minute radio spots that were broadcast on a San Francisco radio station between 1975 and 1977. These radio messages must have been even more perplexing to the uninitiated than the average Creative Initiative pronouncement, since they appeared in isolated segments without context and without transition from one idea to the next. Because they were written for a general audience, moreover, they had no religious references, making many of them sound like all-purpose, positive-thinking pieces of psychology and philosophy.

For example, spot number ten addressed the issue of "authority." To Creative Initiative, "authority" meant only one thing, surrendering individual will to the authority of God. The radio spot said that although people wanted to be number one, they had to realize they were really number two because they were governed by the laws of nature. One has to obey the laws of nature, continued the spot, "because to be obedient means you've discovered the difference between thinking you're number one and knowing you're number two."[26] Similarly, the spot that discussed the great paradox of Jesus never actually mentioned him. It began with the question, "What is the meaning of life?" and ended with the advice, "we are fulfilled by giving. We find life by surrendering it."[27] Among the other topics covered were the presence of the masculine and feminine in all people, the need to make a decision to act (four times), the dangers of materialism, the need for spiritual fulfillment, and so forth.

Dramatizing their message and presenting it to the general public was Creative Initiative's way of casting their seed widely. If the success of the efforts is to be judged by the number of people attracted to the movement, then most of the seed would seem to have fallen on fallow ground. Yet, recruiting new members was only a secondary purpose of the plays, films, and radio spots. By going public in an aggressive way with their ideas, Creative Initiative was also trying to legitimize itself. If outsiders could be convinced of the validity of the movement's principles, then the effort would be achieving two goals at once. First, Creative Initiative would be spreading its doctrine in accordance with its own declared purpose to educate the world with the teachings of the third age. Second, and this was never made explicit, to the extent that outsiders were exposed to their ideas and came to see them as legitimate, even if the outsiders did not actually accept them, the movement was creating a more receptive environment for its own people and thereby decreasing the social cost of being a member. Like any other kind of publicity—and the group certainly did not shy away from opportunities to tell its story to the press—the dramatized messages made insiders who saw them feel as though their group had gained some social legitimacy.

Reaching out to the Black Community

Among the efforts made by Creative Initiative to reach out to people in the larger community, their involvement with two black churches in the predominantly black town of East Palo Alto holds a special place. Because they genuinely and fervently believed that they could create a world in which there was unity among the nations, religions, and races, they also believed that it was incumbent upon them to live lives compatible with that view. To accomplish the first goal, as we shall see, they actively pursued programs that promoted internationalism. The goal of unifying the religions was, at first, dealt with by declaring themselves an ecumenical movement. Even when that failed, they continued to insist that their New Religion was really an amalgam of existing faiths whose doctrines they honored in their work. The third goal, unifying the races, was more difficult because nonwhites in general and blacks in particular did not fall into the socioeconomic categories from which they drew their members. There were always a few Asians in the group, but Hispanics, like blacks, were conspicuously absent.

The absence of ethnic and racial minorities was certainly not due to any lack of intellectual commitment to the cause of brotherhood on the part of the movement. A "Ten Commandments of Good Will" produced in 1963 described the attitude toward race relations that the group expected from its members. Those subscribing to this creed promised to "honor all men and women regardless of their race or religion." They promised, in addition, to stand up for people who were persecuted and to challenge the idea of racial superiority. Couched in the extreme language of the early New Religion period, persons accepting the commandments promised to obey them until their "dying day" and not to "be divorced from this purpose by threats of personal violence or social ostracism."[28]

Emilia's active work with black groups went back at least to 1950 when she and some of the others in Sequoia Seminar became involved with the AME Zion Church in East Palo Alto. Del Carlson led the church choir, and Emilia worked with the church, first on their Negro History Week event, and then on various other projects dealing with the issue of racial prejudice.[29]

Cooperation with black churches took on a profounder significance after 1962. In 1965, the cook at Ben Lomond told Emilia that a deacon had stolen money from her church that was to be used for remodeling. Emilia offered to help raise the missing money and was introduced to "Mother" Branch, president of Palo Alto Church Women United, an ecumenical group, and wife of "Father" James Branch, the church's minister. Creative Initiative donated fifteen hundred dollars to Saint John Missionary Baptist Church and, as part of their increasing involvement, arranged to have nine paintings installed in the church. All the paintings contained New Religion iconography, including illustrations of the "Six Great Religions" and the "Cross of Fulfillment," a metal version of which was prepared for but never placed on the church roof.[30]

A paper distributed to the members of the New Religion in the spring of 1965 made clear the tremendous importance that Emilia (the paper was almost certainly written by her) placed on the movement's relationship with Saint John. The paper opened with the statement, "St. John's Baptist Church is being used by God as the birthplace of the new or Second Coming of Christ." It went on to explain that "the Book of John, the fourth book of the New Testament, is the book which unfolds the third dispensation. It is therefore proper that this first occasion of formally establishing the invisible church built without hands should take place in a church named St. John." That event was to occur on Good Friday, April 16, at a service that symbolized the coming together of the races in cooperation.[31] Almost one hundred members of the movement who were present accepted an invitation to go forward and join the church. Forty of them were subsequently given a traditional full-immersion baptism. The people from Creative Initiative did not intend this act to mean that they were becoming Baptists, but rather that they were engaged in work that embraced all denominations. For their part, both Mother and Father Branch were given special ad hoc initiation ceremonies into New Sphere, and several women from the black church were also given " 'mild' identification," apparently without going through the usual courses.[32] Although quasi-unity between the two groups could not last long—the church did not want to be subsumed into Creative Initiative, and the people in the movement had their own agenda for action—relations between the two groups remained warm, if increasingly detached, until 1968. That year, Creative Initiative became a cosponsor of an "African heritage" festival that was going to be held in East Palo Alto in late April to celebrate "the arts and culture of Africa." After working out some initial disagreement as to where the fair would be held and whether or not it was a "black nationalist" event, plans went forward involving people from Saint John, from the East Palo Alto AME Zion Church, from a black women's group called the Strivers, and from several Stanford University student groups.[33]

Unfortunately, early in the month, before the fair could be held, Martin Luther King, Jr., was assassinated. Working overnight, the Rathbuns and Creative Initiative along with their friends in the black community organized a peaceful memorial march. Harry and Emilia were in the front rank of the demonstration. Feelings in the black community were inflamed, nevertheless, and several of the black women who had been working on the fair were reportedly threatened by black men with pistols and told not to cooperate with whites. For this reason the Strivers withdrew from participation in the fair. The loss of support from this middle-class black women's group combined with the mood of unrest following the assassination caused the fair to be canceled. Creative Initiative's active phase of black–white cooperation died along with the African Heritage festival.[34]

The attempts to integrate a black church into the New Religion of the Third Age had been a failure, and so had the more modest effort to cooperate with black groups in celebrating the cultural heritage of Africa. As Creative Initiative moved into the 1970s, members turned their attention away from the dispossessed, with whom they had never had much success, toward their natural constituency in the white upper-middle class. In a certain sense they were actually following the advice of many black activists who told them if they really wanted to help they should change the attitudes in the white community. They told a black officer of the Ford Foundation in 1970, "We are after significant attitude changes in white communities. We believe this is absolutely essential to . . . help produce the concrete changes that must be made quickly in the underprivileged parts of our society."[35]

The National Voluntary Service Movement

The collapse of Creative Initiative's active involvement with the black community in 1968 coincided with the emergence of their first full-scale social action project, the plan for a national voluntary service corps of young people. The inception of the national voluntary service scheme, in fact, was closely linked to Creative Initiative's involvement with the militant black community.[36] Early proposals for the service project announced that it would have to reach "black students who make up the vanguard of black activist movements," or else it would "make very little impact on the country's consciousness."[37] As they promoted their pilot program through the spring of 1968, the emphasis was always on ways in which the program could further racial harmony among youth. They went so far as to announce that the first project would take place in San Francisco, where eight white college students from Stanford and eight ghetto youths would work together on unspecified projects chosen by a black activist group called the Mission Rebels.[38] The dissolution of Creative Initiative's tenuous link to the militant black community after King's assassination did not stop the voluntary service drive, although it did put an end to most of the hopeful rhetoric about solving the problems of poor youth.

Unlike the media efforts and the work with the black churches, the national service project did not have an obvious religious subtext. Like them, however, it was strongly educational in nature and aimed at the outside world. Part of its purpose, as in all Creative Initiative projects, was to draw attention to the work of the movement. Yet the national service project was action oriented and served as a model for the subsequent civic activities that followed in the 1970s.

Emilia originally suggested the idea for a voluntary national service corps during a "brainstorming" session in the autumn of 1967, and it was quickly adopted by the hub leadership. Obviously there could be no hope of spreading the concept to the youth outside the movement unless the children of Creative Initiative members were fully committed to it. Therefore, in April 1968, when they were gearing up for a major publicity campaign, Creative Initiative teenagers were told that they either had to become active in the new project or drop out of the movement's teen programs. There was one report that as many as a quarter of the teenagers balked at becoming part of the new project, but eventually most joined the support group called "Youth for Positive Action."[39]

Although it was not made explicit, there was a quid pro quo aspect to the demand that teens participate in the national service campaign. After all, they were the ones who would benefit if it were successful, because one of the major objectives of the project was to create an alternative to the military draft and service in the Vietnam War. Harry told the press that he hoped local draft boards would exempt young men who worked for the new program and that he expected that the draft law would eventually be changed to require such exemption. "The difference between us and VISTA and the Peace Corps," said Harry, "is that they are not committed to changing the draft system."[40]

Creative Initiative sought funding for the "Involvement Corps" by appealing to the business community. They explained that they wanted to set up a demonstration project in the Bay Area to "show what can be accomplished by dedicated young people under private leadership and financing." They acknowledged that they were following the lead of VISTA and the Peace Corps but claimed that "government cannot do the job alone" and that the Involvement Corps would show how the private sector could expand the example of the government's projects. It was, nevertheless, not at all clear how Creative Initiative's voluntary service would differ appreciably from the existing federal organizations, other than the fact that it originally planned to recruit large numbers of poorly educated black youth to work with white, middle-class young people.[41]

The core of the first demonstration project was to be made up of Stanford students, many of whom were children of Creative Initiative members. In October 1967, students, faculty, and staff affiliated with the movement formed a campus group called the "Community for Relevant Education" (CRE).[42] Modeling their approach on the psychological deconditioning sessions that the movement had used for years, CRE established a program of "relevance groups" at Stanford through which students could become more aware of their feelings. Public descriptions emphasized the value of people learning to trust one another and developing a sense of power to act. Ironically, one of the criticisms that CRE members aimed at other campus encounter groups was that they were "process oriented," whereas CRE's relevance groups were "action oriented."[43] This was indeed a new departure for a group whose entire history had been one of avoiding social action in favor of an educational process designed only to change the individual.[44]

Nonmembers criticized the two hundred CRE students for being elitist, intolerant, and counterrevolutionary, but the most common complaint was that CRE was a religion or a sect.[45] Here, of course, the critics were correct. *The Stanford Daily* reported a rumor that CRE members were required to sign a paper of commitment after completing a five-week course of relevance groups but it said it could find no proof.[46] In fact, CRE had drawn up a pledge of commitment that, although it avoided any explicit religious terminology, was the functional equivalent of the pledge that people took when they entered the New Religion. The CRE "Statement of Position" asserted that one person could make a difference in the world; that personal relationships could be honest and direct; that people had to be helped to achieve their highest potential; that work toward the cooperation of all races, religions, and nations was the greatest service a person could perform; and that all conditioned responses had to be tested against reality. The signer pledged "to be part of a force of enlightened, committed, caring people capable of building a really loving world" and promised to be "a new kind of universal citizen" who would "free the human race to achieve its highest manifestation."[47]

By presenting itself as a secular effort, CRE was reducing the social cost of joining. The effort to create a national voluntary service project was sincere, but underlying it, as with all Creative Initiative activities, was the desire to spread the group's beliefs. Useful as they might be, social action projects were always seen as part of a greater educational effort. In the middle of all the publicity promoting CRE, the Rathbuns could still assert that when people actually understood the meaning of their philosophy, "the familiar question: 'But what are we going to *do* when we have the trained and committed community?' becomes irrelevant because one is already in action if he has become committed to the goal inherent in the philosophy."[48] They were apparently untroubled by the fact that these statements were made during a period when CRE and Creative Initiative were pushing national service—that is, *real* action in the community, not just "education." After all, CRE said that it had *two* purposes: one was, in effect, spreading the philosophy of Creative Initiative, but the second was promoting the national service program.

Like so many Creative Initiative projects, national service started with great expectations. A thirty-four page "Training Manual" drawn up at the beginning of 1968 (for internal distribution only) listed as the first goal of the project: "to shift the attitude of this country, and eventually of the world, from one of narrow self-interest to one of positive and willing contribution to build the earth for all people." In addition to making it a force for better race relations, they hoped eventually to make national service a part of the educational system nationwide. They believed these goals would be achieved because Creative Initiative would generate "a groundswell of support for National Service of such magnitude and fervor that political forces will naturally support the needs of the program."[49]

The proposal laid out every step in their hypothetical program, from the way it would deal with military service to the cost per volunteer. Creative Initiative's role was to act as a catalyst, and to that end they created a separate legal entity, the National Service Foundation (later called the National Initiative Foundation) to oversee the work. When fully implemented, national service, as its name implied, would be a requirement for every young person in the nation, either in the traditional military or in a new civilian capacity. Obviously, before such a drastic step could be taken a demonstration project was necessary. At first Creative Initiative hoped to establish a nationwide pilot program involving fifty thousand young people. Professional consultants who were brought in quickly scaled down the pilot project, however, to a regional endeavor involving a projected five thousand volunteers for the summer of 1968.[50] Only the eager optimism that marked all Creative Initiative programs could have convinced the organizers that they could draw up plans, raise money, recruit five thousand young people, and have them on the job in less than four months.

There were two public launchings of this project, the first in March and the second in April. The March presentation of the national service idea drew upon the movement's two years of theatrical experience with a three-act dramatic presentation called "Building the Earth" staged at the three-thousand-seat Circle Star Theatre in San Carlos, a few miles north of Palo Alto. After films and speeches, several hundred Build the Earth women in rainbow-colored dresses filled the stage to sing a current popular song, "Who Will Answer?" At the end of the song a disembodied voice from the middle of the women spoke: "We are neither the extreme right nor the extreme left—we are the mobilized middle. If people like us won't do it, who will?" Members of the audience were then asked to volunteer to help organize the pilot program.[51]

Then in April the National Initiative Foundation made plans to present the pilot project to the public at a huge pageant in Stanford Stadium—which holds a hundred thousand people—with "speakers of national prominence," black and white marching bands, and an upbeat program that would cause grown men to stand and weep.[52] Fortunately, perhaps, for Creative Initiative, the stadium was unobtainable, because it was unlikely they could have attracted anything close to a hundred thousand people. They had to settle instead for Stanford's Frost Amphitheater, which seats ten thousand. In the meantime, of course, the possibility of the national service movement working closely with the black community had evaporated in the face of the unrest following King's assassination. Undaunted, they went ahead, and on the appointed day in May they managed to fill the amphitheater. No speakers of major national prominence appeared, but otherwise the pageant was clearly up to Creative Initiative's standards. Entitled "Build the Earth," it featured several Stanford bands, speeches, poems, national and state flags, foreign students in their native costumes, and international folk dancers. The finale consisted of Build the Earth women in their ubiquitous rainbow dresses releasing matching balloons that, after abbreviated flights, soon settled down into the crowd, most having lost their helium in the hot afternoon sun.[53]

The half-filled balloons bobbing listlessly just above the crowd were an unpropitious omen. Back in February the organizers had talked bravely of five thousand volunteers, scaled down from fifty thousand. At the May pageant itself the names of fifteen volunteers were announced, although the office claimed that there were a total of forty applications. Internal communications indicate the number was more like twenty-five. When all the dust (and balloons) had settled, fewer than a dozen people actually went out onto the first projects. Months of labor, thousands of work hours, reams of publicity, and the full-time employment of two people—one Creative Initiative man (Donald Fitton, the first full-time paid Creative Initiative worker) and an outside specialist—plus additional input from two professional consultants, placed eleven young people in a variety of local service projects. Three of the eleven volunteers were women and two were black. Half of them were, as advertised, placed with black-led action groups in San Francisco.[54]

As far as Creative Initiative was concerned, the whole experiment with national service came to an end in October 1968 when they formally severed their ties with the Involvement Corps. Leadership of the group was turned over to one of the outside consultants who had been hired to help the foundation with the experiment. The members of the Creative Initiative community in turn were told that their continued involvement with the program would be a matter of personal choice, for although the movement still supported the corps and the idea of national service, they had fulfilled their goal by launching the program and wanted to move onto other projects.[55]

The Question of Civic Action

The national service experiment demonstrated a recurrent tension in the Creative Initiative movement betweeen the homocentric and the sociocentric. Going back at least to 1946 and the break with the Canadian radicals, the Rathbuns' belief was that changed people would change society rather than the other way around. Recruiting material had emphasized repeatedly that they were not seeking to attract people whose primary interest was political action. "We are looking for people who are concerned with the *human dimension*," said a 1971 recruiting memo. "While we certainly do not reject politically or ecologically oriented individuals," it continued, "we frequently only frustrate them because we do not take action in the outer world in a way they can appreciate and which satisfies their major concern."[56]

In practice, however, it was sometimes very hard not to slip into civic and political action. Indeed, unless the Creative Initiative movement actually tried to do something, how could they know when enough people had been changed to establish that vital "creative minority" that would reform society? Because of this ambivalent but continuing link with the social gospel tradition, Creative Initiative could never simply turn its back on social action. The ultimate litmus test of the validity of their kind of homocentric approach to reform was social and political change. So when they strayed into the area of civic action, as they did with national service, they may have been unconsciously trying to validate their approach by doing exactly what they always said they shouldn't spend time doing, becoming involved in politics.

The first formal involvement with political issues had come in early 1967 when the men (action in the political sphere was always dominated by the men) began to formulate a position on "The New Politics." The men engaged in this exploratory project felt that they had to change worldwide political ideology from competition to cooperation.[57] In July of 1967 the New Politics task force produced a draft paper entitled "Statement of Political Position" and a timeline for accomplishing its goals. The first part of the position paper called for international cooperation and, because it was an existing body whose ideals embodied the philosophy of the group, the paper named the United Nations as the logical vehicle for bringing about this goal.[58] Their three-year timeline projected a series of steps at home and abroad culminating in 1970 with a world conference. Like so many of Creative Initiative's projects, the conception was extremely ambitious. They planned to have teams of trained contacts spreading out through the "seven power sectors" of the United States ("Left, Right, South, Mid-West, Industry, Labor, Church") and the "seven cultures" of the world ("India, USSR, UK, Western Europe, South America, Japan, Africa") and expected the effort also to expand geometrically as they moved.[59] The New Politics campaign never got beyond the designing stage and the great plan remained a paper promise.

Two years later, however, directly after the end of the national service experiment, the group did formulate a program to take direct action in the civic arena, but on a much more modest level than the seven power sectors and the seven cultures. Their target was Palo Alto, and their goal was to "humanize" the city. The "Palo Alto Initiative," as it was called, began in January 1969 when Creative Initiative conducted a survey of community leaders to determine what they thought were the most pressing problems in the city.[60] Tabulating the responses, Creative Initiative determined that there were five areas that needed attention: long-range civic planning, improved black–white relations, dissatisfied young people, nonrelevant education, and community apathy.[61]

Perhaps because their recent experience with the national service program had convinced them that community resistance stemmed from the failure of people to accept Creative Initiative's philosophy, all the problems identified by the survey, except civic planning, were seen as attitudinal and therefore susceptible to correction through education. "Palo Alto," they concluded, "is a symptom of what is going on throughout the entire world." They felt they had to show the city how to realize that "home" was the planet and their "race," mankind. All that was needed to accomplish this was to expose the people in the city to the *truth* and, they reaffirmed, they were "willing to tell the truth even at the risk of our lives, our fortunes, and our sacred honor."[62] The plan was to "revolutionize the educational system in Palo Alto."[63] Creative Initiative sketched out a curriculum, wrote up a rationale, and contacted the principal of one of the Palo Alto high schools. They offered to set up a pilot program at the school for volunteer students and faculty.[64] Apparently neither that overture nor another to the board of education was favorably received. A subsequent memo referred to "a general up-tightness on the part of the [school] staff regarding 'sensitivity training"—which was apparently how they viewed the Creative Initiative proposal—and complained that the school administrators "did not, as yet, recognize us as experts in the field of education."[65]

Eternally optimistic and undeterred by weak response to the civic initiatives of 1969, the movement entered the new decade with their political views intact. A "Statement on Politics" drawn up in 1970 listed the major problems of the nation as peace, "responsiveness," and ecology, and predicted, "If a majority of people in America wanted to shift the use of our national resources from war and destruction to human development and environmental preservation, government would inexorably fall into line."[66]

One of the first political education programs that Creative Initiative proposed for the new decade was based on the upcoming bicentennial of the American revolution. Hoping, as they did at the beginning of each new administration, to entice the president into supporting one of their projects, they contacted Richard Nixon both before and after his second inauguration in 1972. The flowery letters sought to describe how the president's values and those of the foundation coincided and urged him to meet with them so that they could explain their ideas for the bicentennial.[67] They had previously suggested a series of specific ideas for projects to be launched as part of the bicentennial celebration. Although the calls for a peace academy, a department of unity, and a world unity corps may have been unrealistic, they were an earnest effort to develop a meaningful theme for a celebration that eventually was almost universally condemned as dull and directionless.[68]

Undeterred by the lack of positive response from the federal government, Creative Initiative placed the new project in the highest-priority category—which, in fact, was the only category that Creative Initiative had. The membership was told that they would have to make a "*total shift*" in their approach to the bicentennial and visualize themselves "involved in a war for survival for the next two years (a war *for* unity and *without* violence)." "Can you imagine yourself going into battle half-heartedly?" asked the rhetorical call for action. It continued, "The reality is that the only way we can reach the world through '76—or at all—is to believe at the center of our being that our survival *is* at stake and to act accordingly."[69]

The call for action urged members to think about ways to implement the proposed theme, "Rebirth '76," which would promote the bicentennial celebration as the gateway to "Century Three."[70] The idea of a third century echoed Creative Initiative's belief in a third age and, to emphasize that connection further, they took the motto on the reverse side of the Great Seal of the United States, *novus ordo seclorum* ("a new order of the ages"), as the slogan of their bicentennial program. The movement drafted a full-scale plan of action that included: "interchanges" among students, families, and community specialists; international contests on the theme of "interdependence"; a new educational curriculum for the country's schools; and, finally, both a full-length film and a "full-scale musical drama for the stage, entitled 'Reunion.' " The play would be "presented professionally in Washington, and other key national capitals throughout the world."[71]

Since the project they envisioned was expected to cost more than three hundred thousand dollars, they applied for funding to various foundations. A report in September of 1973 to the one foundation that did grant them fifteen thousand dollars reveals that in the end almost none of the projects they had proposed for the bicentennial celebration had been implemented.[72] In fact, by the time 1976 actually arrived, almost all projects for the bicentennial celebration had been left behind as the group became involved in another set of political activities, mostly having to do with ecology. They did, however, compose and circulate a "Declaration of Interdependence" that emphasized the unity of human beings and their environment and rejected nationalism, violence and war, and exploitation of people or the environment.[73]

Energy and Ecology

The movement's stress on environmental issues did not suddenly appear fully formed in the mid-1970s. In the late 1960s, echoing the concerns of organizations such as Zero Population Growth, Creative Initiative had called on their members and the public to support population limitation. The women's ecology task force, established in the spring of 1969, issued a flyer entitled "Overpopulation Newsletter." It consisted of a series of short news items almost all of which supported liberalizing antiabortion laws. The newsletter ended by urging readers to write to their federal and state representatives to support "just abortion and voluntary sterilization laws, which would be open to all with fees to be determined by financial ability to pay."[74] In July 1969 Build the Earth put together an ecology exhibit composed of a series of sixteen free-standing display panels with very professional pictures and graphics. First erected at a Palo Alto shopping mall, it was later shown in museums and schools in the Bay Area. The display emphasized the contrast between the finite capacity of the earth to produce food and the apparently infinite capacity of people to reproduce; it predicted that unless something were done to reduce the birth rate, starvation would be the inevitable result.[75] In 1970, when a special "committee of 90" men drafted a series of suggested position papers on issues of concern, the "politics" statement included an unqualified call for all forms of population control including "massive education, tax penalties for more than two children, free sterilization, intensified research on safe and convenient contraceptives, and unconditional abortion."[76]

There was a hiatus in the public education programs during the early 1970s while the group focused on the theatrical productions. Then, in 1975, Creative Initiative returned to the ecology movement, shifting their emphasis from population control and recycling to energy. The energy issue involved them directly in political activities and led up to the crisis that preceded their reorganization into Beyond War.

Operating as Build the Earth, Creative Initiative created a special task force called "Project Survival" at the beginning of 1975. They were motivated, they said, by hearing British economist E. F. Schumacher speaking at Stanford University. Shumacher's book, *Small Is Beautiful,* further stimulated them to investigate the energy problem, and they chose the nuclear power issue as an appropriate focus for action.[77] From February to March, Project Survival sponsored twelve community forums at which the issue of nuclear power was discussed. These meetings presented both sides of the issue, including people and films from the nuclear power industry, while an accompanying questionnaire tried to determine popular attitudes toward nuclear power.[78] Creative Initiative was far from neutral on the subject, however, and the appearance of objectivity was quickly abandoned. Within months they were distributing flyers listing the long-term dangers of radioactive plutonium waste from reactors and predicting grave consequences for the future unless the production of nuclear energy were halted. They concluded one early list of antinuclear arguments with the statement: "Because of these facts we feel the issue of nuclear power is a moral one."[79]

The more explicitly political side of the nuclear project went through the same rapid transformation from nominally objective to unabashedly partisan in just a few months. In March, the movement circulated a petition calling on the government to create a special commission, "representative of all the people of California, to inquire into the question of nuclear power in our state." The rest of the document maintained the same even-handed tone, noting that nuclear power had both benefits and dangers, supporters and opponents, and that the decision should not be left to the power industry or to scientists. Since the issue was moral and ethical as well as technological and economic reasoned the petition, the decision had to be made by everybody based on all the facts.[80]

By April, the movement had moved to outright antinuclear advocacy. One of the early announcements for an "educational presentation" was headlined, "WE ARE IRREVERSIBLY COMMITTED TO ONE MILLION DEATHS FROM NUCLEAR RADIATION." In the face of so palpable and immediate a danger, the flyer explained, "we must take immediate action. All other problems of human welfare take second place."[81]

On May 9, five hundred women staged a demonstration in Los Angeles to draw attention to the petition campaign. In a newspaper interview several spokeswomen for the march admitted that although the petition only called for an investigation, they were opposed to nuclear power.[82] Their point of view was obvious from the march itself: demonstrating at the Department of Water and Power, they carried signs saying "Plutonium Kills," "Energy Conservation not Nuclear Proliferation," "People Need the Truth About Nuclear Waste," "Children Need a Future, Not a Radioactive Legacy," and "God Gave Us a Finite Planet, Let Us Not Destroy It."[83] Aside from the fact that all the demonstrators were women, with the vast majority middle-aged and white, there was one other aspect that set this march apart from the usual demonstration: they were all dressed in pantsuits that were the colors of the rainbow and each had a matching scarf tied through her hair. They explained that the rainbow was God's sign to Noah that he would not destroy the earth and their sign that they accepted the responsibility to also persuade people not to destroy the earth.[84]

Petition drives were staged in more than half a dozen cities around the state. In Fresno and San Francisco they were accompanied by marches using the same signs and colored costumes as were used in Los Angeles. The highly disciplined demonstration in San Francisco so unnerved one Pacific Gas and Electric counterdemonstrator that he commented, "It's like watching the Hitler youth corps."[85] He was subsequently reprimanded for his remark and apologized to Creative Initiative. But these regional marches were just warmups for the grand finale demonstration in Sacramento. The women had managed to collect 345,000 signatures on their "call for information" petitions, and they went to the state capital to present them to the governor in typical Creative Initiative style. Drawing on their years of experience producing "Bless Man" and "Thirteen Is a Mystical Number," they pulled out all the stops.

More than four thousand enthusiastic and costumed demonstrators went to Sacramento on May 21, 1975. Led by four hundred women forming the inevitable pastel rainbow, they marched from a local park to the Capitol Mall. There the "rainbow women" formed a backdrop to an invocation by American Indians (in costume) and four costumed women representing the four races of the earth. An Indian representative called upon the crowd to "hear a prophecy of my people." "The Great Spirit will return," he predicted, going on to assure the audience that the "War of Light" would vanquish the "Sons of Darkness." Unprompted, he then proceeded to outline the fundamental tenets of Creative Initiative philosophy. He told the people to "go to the mountain-top of consciousness and learn to be 'Warriors of the Rainbow.' " He told them to fight with truth and not with violence. He foretold the emergence of understanding, kindness, and the end of destruction, and finally he called upon them to help bring about a "new order of the ages."[86]

Each of the four costumed women then stepped forward and, after a statement of reconciliation and concern was read for her, released a dove. The black woman forgave the whites. The woman representing the "red" and "brown" races called for the protection of "Mother Earth." The Asian woman denounced war with particular reference to the war in Vietnam. While the white woman denounced war and waste, saying, "We do not want an industrial–military complex running our nation. . . . We do not want more affluence, more electric gadgets, bigger automobiles, more energy. We want simplicity and conservation." It went on in this vein for two and a half hours. A hundred and one men in white pants with gold sashes and rainbow-colored shirts carried beautifully designed banners bearing symbols of life. After speeches and the presentation of the petitions to the chairman of the California Energy Commission, additional men with flags joined those with the banners and, in turn, became part of an ever-growing tableau that included women with baskets of fruit, grain, and flowers, and a huge globe. The afternoon's activities ended with the singing of "America, the Beautiful" and a Creative Initiative anthem, "Mankind, Arise."

Press reaction to the Sacramento demonstration was generally quite favorable. A commentator from a local school wondered about the demonstrators singing "America, the Beautiful" after they had spoken of uniting nations, races, and religions, but she was otherwise greatly impressed.[87] A bemused reporter from the *Sacramento Union* couldn't make up his mind whether the pageant was closer to the model of Busby Berkley or Joseph Goebbels but concluded that neither could have done a better job.[88] The *Union* reporter's reaction was a rather typical one for outsiders when first confronted with Creative Initiative. On the one hand the group seemed to stand for everything that was good—peace, brotherhood, and a clean environment—but on the other hand there was something disquieting about a movement that could convince mature adults to dress up in elaborate uniforms and costumes and march in highly structured formations to further those same ideals.

Other antinuclear-power forces had already qualified an initiative, "Proposition 15," for the June 15 ballot. If passed, Proposition 15 would have placed nuclear power plants in the state under tighter controls for safety and disposal of nuclear waste, and it would have eliminated the limit on liability for nuclear power plants.[89] Because initiatives were considered "political" and the various legal entities that made up Creative Initiatives in 1975 (Sequoia Seminar, Build the Earth, and the National Initiative Foundation) were all tax-exempt, they could not legally partake in any partisan political activity. That problem was resolved in July 1975 when Creative Initiative created a new organization, "Project Survival," through which people could work in support of the "nuclear safeguards initiative," as its supporters called it, without endangering the tax status of the preexisiting entities.

A skeleton crew remained in the established groups to run some seminars and tend to the correspondence, but virtually all regular activities ceased as members of Creative Initiative directed their considerable energy and single-minded purpose to supporting the antinuclear initiative. Not everybody was pleased with the move. One member, who was employed by the nuclear power industry, worried that the suspension of all youth activities would deprive his children of support for the values he had been instilling in them. He pointed out, with considerable logic given Creative Initiative principles, that supporting a coercive law was not in the spirit of the movement. He argued that people would change their energy consumption behavior only when they had changed their thinking and that attempts to force such change from without were doomed, like Prohibition, to failure. Yet, as a true member of the community, he concluded that he would have to go along with whatever the group decided to do and promised, "I will give what I see and act with totality in whatever direction we proceed."[90]

The decision to give up almost all of the regular recruiting and educational work in order to devote all resources to the nuclear power issue foreshadowed the move made seven years later to abandon the New Religion and become Beyond War. Because the initiative drive was limited by its very nature and would be over, one way or the other, after the election in June, the decision to work for Proposition 15 was not as drastic as the decision to reorganize as Beyond War. Nevertheless, the group's willingness to digress dramatically from its previous course and to undertake a task that was actually contradictory to one of its underlying principles was indicative of a flexibility that sometimes seemed to set the movement at odds with itself.

Opponents of Proposition 15 occasionally tried to paint the entire project as part of a sinister conspiracy devised by Creative Initiative itself (it began using that name during this period). Whether it was a conspiracy, as some contended, or merely an expression of the fervor of a group of "true believers," as some newspaper articles implied, it was obvious to most outsiders that Creative Initiative's activity on behalf of the state proposition went well beyond that usually expected from supporters of a political issue.[91] Although members of Creative Initiative founded and dominated Project Survival, the movement had a life of its own with more than ten thousand affiliated people who had no connection with Creative Initiative either before or after the campaign, and, according to participants, no attempt was made to use the antinuclear power drive to recruit members for Creative Initiative.[92]

Although there were no paid workers on Project Survival, of the more than five thousand people who participated, some men, as well as the usually large contingent of women, worked full-time for the initiative.[93] The greatest personal sacrifice, as well as the most spectacular statement of personal commitment, came from three engineers who worked for General Electric Nuclear Systems in San Jose. Each had independently come to the decision to leave his employment in the nuclear power industry, but because they knew one another both from work and their involvement in Creative Initiative, they decided to act in unison. In a highly publicized news conference in February 1976 they all resigned, citing their concern about the dangers of nuclear power and their inability to work any longer in good conscience for a company that was contributing to a situation they believed endangered all humankind.[94] In the wake of these resignations, some other engineers who were members of Creative Initiative but did not support Proposition 15 reported that they were told they would have to leave the movement unless they could get behind the campaign. Although that "shape up or ship out" ultimatum was eventually rescinded, here, as in so much of the sect's activity, conformity was expected as a sign of commitment.[95]

Project Survival disbanded after the proposition's defeat, and Creative Initiative resumed its full schedule of preproposition activities. The conclusion of this experiment with political activism did not, however, mark an end to the group's concern with ecology. The environmental movement was still running strong in California, and Creative Initiative seemed willing to ride that wave as far as it would go. A flyer from some time after 1976 placed the ecology issue in perspective from Creative Initiative's viewpoint. A page and a half of the handout listed the usual problems of water pollution, air pollution, and the limited supply of natural resources. Then it went further, however, lumping together with these environmental dangers such other problems as the stockpiling of nuclear weapons, divorce, suicide, alcoholism, drug addiction, television violence, pornography, child abuse, and venereal disease. They were all part, said the flyer, of "the whole deterioration of our human environment."[96] By not separating ecology from other social problems, Creative Initiative was able to regard its continued activity in that area as both an educational tool and as an expression of its personal commitment to living lives in harmony with people and nature.

In the years between the failure of the nuclear power safety drive and the emergence of Beyond War, the community engaged in three highly visible public campaigns centered on the ecology issue. In 1977 Creative Initiative formed an organization called the "Palo Alto Youth Conservation Corps." Unlike the national service project, the Youth Conservation Corps had no national plans. Essentially it was a three-week summer program for fifteen- and sixteen-year-old children of Creative Initiative members. Dressed in green polo shirts and riding their bicycles, the twenty-six members of the corps canvassed Palo Alto trying to get citizens "to do one thing more" to conserve water and energy.[97]

In 1979 and 1980 Creative Initiative launched its penultimate campaign in the ecology field. Like the earlier efforts, this one was aimed at conserving energy, but unlike the three-week teenage program in the summer of 1977, it involved the whole community and was a full-bore effort. It began in May 1979, contined through the summer and fall, and was revived briefly during the following summer. Called "Energyfast," the project was an attempt to get people in the Bay Area to cut back on their consumption of energy. Carrying signs that said "Children are the endangered species," "Cooperate now for survival," and "Save energy," a thousand rainbow-suited women introduced the project by marching through downtown San Francisco to a rally in Union Square. There, Creative Initiative spokeswoman Phyllis Kidd reminded the lunchtime crowd that they were the same people who had demonstrated five years earlier against nuclear energy and had been laughed at on the street and defeated at the polls. She said that many people had asked where they had been for five years, and the answer was "we have been studying and investigating. What we see strikes horror in our hearts for the future." Their role, said Kidd, was what it had always been: "to act and to educate the people who have not heard, so they can join with us."[98]

Energyfast used two devices to induce people to participate in the program. The first employed the shock strategy that grew out of Creative Initiative's apocalyptic vision. One flyer began, "People are outraged by the lack of cooperation . . . for survival of life on this planet." Then in bold letters it proclaimed, "Children are the endangered species!" It listed the dangers of nuclear war, waste of energy and natural resources, and poisons in the air, water, and food. It concluded with the terse warnings, "We only have one planet. Our resources are going fast. Life is in danger. Cooperate now for survival."[99] The second, more moderate approach emphasized the need for people to take voluntary action and listed the kinds of changes in transportation and home life that could lead to energy savings. Another flyer that advocated this more positive approach ended with the familiar call for geometric growth. "If each person got one more person each week to Energyfast," it explained, in fewer than six months the population of California would be recruited, and in just seven months the entire population of the United States would be participating.[100]

Energyfast for 1979 reached its conclusion with a full-scale Creative Initiative celebration in Palo Alto's city hall plaza. "International Energy Conservation Day," as they called it, featured half a dozen speakers joined by representatives from fifteen countries and more than sixty other dignitaries who lent their support to the program. There was also the usual Creative Initiative rainbow theme, this time augmented by the

Palo Alto High School marching band, several other bands, and "giant costumed animals." The parade was followed by an ecology fair at a local park.[101]

Despite a presidential citation awarded at White House ceremonies, Creative Initiative was turned down for a state grant to expand the project. The Energyfast idea was revived briefly the following summer; nevertheless, when the public was invited to visit the homes of six Creative Initiative members to see how they had used various conservation measures, including solar heat, to cut down on their use of energy.[102] The failure to expand Energyfast did not discourage the group's environmental efforts; they turned instead to a final effort in the ecology field that once more drew them to the edge of politics.

In July of 1980 a report entitled "Global 2000," prepared at the request of President Jimmy Carter by thirteen different government agencies, was released to the public. Although Creative Initiative believed that the report's gloomy prognostications about population, resources, and the environment were not pessimistic enough, its generally negative outlook did support Creative Initiative's own dire predictions, and the movement immediately included the document in its ecological program.[103] Since the release of "Global 2000" occurred during the 1980 presidential race, Creative Initiative "decided to create a small action task force of about 30 full-time volunteers whose singular task [would] be to impel the candidates to respond to the crucial issues raised by Global 2000."[104]

Dubbing themselves "Global 2000: The Challenge to Change," the special task force began their new endeavor by opening a storefront headquarters on University Avenue, Palo Alto's main street. Posters of presidential candidates Carter, Reagan, and independent John Anderson were pasted on the windows under a banner that asked, "When will the candidates discuss the real issues?"[105] Creative Initiative's Global 2000 project folded with the election but did survive briefly in the form of a "Global 2000 Course" in the winter of 1980–1981.[106]

Drugs and Television

Although he had never consumed alcoholic beverages, Harry Rathbun's long association with Alcoholics Anonymous and, through it, his firsthand knowledge of the destructive effects of drinking had turned the Rathbuns against alcohol quite early in their careers of religious work. Although drinking was discouraged, in effect prohibited, at meetings as early as the Sequoia Seminar days, smoking was tolerated at least through the 1950s. But tobacco eventually joined alcohol as substances shunned by members of Creative Initiative. There was no single explicit reason given for the prohibition of alcohol and tobacco—only a series of explanations that ranged from the waste of farmland and grain to the negative impact on the individual's health and relationships. Using the ecological metaphor, ingestion of such substances was frequently referred to as pollution of the body. And, although tobacco and alcohol were often mentioned negatively in passing during discussions of other subjects, they were never the focus of any public action on the part of the group.

Illegal drugs, however, were featured in several public displays sponsored by Creative Initiative. Although they certainly never spoke about it publicly, the fact that a number of the upper leadership group had briefly experimented with LSD in the late 1950s, when it was legal, gave them a position of some authority when they spoke to the children of the movement hoping to keep them from using illegal drugs. The most elaborate antidrug display was created in 1970 for Mayfield Mall, a major Palo Alto shopping center and later set up at the state capitol in Sacramento. The display occupied half the mall and took almost half a year to build. It described effects of both alcohol and tobacco as well as those of illegal drugs. Betsy Scarborough, the Creative Initiative person who spearheaded the project, explained the movement's position by saying that drugs were used by people who were "uncomfortable with themselves and cannot express their feelings." She went on to say, "I believe that each of us has our own share of creative potential."[107]

If alcohol, tobacco, and drugs were pollutants for the body, then television was pollution for the mind. In 1974 the "parent education team" of Creative Initiative circulated a letter that urged members to participate in a project being run by ABC to gather information on what parents thought of children's television programs.[108] There was no particular followup to this suggestion until 1977, when the "Woman to Woman Building the Earth" segment of Creative Initiative organized a one-year program called "Women's Network" to try to improve the quality of television. Unlike most of the public programs run by the movement, in which the ideological motivation was fairly clear even if it were not made explicit, the rationale for Women's Network remains obscure. One can surmise that ultimately the women hoped to attract more people to the movement—for that was always one of the goals of any program aimed at the public. In fact, the only document we could find that lists the purposes of Women's Network does not even mention television but rather reads like a general description of Creative Initiative itself. The group's objective is listed as building "a network of women who will work together to build a better world for the children and all life."[109]

In their attempt to improve television programming, the group held public meetings, handed out information sheets, and urged people to write both to the networks and to advertisers making their feelings known. In addition, they sponsored a speech by Nicholas Johnson, the outspoken former FCC commissioner who called television a "vast wasteland," and they published several versions of a handout called "Guidelines for Conscious Viewing."[110] Most of the suggestions were reasonable and nondogmatic, advising that parents be aware of what their children watch, discuss the programs with them, and not allow television to interfere with other activities within the family. Finally, the Women's Network distributed a petition through which broadcasters were urged to adhere to their own code and stop airing shows that assaulted "the human mind by the showing of excessive violence, aberrated sex, and a loss of respect for the individual person."[111]

Women's Network lasted almost one full year. There is no indication that anything like a hundred thousand women were enrolled by the target date of 1978. They decided to disband the effort and move on, nevertheless, urging those who were interested in staying with the television issue to contact the Committee on Children's Television.[112]

The Role of Public Action

The television effort, like every other public program sponsored by Creative Initiative, proved to be ephemeral. Great enthusiasm and grandiose predictions were followed by a strong burst of effort that was never sustained. No matter what the results, and they were frequently modest by any standards and far short of the group's own predictions, success was declared and a new direction taken. Sometimes the project lasted only a couple of months, like the Palo Alto Initiative, and sometimes a few years, like the Bless Man shows. Usually, however, the life cycle of public activities was around a year.

Each of the projects appears to have been a small-scale recapitulation of the movement as a whole; great expectations followed by furious effort, ending, if not in failure, then at least in unfulfilled expectations. According to their own philosophy, the essence of progress (continued evolution) was flexibility and freedom from preconceived patterns. By constantly changing their short-range focus and, at greater intervals, by changing their community name and image, they were living out their own ideology. By making inconstancy a constant the community was able to avoid the challenge of reality. If they had set hard and fast long-range goals, then their progress—or lack thereof—could have been easily measured, and they would have been faced with the dilemma of how to alter their beliefs or behaviors to achieve their stated ends. But by keeping the group in a state of flux, never lingering long at any one place, they could provide the membership with ever new goals and excitement and the appearance, if not the reality, of accomplishment.

The public presentations also functioned within the sect to give people a way to interact with the outside world other than the one-to-one proselytizing that was their main method of attracting new members. Creative Initiative was sufficiently outside of the mainstream to have to keep religious practices and values quiet, if not actually secret. Yet by incorporating many of those religious values into various presentations and projects, they were able to "practice" their religion in public without risking rejection. Thus, the various campaigns and programs were a way for community members to reinforce their own beliefs by affirming them in public. At the same time, the public programs allowed them to fulfill one of the basic tenets of the New Religion: that all members work actively to spread their ideas to outsiders.

Like all committed revolutionaries (and they never doubted that they were revolutionaries, albeit peaceful ones) the members of Creative Initiative truly believed that victory was imminent. All that was needed to bring about the change they sought was a push in the right direction by a visionary minority who perceived reality while the rest of society was still caught up in a false consciousness. Their homocentric beliefs restrained them from becoming too deeply involved in purely political activities, but invariably most of the public issues they espoused had political implications, and they were not always successful in avoiding the lure of political activity. Even when their own actions were not actually political, they frequently demanded that public officials take specific actions to alleviate the targeted problems, be it television violence, international violence, or violence against the environment. Although they did not always say so explicitly, it was always assumed that nothing politicians did could ultimately solve the problems unless the people had a change of heart, and all their "educational" campaigns had that as their real purpose.

8

A World Beyond War

When Creative Initiative decided to suspend most of its regular activities in 1975 so that it could throw its effort behind the drive to control nuclear power plants, it unwittingly initiated a process that led to the second-most profound change in the history of the movement. The first great transformation had taken place when Emilia had her religious vision and the study group became a new religion. The second change occurred in 1982 when the group decided to give up the religious activities that had been developed over forty-five years and secularize the movement. This would appear to be an unprecedented move for a religion. Religiously affiliated institutions, such as colleges, sometimes become secularized, but for a "church" to divest itself of all religious forms and functions, including the place of God in the organized structure, is unique.

Richard Rathbun and the New Generation

Because the ballot initiative to control nuclear energy was political, as a tax-exempt foundation Creative Initiative was not permitted to become involved with it. To comply with the restriction, they created a separate organization, Project Survival, to carry on the anti-nuclear effort. James Burch, the president of the Creative Initiative Foundation, resigned that post so that he could direct Project Survival.

A new president was needed for the foundation, and Burch's place was filled by Rathbun's son, Richard.

Richard was Harry and Emilia's second child, born in 1940, seven years after his sister Juana Beth. Following a brief period of doubts as a young adult, Juana moved into the Creative Initiative inner circle and became very involved with her mother in formulating the ceremonies of the New Religion period. She did not, however, have her mother's charismatic personality and, in any event, a woman would not have been considered an appropriate leader for the group. By the late 1970s, much of the control of the group had shifted from women to men in accordance with their belief that women were the source of new insights and understanding but men would carry those visions to fruition. Richard was the apple of Emilia's eye, and she believed that he had the kind of spiritual sensitivity and personal style that would enable him to lead the movement successfully.[1]

Richard did not participate in the movement as he grew up. He did, of course, absorb a great deal simply by virtue of being his parents' child. As a youngster he went with them to seminars conducted by Sharman and then later to the summer seminars they led. But Richard had a strong independent streak and remained as aloof from the movement as possible, which was not too hard since he completed high school and most of college before the group had begun their programs to involve children.[2]

After graduating from Stanford, he joined the Peace Corps and worked in a small Nepalese village for several years. His long road home took four more years of travel through India and Africa with his wife Carolyn, who had traveled to Nepal to marry him. Other than a staff position in the Peace Corps, he held his only regular job in South Africa where he worked as an architect designing churches. He says that the experience made him realize that he did not want to spend his life designing buildings because there were more important issues to be dealt with. He thought about entering law school and then going on in politics when he returned to the United States, but instead he rebuilt his parents' home, which had been destroyed in a fire, and then took on the presidency of the movement in 1975.[3]

To some extent Harry and Emilia had viewed Richard as the heir apparent to the leadership of the movement, and Richard and Carolyn say they have not had children in part because they wish to avoid the possibility of a three-generation dynasty.[4] Harry, no less than Emilia, thought that Richard had special qualities that would allow him to lead.

"I truly believe that you have a destiny," Harry wrote to Richard in 1971. "You have gifts by natural endowment which give you advantages that cannot be learned." He went on to assure Ricahrd that, although he may have found school work difficult, he did have "an attractiveness to people which is called charisma." While Richard was trying to figure out what to do with his life, Harry was continuously urging him to become active in the movement. "You have seen [i.e. imagined] yourself as head of the country," Harry wrote to him. "This [movement] could well lead to that but in a different way than through politics."[5]

Harry's admiration for what he thought were Richard's special qualities derived from the contrast that he saw between himself and his son. "The qualities you inherited from your mother are a tremendous asset which will stand you in good stead," he told Richard, thereby implying that those same qualities did not come from him. In fact, Harry had doubts about his own abilities—an opinion not shared by most of those who studied the gospels with him. Repeatedly, Harry referred to himself as "passive" and as having an "inferiority complex" in his letters to Richard, and asked for Richard's understanding for his failures as a father. Richard apparently felt alienated from his father and felt that Harry's passivity was the result of Emilia's domination. But Harry always insisted that his character weaknesses, if indeed they were such, predated his marriage and that Emilia had been his guide to seeing his problems and working his way out of them.[6]

During Richard's six-year sojourn abroad, Harry suggested a number of possible ways that he might find a place in the movement. At one point Harry thought Richard could become an instructor in the AMR program, a series of personal development courses for which higher than usual fees were charged and which the movement considered opening to outsiders. Later, at the urging of the group, which had been impressed with Richard's photographs, he suggested that Richard purchase a movie camera and take stock footage that they could use in their various public presentations. Richard accepted that suggestion and thus first became formally involved in Creative Initiative as a photographer.[7]

At about the same time that Richard assumed the presidency, other new faces began to appear in the inner leadership circle. Like the first generation, these new leaders rose because of their fervent belief in the movement's philosophy and willingness to commit themselves totally to its ends. They also had to get the consent of the senior leadership including Emilia and Harry, who were giving up more and more of their influence over Creative Initiative but remained the admired and respected founders.

Even with Richard as titular head of the movement, Emilia was uneasy about the state of the New Religion. On the surface the group appears to have returned to its traditional pattern in 1977 after the defeat of the nuclear-power ballot measure. Although the usual courses, seminars, and community activities were resumed, Emilia said she felt there was insufficient commitment on the part of those who were active in the movement. The fervor of "totality" that had marked the 1960s and 1970s seemed to be drying up. Perhaps the excursion into the political arena had diluted the singleness of the religious purpose or perhaps Emilia's disappointment and regret were the feelings of a leader in her old age recognizing that her life-long goals were not apt to be realized any time soon.

In 1978 Emilia told a group of high-level members, "These people, this bunch is all we'll ever have. We must maximize these. We're supposed to have a thousand by now, but we have to move with what we have."[8] Her remarks came after a dramatic attempt to rekindle community idealism. It had been more than thirty years since the Rathbuns had branched out on their own, and more than fifteen years since they had founded the New Religion of the Third Age, but still they had not achieved the mystical one thousand totally dedicated people. From the earliest days of the New Religion the group had made a thousand members their proximate goal. No one was sure exactly what would happen if and when they had the thousand, but there was a widespread belief that God would give them further instructions at that point. Despite the fact that thousands of people had passed through their courses, no further instructions had come because the goal of one thousand fourth-level members had never been reached. It had been clear that something was needed to renew the sense of commitment and direction that had marked the early years, and to resume progress toward gathering the thousand dedicated souls.

At the end of 1977, Emilia and the inner leadership concluded that the movement had to undergo a major reassessment to insure a greater commitment to totality. "Too many people . . . have refused to make the basic religious decision and failed to work the process in their own lives," they said. A notice announcing that "our work is in serious crisis" was sent to all members in January 1978, informing them that "as of today there is no longer a Creative Initiative 'community.' Only individuals. All meetings are cancelled. All specialties are disbanded. The office will be closed indefinitely."[9]

In fact the reality was less dramatic than the announcement. A skeleton staff remained active to run introductory programs for new members, and there was never any intention of actually dissolving the movement permanently. Rather, the action was designed to revive the level of dedication—it was Creative Initiative's version of the Great Cultural Revolution, an attempt to artificially recreate the drama of the original event for a generation that had not experienced it. It was also the way for the group to purge itself of people who were then less totally dedicated to the cause. By dissolving the organization and then having people reapply for membership, those with only marginal commitment could be left behind without actually having to be expelled. Although members say that nobody was ever asked to leave, six hundred people, one-third of the membership, never returned to the group after the dissolution.[10]

However heroic the cure, it does not seem to have worked. There were fewer courses and fewer public activities in 1979 than in previous years, and fewer yet in 1980. The sense of crisis that leaders continued to feel was reflected in material for an experimental advanced course on Jesus that was run in 1981. The introduction to the course began (just one year before secularization) by affirming that "The teachings of Jesus have always been the foundation upon which our work is based." The material went on to say that during the previous several years it had become clear that "disappointingly few of those who have been involved for a considerable length of time in our 'process' have really entered the religious life." Something had to be done to speed up the educational process and get people committed to a religious life in which people would accept that "Jesus of Nazareth is the Supreme teacher, demonstrator and exemplar of THE WAY."[11]

The leaner, more dedicated movement that emerged after the dissolution had not been the answer, and neither were the experimental Jesus courses tried in 1980 and 1981. The problem remained because it had not been properly identified. The real problem was not a lack of commitment but an inability to grow. Creative Initiative, in the form it had taken through the 1960s and 1970s, seems to have exhausted the reservoir of potential members. Its focus on upper middle class whites and its continued demand for total dedication to the group meant that it was unable to grow to the desired thousand totally committed members.

The major focus of Creative Initiatives' public activities in the years after Project Survival continued to be on the ecology issues, specifically Energyfast and on the Global 2000 project. They believed that by bringing the dangers that threatened earth to peoples' attention, Creative Initiative could attract individuals who would then continue their affiliation through involvement with the New Religion. Although this focus on ecology did not work any better than previous devices for attracting new people, in 1981 the ecology issue, the nuclear power issue, and the group's long-standing antiwar position finally coalesced, and Creative Initiative found a new direction for a new generation and a new era.

The Antiwar Tradition

The decision to focus exclusively on the antiwar issue had deep antecedents. Opposition to war had been a significant motif in the Rathbuns' work since Harry's high school valedictory address in 1911. With the coming of the atomic age in 1945, the possibility of manmade nuclear Armageddon became a recurring theme in the movement's apocalyptic predictions. There was little that the movement could do in opposition to war as long as they were a gospel study group but, after they became a sect with a more complex set of social functions, new options were available.

Creative Initiative had always believed that women, as the creators of life, were instinctively opposed to war. A piece that was clearly Emilia's, written sometime in the late 1960s, declared, "Within woman, deeply buried, as fire is buried at the center of the earth, exists an inborn, passionate desire—to live without the fear of war." It was men who destroyed, and it was women's special mission to transform men from warmakers to peacemakers. The same paper said, "We call on men in every land, in every clime, to 'Build the Earth,' to stop the pain, to end the rape, the killing, and turn the corner of the age; ascend the mountain, gain a broader view."[12] Thus, the movement's antiwar activity, like almost everything else it did, was begun by the women.

The group's first organized antiwar activity came in 1967 when the women sponsored a "minute for peace." Operating under the name "Woman to Woman Building the Earth for the Children's Sake," about two hundred women and children gathered at the Ferry Building in San

Francisco three days before Christmas to sing seasonal and peace songs and to observe "a minute of silence for the children's sake." The positive response from people and extensive publicity from Bay Area newspapers, television, and radio stations prompted them to expand their efforts.[13]

In May, twenty-four members of the movement joined several hundred other women in signing an advertisement published in the *Palo Alto Times* calling for "an end to killing." Like the minute for peace, the advertisement was obviously aimed at the war in Vietnam, although that conflict was not specifically mentioned. The advertisement was actually placed by Another Mother for Peace and featured their logo and slogan: "War is not healthy for children and other living things." In July a delegation of movement women traveled to Los Angeles to see if Build the Earth and Another Mother for Peace could cooperate in further antiwar efforts. No joint activities ensued because some members of Build the Earth were suspicious that several women in Another Mother for Peace "were connected with the Communist movement in this country."[14]

Although they were concerned about American Communists, Creative Initiative women were nevertheless willing to develop contacts with people from Communist countries. The women in the movement met with visitors from Eastern Europe in 1969 and again in 1970, stressing the importance of international friendship as a way to maintain peace. The first event featured an international fashion show that was used to raise funds for a visit by a delegation from the Czechoslovak Women's Council. Shirley Temple Black provided the commentary.[15] The following year a group of Build the Earth women held dinners, receptions, and a public serenade for a contingent of Soviet women whom they had invited to visit the United States when some of the Build the Earth women had been on a visit to the Soviet Union.[16]

Three years later, the group embarked on its most extreme activity in the antiwar arena. On October 12, 1973, over five hundred women in rainbow-colored costumes with long flowing skirts marched through San Francisco's Union Square carrying placards calling for an end to the Arab–Israeli war. They visited the Israeli Consulate and the Arab Information Center and presented their plea for peace in the Middle East.[17]

Their unconventional approach did not stop with their costumes. Distressed that the Arab–Israeli conflict might mean that "we could be on the brink of World War III," they took a step that publicly revealed the depth of their personal commitment and risked exposing themselves to charges of being a "cult" and out of touch with reality. Having read that the people on both sides were demanding blood, a number of women decided during their drive up to the city to offer their own blood if that could prevent innocent civilians from dying. Twenty of the women publicly offered to sacrifice their lives to bring about a cease-fire. According to Virginia Fitton, probably the second most influential woman leader behind Emilia herself, "to show our concern, 10 women have offered their lives to each side to be shot to bring about the laying down of arms."[18] If they hoped to shock the combatants with their commitment they were partially successful since the Israeli consulate said he found the offer "shocking." Although it was a spur of the moment decision, it did reflect the commitment to totality that transformed people were supposed to exhibit.[19] A week later, six hundred men in business suits participated in a similar march, a sight that was probably as unexpected as the rainbow-colored clothing of the women.[20] Finally, in 1976, during the height of the fighting in Northern Ireland, Build the Earth organized a march of two thousand members in San Francisco, in support of the effort by Irish women to bring about an end to the conflict there.[21]

Thus, when the forces of circumstance turned the group's attention to the nuclear war issue in 1980, they had a long history of strong antiwar activity upon which to draw. War, after all, was the most likely and most immediate threat to the continued existence of the human race and, as a movement that viewed itself as a counterforce to Armageddon, Creative Initiative found it easy to shift all their effort to that single issue. Unlike all the previous single-purpose mobilizations, this one stuck. They did not grow tired or disappointed and start looking for another cause to champion because this time they burned their bridges behind them. By eliminating every organized vestige of religious activity, they made the success of the new Beyond War effort the only way to continue the life of the movement. Although older members of the group did not reject the possibility of returning to a religious framework sometime in the future, most of the younger people saw the shift as irreversible. What had been a New Religion for the Third Age, was now a secular group working for peace.

The Decision to Secularize

At first, Beyond War was merely another new project for Creative Initiative. It was not a separate entity, and all Creative Initiative's other courses and religious activity were kept intact. Increasingly, however, the secular began to dominate the religious. The collective religious activities, ceremonies, and rituals were gradually dropped, but the theistic underpinning and individual religiosity were temporarily intact. Most of the people from the Los Angeles area who attended a seminar with Harry and Emilia in June 1983, well after Beyond War had begun, could still state that the experience had deepened their religious commitment. "I have chosen to be identified with God," reported one person, "God is #1 in my life." Another wrote, "The change in me was the feeling of having now found a goal for my life—doing the will of God . . . and bringing the Kingdom of God about on earth." Others spoke about the seminar enhancing their understanding of the use of meditation and prayer.[22] As late as March 1985 general meetings of the Beyond War leaders at Ben Lomond were still begun with prayers.[23]

A transition was being made, nevertheless, and large numbers of new people were becoming involved who had no background in the New Religion aspect of the movement, and no attempt was made to indoctrinate them. Old-time Creative Initiative activists could, and some did, celebrate the Sunday candle-lighting ceremony in their homes, and they would hold hands and recite "the Shema of the New Age" when they met together; but for the vast majority of people, the explicitly religious either atrophied or was never there in the first place.

A number of the people who answered our questionnaire remarked sadly that they regretted the end of the religious community. One woman wrote that she and her family missed the "sense of direction we had as a group before" and that they were "struggling a bit to figure out how we will sustain our spiritual/religious lives."[24] Another was actually bitter, calling himself "disillusioned in the abrupt way in which Creative Initiative came to an end." One moment, he complained, they were a community, the next they were just individuals. He concluded, "I truly wonder if we ever really had the warm, loving relationship that I thought we had."[25] As these people's remarks make clear, in the transition from Creative Initiative to Beyond War, the movement ceased to be a sect. The positive social support that was so essential in maintaining sect membership vanished, but then so did the need to repay the high cost of membership, because as a relatively noncontroversial, nonreligious movement, the social cost of membership in Beyond War was not nearly as high as that of Creative Initiative.

Several separate events had prompted the new focus on nuclear war.

First, a number of sources criticized the Global 2000 report as concentrating on other ecological dangers but totally ignoring the threat of atomic weapons. At the same time people in the movement were reading Jonathan Schell's anti-nuclear-war articles in the *New Yorker,* "The Fate of the Earth."[26] Even more important was the influence of the film, "The Last Epidemic," featuring the ideas of Physicians for Social Responsibility and its leader, Dr. Helen Caldicott. Simultaneously, but unknown to each other, groups in Palo Alto and Los Angeles viewed the film and were moved to take some kind of action.[27] Their newfound resolve to switch emphasis from ecology to nuclear war was supported by the coincidental involvement of Caldicott in Creative Initiative.

Caldicott and her husband, William, had first attended a seminar in late 1975 and had been tremendously moved by the experience. She wrote to Harry and Emilia that they both felt "as if a fresh wind had swept through our lives."[28] Three years later, she was still deeply involved in the movement. In an interview with the *New York Times,* William Caldicott said of Creative Initiative, "It's become the prime focus of our lives over the last few years, even more so than the nukes." The reason for their involvement lay in the role that the group had played in saving their marriage. Both agreed that had it not been for their participation in Creative Initiative seminars, they would have been divorced. Demonstrating the influence of Creative Initiative ideas, they explained that they had been hypocritical by going out and trying to influence other people when their own marriage and family were a "mess." Creative Initiative, they said, had taught them to be honest with each other and to communicate their feelings. Finally, Helen Caldicott said that she had changed her approach as a result of her experience with the movement. Previously she had worked out of a feeling of hatred that, she said, only engendered hostility from the other side. Now she was working through love.[29]

At first, there was some effort to maintain a dual system with religious ceremonies continuing for the old members while new members operated on a completely secular basis. It was clear after a year or so that such an arrangement would never work. New members would either be put off by the religious aspects of the work that the old members were continuing or would feel excluded. In either case the two-tiered structure would guarantee division and probably dissension. To resolve the issue, the ceremony committee drew up a terminal ceremony, a ceremony to mark the end of ceremonies, and even that was anticlimactic. Rather than meeting to bring closure to an era that had lasted twenty years, the final ceremony, as described in chapter 3, was a meditation that each person said individually. By doing so they were acknowledging that the movement was no longer a community but a collection of individuals.

Relieved of its religious trappings, the movement was able to grow at a rate it had only dreamed of previously. The group had always known that its unorthodox beliefs had acted as a deterrent to new people who were otherwise in sympathy with its social ideas, which is the reason it had always been reticent about explaining the religious aspects of its work in public presentations. After 1982 it no longer needed to downplay this dimension. Although people still wondered about what motivated the high level of commitment participants exhibited, and Beyond War was still sometimes accused of being a cult, what had been an arcane body of knowledge revealed in progressive stages no longer existed, except in history. They could even say—as they always had, but this time more straightforwardly—that they had no guru or dominant leader and all decisions were made "from the ground up."[30]

The group still does not make a point of explaining its origins. In fact, the major reservation that Creative Initiative leaders had about cooperating with us on this study was the fear that newcomers to Beyond War, who greatly outnumber the Creative Initiative veterans, might be put off by the details of its religious past. Nevertheless, reporters writing about Beyond War are usually told that the group grew out of Creative Initiative, a nondenominational, spiritual, personal-enrichment movement that studied the teachings of Jesus as a man but not as a savior.[31] Virginia Fitton, one of the most senior Creative Initiative leaders, has gone so far as to acknowledge that Creative Initiative was a religion "in the sense that it became a way of life" and that members had eschewed alcohol and tobacco, although not on moral grounds.[32]

When they get together, the Creative Initiative veterans will still sometimes open their meetings with prayer and testimony, and a few of the people who have been active in the movement since the earliest days of Creative Initiative still harbor the hope that at the right time religion will return.[33] Richard Rathbun and others of the new generation of leaders, however, argue that Beyond War is seeking the same goals as Creative Initiative and that the new movement, no less than the old, is a way of loving and obeying the will of God. Therefore, they claim, it is unnecessary to revive the religious forms so long as they are practicing the religious content.[34]

Beyond War

The new organization is not a sect. It does not have a charismatic leader. Due to ill health, Harry retired almost completely from active participation in the five years before his death in 1987, and Emilia took on the role of revered but less-active elder, although she can still totally dominate a meeting when she wants to through the sheer force of her personality.[35] Richard is the president, and members often feel it is necessary to check with him before making decisions. His ideas of the moment seem to dominate leadership thinking in much the way that Emilia's did previously, but there is no sense of his having a connection to the supranatural in the same way as his mother.[36] Beyond War appears to be, in fact, what Creative Initiative always said it was: a nebulous organization without formal membership and with only the loosest of leadership.

So imprecise is their sense of organization that participants are usually more comfortable describing what Beyond War is *not*. They say it is not antimilitary, it is not pacifist, members are not activists, it is not a peace group. Virginia Fitton says it is not even an organization but rather "more of an organism."[37] Functionally, Beyond War is profoundly different from Creative Initiative because it does not provide its members with a structured community. Informally, of course, so many people devoting so much time and energy to a common cause inevitably develop some sense of community. But the feeling of belonging that people have in Beyond War is more akin to that felt by members of any other affinity group than that felt by members of a religious sect.

What ties Beyond War to its past is its philosophy. By dropping the study of Jesus, the group has severed its most important link to the Sharman era. But it retains many of the principles that had evolved from the study of Jesus as Teacher and, in those ideas, the ideological tradition is still clearly visible. The presentation of those principles has been denuded of the religious justifications and, in many cases, of the underlying philosophical rationale as well. In this sense, the Beyond War approach is similar to the introductory programs that were run by Creative Initiative, in which the public was exposed to their ideas in nonreligious language. There is a significant difference, however. In the Creative Initiative period, the pared-down version was used as a foretaste of the richer feast to come. In the Beyond War period the philosophy as it is presented to the public is all the philosophy there is. The

gnostic approach of revealing increasingly more arcane levels of knowledge is gone. The philosophy that is presented is, nevertheless, almost
entirely based on the ideas developed during the New Religion period.
Although they have been softened in most cases, they are still completely recognizable.

Both the old and the new movements are predicated on the assumption that the world is traveling quickly down the road to total destruction. In Beyond War, this apocalyptic vision is invariably presented by
way of a quotation from Albert Einstein: "The unleashed power of the
atom has changed everything save our modes of thinking and we thus
drift toward unparalleled catastrophe."[38] Not only does the quotation
contain the threat of worldwide destruction, but it also implies the
solution: all we need to do is change our mode of thinking to match the
new mode of destruction and we will be able to control it. "A new way
of thinking" has become Beyond War's operative slogan and is the
current expression of the Creative Initiative belief that the world could
be saved by people who consciously decided to change themselves and
obey the will of God.

A new twist on the apocalyptic vision is the group's contention that
nuclear war is inevitable unless people change their way of thinking.
Using the arguments of one of their members, Professor Martin Hellman of Stanford, they contend that any conflict, no matter how small,
contains the potential for nuclear Armageddon because there is always
the danger of the great powers becoming involved. Hellman argues that
each conflict is like a spin of the chambers in a game of Russian roulette.
No matter how small the chance, no matter how many chambers there
are in the theoretical gun, if the trigger is pulled often enough there is a
mathematical certainty that the gun will fire.[39] The only way to stop this
suicidal game, they contend, is to create a world in which no conflicts
are resolved through violence and, therefore, the trigger is never
pulled.[40]

The essential premise of the belief system, going back to Sharman,
was the existence and goodness of God. Creative Initiative sought to
prove this concept by describing God as the first cause everywhere
immanent in His creation. Indeed that creation was of God and, therefore, creation was good.[41] As a secular movement, Beyond War cannot
build its argument on a theistic premise, but it can, and does, retain the
monistic world view that derived from the assumption of God as first
cause. "We live on one planet with one life-support system. We all
breathe the same air, drink the same water. We are part of one human

family," said the first edition of the Beyond War handbook.[42] The slogan, "We are one," has been revived and used in Beyond War work, and its implications have been pushed to new limits. The handbook informed its readers, "Lift your little finger and the stars move—ever so slightly, but they move. When the stars move, you are affected—ever so slightly, but you are affected."[43] They conclude from this that no person and no nation can exist in isolation, and therefore whatever harms anyone or anything on the planet harms everyone and everything.

In the Creative Initiative period scientific thinking in general and evolution in particular played a large part in explaining how God's plan for humankind worked. Obviously, without any explicit references to God or Jesus, the Beyond War movement no longer has to justify either its theology or its study of the gospels with scientific rationalization because both have been eliminated. Both scientific terminology and the central role of evolution nevertheless remain in the revised approach. Quotations from prominent figures and analogous examples from science are presented as supporting evidence in Beyond War publications, and the scientific examples are designed to make their ideas appear more factual than theoretical.

Evolution is no longer presented as the method through which people can become a new species in a third age. In fact, the whole concept of a third age or third dispensation, has been dropped. Evolution is now presented as essential to obtaining the "knowledge" that is the first step in a three-step process that has replaced the old seven steps of Challenge to Change. The second step is "decision" and the third is "action." Beyond War argues that most people lack the knowledge necessary to insure survival and that the first place to look in order to gain the necessary understanding is the process that produced us all, evolution. Evolution, as used in Beyond War, is a pale shadow of the dynamic concept that underlay Creative Initiative. They still argue that human beings need to continue to evolve in order to meet a changing environment. But continued evolution is now usually described as the evolution of ideas only. Almost all mention of mutations, new races, and rising to a new spiritual plane are gone.[44] Occasionally, however, echoes of the past do creep into Beyond War presentations. Speaking to a large men's convocation in 1984, one leader said, "we are in a peduncle between phylums on the tree of life. Other great phylum changes have been unconscious. This one is different in kind in that it is a conscious change."[45]

Gone too is any mention of the Kingdom of God. That specifically religious phrase with its origins in the New Testament obviously has no place in a secular movement. Yet a secularized version of the Kingdom of God is still the goal of the group. No name is given to it, and it is referred to only tangentially, but the goal of the movement is "a world beyond war," a world in which people will resolve their conflicts creatively and without violence, a world in which they will see one another not as potential enemies but as fellow partners in the process of improving the quality of life on earth. To achieve their goal of a world in which no one casts another person as an enemy, Beyond War explains that people have to expand beyond their particularistic identification. This is the Beyond War analog of the process in Creative Initiative of surrendering the individual ego. Particularistic "identification" is the new word for "frame of reference."[46]

Once people have understood and obtained the knowledge that human beings can move forward by building on the ideas of others, that it is not necessary to pose enemies and that conflicts can be resolved without violence, then they are ready to move to the second step, "decision." "Decision" takes the place in Beyond War of "transformation" in Creative Initiative. Transformation, however, consisted of giving up the individual will to obey the will of God, whereas "decision" involves only a determination to adopt what is now called "a new way of thinking." Yet, since Beyond War believes that individuals cannot make the "decision" until they have expanded beyond their personal identification, the process is a parallel of the old Creative Initiative process.

There is an additional similarity between the old surrender to the will of God and the new decision to move beyond war—totality. "A true decision must be total," the Beyond War handbook tells its readers. "Unless we totally reject war as an old, obsolete approach, we will not discover how to move beyond war." The decision is further described as one between "yes" and "no" and between "life" and "death."[47] It is a version of positing the old good and evil dichotomy in which each person can only decide totally yes or totally no; there is still no middle ground in the dualistic universe. Choices are presented as the "old mode" and the "new mode." The old mode consists of thinking in terms of limited identification, exclusiveness, blaming enemies, killing, destroying, war, and extinction. The new mode is the opposite of each of these, identification with the whole, inclusiveness, taking personal responsibility, cooperation and building, rejecting war, and choosing life.[48]

Just as Creative Initiative members were expected to "live the life" personally before they could do so collectively, so Beyond War people are told, "A world beyond war is possible only if we make a personal commitment to live our lives in accordance with the new mode of thinking." Then, reiterating a favorite phrase from the earlier era, the handbook states, "The message and the messenger must be consistent." Each person is asked to pledge that he or she will resolve conflict without violence, maintain a spirit of goodwill, not become preoccupied with enemies, and work with others to build a world beyond war.[49] Group leaders explain that members are expected to resolve conflicts both inside and outside the family without resorting to confrontation and violence.

The heavy emphasis on marriage-for-life and the discouraging of single members that existed in Creative Initiative has been toned down considerably. Single and divorced people are welcome in the movement, but some participants still find a strong, if informal, emphasis on couples and the family. One participant in a Beyond War meeting found their philosophy "pervaded by a peculiarly fundamentalist mindset about the family." The talk about "family discipline," of strengthening spousal relationships and doing something about the 50-percent divorce rate, all seemed to her more akin to a traditional church than to an antiwar movement. She said she was queried no fewer than three times about her own marital status and was told by one woman, "We believe marriage is very, very important."[50]

The ghost of Creative Initiative shows itself in other aspects of Beyond War's view of the sexes. Although Jung is not mentioned in the new group's literature, the ideas about gender differences were still being used until recently. One striking example of the continued belief in distinct gender roles occurred in the 1984 convocations: one for men and another for women. Participants at the women's convocation in Palo Alto and similar symposia in other areas were told that they were participating in a "rite of passage" for women that marked their new status as a women's collective that would lead humankind to a new way of thinking.[51] They were also told that men and women had different moral imperatives, and that it was women's role to "care for life and alleviate suffering."[52]

The announcement for the men's meeting explained that in the past men had gathered to hunt and to fight wars but that now they had to come together to become "new warriors" for peace.[53] In language that was very reminiscent of Creative Initiative, one of the speakers told the

audience, "After sexism is stripped away, there is still something different [between men and women] and they have important and different
roles to play in any cohesive society."[54]

To remind themselves of the pledge to resolve conflicts peacefully,
participants are asked to wear a small enamel pin in the shape of the
earth. The little card that comes with the pin says, "When you wear this
pin, remember, pray or meditate on this thought until it becomes a
reality."[55] The reference to meditation and prayer on the pin card is one
of the very few and faint echoes of the religious era. Yet if one looks
carefully they do show up here and there, in such understated ways that
only those familiar with the New Religion would catch the allusions.
They exist because the new movement is an evolutionary descendent of
the old and both vestigial and functional structures remain. After describing the process of deciding to adopt the new way of thinking and
apply it to daily life, for example, the handbook notes that "only a few
rare individuals in human history have held to these high principles" but
that "the future of the world depends on many people holding these
principles and working together."[56] The reference to a "few rare individuals" is an oblique reference to Jesus, and the second comment about
"people working together" in the same way as the few unique individuals is an echo of the belief that the community was a collective messiah.
Except that now, there is no community in the old sense, only a collection of individuals trying to persuade other individuals to think as they
think.

The third step in the three-step process is "action." Beyond War
teaches that once individuals have changed their own personal ways of
thinking they need to move on to teach others how to do the same
thing. As in Creative Initiative, action consists of spreading the word.
Defending this homocentric approach to social change, the handbook
asks rhetorically, "Are education and building agreement action?" and
answers "Absolutely—even though they are not usually recognized as
such." The argument here is the perfectly reasonable one that before any
kind of legislative action can be taken there has to be a popular consensus, or else, like Prohibition, the law is bound to fail.[57] Like Creative
Initiative, Beyond War specifically rejects the "illusion" that someone
else (a savior, a political leader) will prevent war and argues that the
single person can make a difference, so long as he or she works with
others of like mind.

To explain how the new consensus in opposition to war will take
hold, Beyond War argues that a few "innovators" (previously called the

"creative minority") can hope to influence the entire nation. They cite research studies that show if 5 percent of a population believes something the idea becomes "imbedded," and when 20 percent accept a new idea it becomes "unstoppable." Thus, it is the job of the innovators to try to convert that first 5 percent, who in turn will keep the flame alive until the majority is eventually won over. The conclusion it draws from this theory of social change is that Beyond War needs to focus its energy on those people who are open to change and not "spend time vainly trying to convince laggards."[58] In order to get the 5-percent adoption rate, Beyond War estimates that its message may have to reach as much as 50 percent of the population, and thus the essential task of the movement is getting the message out to as many people as possible, but ideally to the "innovators" and "early adopters" who are more open to new concepts.[59] Although it does not appear in their published material, members still use the geometric progression model to encourage one another about the possibility of contacting huge numbers of people. At one meeting, in fact, an optimistic member predicted that if they could keep up their rate of contacts they will have reached over six million people by the 1992 election.[60]

Since they believe that the way to move the world beyond war is to educate as many people as possible, Beyond War has been organized from the beginning to be an engine of growth. One of the earliest written plans for the new movement set the familiar goal of building a base of a thousand people who would work to bring a world beyond war. All early efforts, luncheons, presentations, interviews with national figures, production of films and other materials, and creating the Beyond War Award, were aimed at garnering that elusive thousand.[61] This time, however, there was no longer a multiyear course of study that had to be followed, people did not have to be "identified" and go through an initiation process, and becoming active in the new group did not involve the same high social costs as joining Creative Initiative. Thus the magic number was quickly reached, and growth continued in leaps and bounds.

In 1984, Beyond War sent seventeen "missionary families" to eleven states to begin local groups. These volunteers either retired or took leaves of absence from their jobs so that they could devote full time to spreading the Beyond War message. By 1985 more than four hundred people, including fifty men, worked as full-time volunteers for the movement, and they had an active following of more than eighteen thousand people in thirty-eight states.[62]

Although Beyond War has brought in thousands of new members in the last few years, the composition of the group, except for larger numbers of single people, appears essentially unchanged. They are still mostly white, upper middle class people looking for something to give their lives meaning.[63]

Politically they seem to be mainstream liberals whose hearts are in the right place but who have never actively participated in any kind of political movement. Joining Beyond War allows them to make a commitment without getting them involved in anything too controversial. Indeed, making the commitment sometimes seems more important than the actual cause involved. Some of the members are "seekers" who have moved on to Beoynd War after stops in other New Age organizations. Others are getting involved for the first time, and the experiences they report sound more like religious conversions than decisions to join a peace group. New members have said of their participation: "A total change in the course of my life," "I've never been involved in anything that makes me feel so whole," "I was looking for something larger than myself to be part of."[64] Their comments reflect a commitment not to a movement but to a way of life, which, of course, is precisely what Beyond War seeks. Like Creative Initiative, Beyond War is not a movement that has a specific social or political agenda. It wants people to change their lives and believes that other social and political changes will follow inevitably. In other words, Beyond War is still homocentric, as the movement has been since the 1945 fight at Camp Minnesing.

For some participants Beyond War retains sectlike elements. Those looking for a purpose in life join it for many of the same reasons people joined Creative Initiative. Once in, they adopt many of the same ideas that were basic to the older movement. Although Beyond War lacks Creative Initiative's theistic core, it functions like a quasi-religion for many of its adherents. The philosophy still holds total commitment as a theoretical ideal; people are still urged to adopt a new life style and a new way of thinking; and some people still relate to the movement in a sectarian manner. Its ideology guides their lives, and those who fully adopt it feel as if they have been given a new purpose and direction. For these people, Beyond War becomes the center of their lives, and they are as fully involved in attending and hosting meetings as were their predecessors in Creative Initiative.

If we go back, however, to the economic distinction between church and sect, it becomes apparent that the emergence of Beyond War also marks a dramatic shift toward the church end of the spectrum. In this model, the sect makes great demands on people but also provides them with significant benefits. The church, however, neither asks nor gives as much. In that sense, there is little in the economic definition of a church that distinguishes it from most secular membership groups, and it was therefore inevitable that when the religious Creative Initiative dissolved in favor of the secular Beyond War it would become more "churchlike." Although some, perhaps many, Beyond War activists find a sense of life-purpose in the group, deep dedication is no longer required for affiliation. The tightly knit community of believers that provided spiritual and temporal benefits in return for total commitment to the group is no more. Deep individual involvement is still possible, but participation can also involve nothing more than subscribing to the newsletter. There is no mechanism for either building or testing commitment.

Ironically, a recent analysis of Beyond War by scholars who were unaware of its religious origins, criticized it for failing to have a basis in "firm ethics based *outside* modern consciousness." "Secular humanism and the defense of a privileged class are not strong places from which to offer a critique of present society and fashion a vision of a redemptive community of the future," they concluded.[65] Unknowingly they were criticizing the movement for failing to have that which they had only recently discarded. On the one hand, this secularization has allowed the movement to grow dramatically, but on the other hand, it has meant that they can never be sure just who is with them and to what extent. From a tightly controlled sect, they evolved into an open-structured New Age movement that stresses positive thought and gives people a sense of being able to do something about the dangers that face the world. Whether that will be enough to sustain the group over the long run remains to be seen.

Notes

A Note on Sources

1. Creative Initiative Archives—These historical records of the Creative Initiative movement are currently held at the Beyond War headquarters in Palo Alto, California. When we used them, they were stored in a disorganized state at the home of Harry and Emilia Rathbun. Because they were subsequently moved and reorganized by a team of Creative Initiative workers, it is impossible to include a specific box or folder number in the citation. This archive is not open to the public.

2. Sharman Papers—When we used them, the papers of Henry B. Sharman, which had been inherited by the Rathbuns, were stored at their community center in Portola Valley. The papers were later donated to the Public Archives of Canada, Manuscript Division, Ottawa, Ontario. Because the Canadian Archives reorganized the material we were unable to give box or folder numbers in the citations.

3. Personal Papers—A number of people, including James and Wileta Burch, Betty Eisner, Del Carlson, and Emilia Rathbun, gave us access to material that remains in their personal possession. We have referred to such material as "personal papers."

4. Questionnaires—In 1986 the movement distributed a questionnaire for us. More than four hundred people responded to our request for specific demographic data and open-ended responses on the nature of their religious experience. We assigned numbers to those questionnaires from which we quote directly, and it is to those numbers that we refer in the notes.

Introduction

1. Thomas Robbins, "The Transformative Impact of the Study of New Religions on the Sociology of Religion," *Journal for the Scientific Study of Religion,* 27 (March 1988): 12–31.

2. See, for example, Thomas Robbins, Dick Anthony, and James Richardson, "Theory and Research on Today's 'New Religions,' " *Sociological Analysis* 39 (1978): 95–122; Thomas Robbins, "Sociological Studies of New Religious Movements: A Selective Review," *Religious Studies Review* 9 (July 1983): 233–239.

3. The classic of this genre is L. A. Festinger, H. W. Riecken, and S. Schachter, *When Prophecy Fails: A Social and Psychological Study of a Modern Group that Predicted the Destruction of the World* (New York: Harper, 1956); for some other examples see John Lofland, *Doomsday Cult: A Study of Conversion, Proselytization, and Maintenance of Faith* (Englewood Cliffs, N.J.: Prentice-Hall, 1966); Rex Davis and James T. Richardson, "The Organization and Functioning of the Children of God," *Sociological Analysis* 37 (Winter, 1976): 321–339; David G. Bromley and Anson D. Shupe, Jr., *"Moonies" in America* (Beverly Hills, Calif.: Sage, 1979); J. Stillson Judah, *Hare Krishna and the Counterculture* (New York: Wiley, 1974); James V. Downton, *Sacred Journeys: The Conversion of Young Americans to Divine Light Mission* (New York: Columbia University Press, 1979); Robert W. Balch, "Looking Behind the Scenes in a Religious Cult: Implications for the Study of Conversion," *Sociological Analysis* (Summer, 1980): 137–143.

4. Max Weber, *The Protestant Ethic and the Spirit of Capitalism* (London: Unwin University Books, 1930), 144–154; Ernst Troeltsch, *The Social Teaching of the Christian Churches,* 2 vols., trans. Olive Wyon (London: George Allen and Unwin, 1931).

5. H. Richard Niebuhr, *The Social Sources of Denominationalism* (New York: Henry Holt & Co., 1929).

6. See for examples, Benton Johnson, "A Critical Appraisal of the Church–Sect Typology," *American Sociological Review* 22 (February 1957): 88–92; Calvin Redekop, "A New Look at Sect Development," *Journal for the Scientific Study of Religion* 6 (September 1974): 345–352; Andrew M. Greeley, *The Denominational Society* (Glenview, Ill.: Scott, Foresman, 1972); Milton Yinger, *The Scientific Study of Religion* (New York: Macmillan, 1970); Bryan R. Wilson, *Religious Sects* (New York: McGraw-Hill, 1970); Alan J. Winter, *Continuities in the Sociology of Religion* (New York: Harper & Row, 1977).

7. Benton Johnson, "On Church and Sect," *American Sociological Review* 28 (August 1963): 539–549; see also Benton Johnson, "Church and Sect Revisited," *Journal for the Scientific Study of Religion* 10 (1971): 124–137.

8. Rodney Stark and William Sims Bainbridge, *The Future of Religion: Secularization, Revival and Cult Formation* (Berkeley and Los Angeles: University of California Press, 1985), 19–96.

9. Ibid., 53–63.

10. Laurence R. Iannaccone, "A Formal Model of Church and Sect," *American Journal of Sociology* 94, Supplement (1988): S241–S268; Gary S. Becker, *The Economic Approach to Human Behavior* (Chicago: University of Chicago Press, 1976).

11. Iannaccone, "A Formal Model," S260.

12. Stark and Bainbridge, *The Future of Religion*, 24–26; Roy Wallis, "The Cult and Its Transformation," in Roy Wallis, *Sectarianism* (New York: Wiley, 1975), 35–49; Allan W. Eister, "Culture Crises and New Religious Movements: A Paradigmatic Statement of a Theory of Cults," in Irving I. Zaretsky and Mark P. Leone, *Religious Movements in Contemporary America* (Princeton, N.J.: Princeton University Press, 1974), 612–627; Andrew J. Pavlos, *The Cult Experience* (Westport, Conn.: Greenwood Press, 1982).

13. Wileta Burch to Steven Gelber, March 1, 1989.

1. Genesis

1. For the sake of clarity, we will usually refer to the Rathbuns' movement as Sequoia Seminar prior to 1962, as Creative Initiative for the period between 1962 and 1982, and as Beyond War after 1982. Occasionally, however, we will use one of their numerous other names, particularly if we are also quoting material in which they use another name.

2. *This One Thing: A Tribute to Henry Burton Sharman* (Toronto: Student Christian Movement of Canada, 1959), 27–28; Donald L. Kirkey, "This One Thing I Do" (unpublished MS, 1986), 16.

3. Ibid.

4. Ibid., 9, 27.

5. Ibid., 28.

6. "The Genesis of the Jesus Study Group: A Paper on the Work of H. B. Sharman Written in 1935 by an Anonymous Author," 1935: 1, Creative Initiative Archives. Harry Rathbun believed the piece was written by Abbie Lyon Sharman, Henry Sharman's wife. The title is slightly confused, but it is clear the author is referring to Henry Drummond, *Natural Law in the Spiritual World* (New York: A. L. Burt Co., 1892).

7. "The Genesis of the Jesus Study Group," 31; Donald Layton Kirkey, Jr., " 'Building the City of God': The Founding of the Student Christian Movement of Canada" (M.A. thesis, McMaster University, 1983), 107.

8. *This One Thing*, 31. The precise chronology is not clear. An undated YMCA announcement during Sharman's graduate-school days refers to four years as SVM general secretary and two years as YMCA Bible study secretary; "The Life of Christ," *Winter Term Announcement* (Central Department, YMCA of Chicago, n.d., c. 1901–1906), n.p., Henry Burton Sharman Papers.

9. *This One Thing*, 34.

10. "The Genesis of the Jesus Study Group," 4.

11. *This One Thing,* 34; for greater detail see Kirkey, "This One Thing I Do," 18–19.

12. "The Genesis of the Jesus Study Group," 5; "Interview on McGill Rock," August 1941, Creative Initiative Archives.

13. Ibid., 35.

14. Ibid., 35, 36; Cyrus LeRoy Baldridge, *Time and Chance* (New York: John Day Co., 1947), 76–78.

15. *This One Thing,* 37–38.

16. Henry Burton Sharman, *Records in the Life of Jesus* (New York: Association Press, 1917).

17. Interview with Harry and Emilia Rathbun, October 28, 1985, Palo Alto, Calif.

18. Henry Burton Sharman, *Jesus in the Records* (New York: Association Press), 1918.

19. *This One Thing,* 45–46, 49; for a complete discussion of Sharman's work in this period see, Kirkey, "This One Thing I Do," 24–28.

20. "The Life of Christ," Sharman papers.

21. Henry Burton Sharman, "Why Study the Life of Jesus?" *The Intercollegian* 36 (November 1918): 4.

22. "The Application of the Scientific Method to the Study of the Records of the Life of Jesus," Sharman Papers; also in Earl Willmott, et al., "Leaders Handbook," 1946: A-5, Creative Initiative Archives.

23. Mary McDermott Shideler, *"Via Crucis:* A Study of the Philosophy of Henry Burton Sharman," Sharman papers.

24. "The Application of the Scientific Method," A-5.

25. Ibid., A-6.

26. Ibid., A-9.

27. Rathbun interview, October 28, 1985.

28. Shideler, *"Via Crucis,"* 29.

29. Ibid., 2.

30. Ibid., 3.

31. Ibid., 6.

32. Abbie Sharman to Sophia Fahs, July 23, 1942, Sharman papers.

33. Ibid.

34. Ibid.

35. Ibid.

36. "Prayer by Dr. H. B. Sharman," n.d.: 11, Creative Initiative Archives. This is apparently a verbatim transcript of Sharman's response to a question at a seminar.

37. Ibid., 12, original completely underlined.

38. Ibid., 13.

39. "Alpha Psi Zeta Foundation," n.d., Sharman papers.

40. Ibid.

41. Shideler, 28.

42. Henry B. Sharman, memo, November 7, 1936, Creative Initiative Archives.

43. Ibid.

44. Ibid.

44. Rathbun interview, October 28, 1985.

46. "Iota Sigma Seminar, 1945, at Camp Minnesing in Algonquin Park Ontario, Canada," Sharman papers.

47. *Minnesing* (resort brochure, 1946), Creative Initiative Archives.

48. "Alpha Psi Zeta Foundation," 1933: 4–5, Sharman papers.

49. *This One Thing,* 49.

50. "Alpha Psi Zeta Foundation," 1933: 2.

51. Rathbun interview, October 28, 1985.

52. Frances Horn, *I Want One Thing: An Autobiography* (Marina del Rey, Calif.: De Vross & Co., 1981).

53. H. B. Sharman to Members of the Central Group, quoted in Earl Willmott, circular letter to the Central Group, no. 4, November 21, 1944, copy in possession of the authors; Alexander Grant, "Report on the Winter's Work, 1941–42," September 3, 1942, Sharman papers; H. B. Sharman to Alex Grant, quoted in Earl Willmott, circular letter to the Central Group, special no. 7A, January 20, 1945, copy in possession of authors; Harry Rathbun to Earl Willmott, "For Earl—Personal and Confidential," January 19, 1945, Creative Initiative Archives; Harry Rathbun to Earl Willmott, January 19, 1945, Creative Initiative Archives; Earl Willmott to Central Group, September 6, 1944: 2, copy in possession of authors.

54. Earl Willmott to Central Group, circular letter, September 6, 1944, copy in possession of the authors.

55. "Meeting of Those Interested in Seminars and Method of Leadership, 8th August, 1944, Camp Minnesing" and "Alpha Psi Zeta Foundation, Minutes of Meeting, Camp Minnesing, 20.8.44," Sharman papers. The seven members of the Central Group were "Bill Archibald, Department of Physics, Dalhousie University, Halifax; Bert Baily, teacher of Biology in Westtown School, near Philadelphia; Alex Grant, formerly SCM secretary at McGill, for the last three years promoting and leading Jesus study groups in the universities of western Canada; Ralph Odom, recent graduate of Garrett Biblical Institute, Evanston, now at Pacific School of Religion, Berkeley; Dryden Phelps, graduate of Yale and Yale Divinity, teacher in departments of English and Religion in West China Union University for over twenty years; Dora Willson, teacher at Pendle Hill; and myself, Earl Willmott, graduate in civil engineering and later Education, work with students in West China for over twenty years. Glenn Olds, recent graduate of Garrett Biblical Institute, a Methodist minister; and Harry Rathbun, graduate in Engineering and Law, professor of International Law at Stanford University, Cal.," Earl Willmott to Central Group, no. 6, January 12, 1945, copy in possession of authors. To these were added "Herman Clark, professor of Physical Science at Willamette University, Salem, Oregon; Bob Chipman, professor of Physics in Queens University, Kingston, Ontario, and Jack McMichael, formerly leader in student organizations in America, SCM rep to China and now secretary of the Methodist Federation for Social Service." "Alpha Psi Zeta Foundation, New Circular Number One," c. January 1945, Sharman papers.

56. "Alpha Psi Zeta Foundation, Minutes of Meeting, Camp Minnesing, 23.8.44," Sharman papers.

57. Quoted in Earl Willmott, circular letter to Central Group, no. 4, November 21, 1944: 3, copy in possession of authors.

58. See for example, the description of proposed activities in "Report of the Promotion Committee" [Camp Minnesing, 1944], Sharman papers.

59. "Earl Willmott to Central Group, no. 6," January 12, 1945, copy in possession of authors.

60. Ibid.

61. Harry J. Rathbun to L. E. Willmott, Western Union Night Letter, January 15, 1945, copy in Creative Initiative Archives.

62. "Earl Willmott to Central Group, no. 8," January 17, 1945, copy in possession of authors.

63. Ralph [Odom] to Earl Willmott, February 28, 1945, copy in Creative Initiative Archives.

64. Harry Rathbun to Earl Willmott, January 19, 1945, Creative Initiative Archives; also, "Earl Willmott to Central Group, no. 8," January 17, 1945: 7.

65. For support for commitment as a precondition of participation, see Glenn Olds to Earl Willmott, n.d., copy in Creative Initiative Archives.

66. Ibid.

67. Ralph Odom to Earl Willmott, February 28, 1945, copy in Creative Initiative Archives, emphasis in original; Ralph and Martha Odom had independently conceived of the idea of a separate religious community and written to the Rathbuns about it, Martha and Ralph Odom to Harry and Emilia Rathbun, March 21, 1945, Creative Initiative Archives.

68. Ibid.; Harry Rathbun to Glenn and Eva Olds, January 29, 1945, Creative Initiative Archives.

69. Dryden Phelps, "Letter to the Central Group Relating Conversations in Berkeley with Rathbuns and Odoms: and with Dr. Sharman; and Dealing with Recent Issues Relative to the Foundation," March 13, 1945: 1, copy in possession of the authors.

70. Ibid.

71. Ibid., 2; the full spectrum of Earl Willmott's left-wing political views are set forth in a letter he wrote just before returning to China in 1946, Earl Willmott to Dear Ones Soon-to-be-left-behind, June 1, 1946, Creative Initiative Archives.

72. Interview with Harry and Emilia Rathbun, October 14, 1984, Palo Alto, Calif.

73. Kirkey, "This One Thing I Do," 18, 33.

74. Interview with Harry and Emilia Rathbun, November 4, 1984, Palo Alto, Calif.

75. Bill Archibald to Henry B. Sharman, n.d., c. April 4, 1945, Sharman papers; Bruce Collier to Henry B. Sharman, March 28, 1948, Sharman papers.

76. Harry and Emilia Rathbun to Glenn and Eva Olds, January 29, 1945.

77. Earl Willmott, "Alpha Phi Zeta Foundation Discussions at Camp Minnesing 1945," 1, copy in possession of the authors.

78. Ibid., 3.

79. Ibid., 4.

80. Interview with Harry and Emilia Rathbun, November 11, 1984, Palo Alto, Calif.

81. Willmott, "Alpha Phi Zeta Foundation Discussions," 5–6.

82. Ibid., 10–12.

83. Ibid., 13–14; most of this description of events was taken from Earl Willmott's notes on the meetings. The Rathbun faction criticized them as being biased and incomplete, preferring instead a report by Alex Grant (who sided with the Rathbuns) that never mentions the Communist issue but focuses exclusively on organizational issues, Harry Rathbun to Bert Bailey, December 30, 1945; Harry Rathbun to Glenn Olds, November 2, 1945; Henry B. Sharman to Harry Rathbun, November 16, 1945; Alex Grant to Fellow Members of the Central Group, October 4, 1945, Creative Initiative Archives.

84. Earl Willmott, et al., to Co-worker with the Records, March 5, 1946, Sharman papers; Earl Willmott, et al., "Leader's Handbook," Creative Initiative Archives.

85. Henry B. Sharman to [Howard L.] Bronson, November 9, 1948, Sharman papers; Dora Willson, circular letter, June 1947, Sharman papers; Juliet D. Roby, circular letter, February 1949, Sharman papers; *This One Thing*, 71; Dora Willson and Elisabeth Trimmer, newsletters, c. 1946–1948, Creative Initiative Archives.

86. "Unpredictable," *Time* (January 1, 1951): 51; "Return of a Missionary," *Time* (February 4, 1952): 45; "Missionary Recalled to Explain Letter," *The Christian Century* (January 3, 1951): 5; Dryden Phelps to Harry Rathbun, November 13, 1975, Creative Initiative Archives.

87. Alvyn J. Austin, *Saving China: Canadian Missionaries in the Middle Kingdom 1888–1959* (Toronto: University of Toronto Press, 1986), 314.

88. Ibid., 318–319.

89. Kirkey, "This One Thing I Do," 56–59.

90. Elizabeth B. Howes, "Appendix," in Walter Wink, *The Bible in Human Transformation: Toward a New Paradigm for Biblical Study* (Philadelphia: Fortress Press, 1973), 84–90.

91. Rathbun interview, October 14, 1984; "Biographical Information on Harry J. Rathbun, Professor of Law, Emeritus, at Stanford University," Creative Initiative Archives.

92. Ibid.

93. Ibid.

94. Ibid.

95. Harry Rathbun, "The Trend Toward Peace," valedictory address to the Mitchell High School Commencement, June 1, 1911, Creative Initiative Archives.

96. Rathbun interview, October 14, 1984; "Biographical Information."

97. Harry Rathbun, et al., Dear Friend circular letter, October 29, 1941, Creative Initiative Archives.

98. Rathbun interview, October 14, 1984.

99. Ibid.

100. *Palo Alto Times* (December 25, 1959): n.p., clipping in Creative Initiative Archives.

101. Rathbun interview, November 4, 1984.

102. Rathbun interview, October 14, 1984; calculations in folder marked "HJR, course info.," 1953, Creative Initiative Archives.

103. Harry Rathbun to J. E. Wallace Sterling, June 15, 1962, Creative Initiative Archives.

104. Ibid.

105. Tro Harper, "Bull Session: We Who Are About to Graduate," *Stanford Daily* (April 2, 1937): 6.

106. Rathbun interview, November 4, 1984; *San Francisco Chronicle* (July 20, 1977): 16.

107. *Stanford Daily* (June 2, 1950): n.p., clipping in Creative Initiative Archives; *Palo Alto Times* (December 25, 1959): n.p., clipping in Creative Initiative Archives.

108. Betty Eisner to Henry B. Sharman, July 30, 1946, excerpt in Creative Initiative Archives.

109. Rathbun interview, October 14, 1984.

110. [Harry Rathbun], "The 4 Absolutes," January 18, 1974: 4, notes, Creative Initiative Archives.

111. Interview with Emilia Rathbun, September 21, 1984, Palo Alto, Calif.

112. Ibid.

113. Ibid.

114. Ibid.

115. Ibid.

116. Donald Kirkey interview with Harry and Emilia Rathbun, October 5, 1982, Palo Alto, Calif.

117. Ibid.; interview with Emilia Rathbun, September 21, 1984.

118. Ibid.; chronology of lives of Henry B. Sharman and Harry and Emilia Rathbun, c. 1978, Creative Initiative Archives.

119. *The Stanford Daily* (June 27, 1933): 1; the group even attempted to hire a professional manager, Harry Rathbun to Carolyn E. Ware, March 6, 1934, Creative Initiative Archives.

120. Rathbun interview, September 21, 1984.

121. Ibid.

122. Ibid.; Frances Horn, *I Want One Thing: An Autobiography,* 31, 55–57, 61–63.

123. Ibid.

124. Ibid.

125. Ibid.; Emilia Rathbun to Henry B. Sharman, September 20, 1948, Creative Initiative Archives.

126. Ibid.

127. Ibid.

128. Rathbun interview, October 14, 1984.

129. Harry Rathbun to Henry B. Sharman, October 30, 1948, Creative Initiative Archives.

130. "The Sierra Seminar: A Study of the Life of Jesus to Discover the Source of His Achievement," 1935, Creative Initiative Archives; "Iota Sigma Seminar at Camp Minnesing in Algonquin Park, Ontario, Canada," 1936, Creative Initiative Archives.

131. "Southwest Seminar, Capitan, New Mexico," 1942, Creative Initiative Archives.

132. Earl Willmott and others to Co-Worker with the Records, March 5, 1946, Sharman papers; Dora Willson to Dear Friends, June, 1947, Sharman papers; Dryden Phelps to Dear Friends, April 15, 1953, Creative Initiative Archives.

133. "Sequoia Iota Sigma Seminar," announcements for 1946, 1947, 1948, 1949, 1950, Creative Initiative Archives.

134. Handwritten notes, October 18, 1945, Creative Initiative Archives; interview with Harry and Emilia Rathbun, December 2, 1984, Palo Alto, Calif.; John F. Woolverton, "Evangelical Protestantism and Alcoholism 1933–1962: Episcopalian Samuel Shoemaker, the Oxford Group and Alcoholics Anonymous," *Historical Magazine of the Protestant Episcopal Church,* 52, no. 1 (1983): 53–65; Harry Rathbun, "The Twelve Steps of Alcoholics Anonymous," n.d., c. 1946, Creative Initiative Archives.

135. Ibid.

136. Harry Rathbun to Henry J. Kaiser, December 8, 1945, Creative Initiative Archives.

137. Emilia Rathbun to Henry B. Sharman, October 11, 1948, Creative Initiative Archives.

138. Harry Rathbun to Merle Dennis, May 25, 1950, Creative Initiative Archives.

139. *San Jose Mercury News* (August 6, 1950): n.p., clipping in Creative Initiative Archives; Rathbun to Dennis, May 25, 1950; Leon and Lucille Carley to Sequoia People, July 3, 1950, Creative Initiative Archives.

140. "Sequoia Iota Sigma Seminar," announcement, 1946, Creative Initiative Archives.

141. "Sequoia Seminar, Report for 1959," 1, Creative Initiative Archives; repeated verbatim in "Sequoia Seminar, Report for 1960," 1, Creative Initiative Archives.

142. "Philosophy of Jesus as Teacher Study Group," First Congregational Church, Redwood City, California, c. 1956, Creative Initiative Archives; "Sequoia Seminar Planning Commitee, Minutes of Meeting, 3/17/56," Creative Initiative Archives.

143. "Leadership Seminar—1955, Discussion on Leadership," Creative Initiative Archives.

144. "S.S. Newsletter," November 1958: 2, Creative Initiative Archives.

145. Interview with Emilia Rathbun, Richard Rathbun, Donald Fitton, and others, September 16, 1987, Palo Alto, Calif.

146. "Sequoia Seminar, Organizing and Operating Principles," December 24, 1955, Creative Initiative Archives.

147. "Sequoia Seminar, Operating Committees," May 13, 1956, revised October 3, 1956, Creative Initiative Archives.

148. "S.S. Newsletter," February, 1956, Creative Initiative Archives.

149. Hayden R. Anderson, "To the Policy Group of the Sequoia Seminar," May 28, 1959, Creative Initiative Archives; "Sequoia Seminar: Minutes of Planning Group Meeting, July 18, 1959," Creative Initiative Archives.

150. Sequoia Seminar rollbooks, 1947, 1948, 1955, Creative Initiative Archives.

151. "On Inviting People to Make a Study of the Records of the Life of Jesus at a Summer Seminar," n.d., c. 1959, Creative Initiative Archives; "Sequoia Seminar Planning Group, Brainstorming Ideas from Meeting of 2/21/59," Creative Initiative Archives.

152. Sequoia Seminar rollbooks, 1947–1959, Creative Initiative Archives.

153. "S.S. Newsletter," May 1957: 3, Betty Eisner papers.

154. "S.S. Newsletter," n.d., c. 1956: 1, Betty Eisner papers; "S.S. Newsletter," February 1959: 5, Betty Eisner papers.

155. Earl Willmott to Donald Kirkey, n.d., copy in authors' possession.

156. Will of Henry B. Sharman, Sharman papers.

157. Howard L. Bronson to Harry J. Rathbun, January 28, 1952, Creative Initiative Archives.

158. Newsletter, August 1951: 7, Betty Eisner papers; George Bahrs, et al., circular letter, November 16, 1954, Creative Initiative Archives.

159. "Sequoia Seminar Foundation, Statement of Income and Expenses, 1955," in "Sequoia Seminar Planning Committee, Minutes of Meeting, March 17, 1956," Creative Initiatives Archives.

160. "Sequoia Seminar, Report for 1957," Betty Eisner papers; Sequoia Seminar annual reports, 1958–1961, Creative Initiative Archives.

161. Sequoia Seminar rollbooks, 1947–1956, Creative Initiative Archives, "Sequoia Seminar, Report for 1960," "Sequoia Seminar, Report of 1961," Creative Initiative Archives.

162. "Sequoia Seminar Planning Group, Brainstorming Ideas from Meeting of 2/21/59," Creative Initiative Archives.

163. "Sequoia Seminar, Report for 1957," Betty Eisner papers; "Sequoia Seminar, Report for 1958," Creative Initiative Archives; John Levy, circular letter, June 15, 1957, Betty Eisner papers.

164. "Sequoia Seminar, Report for 1959," 2, Betty Eisner papers.

165. Ibid.; "Sequoia Seminar Planning Group, Brainstorming Ideas from Meeting of 2/21/59," Creative Initiative Archives.

166. "Sequoia Seminar Planning Group . . . of 2/21/59."

2. Philosophy and Action in a Proto-Sect

1. Emilia Rathbun to Henry B. Sharman, October 11, 1948, Creative Initiative Archives.

2. Henry B. Sharman to Howard Bronson, November 9, 1948, Sharman papers.

3. Henry B. Sharman, "Introductory Lecture: The Choice Is Always Ours," September 6, 1948, Creative Initiative Archives.

4. Harry Rathbun to Buckley, November 7, 1941, Creative Initiative Archives.

5. Harry Rathbun to Merle E. Dennis, August 13, 1953, Creative Initiative Archives.

6. Sequoia Seminar rollbook, 1948, Creative Initiative Archives.

7. Interview with David and Nancy Manning, September 3, 1985, Carmel, Calif.

8. See for example, the letter from a father whose son was taking leave from medical school, Orion D. Wray to Harry Rathbun, March 14, 1948, Creative Initiative Archives; interview with Harry and Emilia Rathbun, November 25, 1985, Palo Alto, Calif.

9. *Palo Alto Times* (March 18, 1948): 7.

10. "Students Concerned, committed to unlimited responsibility—An Educational Project," c. 1948, Creative Initiative Archives. This is one of several similarly titled statements issued by Students Concerned.

11. "Students Concerned, Committed to Unlimited Responsibility for making real One World, An Educational Project," Creative Initiative Archives; "Students Concerned, committed to unlimited responsibility—An Educational Project."

12. "Students Concerned, committed to unlimited responsibility—An Educational Project."

13. "Students Concerned, An Educational Project: Committed to unlimited responsibility for making One World," Creative Initiative Archives.

14. "Students Concerned: An Educational Project," Creative Initiative Archives.

15. "Students Concerned, Committed to unlimited responsibility for making real One World: An Educational Project," Creative Initiative Archives.

16. "Students Concerned, An Educational Project: Committed to unlimited responsibility for making real One World," Creative Initiative Archives; interview with David and Nancy Manning, September 3, 1985.

17. Francis Geddes to Harry and Emilia Rathbun, January 27, 1953, Creative Initiative Archives; see also, David E. Manning, letter to the editor, *Stanford Daily*, n.d., 1949: 49, clipping in Creative Initiative Archives.

18. Del Carlson, cartoon book and journal, c. 1948, Del Carlson papers, private collection.

19. Interview with Emilia Rathbun, November 25, 1985, Palo Alto, Calif.

20. Leola Baer, ed., "Dear Seminarians," newsletters, February 1951, August 1951, January 1952, Betty Eisner papers.

21. Notes, Continuation Seminar, 1952: 8, Creative Initiative Archives.

22. "Sequoia Seminar 1953," Creative Initiative Archives.

23. "1952 Continuation Seminar," July 1952, Creative Initiative Archives.

24. Emilia Rathbun, "Dear Brethren," c. 1959, Creative Initiative Archives.

25. Leola Baer, "Dear Seminarians," newsletter, August 1951, Betty Eisner papers.

26. "Sequoia Seminar, Schedule of Summer Seminars," 1958, 1959, Creative Initiative Archives.

27. "Offerings of Sequoia Seminar for the Summer of 1956," Creative Initiative Archives.

28. "S.S. Newsletter," February 1956, Betty Eisner papers.

29. "Sequoia Seminar, Report for 1960," Creative Initiative Archives.

30. Helen R. H. Nichol, "Sequoia Seminar," June 14–27, 1959: 3, Creative Initiative Archives.

31. Frances Horn, *I Want One Thing* (Marina del Rey, Calif.: De Vross & Co., 1981), 62–63; Elizabeth Boyden Howes to Steven Gelber, February 12, 1987.

32. Howes to Gelber, February 12, 1987.

33. John A. Sanford, ed., *Fritz Kunkel: Selected Writings* (New York: Paulist Press, 1984), 3–31; "Chronology," Creative Initiative Archives.

34. For a complete discussion of the history of the Oxford Group see, Elston John Hill, "Buchman and Buchmanism" (Ph.D. diss., University of North Carolina at Chapel Hill, 1970); also, Allan W. Eister, *Drawing Room Conversion: A Sociological Account of the Oxford Group Movement* (Durham, N.C.: Duke University Press, 1950), 28–65.

35. Henry B. Sharman to Abbie Lyon Sharman, April 29, 1932, Sharman papers.

36. Interview with Harry and Emilia Rathbun, October 28, 1985, Palo Alto, Calif.

37. Ibid.

38. Interview with Emilia Rathbun, September 21, 1984, Palo Alto, Calif.; Harry Rathbun to Frederick S. Howes, November 27, 1935, Creative Initiative Archives.

39. Hill, "Buchman and Buchmanism," 284–295, 363–366.

40. *Palo Alto Times* (September 28, 1939): 5.

41. Harry Rathbun and others to Dear Friends, October 29, 1941, copy in Creative Initiative Archives.

42. Hill, "Buchman and Buchmanism," 55–57; Robert L. Harris, *What Is the Oxford Group* (San Francisco: The Church Book Shop, n.d.), pamphlet in Creative Initiative Archives.

43. "Spiritual Responsibility, Am I Prepared for It?" typescript marked "O.G. [Oxford Group] Adele Beard," 1936, Creative Initiative Archives.

44. "Gerald Heard: Author, Historian, Philosopher, Lecturer," publicity flyer, c. 1950, Creative Initiative Archives.

45. "Residence at Trabuco," 2, Creative Initiative Archives; "The Way of Life at Trabuco," Creative Initiative Archives.

46. Interview with Harry and Emilia Rathbun, November 18, 1984, Palo Alto, Calif.

47. Ibid.

48. Harry Rathbun to Betty Eisner, August 10, 1946, Eisner papers.

49. Howard Louis Love, "Gerald Heard's Natural Theology in Relation to

the Philosophy of Henri Bergson" (Ph.D. diss., Boston University, 1962), 77–92.

50. Ibid., 112–127.

51. Ibid., 128–132.

52. Gerald Heard, *A Preface to Prayer* (New York, Harper & Brothers, 1944), xiv.

53. Love, "Gerald Heard," 213–232.

54. Heard conducted a seminar specifically for Sequoia Seminar participants for a weekend in 1954 and for two weeks in 1955. "Sequoia Seminar, Week-End Seminar-Retreat with Gerald Heard, Ben Lomond—April 10–11, 1954," Creative Initiative Archives; "Sequoia Seminar, Leadership Seminar, August 1 to 14, 1955," Creative Initiative Archives; John L. Levy, "Gerald Heard Seminar—1955: A Personal Evaluation," Creative Initiative Archives.

55. "Sequoia Iota Sigma Seminar: A Critical and Constructive Contribution to Individual Man's Most Central Need," 1946, Creative Initiative Archives.

56. "Sequoia Iota Sigma Seminar: Devoted to discovery of the answer to the world's most pressing problems," 1948, Creative Initiative Archives.

57. "Sequoia Seminar," c. 1956, Creative Initiative Archives.

58. "Sequoia Seminar," 1956: 2, Creative Initiative Archives.

59. Ibid.

60. Henry B. Sharman, "Introductory Lecture," seminar at Carmel, Calif., September 6, 1948, Creative Initiative Archives.

61. Notes, Continuation Seminar, 1952: 35, Creative Initiative Archives.

62. Ibid., 30.

63. "Sequoia Seminar Planning Committee, Minutes of Meeting," March 17, 1956: 4–5, Creative Initiative Archives.

64. Interview with Del Carlson, September 1, 1985, Palo Alto, Calif.

65. "Sequoia Seminar, Post Seminar Groups, Leadership Handbook," c. 1959: 6, Creative Initiative Archives.

66. Ibid., 10.

67. Notes, Continuation Seminar, 1952, 21–23.

68. "Sequoia Seminar, Post Seminar Groups, Leadership Handbook," 10–12.

69. Ibid., 16.

70. Ibid., 29.

71. Ibid., 30.

72. Ibid., 35.

73. Harry Rathbun, "What's Ahead," c. 1947, Creative Initiative Archives.

74. Harry Rathbun, "The Future of Man," 15–17, sermon to the Unitarian Church of San Mateo, April 1966, Creative Initiative Archives.

75. Harry Rathbun, *The Pursuit of Happiness,* speech to the Eighteenth Stanford Business Conference, July 20, 1959: 5, Creative Initiative Archives.

76. Rathbun, "What's Ahead," 8.

77. Harry Rathbun, "Youth's Ideals in a World at War," speech to Junior College Deans' Section of the National Association of Deans of Women, February 20, 1942: 6, Creative Initiative Archives; Sinombre [Harry Rathbun],

"Primer for Living: A Manual of Discipline for the Passengers and Crew of Spaceship Earth," 1975: 70, Creative Initiative Archives.

78. Harry Rathbun, "Human Challenge of the Nuclear Age," speech to Ninth Annual Better Business Relations Conference, September 25–29, 1960: 1, Creative Initiative Archives.

79. Ibid.

80. Rathbun, "Youth's Ideals in a World at War," 11, emphasis added.

81. Personal comment, Sequoia Seminar rollbook, 1953: 36, Creative Initiative Archives.

82. Rathbun, "Youth's Ideals in a World at War," 9.

83. Interview with John Levy, February 20, 1985, San Francisco, Calif.

84. Memo, c. 1950, Creative Initiative Archives.

85. Telephone interview with Betty Eisner, September 9, 1985; newsletter, August 1951: 3, Creative Initiative Archives.

86. Notes from Continuation Seminar, 1952: 7, Creative Initiative Archives.

87. Ibid.

88. "S.S. Newsletter," September 1966, Betty Eisner papers.

89. "Some Notes on the Group Understanding of Dreams," c. 1957, Creative Initiative Archives.

90. "Sequoia Seminar, Report for 1957," 3, Creative Initiative Archives.

91. "Dear Sequoia Seminarian," January 15, 1958: 2–3, circular letter, Betty Eisner papers; also "Dear Sequoia Seminarian," February 6, 1959: 1–3, circular letter, Creative Initiative Archives.

92. Emilia Rathbun, "Dear Brethren," c. 1959, Creative Initiative Archives.

93. Carlson interview, November 1, 1985.

94. Walter Truett Anderson, *The Upstart Spring: Esalen and the American Awakening* (Reading, Mass.: Addison-Wesley, 1983), 59–62.

95. Interview with Willis Harman, August 23, 1985, Stanford, Calif.

96. Harmon interview; Eisner interview; interview with Ray and Pat Jacobsen, August 5, 1985, Palo Alto, Calif.

97. Harmon interview; Levy interview; interview with Jean and Louis Sloss and Norma Lyman, August 2, 1985, Forestville, Calif.; Anderson, *Upstart Spring,* 72.

98. Herman Clark to H. L. Bronson, December 5, 1958, copy in Creative Initiative Archives; Harry Rathbun to the Trustees of the Sharman Will, December 15, 1958, Creative Initiative Archives.

99. H. L. Bronson to Harry Rathbun, January 7, 1959, Creative Initiative Archives.

100. Glenn Olds to Harry Rathbun, January 13, 1959, Creative Initiative Archives.

3. The New Religion of the Third Age

1. Interview with Emilia Rathbun and Virginia Fitton, February 19, 1988, Palo Alto, Calif.

2. Ibid.

3. Interview with Elsie Westfall, July 5, 1987, San Jose, Calif.

4. Rathbun and Fitton interview.

5. Interview with John Levy, February 20, 1985, San Francisco; interview with Del Carlson, September 1, 1985, Palo Alto, Calif.

6. Ibid.

7. Interview with Harry and Emilia Rathbun, December 23, 1984, Palo Alto, Calif.

8. Interview with Harry and Emilia Rathbun, November 18, 1984, Palo Alto, Calif.

9. Rathbun and Fitton interview.

10. [Harry Rathbun], "The 4 Absolutes," notes, January 18, 1974, Creative Initiative Archives.

11. Frances Horn, *I Want One Thing: An Autobiography* (Marina del Rey, Calif.: De Vross & Co., 1981), 64–65.

12. Fred Howes to Henry B. Sharman, August 8, 1937, Sharman papers; Fred Howes to Elizabeth Howes, March 21, 1940, copy in Sharman papers; Fred Howes to Henry B. Sharman, February 1, 1941, Sharman papers.

13. Elizabeth Boyden Howes to Henry B. Sharman, November 16, 1939, Sharman papers.

14. Henry B. Sharman to Elizabeth Boyden Howes, November 18, 1939, Creative Initiative Archives.

15. Elizabeth Boyden Howes to Henry B. Sharman, December 21, 1939, Sharman papers.

16. Dora Willson to Elizabeth Boyden Howes, February 8, 1940, Creative Initiative Archives.

17. Carlson interview: interview with Louis and Jean Elsa Sloss and Norma Lyman, September 13, 1985, Forestville, Calif.; interview with Gordon and Joyce Tappan, August 2, 1985, Sonoma, Calif.

18. Rathbun and Fitton interview.

19. "1952 Continuation Seminar," July 5 to July 19, 1952, Creative Initiative Archives.

20. Tape-recorded discussion between Del Carlson and Emilia Rathbun, December 31, 1958, copy in possession of authors.

21. Ibid.

22. Ibid.

23. Sloss and Lyman interview.

24. Ibid.; interview with John Levy, January 20, 1985, San Francisco.

25. Rathbun and Fitton interview.

26. Rathbun interview, November 18, 1984.

27. Ibid.

28. Carlson interview.

29. Rathbun interview, November 18, 1984.

30. Rathbun and Fitton interview.

31. Ibid.

32. Ibid.

33. Ibid.

34. Telephone interview with Betty Eisner, July 5, 1985; Carlson interview; Levy interview; Rathbun and Fitton interview.

35. Emilia Rathbun, "key words," May 8, 1960, Rathbun papers.

36. Ibid.

37. Carlson interview.

38. Emilia Rathbun, "key words."

39. William Proctor to Emilia Rathbun, February 2, 1985, Creative Initiative Archives.

40. Rathbun interview, November 18, 1984.

41. Ibid.

42. In this case she may have been following a pattern common among creative people. See, George Pickering, *Creative Malady: Illness in the Lives and Minds of Charles Darwin, Florence Nightingale, Mary Baker Eddy, Sigmund Freud, Marcel Proust, Elizabeth Barrett Browning* (London: George Allen & Unwin, 1974).

43. Rathbun interview, November 18, 1984.

44. Ibid.

45. Ibid.

46. Interview with Harry and Emilia Rathbun interview, November 25, 1985, Palo Alto, Calif.

47. Rathbun interview, November 18, 1984.

48. Rathbun interview, November 25, 1985.

49. Rathbun interview, November 18, 1985.

50. Emilia Rathbun, "My Commitment Is to God Himself . . . ," meditation, n.d., Rathbun papers.

51. Rathbun interview, November 25, 1985.

52. Emilia Rathbun, "Luke 13 vs. 28–30; Explanation," c. 1976: 1, Rathbun papers.

53. Emilia Rathbun, "Once my soul was born . . . ," c. 1962, Rathbun papers.

54. Emilia Rathbun, "There is a Gnostic plane . . . ," Rathbun papers.

55. Emilia Rathbun, "There is authority," c. 1962, Rathbun papers.

56. Rathbun interview, November 18, 1984.

57. Rathbun and Fitton interview.

58. Ibid.

59. Rathbun interview, November 18, 1985.

60. "The Passing of the Portals of the Temple," n.d., Creative Initiative Archives.

61. Rathbun interview, November 24, 1984.

62. "Dawn Ceremony," Ceremony Book, Creative Initiative Archives.

63. Interview with Harry and Emilia Rathbun, December 2, 1984, Palo Alto, Calif.

64. Ibid.

65. Interview with Donald and Virginia Fitton, January 25, 1985, Palo Alto, Calif.

66. "The Blue, Blue Lake," c. 1962, Creative Initiative Archives.

67. "The First Paper," c. 1962, Creative Initiative Archives.

68. Rathbun interview, December 2, 1984.

69. Ibid.

70. Ibid.

71. Ibid.

72. Ceremony Book, Creative Initiative Archives.

73. "The Able Ceremony," Ceremony Book, Creative Initiative Archives.

74. Rathbun interview, November 18, 1984.

75. "The Able Ceremony."

76. Ibid.

77. See chap. 5.

78. Beverly Sorenson, "Dr. Robert G. Albertson," Creative Initiative Archives.

79. Ibid.

80. Rathbun Interview, December 2, 1984.

81. *The Gospel According to Thomas,* trans. A. Guillaumont, et al. (New York: Harper & Row, 1959), 99:21–26.

82. Rathbun interview, December 2, 1984.

83. See, for example, Max Weber, "The Sociology of Charismatic Authority," in *From Max Weber: Essays in Sociology* (New York: Oxford University Press, 1946), 245–252.

84. Raymond Trevor Bradley, *Charisma and Social Structure: A Study of Love and Power, Wholeness and Transformation* (New York: Paragon House Publishers, 1987).

85. Ibid., 51.

86. Ibid., 57.

87. Ibid., 70.

88. Ibid., 71.

89. Ibid., 71.

90. Ibid., 101–127.

91. Ibid., 112.

92. Ibid., 113.

93. Ibid., 116.

94. Rathbun interview, November 25, 1985.

95. Bradley, *Charisma,* 178.

96. "First Spring Maiden Ceremony," Ceremony Book. These ceremonies developed in greater detail over time—for example, the "Spring Maiden Ceremony" 1970–1971, Creative Initiative Archives; telephone interview with Pixie Hammond, July 15, 1988.

97. "Eagle Program," 1970, Creative Initiative Archives.

98. "The Eagle Ceremony," n.d., Creative Initiative Archives.

99. Rathbun interview, December 23, 1984.

100. "The Secret of Light," 1965, mimeographed program, Creative Initiative Archives. The full text of the program was included in an illustrated cartoon version for distribution to children.

101. *Palo Alto Times* (December 11, 1967): II, 13; *Christmas House,* 1967, Creative Initiative Archives.

102. The most obvious of these later events were "Bless Man" and "13 Is a Mystical Number." See chap. 7.

103. Rathbun interview, December 23, 1984.

104. Interview with James and Wileta Burch, December 26, 1984, Palo Alto, Calif.

105. Interview with Donald and Juana Mueller, August 8, 1985, Long Beach, Calif.

106. Somewhat confusingly, the term was also used to designate those who had passed through the seminar process to the point of initiation. Subsequently, the Passover Ceremony was repeated annually for a number of years, providing an occasion for the incorporation of new members and a renewal of vows for those already associated with the group.

107. "Passover Ceremony," 1978, Creative Initiative Archives.

108. Ibid.

109. Mueller interview, August 8, 1985.

110. "Why We Have a Blessman Calendar," 1977, Creative Initiative Archives; "Overview of the Symbolism in the Adam/Eve Ceremony," c. 1978, Ceremony Book; "Ceremony of the 12," n.d., Ceremony Book; "Days of Meditation and Prayer," 1976, Creative Initiative Archives; "Mary Ceremony, 1977," Ceremony Book; "Days of Awe Ceremony," 1980, Creative Initiative Archives; "New Beginnings, Overview," c. 1978, Creative Initiative Archives.

111. "Preparation for Candles of Light Ceremony: Leader's Guide," 1979, Creative Initiative Archives.

112. Mueller interview, August 8, 1965.

113. Ibid.

114. Ibid.

4. Surrendering: The Process of Personal Transformation

1. Harry Rathbun, "Self-Help Manual for a Life of Rich Meaning, designed for those blessed with the Divine Discontent, to Accompany the study of the book, *Creative Initiative: Guide to Fulfillment* and other supplementary readings which help toward enlightenment," 1978: 17, Creative Initiative Archives.

2. "A Seminar Outline—revised June 4th," 1974: 1. Creative Initiative Archives.

3. See for example, "Syllabus for the Unitive Principle: God and Man Curriculum Series," 1972: 7, Creative Initiative Archives; "God, Soul, Reality, God as Secondary Manif[estation]," 1, small handwritten notebook, Creative Initiative Archives.

4. Emilia also used the expression "now-present-in-the-flesh-Christ," "Purpose of the Jesus Seminar," n.d.: 2, typescript, Creative Initiative Archives.

5. "We Are One," c. 1973, Creative Initiative Archives; see also, "From the

beginning of time . . . ," n.d.: 4, Creative Initiative Archives; and "Star of Fulfillment, Quest for Meaning Seminar," June 1979: 2, Creative Initiative Archives.

6. [Emilia Rathbun], "We believe that this is a historical time . . . ," c. 1966, James and Wileta Burch papers.

7. Rathbun, "Self-Help Manual," 17.

8. "Meditation on God," 1979, Creative Initiative Archives.

9. "A Seminar Outline—revised June 4th," 1974: 1, Creative Initiative Archives.

10. "What Is God," 1979: 2, Creative Initiative Archives.

11. "Thoughts on beauty for leaders to ponder," n.d., Creative Initiative Archives.

12. "The Teaching of Jesus: Course I," 1980: 6, Creative Initiative Archives.

13. "Challenge to Change: Series of 7 Sessions," October–November 1969: 2, Creative Initiative Archives.

14. Harry Rathbun, "A Skeptic Quizzes God: Fifteen Imaginary Conversations on Matters of Moment, c. 1980, "Seventh Conversation," 4, Creative Initiative Archives; virtually the same thing is repeated in Rathbun, "A Skeptic Quizzes God," "Ninth Conversation," 1; see also Harry Rathbun, *Creative Initiative: Guide to Fulfillment* (Palo Alto, Calif.: Creative Initiative Foundation, 1976), 13.

15. "Introduction to Personal Fulfillment, Three Session Course, Leader's Manual," 1977: 6, Creative Initiative Archives.

16. Teilhard's ideas are most completely spelled out in Pierre Teilhard de Chardin, *The Phenomenon of Man* (New York: Harper & Row, 1955, 1959), but are repeated in many of his other works including, *The Heart of Matter* (New York: Harcourt Brace Jovanovich, 1976, 1978), *Activation of Energy* (London: William Collins Sons, 1963, 1970), and *Building the Earth* (Wilkes-Barre, Pa.: Dimension Books, 1965), which was used as a textbook for some early courses; "New Sphere, Leaders' Manual," February 1966: 7–9, Burch papers; the influence of Teilhard is also evident in the Evolution of Consciousness Program that was based heavily on *The Phenomenon of Man*—see, "E.O.C. Program," c. 1972, Creative Initiative Archives; also "New Curriculum, Orientation Session #1," n.d.: 10, Creative Initiative Archives.

17. "The Story of Man's Evolution," June 1967: 1–2, Creative Initiative Archives; Rathbun, *Creative Initiative: Guide to Fulfillment,* 11–12.

18. Rathbun, *Creative Initiative: Guide to Fulfillment,* 11–12.

19. "Introductory Weekend Curriculum, September 1979," Creative Initiative Archives.

20. Joseph Campbell, *The Hero with a Thousand Faces* (Princeton, N.J.: Princeton University Press, 1972).

21. Frieda Fordham, *An Introduction to Jung's Psychology* (New York: Penguin Books, 1953), 77–79.

22. Ibid.

23. [Rathbun], "Primer for Living," 12.

24. "The Challenge of Time," Revised Curriculum, March 29, 1973: 5, Creative Initiative Archives; see also, [Rathbun], "Primer for Living," 14.

25. "Tree of Life, Supplemental Materials," "Evolution & the Function of Emotion in Higher Man," c. 1972, Creative Initiative Archives.

26. [Rathbun], "Primer for Living," 12; "Affirmation," c. 1966, Burch papers.

27. "Identity Year—Level I (Pre-Jesus), Overview," 1979: 1, Creative Initiative Archives, emphasis added.

28. "The Position on Which We Stand," Burch papers, emphasis added.

29. "The Challenge of Time, Series of 5 sessions, October 27–December 5, 1969," 4, Creative Initiative Archives.

30. Teilhard de Chardin, *The Phenomenon of Man,* 103–140.

31. "Evolution of Consciousness: Concept Outline," November 3, 1972, Creative Initiative Archives.

32. "New Sphere: An Experiment in Self-Directed History," April–May, 1967: 1–4, 6–7, Creative Initiative Archives.

33. "We are a community . . . ," c. 1966, Burch papers.

34. Teilhard de Chardin, *The Phenomenon of Man,* 180–213; Henry R. Luce, "A Great Thinker's Joyful Vision: The Spiritual Perfection of Mankind," *Life* (October 16, 1964): 12.

35. Wileta Burch, "Wednesday Night Put-Out: 'A' Seminar, 1973," 3, Burch papers; see also "Introduction to Personal Fulfillment, Three Session Course, Leader's Manual," 1977: 10, Creative Initiative Archives; Rathbun, *Creative Initiative,* 14–15; Curriculum for "Wholeness series," n.d.: 3, Creative Initiative Archives; see also, "The Levels of Perception," 1968: 1, Creative Initiative Archives.

36. Rathbun, *Creative Initiative,* 15; small handwritten notebook, n.d., Creative Initiative Archives; see also "The Challenge of Time, Leader's Syllabus," 1964: 15, Creative Initiative Archives; and "The Flowering of the Soul: What does it mean? How can it happen?" c. 1980, typescript course outline, Creative Initiative Archives; "The Challenge of Time, Leader's Syllabus," 1974: 9, Creative Initiative Archives.

37. "Book of John," 1976: 14, Creative Initiative Archives.

38. Ibid.; [Rathbun], "Primer for Living," 49.

39. "Syllabus for the Unitive Principle: God and Man, Curriculum Series," 1972: 15–16, Creative Initiative Archives; see also, "B Curriculum, Outline for Overview," August 24, 1971, Creative Initiative Archives.

40. "B Curriculum, Outline for Overview," 17.

41. Ibid.

42. Emilia Rathbun, talk to "A" Seminar, June 23, 1971, Burch papers.

43. "Notes from Jesus III Seminar, 11/5/78–11/10/78," 28, Burch papers.

44. "Agenda," pt. 5, "Prayer," January 1965, Burch papers.

45. "Prayer and Third Level Existence," c. 1963, 1–2, Creative Initiative Archives; "Prayer," c. 1965, Creative Initiative Archives.

46. "The Challenge of Time," 1976: 9, Creative Initiative Archives.

47. [Rathbun], "Primer for Living," 90, 93.

48. "The Levels of Perception," chap. 6, "Social Outcome: The Seventh Stage," 1968, Creative Initiative Archives.

49. "The Kingdom of God, (Jesus as Teacher, Section 34)," 1977: 1–2, Creative Initiative Archives.

50. "Critical Approach to the Records," "Withdrawal of Jesus to the Wilderness," n.d.: 2, Creative Initiative Archives.

51. Ibid., 3.

52. "Our Philosophy," n.d., mimeographed fragment, Creative Initiative Archives; "Statement on Goals," n.d.: 1, Creative Initiative Archives; "Challenge to Change, Overview," n.d.: 1, Creative Initiative Archives; "The Challenge of Time," March 29, 1973: 8, Creative Initiative Archives.

53. "The Levels of Perception," chap. 6, "Social Outcome," 1968, Creative Initiative Archives; see also, Jim Burch, talk to men's symposium, May 15, 1966: 2–3, Burch papers.

54. "Statement on Goals," n.d.: 1, Creative Initiative Archives.

55. "Authority, Mission, Integrity," 1972: 2, Creative Initiative Archives.

56. "New Curriculum, Orientation Session #2," n.d.: 10, Creative Initiative Archives.

57. See chap. 1, 17–26.

58. See for example, [Rathbun], "Primer for Living," 64; "Authority Seminar," "God as Creator and Authority," 1979, Creative Initiative Archives; also Rathbun, *Creative Initiative,* 76–77; "Syllabus for the Unitive Principle: God and Man, Curriculum Series," 1972: 3, Creative Initiative Archives.

59. "C—Seminar, 1974: A Transitional Seminar from the Psychological to the Religious," "God Image," 1974, Creative Initiative Archives.

60. "Critical Approach to the Records," "The Authority Issue," n.d.: 1, Creative Initiative Archives.

61. "A Seminar Outline—Revised June 4th," "Authority," 1974, Creative Initiative Archives.

62. Ibid., emphasis added.

63. [Wileta Burch?], "Notes from Jesus III Seminar, 11/5/78–11/10/78, plus discussion on Love, resistance, hate; Origin of evil; Resolving conflict, from January 1979," vii, Burch papers.

64. Ibid., 2.

65. "The Teaching of Jesus: Course I," 1980: 10, Creative Initiative Archives; Rathbun, "A Skeptic Quizzes God," "Fifteenth Conversation," 22; [Rathbun], "Primer for Living," 72.

66. [Rathbun], "Primer for Living," 61–62; almost all the points on love are also repeated in Rathbun, *Creative Initiative,* 95–100.

67. Earle Reynolds, *The Center Is Quaker: A Personal History of Ben Lomond Quaker Center* (Ben Lomond, Calif.: privately printed, n.d.), 14–15.

68. [Rathbun], "Primer for Living," 62.

69. Ibid.

70. "Authority Seminar," 1979: 8, Creative Initiative Archives.

71. "Positive Self-Assessment," 1977, Creative Initiative Archives.

72. This course reached its culmination in 1976 as the Attitude Motivation Responsibility (AMR) Course, "Self-Assessment"; see "Attitude Motivation

Responsibility, Course #1076, Self-Assessment," 1976, Creative Initiative Archives.

73. For an early example where the process was called "reconditioning," see "New Sphere, Syllabus," February 1966: 3, Burch papers.

74. "The Personal Journey and the Religious Life, Facilitator's Guide and Assignments for Participants," 1982: I–III, Creative Initiative Archives.

75. Questionnaire 13, summer, 1986.

76. Questionnaire 14, summer, 1986.

77. Questionnaire 9, summer, 1986.

78. Questionnaire 10, summer, 1986.

79. Questionnaire 15, summer, 1986.

80. Questionnaire 27, summer, 1986.

81. "The Challenge to Change, Overview," n.d.: 1, 81, Creative Initiative Archives; "The Challenge of Time," revised curriculum, March 29, 1973: 12, Creative Initiative Archives; late in their work they referred to conditioning as the "existential self," Rathbun, *Creative Initiative*, 42–43.

82. [Rathbun], "Primer for Living," 19.

83. "Women's Destiny: An Enlightened Mind," 1982: 5, Burch papers.

84. "Jesus Seminar, 1977," "The Baptism Experience," Burch papers.

85. Rathbun, *Creative Initiative*, 67.

86. "C—Seminar, 1974: A Transitional Seminar from the Psychological to the Religious," "God Image," 1974; see also "Life of the Spirit," "Chapter V—Nature," 1968, Creative Initiative Archives; "Overview Putout: The Symbol with Reference to the Individual, Phase Two of Putout," fragment, c. 1970, Creative Initiative Archives.

87. "Leader's Setting," n.d.: 87, fragment, Creative Initiative Archives.

88. "Quest for Meaning Seminar, Leader's Guide," c. 1977: 1, Creative Initiative Archives.

89. "Leader: This Wholeness Series . . . ," n.d.: 3, mimeographed fragment, Creative Initiative Archives.

90. Elston John Hill, "Buchman and Buchmanism" (Ph.D. diss., University of North Carolina at Chapel Hill, 1970), 53–60, 202–212.

91. Ibid., 2.

92. [Rathbun], "Primer for Living," 63; Rathbun, *Creative Initiative*, 99.

93. "The Human Enterprise," 1979: 2, Creative Initiative Archives; "God, Soul, Reality," n.d.: 6, notebook, Creative Initiative Archives.

94. "New Sphere: An Experiment in Self-Directed History," April–May 1967: 5, Creative Initiative Archives.

95. "Notes from Jesus III Seminar," 11, Burch papers.

96. Questionnaire 12, summer, 1986.

97. Questionnaires 22, 30, summer, 1986.

98. Questionnaire 23, summer, 1986.

99. Questionnaire 30, summer, 1986.

100. Questionnaire 12, summer, 1986.

101. Questionnaire 23, summer, 1986.

102. Questionnaire 31, summer, 1986.

103. Elliot Aronson, "Dissonance Theory: Progress and Problems," in

R. Abelson, et al., *The Cognitive Consistency Theories: A Source Book* (Chicago: Rand McNally, 1968); Leon Festinger, *A Theory of Cognitive Dissonance* (Evanston, Ill.: Row, Peterson, 1957).

104. Questionnaire 4, summer, 1986.

105. Questionnaires 12, 22, summer, 1986.

106. "Jesus Seminar, 1977," "The Authority Issue," 2, emphasis in original.

107. "New Sphere: An Experiment in Self-Directed History," April–May 1967: 3, Creative Initiative Archives.

108. "Violence Curriculum, Outline of Main Topics," c. 1971: 1, Creative Initiative Archives.

109. [Rathbun], "Primer for Life," 66.

110. "Book of John," 1976: 1, Creative Initiative Archives; see also, "Purpose of Jesus Seminar," n.d.: 2, Creative Initiative Archives.

111. "Notes from Jesus III Seminar," 76.

112. "Notes from Jesus III Seminar," v.

113. "The Teaching of Jesus: Course I," 1980: 4, Creative Initiative Archives.

114. "Authority Seminar," 1979: 11, Creative Initiative Archives.

115. "The Challenge of Time, Leader's Syllabus," 1974: 11, Creative Initiative Archives; see also, Rathbun, *Creative Initiative,* 59–60.

116. "Prayers and Third Level Existence," c. 1964: 3, Creative Initiative Archives.

117. "Decision: The Key to Change," 1979: 5, Creative Initiative Archives; "Curriculum for Relevant Education Series," Fall, 1968: 2, Creative Initiative Archives.

118. "Kingdom of God Versus Kingdom of Man," January 11, 1982: 1, 3, Creative Initiative Archives.

119. Dick Anthony and Thomas Robbins, "Spiritual Innovation and the Crisis of American Civil Religion," *Dedalus* 111 (Winter, 1982): 216–218.

120. Ibid., 221–229.

121. "Responsibility," c. 1967: 3, Burch papers.

122. "Women's Destiny in an Age of Chaos," "Meeting #3, Man as Cause," Creative Initiative Archives.

123. [Richard Lagerstrom], "We'll begin . . . ," "Opening—3," c. 1967, Creative Initiative Archives.

124. "A Time for Decision," October 27, 1973: 1, Creative Initiative Archives.

125. Ibid., 2.

126. "Unitive Principle Curriculum: The I–Thou Relationship," 1974: 8, Burch papers.

127. Ibid.; chart of pass over, c. 1977, Creative Initiative Archives.

128. "Unitive Principle Curriculum," 3.

129. "Prayer and Third Level Existence," c. 1963: 1, Creative Initiative Archives; "Challenge to Change Groups," 1967, history notebook, Creative Initiative Archives.

130. "Quest for Meaning Course Descriptions," 1976, flyer, Creative Initiative Archives; "Preparation for the New Religion," 1978: 2, Creative Initiative

Archives; "Leader's Guide, Quest for Meaning, Introductory Weekend Seminar," 1981, Creative Initiative Archives, "The Human Enterprise," 1979, Creative Initiative Archives; "Perspective in a Changing World," November 3–December 5, 1969, Creative Initiative Archives; "The Challenge to Change," 1976, Creative Initiative Archives; see also for example, "Life of the Spirit," 1968: 1, Creative Initiative Archives; "Jesus as Teacher Series for Intermediate Leaders," Winter, 1969, Creative Initiative Archives; "C/C Training Days," September 8, 15, 22, 1973, Creative Initiative Archives. The seven-step structure first introduced in Challenge to Change became a standard that was frequently used to explain other material in more advanced courses and to justify specific actions, especially conservation, during the late 1970s.

131. "Purpose in Having Challenge to Change Groups," June 1967: 1, Creative Initiative Archives.

132. See for example, "The Levels of Perception," 1968, Creative Initiative Archives.

133. P. W. Martin, *Experiment in Depth: A Study of the Work of Jung, Eliot and Toynbee* (New York: Pantheon Books, 1955).

134. "Woman in Myth and Mystery, Presentations and Series, Holistic," "Course," 1972: 1–2, Burch papers.

135. Fordham, *An Introduction to Jung's Psychology,* 25–27; Martin, *Experiment in Depth,* 1–16.

136. "Old Testament Seminar," 1977: 1, Creative Initiative Archives.

137. "Life of the Spirit," 1968, chap. 3: 3, Creative Initiative Archives.

138. "Life of the Spirit," chap. 3: 4.

139. "C Seminar, 1974," "Symbols in the Myth of Moses," 2, Burch papers.

140. Ibid., 1–3.

141. "C Seminar," "Moses," 1973: 4, Burch papers; "C Seminar 1974," "The Myth of Moses," Burch papers.

142. "C Seminar, 1974," "Comparison of Consciousness as Expressed in the Old and New Testament," Creative Initiative Archives.

143. "Why Study Jesus?" 1968, Creative Initiative Archives; see also, Harry J. Rathbun, "On Critical Work," n.d.: 1–2, Creative Initiative Archives; "Appendix A, Background of Jesus as Teacher Approach," 1976: 1–3, Creative Initiative Archives.

144. Ibid., 1–9.

145. William G. Perry, Jr., "Cognitive and Ethical Growth: The Making of Meaning," in Arthur W. Chickering and associates, eds., *The Modern American College* (San Francisco: Jossey-Bass Publishers, 1981), 76–116.

5. Men, Women, and Children

1. Sinombre [Harry Rathbun], "Primer for Living: A Manual of Discipline for the Passengers and Crew of Spaceship Earth," 73: 1975,

Creative Initiative Archives; see also, "Masculine, feminine principles: God and Mankind," Fall, 1973, Creative Initiative Archives.

2. Frieda Fordham, *An Introduction to Jung's Psychology* (New York: Penguin Books, 1953), 52–60.

3. "Outline for the 'A' Seminars of 1973," 13–14, Creative Initiative Archives.

4. "A Seminar Outline—Revised June 4th," "Masculine and Feminine Principles as Experienced in a Person," 1974, Creative Initiative Archives; Harry says essentially the same thing in an early draft of his book, see [Rathbun], "Primer for Living," 13–14, but tones the position down considerably in the published version, Harry Rathbun, *Creative Initiative: Guide to Fulfillment* (Palo Alto, Calif.: Creative Initiative Foundation, 1976), 103–104.

5. "Outline for the 'A' Seminars of 1973," 16.

6. Ibid., 18; see also "Women in Myth and Mystery," "Anima–Animus," 1974: 2, James and Wileta Burch papers.

7. Emilia appears to have been particularly influenced by the interpretation of Jung in P. W. Martin, *Experiment in Depth: A Study of the Work of Jung, Eliot and Toynbee* (New York: Pantheon, 1955), which was frequently cited in Creative Initiative recommended reading lists.

8. Used in this context "transition to Community" meant Creative Initiative becoming a functioning unit in the Kingdom of God.

9. "Notes from Jesus III Seminar, 11/5/78–11/10/78," 52, Burch papers.

10. "Woman in Myth and Mystery, Presentations and Series, Holistic," 1972, Burch papers.

11. [Rathbun], "Primer for Living," 14.

12. "Woman in Myth and Mystery."

13. Ibid.

14. Ibid., 4.

15. "Woman in Myth and Mystery," "Blessman—The New Identity," 1974: 1, Burch papers.

16. "Women in Myth and Mystery," "Bless Man—The New Identity (Part II)," 2–4, Burch papers.

17. Ibid., 6.

18. "For the Children's Sake," c. 1968, 5, mimeographed newsletter, history notebook, Creative Initiative Archives.

19. Ibid., 5.

20. "A Relevant Education Seminar," c. 1968, flyer, Creative Initiative Archives; see also "Build the Earth began in 1962 . . . ," c. 1968, Burch papers; *San Jose News* (December 1, 1967): 29.

21. Questionnaire 20, summer, 1986.

22. "Young Mothers—1970," October 22–November 12, 1969: 2, Creative Initiative Archives.

23. "Woman, the Image, the Self," "Masculine/Feminine Talk," c. 1974, Burch papers.

24. "Facilitator's Guide, Marriage AMR—1977," 5, Creative Initiative Archives.

25. "There is a seed in the heart . . . ," April 1968, Creative Initiative Archives.

26. "Basic Script, Women's Mass Meeting," June 7, 1966, Burch papers.

27. "There is a seed in the heart . . . ," 1.

28. "Marriage and the Religious Life, Facilitator's Guide and Assignments for Participants," 1982: 10, Creative Initiative Archives.

29. "Notes from Jesus III Seminar," 35.

30. "Women's Destiny in an Age of Chaos," 1971, Creative Initiative Archives.

31. "Outline—Woman Realized," Creative Initiative Archives; see also, "Woman: The Great Controversy," "Woman Through Time, Woman as Civilizer," November 1978, Creative Initiative Archives.

32. "Woman's Destiny in an Age of Chaos."

33. "Young Mothers—1970," "Last Talk," October 22–November 12, 1969, Creative Initiative Archives.

34. "Responsibility," February 27, 1970, Creative Initiative Archives.

35. "New Women, Where am I, Who am I, Where am I going?," c. 1966: 1, Creative Initiative Archives; "For Leaders," c. 1966, Creative Initiative Archives; Questionnaire 10, summer, 1986.

36. *San Jose News* (December 1, 1967): 29.

37. [Emilia Rathbun], "Everything in the present day . . . ," n.d., Emilia Rathbun papers.

38. *Sunnyvale Scribe* [Calif.] (July 16, 1975): 9.

39. "Basic Script, Women's Mass Meeting," paper no. 1.

40. "1952 Continuation Seminar," July 1952: 27, Creative Initiative Archives.

41. "Introductory Weekend, Journey to Fulfillment," 1976: 2, Creative Initiative Archives.

42. Questionnaire 7, summer, 1986. They did, however, hold special courses for singles, including a "relationship" course modeled after the marriage courses; "Relationships and the Religious Life," 1980, Creative Initiative Archives.

43. Questionnaire 8, summer, 1986.

44. "Facilitator's Guide, Marriage AMR—1977," "Course #2076, Marriage Relationship," 1, Creative Initiative Archives.

45. "Women in Creative Relationships," 1977: 3, Creative Initiative Archives.

46. "Marriage—Los Angeles," n.d., notes, Creative Initiative Archives.

47. "Morning on Marriage," n.d., c. 1976, notes, Creative Initiative Archives.

48. "Curriculum for Relevant Education Series," Fall, 1968: 3, Creative Initiative Archives.

49. "Women in Myth and Mystery," "Bless Man—the New Identity (Part II)," 1976: 6, Burch papers.

50. Questionnaire 10, summer, 1986.

51. Marie N. Robinson, *The Power of Sexual Surrender* (Garden City, N.Y.: Doubleday & Company, 1959), 148–154.

52. Ibid., 215.

53. "Dynamics of Marriage," August 4, 1971: 8, Creative Initiative Archives.

54. "Facilitator's Guide, Marriage AMR—1977," "Handout for Meeting #3," 2, Creative Initiative Archives.

55. Melvin Anchell, *Understanding Your Sexual Needs* (New York: Frederick Fell, 1968).

56. "Dynamics of Marriage," September 7, 1973: 2, Creative Initiative Archives.

57. Anchell, 18–33.

58. Ibid. See for example, 14–15, 49–53, 90–95, 105, 216–217, 262–268.

59. "Jesus Seminar, 1977," 26, Creative Initiative Archives.

60. "The New Religion, Contemporary Abstracts from the Old Myths, Series I, Lecture 3, Abraham," 1975: 2, Creative Initiative Archives.

61. " 'Thrust' Coordinating Men," "Statement on Politics (Rough Draft)," May 4, 1970: 2, Creative Initiative Archives.

62. "C—Seminar, 1974," "The Four Absolutes," Burch papers.

63. "Introduction to the Life of the Spirit, Discourse on the Standards of Righteousness," "Meeting 4," 1979, Creative Initiative Archives.

64. "Notes from Jesus III Seminar," 67, Burch papers.

65. See chap. 3.

66. Interview with Marilyn Nyborg, December 29, 1986, Sunnyvale, Calif.

67. Child questionaire 6, summer, 1986.

68. Raymond Trevor Bradley, *Charisma and Social Structure: A Study of Love and Power, Wholeness and Transformation* (New York: Paragon House, 1987), 116–117.

69. An example of an all-male course was, "The Spirited Man," November 10–December 14, 1969, Creative Initiative Archives; also the "Invitational San Damiano Retreat for Men Seminar Leaders," October 5–7, 1973, mimeographed, Creative Initiative Archives; although there must have been many more, aside from some introductory talks, these are the only two purely men's meetings for which records exist, some indication of their rarity.

70. "The Spirited Man," 2.

71. "Parenting: How to Parent in a Stressful World," 1981, 10–11, Creative Initiative Archives.

72. "A Parent in the New Age," n.d., c. 1969, Creative Initiative Archives.

73. "Family Outings Involving the Children," July 1968: 3, 5, Creative Initiative Archives.

74. "Notes from the Jesus III Seminar," 11.

75. "Family Outings Involving the Children," 2.

76. Child questionnaire 5, summer, 1986.

77. Questionnaire 26, summer, 1986.

78. "Financial Information for 1973 Seminars," 2, Creative Initiative Archives.

79. Interview with Emilia Rathbun, Richard Rathbun, Virginia Fitton,

Donald Fitton, Beverley Sorensen, and others, September 15, 1987, Palo Alto, Calif.

80. "Sequoia Seminar, Some Proposals Regarding the Long-Range Program," June 3, 1961: 2, Creative Initiative Archives; "Sequoia Seminar, Report of 1961," 2, Creative Initiative Archives.

81. "Children's Camps for 1969," December 3, 1968: 1, Creative Initiative Archives; "To: Family Leaders," March 26, 1969, Creative Initiative Archives.

82. "Community Summer Camp, Aurora and Arriba!" May 22, 1973, Creative Initiative Archives.

83. "Youth Work, September 1980–June 1981," Creative Initiative Archives; for earlier activities, see "Area Profile Report, San Jose," August 25, 1969: 2–3, Creative Initiative Archives; "Outreach Newsletter," April 1976: 2, Creative Initiative Archives.

84. "Curriculum for 13–15 Year Olds," n.d., Creative Initiative Archives; a very similar pattern of daughters cooking for fathers can be found in "Family Outings Involving the Children," 7.

85. "Dear Continuation Family Leaders," "Program for 7–8–9 Year Old Sons," March 26, 1969, Creative Initiative Archives; "Program for 10–11–12 Year Old Sons"; "Program for Boys, 13 to 15 years," n.d., Creative Initiative Archives.

86. "Eagle Program," January 28, 1970: 1, Creative Initiative Archives.

87. "Dear Aguilas Candidate," February 23, 1979, Creative Initiative Archives.

88. "Eagle Program," 1–2.

89. "Aguilas Brainstorming Meeting: Purpose and Form of Aguilas Program," October 15, 1981: 1, Creative Initiative Archives.

90. "Aguilas Brainstorming Meeting," 1–2.

91. "Dear _____," n.d., Creative Initiative Archives.

92. "Spring Maiden Program," c. 1971, Creative Initiative Archives.

93. "Plans for Spring Maiden Program, 1970–1971," Creative Initiative Archives.

94. "Project Nepal and Youth Evolving Solutions: Proposal for Academic Credit from University of California, Los Angeles," February 1981, Creative Initiative Archives; The Peninsula Times Tribune (June 30, 1979): A-4; "Project Nepal, Project Description," c. 1979, Creative Initiative Archives.

95. "Salvatierra Year Seminar," "Report to Annual Meeting of Sequoia Seminar Foundation," November 28, 1981, Creative Initiative Archives.

96. Questionnaire 11, summer, 1986.

97. "1952 Continuation Seminar," July 1952: 16, Creative Initiative Archives.

98. Rick Kushman, "Part II: Views from the Outside, What is CIF Really About, Anyway?" Palo Alto Weekly (August 7, 1980): 12.

99. Child questionnaire 1, summer, 1986.

100. Child questionnaire 3, summer, 1986.

101. Child questionnaire 5, summer, 1986.

102. Child questionnaires 1, 3, 5, 6, summer, 1986.

103. Child questionnaires 1, 5, summer, 1986.

6. Creating a Community of Believers

1. "An Introductory Paper," c. 1965, Creative Initiative Archives.

2. Harry J. Rathbun, "Some Proposals Regarding the Long-Range Program," June 3, 1961: 2, Creative Initiative Archives.

3. Ibid.

4. "Sequoia Seminar Financial Operations, Fiscal Year 11-1-64—10-31-65," "Sequoia Seminar Balance Sheet, Fiscal Year 11-1-64—10-31-65," Creative Initiative Archives; untitled financial summary, "as of 10-1-71," Creative Initiative Archives; "Asking for Pledges at 1977 Seminars," July 1977, Creative Initiative Archives; "To All Seminar Leaders," from the Finance Committee, 1972, Creative Initiative Archives; Harry Rathbun to Richard and Carolyn Rathbun, June 29, 1971, Creative Initiative Archives; "Financial Information for 1973 Seminars," James and Wileta Burch papers.

5. Kathy McHale, "New Sphere Has Energy and Christian Altruism," *Midpeninsula Observer* (April 8–22, 1968): 6; in 1980 their budget had risen to approximately $350,000 per year, Rick Kushman, "We Are One," *Palo Alto Weekly* (July 31, 1980): 13.

6. *Contra Costa Times* (July 5, 1979): 3.

7. Harry J. Rathbun, "Some Proposals Regarding the Long-Range Program," June 3, 1961: 4, Creative Initiative Archives; Harry and Emilia Rathbun, circular letter, December 23, 1965, Creative Initiative Archives; actually a sliding scale, from 1 percent for those who earned less than $10,000 to 4 percent for those who earned more than $25,000 was suggested, "Outreach Group," c. 1968, "Financial," Creative Initiative Archives; for other suggestions on how to raise funds see, "Funding," July 11, 1972, Creative Initiative Archives.

8. "Identity the Basis of Community: Identification with 'The Community' the basis for Identity," February 2, 1969, Creative Initiative Archives.

9. "The Role of the 'New Community' in Politics," June 23, 1970, Creative Initiative Archives.

10. "Stanford Summer Family Conference (An Experiment in Family Community Living)," c. 1970, Creative Initiative Archives; "Where You Should be this Summer," c. 1970, Creative Initiative Archives.

11. "Where You Should be this Summer," 2–3.

12. *San Jose Mercury News* (March 29, 1987): 10A.

13. *Menlo-Atherton Recorder* (August 17, 1977): 5.

14. Harry Rathbun to Richard and Carolyn Rathbun, March 26, 1973, Creative Initiative Archives.

15. *Menlo-Atherton Recorder* (August 17, 1977): 5; *The Country Almanac* [Woodside] (December 11, 1974): 1; interview with Emilia Rathbun, Richard Rathbun, Virginia and Don Fitton, and others, September 15, 1987, Palo Alto, Calif.

16. Interview with Emilia Rathbun, et al., September 15, 1987; *The Country Almanac* [Woodside] (February 16, 1977): 1.

17. "The Role of the 'New Community' in Politics," June 23, 1970, Creative Initiative Archives.

18. "Economic Aspects," July 25, [1970], Creative Initiative Archives.

19. "Econolution!" 1967, Creative Initiative Archives.

20. "Building the Earth and Economics: Econolution!" July 5, 1967, Creative Initiative Archives.

21. "Econolution Presentation—Asilomar," September 11, 1967, Creative Initiative Archives.

22. "Building the Earth and Economics: Econolution!"

23. Bill McGlashan, "Recommendation to the Hub," c. 1975, Creative Initiative Archives.

24. "Rough Draft, Financial Curriculum," c. 1970, Creative Initiative Archives; "Recommendations of Men's Brainstorming Group Meeting on 9-28-74 on the Subject of 'Freeing Men' and 'Work of Freed Man,' " 1974, Creative Initiative Archives.

25. "Holistic Job Directory," June 4, 1971, Creative Initiative Archives.

26. "Specialization, I. Coordinating Center," c. 1966, Creative Initiative Archives.

27. "New Sphere—Stanford Area," June 20, 1966, Creative Initiative Archives; "For the Children's Sake," c. 1968: 2, mimeographed newsletter, Creative Initiative Archives.

28. Beverly Sorensen, "The Work Becomes New Sphere," in history notebook, Creative Initiative Archives.

29. "Draft Copy—Sept. 1987, Membership of Sequoia Seminar and Creative Initiative," Creative Initiative Archives; Area Profile Reports: Central Peninsula, Northern Peninsula, Oakland, Contra Costa, San Francisco—Marin, Southern Peninsula, Berkeley, all August 1969, typescripts, Creative Initiative Archives; "Reorganization," fragment, March 22, 1974, Creative Initiative Archives; newsletter, May 7, 1974: 3, Creative Initiative Archives; "Outlying Regions," January 1976, Creative Initiative Archives; "Creative Initiative Foundation, People in Community," July 1, 1977, Creative Initiative Archives.

30. Beverly Sorensen, "Foothill Symposium," in history notebook, Creative Initiative Archives.

31. "New Sphere—Symposium for Women," March 21, 1965, outline of eleven talks, Creative Initiative Archives.

32. Harry J. Rathbun, talk to basic seminar, December 27, 1970: 4, Creative Initiative Archives.

33. Ibid., 12.

34. "New Sphere, Training and Enrichment Program, Winter/Spring 1966," Creative Initiative Archives.

35. Donald Fitton to Max M. Fisher, May 13, 1969, Creative Initiative Archives.

36. Letter to John May, San Francisco Foundation, May 7, 1969: 1, Creative Initiative Archives.

37. "We're Looking for a Special Kind of People," brochure, c. 1979, Creative Initiative Archives.

38. See for example, "The Creative Initiative Foundation," 1972, brochure,

Creative Initiative Archives; "The Creative Initiative Foundation," c. 1976, brochure, Creative Initiative Archives, "What am I? Who am I? Where am I going? Creative Initiative introduces the universal process that leads to the answers," c. 1977, brochure, Creative Initiative Archives; "Creative Initiative Foundation," November 1980, Creative Initiative Archives.

39. Harry Rathbun to Richard and Carolyn Rathbun, June 29, 1971: 2, 4, Creative Initiative Archives.

40. Harry Rathbun to Richard and Carolyn Rathbun, July 25, 1972, Creative Initiative Archives.

41. "Sequoia Seminar," booklet, c. 1962, Creative Initiative Archives.

42. "A Correction," [January 1972], Creative Initiative Archives; see also, *San Jose Mercury-News* (January 2, 1972): 75.

43. John Kopczak, "Revolution—Peninsula Style," *The Elephant Committee* 1 (no. 1): n.d., mimeographed; *San Jose Mercury News* (April 25, 1971): n.p., clipping, Creative Initiative Archives.

44. Harry Rathbun, "The Future of Man," sermon to the Unitarian Church of San Mateo, May 1966, Creative Initiative Archives.

45. Beverly Sorensen, note, history notebook, n.d., Creative Initiative Archives.

46. Kathy McHale, "New Sphere Has Energy and Christian Altruism," *Midpeninsula Observer* (April 8–22, 1968): 6.

47. Clipping, unknown newspaper, December 7, 1971, history notebook, Creative Initiative Archives.

48. *Oakland Tribune* (April 13, 1976): 10E.

49. *Oakland Tribune* (April 12, 1976): 8E.

50. Letter to Harry J. Rathbun, July 3, 1982, Creative Initiative Archives.

51. Letter to Harry Rathbun, April 1, 1974: 6, Creative Initiative Archives.

52. Questionnaire 18, summer, 1986.

53. Questionnaire 13, summer, 1986.

54. "This Is New Sphere," c. 1965, Creative Initiative Archives.

55. "Minister—Layman Weekend, Sequoia Seminar," January 21–22, 1966, participant list, Creative Initiative Archives.

56. Lester Kinsolving, "New Sphere Hopes to Change History," *San Francisco Chronicle* (January 28, 1967): 28.

57. "Time for Reality, Church Thrust Program," December–January 1972, Creative Initiative Archives.

58. Interview with Ray and Pat Jacobsen, August 5, 1985, Palo Alto, Calif.: Rick Kushman, "Part II: Views From the Outside, What Is CIF Really About, Anyway?" *Palo Alto Weekly* (August 7, 1980): 13.

59. Questionnaire 16, summer, 1986.

60. Kinsolving, "New Sphere," 28.

61. *Contra Costa Times* (July 5, 1979): 3.

62. *Oakland Tribune* (April 11, 1976): 1, 5.

63. Questionnaire 18, summer, 1986.

64. "New Sphere: An Experiment in Self-Directed History," [1967]: 5, Creative Initiative Archives.

65. "General Statement," c. 1966: 6, Burch papers.

66. Questionnaire 22, summer, 1986.

67. Jim Burch, talk to men's symposium, May 15, 1966: 4, Burch papers.

68. Sinombre [Harry Rathbun], "Primer for Living: A Manual of Discipline for the Passengers and Crew of Spaceship Earth," 1975: 104, Creative Initiative Archives.

69. Ibid.

70. Questionnaire 26, summer, 1986.

71. Questionnaires 12, 26, summer, 1986.

72. Questionnaire 14, summer, 1986.

73. Kushman, "Part II: Views From the Outside," 11.

74. "Challenge to Change Follow-Up: Being, Knowing Doing," 1969, Creative Initiative Archives.

75. "A Seminars," c. 1972, Creative Initiative Archives.

76. [Rathbun], "Primer for Living," 116.

77. "Statement," c. 1967, Creative Initiative Archives.

78. Ibid.

79. "Basic Agreement to Meet the Goal of a Strong Working Foundation," c. 1977, Burch papers; interview with Marilyn Nyborg, January 12, 1987, Sunnyvale, Calif.

80. Rick Kushman, "We Are One," *Palo Alto Weekly* (July 31, 1980): 12.

81. Questionnaire 22, also 16, summer, 1986.

82. Letter to Harry and Emilia Rathbun, June 29, 1975, Creative Initiative Archives.

83. Harry Rathbun to Richard Rathbun, February 15, 1972, Creative Initiative Archives.

84. *Contra Costa Times* (July 5, 1979): 1.

85. Ibid., 13.

86. Letter to Harry J. Rathbun, November 3, 1979, Creative Initiative Archives.

87. Questionnaire 1, summer, 1986.

88. Questionnaire 6, summer, 1986.

89. Questionnaire 4, summer, 1986.

90. Questionnaire 2, also 17, summer, 1986.

91. McHale, "New Sphere Has Energy and Christian Altruism," 6.

92. Sam Harding, "Man and His Job," October 10, 1974, Creative Initiative Archives.

93. *The Washington Post* (March 31, 1983): 1.

94. Questionnaires 16, 20, summer, 1986.

95. Personal evaluation of seminar, 1975, Creative Initiative Archives.

96. *Contra Costa Times* (July 5, 1979): 3.

97. Questionnaire 12, summer, 1986.

98. H. J. R. [Harry J. Rathbun], "Sequoia Seminar, Some Proposals Regarding the Long-Range Program," June 3, 1961, dittoed, Creative Initiative Archives.

99. Ibid., 2.

100. Ibid., 3; "Outreach Group," 1968: 2, Creative Initiative Archives.

101. "Suggestions for Gathering New People for Challenge to Change Groups," c. 1967, Creative Initiative Archives.

102. "To: All Seminarians," February 28, 1966, Creative Initiative Archives; for similar advice on the distribution of brochures, see also "Introductory Year," January 2, 1979, Creative Initiative Archives.

103. "Minutes—Planning Group Meeting," October 11, 1965, Creative Initiative Archives.

104. "Outreach Group," 1968: 3, Creative Initiative Archives.

105. "The Dynamics of Change: A Men's Luncheon Program," April 12, 1967, with note, history scrapbook; "What Is New Sphere," c. 1966, with note, history notebook, Creative Initiative Archives.

106. "The New-Sphere Outreach," October 1966, Creative Initiative Archives.

107. "The Creative Initiative Introductory Evening: Facilitator's Manual," September 1978: 1, Creative Initiative Archives.

108. Ibid., 9.

109. Ibid., 4–8. An earlier, slightly less complete version of these host guidelines appeared in 1968 as part of instructions on how to run Challenge to Change groups, "To: All Challenge to Change Leaders, Subject: Fall, 1968 Involving Process Groups," 1968, Creative Initiative Archives.

110. "Outreach Group," 1968: 1, Creative Initiative Archives.

111. Ibid., 1–2; "Control and Feedback," n.d., Creative Initiative Archives.

112. "The Napa Experience," n.d., Creative Initiative Archives.

113. Harry Rathbun to Richard and Carolyn Rathbun, July 25, 1972, Creative Initiative Archives.

114. "General Basic Principles," January 26, 1972, Creative Initiative Archives.

115. "Dear Outposts and Outlying Areas," May 7, 1974, Creative Initiative Archives; "Outreach Newsletter," August 1974, Creative Initiative Archives.

116. "Preparation of a Comprehensive Plan," c. 1976, Creative Initiative Archives.

117. "Clarification of New Sphere," c. 1965, Creative Initiative Archives.

118. Questionnaire 24, summer, 1986, for example.

119. "Mystical Evolution of the New Sphere, Session I," c. 1966: 8, notes, Burch papers.

120. "Notes from Jesus III Seminar, 11/5/78–11/10/78," 70, also 6, 20, typescript, Burch papers.

121. The Stanford Daily (March 3, 1980): 3.

122. "New Sphere: An Experiment in Self-Directed History," April–May 1967: 7, Creative Initiative Archives.

123. "We're Looking for a Special Kind of People," n.d., brochure, Creative Initiative Archives.

124. Harry Rathbun to Richard and Carolyn Rathbun, April 3, 1970, Creative Initiative Archives.

125. Palo Alto Weekly (August 28, 1980): 17.

126. See also, "What Is Creative Initiative," August 1982: 14, Creative Initiative Archives.

127. "The Creative Initiative Foundation," 1972, pamphlet, Creative Initiative Archives.

128. "Hub Financial Questionnaire," November 4, 1971, typescripts, Creative Initiative Archives; U.S. Bureau of the Census, *Historical Statistics of the United States: Colonial Times to 1970,* pt. 1 (Washington, D.C.: GPO, 1975), 292.

129. Collection of 5 × 8 cards with biographical information, c. 1964, Creative Initiative Archives.

130. All the statistical data in this section is derived from the questionnaires.

7. Public Presentations: Programs and Politics

1. "New Sphere Presents, People, War & Destiny," 1966, announcement, Creative Initiative Archives; "New Sphere Presents, People, War & Destiny," 1967, announcement, history notebook, Creative Initiative Archives.

2. "New Sphere Presents, People, War & Destiny."

3. "First Multimedia Presentation," 1966, history notebook, Creative Initiative Archives.

4. "The First Blessman," 1917, note, history notebook, Creative Initiative Archives.

5. Ibid.

6. *Palo Alto Times* (November 26, 1976): n.p., clipping, Creative Initiative Archives.

7. Photographs of "Bless Man," 1972, history notebook, Creative Initiative Archives; "Bless Man," souvenir booklet, 1973, Creative Initiative Archives.

8. *Pacific Telephone Magazine* (December 1973), cover.

9. *California Living Magazine, San Francisco Sunday Examiner and Chronicle* (December 9, 1973): 28–29.

10. Photograph and caption, 1972, history notebook, Creative Initiative Archives.

11. "Lifestyle," *The Times* (December 5, 1976): n.p., clipping, Creative Initiative Archives.

12. "All Five Performances of 'Thirteen' Sold Out. Two Additional Performances Scheduled," [1972], Creative Initiative Archives.

13. "Thirteen Is a Mystical Number: A Musical Drama of a Living Myth," October 1972, program, Creative Initiative Archives.

14. " 'Thirteen' Curriculum," August 1972, Creative Initiative Archives.

15. "Resource Paper for Concept Groups on '13,' " 1972, Creative Initiative Archives.

16. Script for "Thirteen Is a Mystical Number," 1972, typescript, Creative Initiative Archives.

17. Script for "Thirteen."

18. "Resource Paper for Concept Groups on '13,' " 4.

19. Ibid.

20. *San Francisco Chronicle* (April 16, 1972): n.p., clipping, Creative Initiative Archives; *Palo Alto Times* (April 25, 1972): 15; *Palo Alto Times* (October 18, 1972): 29.

21. " '13', Myth, Living Myth," in " 'Thirteen' Curriculum," August 1972: 6, Creative Initiative Archives.

22. "Angels' Advice: A Young People's Musical Presentation (with some much-needed advice for the inhabitants of Planet Earth)," September 1980, program, in authors' possession.

23. Harry Rathbun to Richard and Carolyn Rathbun, November 2, 1971, Creative Initiative Archives; "No Frames, No Boundaries," c. 1983, advertising flyer for films and tapes, Creative Initiative Archives; Adrian Malone Productions, "A Unique Television Opportunity," August 1981, Creative Initiative Archives.

24. Harry Rathbun to Richard and Carolyn Rathbun, November 2, 1971, Creative Initiative Archives.

25. "NIF Office Report to Area Chairmen," February 4, 1970, Creative Initiative Archives.

26. "Radio :60 #10: 'On Being Number Two,' " 1975–1977, Creative Initiative Archives.

27. "Radio :60 #27, 'Meaning of life,' " 1975–1977, Creative Initiative Archives.

28. "The Ten Commandments of Good Will," December 1963, Creative Initiative Archives.

29. Harry Rathbun to Ruth Hellman, January 24, 1950; Harry Rathbun to Janet Hargreaves, April 19, 1950, Creative Initiative Archives.

30. "St. John's Missionary Baptist Church," n.d., history notebook, Creative Initiative Archives; "Summary of the New Sphere Involvement at St. John Missionary Baptist Church," c. 1966, Creative Initiative Archives.

31. "What Is Going to Happen Good Friday at the Negro Church," 1965, Creative Initiative Archives.

32. "St. John's Missionary Baptist Church," history notebook, Creative Initiative Archives; "Summary of the New Sphere Involvement at St. John Missionary Baptist Church," c. 1966, Creative Initiative Archives.

33. *Palo Alto Times* (February 26, 1968): n.p., clipping, and (March 4, 1968): n..p., clipping, history notebook, Creative Initiative Archives; "African Heritage," note, history notebook, Creative Initiative Archives; "Our African Heritage Festival," 1968, history notebook; "Woman to Woman Building the Earth," newsletter, March 1968: 3, Creative Initiative Archives; "National Initiative Newsletter," April 1968: 1, Creative Initiative Archives.

34. *Palo Alto Times* (April 6, 1968): 3; "African Heritage," history notebook, Creative Initiative Archives; Kathy McHale, "New Sphere's Big 'Put Out' Snares Militant Middle," *Midpeninsula Observer* (April 22–May 6, 1968): 5.

35. Donald Fitton to Roger Wilkins, January 2, 1970, Creative Initiative Archives.

36. "National Initiative Newsletter," April 1968: 1, Creative Initiative Archives.

37. "Training Manual for Proposal on National Service," February 26, 1968: 20, 22, Creative Initiative Archives; National Service Foundation, "Proposal for National Service," March 1968: 1, Creative Initiative Archives.

38. *Daily Commercial News* [San Francisco] (April 8, 1968): 1; *San Francisco Chronicle* (April 8, 1968): 4.

39. McHale, "New Sphere's Big 'Put Out' Snares Militant Middle," 5; "National Initiative Newsletter," May 1968: 3, Creative Initiative Archives.

40. *Daily Commercial News* [San Francisco] (April 8, 1968): 1.

41. "The Involvement Corps, A National Voluntary Service," c. 1968: 2, 4, Creative Initiative Archives.

42. *The Stanford Daily* (April 18, 1968): 5.

43. Ibid.

44. "Curriculum for Saturday—Relevance Groups," CRE Conference, April 19–21, 1968, Creative Initiative Archives.

45. *The Stanford Daily* (April 18, 1968): 5.

46. Ibid.; *The Stanford Daily* (April 29, 1968): 2; "The Relevance Group," April 15, 1968, Creative Initiative Archives.

47. "Statement of Position," c. 1967, Creative Initiative Archives.

48 "Notes on CRE for 1968–9 and Seminar in September," May 29, 1968, Creative Initiative Archives.

49. "Training Manual for Proposal on National Service," February 26, 1968: 1, Creative Initiative Archives.

50. Ibid.

51. McHale, "New Sphere's Big 'Put Out' Snares Militant Middle," 5; *San Jose Mercury* (February 27, 1968): 4; *Palo Alto Times* (February 26, 1968): n.p., clipping, history notebook, Creative Initiative Archives; *Palo Alto Times* (March 4, 1968): sec. II, 13; "Circle Star Presentation," note, history notebook, Creative Initiative Archives.

52. *Palo Alto Times* (March 1, 1968): n.p., clipping, history notebook, Creative Initiative Archives; *San Francisco Chronicle* (April 7, 1968): n.p., clipping, history notebook, Creative Initiative Archives; *San Francisco Chronicle* (April 8, 1968): 4; *Palo Alto Times* (March 29, 1968): n.p., clipping, history notebook, Creative Initiative Archives.

53. "Don't Let Pageantry Confuse You . . . ," flyer from the Women's International League for Peace and Freedom, history notebook, Creative Initiative Archives; *Palo Alto Times* (May 25, 1968): 5; "Build the Earth," program, Creative Initiative Archives; "Build the Earth Pageant—May 26th," history notebook, Creative Initiative Archives.

54. "Build the Earth," May 26, 1968, program, Creative Initiative Archives; "National Initiative Newsletter," April 1968: 1, May 1968: 2, July–August 1968: 1–2, Creative Initiative Archives; *Palo Alto Times* (August 10, 1968): 3; Gary G. Williams, et al., to Glenn A. Olds, December 26, 1968, Creative Initiative Archives.

55. Memo to the membership, October 7, 1968, Creative Initiative Archives.

56. "Challenge to Change Recruiting—Fall, 1971," 1971, Creative Initiative Archives.

57. "The New Politics: Cooperation for the benefit of all men," June [1967], Creative Initiative Archives.

58. "Statement of Political Position," July 7, 1967, Creative Initiative Archives.

59. "World Cooperation for the Fulfillment of All: A New Political Thrust," c. 1967, Creative Initiative Archives.

60. "Palo Alto Initiative," [January 1969], Creative Initiative Archives.

61. "Results of a Survey on Problems and Concerns of Individuals in Palo Alto," February 4, 1969, Creative Initiative Archives.

62. "Notes on Meeting of 2-7-69," Creative Initiative Archives.

63. "Palo Alto Initiative Proposal (Preliminary Outline)," n.d., c. February 1969, Creative Initiative Archives.

64. "Timing and Scheduling for Gunn Experimental Program," January 1968, Creative Initiative Archives; National Initiative Foundation to Robert McClean, [January 28, 1969], Creative Initiative Archives.

65. "Question: How do we develop our proposal . . . ," 1969, Creative Initiative Archives.

66. "Statement on Politics (Rough Draft)," May 4, 1970, Creative Initiative Archives.

67. Donald Fitton to President Richard M. Nixon, December 1, 1972, Creative Initiative Archives.

68. "Synopsis and Thrust of Statement and Proposal to President Nixon," n.d., Creative Initiative Archives; James Burch to President Richard M. Nixon, November 1, 1972, Creative Initiative Archives.

69. "To: All A, B, C, and D Branch Trainers," August 13, 1973, Creative Initiative Archives.

70. Ibid.

71. Proposal for a bicentennial celebration, apparently a grant application, c. 1972, Creative Initiative Archives.

72. Winston Boone to Morris Cox, September 25, 1973, Creative Initiative Archives.

73. "A Declaration of Interdependence," 1976, Creative Initiative Archives.

74. "Overpopulation Newsletter," April 28, 1969, Creative Initiative Archives.

75. "Ecology Exhibit," history notebook, Creative Initiative Archives; *Palo Alto Times* (July 12, 1969): 12, editorial; "Build the Earth," ecology handout, [July 1969], Creative Initiative Archives.

76. "Statement on Politics (Rough Draft)," May 4, 1970: 2, Creative Initiative Archives.

77. *Los Angeles Times* (May 9, 1975): 1.

78. "How Much Do You Really Know About Nuclear Power," meeting announcement, 1975, Creative Initiative Archives; "We are interested in assessing . . . ," questionnaire, 1975, Creative Initiative Archives.

79. "Do You Really Know the Facts About Nuclear Power?" c. 1975, Creative Initiative Archives; "Nuclear Power Plants Create Plutonium," c. 1975, flyer, Creative Initiative Archives.

80. "A Petition," March 5, 1975, Creative Initiative Archives.

81. "A Call to Women for a Decision on Nuclear Power," [1975], Creative Initiative Archives; *Sacramento Bee* (c. 1975): n.p., clipping, history notebook, Creative Initiative Archives.

82. *The Daily Pilot* (May 8, 1975): n.p., clipping, Creative Initiative Archives.

83. *Los Angeles Times* (May 10, 1975): n.p., clipping, history notebook, Creative Initiative Archives.

84. *The Daily Pilot* (May 8, 1975): n.p.; *Los Angeles Times* (May 9, 1975): 1.

85. *San Francisco Chronicle* (May 14, 1975): 2, (May 9, 1975): n.p., clippings, history notebook, Creative Initiative Archives; *Palo Alto Times* (April 28, 1975): n.p., clipping, history notebook, Creative Initiative Archives.

86. "The Time Is Now," May 21, 1975, demonstration program, Creative Initiative Archives; " 'The Time Is Now,' Schedule of Events," May 21, 1975, Creative Initiative Archives, "4,000 Protest Construction of N-Plants," n.d., n.p., newspaper clipping, Creative Initiative Archives.

87. *Community Campus* (June 6, 1975): 6, clipping, history notebook, Creative Initiative Archives.

88. *The Sacramento Union* (May 22, 1975): A6.

89. *Oakland Tribune* (May 3, 1976): 2, (June 6, 1976): 5.

90. Letter to Harry and Emilia Rathbun, July 21, 1975, Creative Initiative Archives.

91. *Chico Enterprise Record* (June 3, 1976): n.p., clipping, Creative Initiative Archives.

92. Interview with Dale Bridenbaugh, Richard Hubbard, and Gregory C. Minor, May 4, 1987, San Jose, Calif.

93. *Independent-Journal* [Marin] (November 29, 1975): 7.

94. Dale G. Bridenbaugh to N. L. Felmus, February 2, 1976; Richard B. Hubbard to Abdon Rubio, February 2, 1976; Gregory C. Minor to Harry H. Hendon, February 2, 1976, Creative Initiative Archives; interview with Bridenbaugh, Hubbard, and Minor.

95. *Oakland Tribune* (April 13, 1976): 10E.

96. "Facts About the Imperative," n.d., Creative Initiative Archives.

97. *San Francisco Examiner* (July 14, 1977): 4; "Project Summary," c. 1977–1978, Creative Initiative Archives; "Will You Do One Thing More?" 1977, Creative Initiative Archives.

98. Phyllis Kidd, "Rainbow March for an Energy Fast," May 10, 1979, Creative Initiative Archives; *San Francisco Chronicle* (May 11, 1979): 38.

99. Flyer, c. 1979, Creative Initiative Archives.

100. "People Ask," n.d., flyer, Creative Initiative Archives.

101. "International Energy Conservation Day," October 27, 1979, program, Creative Initiative Archives; *Palo Alto Times Tribune* (October 20, 1979): n.p., clipping, Creative Initiative Archives; photographs of Energy Conservation Day, 1979, history notebook, Creative Initiative Archives.

102. "You're Invited to the Energyfest House Tour," July 26, 1980, Creative Initiative Archives.

103. "Global 2000—A doomsday report or the most 'optimistic' projection for the next 20 years," n.d., Creative Initiative Archives.

104. "To All Passover People, Global 2000: The Challenge to Change," August 28, 1980, Creative Initiative Archives.

105. *Palo Alto Times Tribune* (November 10, 1980): A1.

106. "Global 2000 Course," January 4, 1981, Creative Initiative Archives.

107. *Palo Alto Times* (May 6, 1970): n.p., clipping, history notebook, Creative Initiative Archives; note, 1970, history scrapbook, Creative Initiative Archives.

108. "To: Regional Youth Coordinators, Holistic Youth Team, Regional Chairmen, Pre-School Staff," October 10, 1974, Creative Initiative Archives.

109. "Women's Network," 1977, Creative Initiative Archives.

110. "Letter Writing," 1977, Creative Initiative Archives; "Improving TV for a Healthier Tomorrow," flyer for Johnson speech, December 1977, Creative Initiative Archives; "TV Guidelines for Conscious Viewing," c. 1977, Creative Initiative Archives; "Woman—Key to the Future," October 1977, Creative Initiative Archives.

111. "A Call for Responsible Television," c. 1977, petition, Creative Initiative Archives.

112. Ibid.

8. A World Beyond War

1. Interview with Harry and Emilia Rathbun, October 14, 1984, Palo Alto, Calif.

2. Interview with Richard and Carolyn Rathbun, February 20, 1985, Palo Alto, Calif.

3. Ibid.

4. Interview with Richard and Carolyn Rathbun, February 2, 1985, Palo Alto, Calif.

5. Harry Rathbun to Richard and Carolyn Rathbun, July 30, 1971, Creative Initiative Archives.

6. Harry Rathbun to Richard and Carolyn Rathbun, July 12, 1970; July 30, 1971; February 15, 1972, Creative Initiative Archives.

7. Harry Rathbun to Richard and Carolyn Rathbun, June 29, 1971; October 10, 1971, Creative Initiative Archives.

8. "Notes from Jesus III Seminar, 11/5/78–11/10/78," James and Wileta Burch papers. There were, in fact, more than a thousand members, almost 1,800 in 1976, but many of them apparently did not meet Emilia's criteria for totality; "Draft Copy—Sept. 1987, Membership of Sequoia Seminar and Creative Initiative," Creative Initiative Archives.

9. "A Time for Decision," c. January 1978: 1, Creative Initiative Archives.

10. "Draft Copy—Sept. 1987, Membership of Sequoia Seminar and Creative Initiative."

11. "Assessment of the Teachings of Jesus: Course I," 1981: 1–3, Creative Initiative Archives.

12. "Within woman, deeply buried . . . ," n.d., Creative Initiative Archives.

13. "Woman to Woman sponsors 'A Minute for Peace for the Children's Sake,' " December 1967, Creative Initiative Archives; *San Francisco Chronicle* (December 23, 1967): n.p., clipping and note, history notebook, Creative Initiative Archives; "For the Children's Sake," c. 1968: 4, newsletter, Creative Initiative Archives.

14. *Palo Alto Times* (May 13, 1967): 32; "Another Mother for Peace," history notebook, Creative Initiative Archives.

15. Press release, c. June 1969, Creative Initiative Archives; newspaper clippings, June 19, 1969; June 24, 1969, history notebook, Creative Initiative Archives.

16. *Palo Alto Times* (October 23, 1970): 14; "Russian Humming Song," history notebook, Creative Initiative Archives.

17. "To: Outlying Areas, Outposts and Contacts," October 17, 1973, Creative Initiative Archives.

18. *Palo Alto Times* (October 13, 1973): 2.

19. Ibid.

20. *San Francisco Chronicle* (October 20, 1973): 6.

21. "We March in Unity with the Women of Ireland," c. 1976, leaflet, Creative Initiative Archives; *Palo Alto Times* (October 25, 1976): 11.

22. Questionnaires, June 1983, Creative Initiative Archives.

23. Meeting of Beyond War leaders, March 1, 1985, Ben Lomond, Calif.

24. Questionnaire 19, summer, 1986.

25. Questionnaire 20, summer, 1986.

26. Richard Rathbun, speech to Men's Convocation, "The New Warrior," November 11, 1984; Jonathan Schell, "The Fate of the Earth," *New Yorker* 57 (February 1, 1982): 44, (February 8, 1982): 48, (February 15, 1982): 45.

27. *Los Angeles Times* (September 15, 1985): IV, 1.

28. Helen Caldicott to Harry and Emilia Rathbun, February 2, 1976, Creative Initiative Archives.

29. *New York Times* (May 25, 1979): 17.

30. *Los Angeles Times* (September 15, 1985): IV, 12.

31. *Metro* [San Jose] (May 9–15, 1985): 7; *Palo Alto Weekly* (July 23, 1986): 26; Susan Faludi, "A Separate Peace," *West* [Sunday magazine of the *San Jose Mercury News*] (May 4, 1986): 33–34.

32. *Los Angeles Times* (September 15, 1985): IV, 13.

33. Beyond War leadership meeting, March 1, 1985, Ben Lomond, Calif.

34. Creative Initiative leadership meeting, January 13, 1985, Ben Lomond, Calif.

35. Beyond War leadership meeting, March 1, 1985, Ben Lomond, Calif.

36. Faludi, "A Separate Peace," 33.

37. Ibid., 11.

38. *Beyond War: A New Way of Thinking* (Palo Alto, Calif.: Beyond War, 1985), i.

39. *Parade Magazine* (August 24, 1986): 18–19.

40. Martin E. Hellman, "On the Inevitability of Nuclear War," Creative Initiative Archives.

41. See chap. 5.

42. *Beyond War,* "Knowledge," 2–3.

43. Ibid., 14.

44. Ibid., 1, 1A, 2.

45. "Men's Convocation," November 11, 1984, drafts of speeches, Creative Initiative Archives.

46. "Convocation talk #2—Saturday morning," November 5, 1984: 6–8, Creative Initiative Archives.

47. *Beyond War,* "Decision," 2–2A.

48. Ibid., 3.

49. Ibid., 3–4.

50. Susan Faludi, "Inner Peaceniks," *Mother Jones* (April 1987): 51.

51. "To: Regional Chairman of regions having a Symposium," October 6, 1984, Creative Initiative Archives; "Woman's Rite of Passage," 2, Creative Initiative Archives.

52. Speech to women's convocation, November 5, 1984, Creative Initiative Archives.

53. "Who Speaks for Earth? The New Warrior," November 11, 1984, Creative Initiative Archives.

54. "Men's Convocation," November 11, 1984, Creative Initiative Archives.

54. Pin card, c. 1985, Creative Initiative Archives.

56. *Beyond War,* "Decision," 7.

57. *Beyond War,* "Action," 3–4.

58. Ibid., 5–7.

59. "Adoption of an Idea," n.d., resource paper, Creative Initiative Archives.

60. Wayne Mehl speaking at Beyond War leaders' meeting, March 1, 1985, Ben Lomond, Calif.

61. "Beyond War Plan," c. 1982, Creative Initiative Archives.

62. "Beyond War Summary," "The Plan for 1984–1985," August 1, 1984, Creative Initiative Archives; "Beyond War coordinators' meeting," De Anza College, January 12, 1985.

63. See for example, *The Washington Post* (March 21, 1983): A1.

64. Interviews at Beyond War United Nations meetings, January 28–30, 1985; Faludi, "Inner Peaceniks," 22; Faludi, "A Separate Peace," 34.

65. Elizabeth Walker Mechling and Gale Auletta, "Beyond War: A Socio-Rhetorical Analysis of a New Class Revitalization Movement," *Western Journal of Speech Communication* 50 (Fall, 1986): 403.

Index

Designer:	U.C. Press Staff
Compositor:	Huron Valley Graphics
Text:	10/13 Galliard
Display:	Galliard
Printer:	Bookcrafters
Binder:	Bookcrafters